Imp Owners Workshop Manual

by J H Haynes

Member of the Guild of Motoring Writers

and R T Grainger

Models covered:

Hillman Imp 875 cc
Singer Chamois, Sport and F.H. Coupe 875 cc
Sunbeam Imp Sport 875 cc
Sunbeam Stiletto 875 cc
Sunbeam Sport 875 cc
Rallye 998 cc
Husky 875 cc
Van 875 cc

ISBN 0 900550 22 8

© J H Haynes and Company Limited 1976, 1980   ABCDE FGH

Printed in England   (022—5F2)

HAYNES PUBLISHING GROUP
SPARKFORD YEOVIL SOMERSET ENGLAND
distributed in the USA by
HAYNES PUBLICATIONS INC
861 LAWRENCE DRIVE
NEWBURY PARK
CALIFORNIA 91320
USA

Acknowledgements

My thanks are due to Chrysler United Kingdom Ltd., for the generous assistance given in the supply of technical material and illustrations; to Castrol Ltd., for supplying the lubrication chart; to the Editor of Autocar for permission to use the cutaway drawing featured on the cover; Champion Sparking Plug Company Limited for the provision of spark plug photographs. The bodywork repair photographs used in this manual were provided by Lloyds Industries Limited who supply 'Turtle Wax', Holts 'Dupli-Color' and a range of other Holts products. Special thanks are due to Mr. L. Tooze and Mr. R.F. Lodge whose experience and practical help were of great assistance in the compilation of photographs for this manual.

Although every care has been taken to ensure all the data in this manual is correct, bearing in mind that manufacturers' current practice is to make small alterations and design changes without reclassifying the model, no liability can be accepted for damage, loss or injury caused by any errors or omissions in the information given.

Photographic Captions & Cross References

For the ease of reference this book is divided into numbered chapters, sections and paragraphs. The title of each chapter is self explanatory. The sections comprise the main headings within the chapter. The paragraphs appear within each section.

The captions to the majority of photographs are given within the paragraphs of the relevant section to avoid repetition. These photographs bear the same number as the sections and paragraphs to which they refer. The photograph always appears in the same chapter as its paragraph. For example if looking through chapter ten it is wished to find the caption for photograph 9:4 refer to section 9 and then read paragraph 4.

To avoid repetition once a procedure has been described it is not normally repeated. If it is necessary to refer to a procedure already given this is done by quoting the original chapter, section and sometimes paragraph number.

The reference is given thus: Chapter No/Section No. Paragraph No. For example chapter 2, section 6 would be given as: Chapter 2/6. Chapter 2, Section 6, Paragraph 5 would be given as Chapter 2/6:5. If more than one section is involved the reference would be written: Chapter 2/6 to 7 or where the section is not consecutive 2/6 and 9. To refer to several paragraphs within a section the reference is given thus: Chapter 2/6.2 and 4.

To refer to a section within the same chapter the chapter number is usually dropped. Thus a reference is in a chapter merely read 'see section 8', this refers to section 8 in that same chapter.

All references to components on the right or left-hand side are made as if looking forward to the bonnet from the rear of the car.

IMP MK I DELUXE SALOON

Introduction

This is a manual for do-it-yourself minded owners of Imps and their many variants. It shows how to maintain these cars in first class condition and how to carry out repairs when components become worn or break. Regular and careful maintenance is essential if maximum reliability and minimum wear are to be achieved.

The step-by-step photographs show how to deal with the major components and in conjunction with the text and exploded illustrations should make all the work quite clear - even to the novice who has never previously attempted the more complex job.

Although Imps are hardwearing and robust it is inevitable that their reliability and performance will decrease as they become older. Repairs and general reconditioning will become necessary if the car is to remain roadworthy. Early models requiring attention are frequently bought by the more impecunious motorist who can least afford the repair prices charged in garages, even though these prices are usually quite fair bearing in mind overheads and the high cost of capital equipment and skilled labour.

It is in these circumstances that this manual will prove to be of maximum assistance, as it is the ONLY workshop manual written from practical experience specially to help Imp owners.

Manufacturer's official manuals are usually splendid publications which contain a wealth of technical information. Because they are issued primarily to help the manufacturers authorised dealers and distributors they tend to be written in very technical language, and tend to skip details of certain jobs which are common knowledge to garage mechanics. Owner's workshop manuals are different as they are intended primarily to help the owner. They therefore go into many of the jobs in great detail with extensive photographic support to ensure everything is properly understood so that the repair is done correctly.

Owners who intend to do their own maintenance and repairs should have a reasonably comprehensive tool kit. Some jobs require special service tools, but in many instances it is possible to get round their use with a little care and ingenuity. For example a 3½ inch diameter jubilee clip makes a most efficient and cheap piston ring compressor.

Throughout this manual ingenious ways of avoiding the use of special equipment and tools are shown. In some cases the proper tool must be used. Where this is the case a description of the tool and its correct use is included.

When a component malfunctions repairs are becoming more and more a case of replacing the defective item with an exchange rebuilt unit. This is excellent practice when a component is thoroughly worn out, but it is a waste of good money when overall the component is only half worn, and requires the replacement of but a single small item to effect a complete repair. As an example, a non-functioning dynamo can frequently be repaired quite satisfactorily just by fitting new brushes.

A further function of this manual is to show the owner how to examine malfunctioning parts; determine what is wrong, and then how to make the repair.

Given the time, mechanical do-it-yourself aptitude, and a reasonable collection of tools, this manual will show the ordinary private owner how to maintain and repair his car really economically.

Contents

Routine Maintenance

The maintenance instructions listed below are basically those recommended by the manufacturer. They are supplemented by additional maintenance tasks which, through practical experience, the author recommends should be carried out at the intervals suggested.

The additional tasks are indicated by an asterisk and are primarily of a preventive nature in that they will assist in eliminating the unexpected failure of a component due to fair wear and tear.

The levels of the engine oil, radiator cooling water, windscreen washer water and battery electrolyte, also the tyre pressures, should be checked weekly or more frequently if experience dictates this to be necessary. Similarly it is wise to check the level of the fluids in the clutch and brake master cylinder reservoirs at monthly intervals. If not checked at home it is advantageous to use regularly the same garage for this work as they will get to know your preferences for particular oils and the pressures at which you like to run your tyres.

5,000 miles

EVERY 5,000 miles (or every six months if 5,000 miles are not exceeded).

1. Run the engine until it is hot and place a container of at least 8 pints capacity under the sump drain plug, undo and remove the drain plug and allow the oil to drain for at least 10 minutes. Clean the plug and its surrounding area and replace the plug tightening it firmly. Place a tray below the oil filter, remove the central domed nut above the filter body, withdraw the filter casing and remove the element. Clean out the casing, fit a new element and fit new sealing rings under the domed nut and between the filter casing and body, before reassembly. Refill the sump with 5½ pints of the recommended grade of oil (see page 10) and clean off any oil which may have spilled over the engine or its components. Check the oil level. The interval between oil changes should be reduced in very hot or dusty conditions or during cold weather with much slow stop/start driving.

2. Check the water pump bracket and mounting bolts for tightness and also the tension of the fan belt which must be tight enough to drive the generator and water pump without overloading the bearings. The method of adjusting the fan belt is described on page 52 and is correct when there is one inch (25 mm) of play at the midpoint position between the crankshaft and water pump pulleys. Check the fan cowl for tightness.

3. Undo and remove the bolt in the centre of the fuel pump cover, lift off the cover, and lift out the gauze filter to clean it with petrol and a soft brush. Renew the cork gasket if it has hardened or broken.

4. The air cleaner, whether of the oil bath or dry element

The oil filter

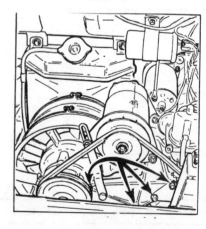

Water pump bracket bolts

types, should be inspected, cleaned and serviced as described on page 55.

5. Examine the engine and the transmission unit for leaks and, if found, determine the cause.

6. Check the carburettor slow running as described on pages 64 (Solex) and 68 (Stromberg) and adjust if necessary.

7. Examine the cooling system, hoses etc., for leaks. Drain, flush and refill the cooling system. Check the radiator core for clogging or damage and remove any obstructions with mild detergent and compressed air. If the engine is over-heating because of a badly clogged radiator it is best to remove it for cleaning.

8. Inspect all hydraulic pipes, hoses and connections for leaks or damage. Inspect the handbrake cable for wear or damage and check the efficient operation of the handbrake. Check the brakes and adjust if necessary. Always test the brakes several times after making any adjustments.

9. Remove the sparking plugs, clean them and reset the gaps to .025 ins. Clean the ceramic insulators and inspect the plug leads for deterioration.

10 Check the distributor contact breaker and adjust if necessary. Loosen the locking screw on the fixed contact and move it by inserting a screwdriver in the notched hole at the end of the plate until there is a gap of .015 ins. Turn clockwise to decrease and anti-clockwise to increase the gap. Tighten the locking screw and check the gap again. At the same time clean any dirt from the inside of the distributor cap and clean the rotor arm. Apply two drops of oil at the centre of the cam spindle and also through the plate to lubricate the automatic advance mechanism. Smear very lightly with grease the cam surface and apply one drop of oil, only, to the moving contact breaker pivot. Wipe off immediately any excess oil or grease.

11 Clean the top of the battery and the battery terminals. Smear the terminals with a silicone compound or lanoline (not grease).

12 Inject a few drops of oil through the aperture at the centre of the rear plate of the generator.

13 Remove the filler/level plug, on the left of the transmission unit, and clean it and its surrounding area. If the level is low top up with the recommended grade of oil (see page 10) until it runs back out of the filler/level hole. Replace the plug and clean off any excess oil.

14 Check the tightness of the rack and pinion steering mounting bolts. Examine for leaks. Check the outer steering column fixing bolts and the inner steering column pinion pinch bolts.

15 Check the pivot bolts on the front and rear suspension mountings and also the bolts between the floor and mountings.

16 The road wheels, if fitted with cross-ply tyres, should be rotated.

17 The door strikers, locks and hinges, the bonnet and engine compartment locks, hinges and catches, and the rear window lock and hinges should all be lubricated by means of an oil can.

18 Check the front wheel 'toe-in' and the alignment of the ball joints.

19 Check the headlamp alignment and the condition of the headlamp seals.

20 Check all lamps, especially the stop/tail lamps, for correct functioning and renew if necessary.

21 Check the windscreen wiper blades for efficient functioning and renew if suspect.

22 Check the operation of the windscreen washer.

23 Check the window winding handles, seat adjustment mechanism, sun visors etc., for ease of movement.

24 Check the alignment of the doors.

25 Give the bodywork and trim a thoroughly good wash and then a wax polish. If chromium cleaner is used to

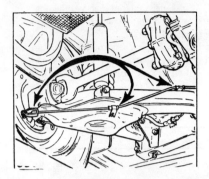

Handbrake cable

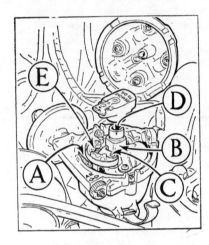

Distributor maintenance

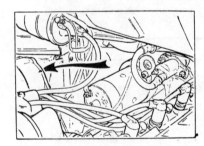

Generator lubrication aperture

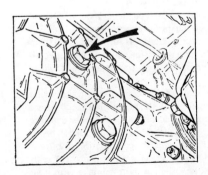

Transmission unit filler plug

remove rust on any of the car's plated parts remember that the cleaner also removes parts of the chromium and therefore must be used sparingly.

26 Remove the carpets or mats and thoroughly vacuum clean the interior of the car. Beat out or vacuum clean the carpets. If the upholstery is soiled apply an upholstery cleaner with a damp sponge and wipe off with a clean cloth.

10,000 miles

EVERY 10,000 miles (or every year if 10,000 miles are not exceeded).
1. Carry out all the operations for the 5,000 miles service.
2. Remove the setscrew in the centre of the crankcase breather, remove the assembly and discard the element. When refitting, the new element should be stuck to the cover inside bottom face with quick setting jointing compound to keep it in place during refitting. The breather outlet pipe must always point upwards. Cars delivered to North America have sealed breather systems which require no maintenance.
3. Renew the sparking plugs ensuring that the gaps are .025 ins.

15,000 miles

EVERY 15,000 miles.
1. Carry out all the operations for the 5,000 miles service.
2. Renew the air cleaner element if a dry type air cleaner is fitted.
3. Examine the carburettor flange, the manifolds and the exhaust system for leaks and check all fixings for tightness.
4. Check the starter motor fixing bolts for tightness.
5. Run the car until it is hot and place a container of at least 8 pints under the transmission unit. Undo the drain plug, clean it and its surrounding area, and replace the plug tightening it firmly. Refill with 4½ pints of a recommended grade of oil, cleaning off any oil which may have spilled.

30,000 miles

EVERY 30,000 miles.
1. Carry out all the operations for the 5,000, 10,000 and 15,000 miles services.
2. Check the rubber engine mountings for any signs of damage or deterioration.
3. Inspect the rubber couplings on the drive shafts for any signs of damage or deterioration.
4. Check all the rubber bushes on the suspension for damage or deterioration.
5. Repack the front hub bearings with grease.
*6. It is a sound scheme to visit your local main agent and have the underside of the body steam cleaned. This will take about 1½ hours and cost about £4. All traces of dirt and oil will be removed and the underside can then be inspected for rust, damaged hydraulic pipes, frayed electrical wiring and similar maladies.
*7. At the same time the engine compartment should be cleaned in a similar manner. If steam cleaning facilities are not available then brush 'Gunk' or a similar cleaner over the whole engine and engine compartment with a stiff brush working it well in where there is an accumulation of oil and dirt. Do not paint the ignition system but protect it with oily rags. As the Gunk is washed away it will take with it all traces of oil and dirt, leaving the engine looking clean and bright.

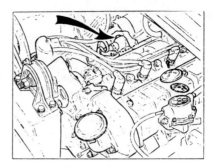

Crankcase breather

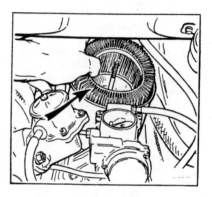

The dry element type air cleaner

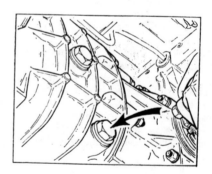

Transmission unit drain plug

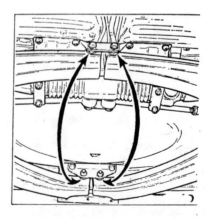

Suspension bushes locations

Safety first!

Professional motor mechanics are trained in safe working procedures. However enthusiastic you may be about getting on with the job in hand, do take the time to ensure that your safety is not put at risk. A moment's lack of attention can result in an accident, as can failure to observe certain elementary precautions.

There will always be new ways of having accidents, and the following points do not pretend to be a comprehensive list of all dangers; they are intended rather to make you aware of the risks and to encourage a safety-conscious approach to all work you carry out on your vehicle.

Essential DOs and DON'Ts

DON'T rely on a single jack when working underneath the vehicle. Always use reliable additional means of support, such as axle stands, securely placed under a part of the vehicle that you know will not give way.

DON'T attempt to loosen or tighten high-torque nuts (e.g. wheel hub nuts) while the vehicle is on a jack; it may be pulled off.

DON'T start the engine without first ascertaining that the transmission is in neutral (or 'Park' where applicable) and the parking brake applied.

DON'T suddenly remove the filler cap from a hot cooling system – cover it with a cloth and release the pressure gradually first, or you may get scalded by escaping coolant.

DON'T attempt to drain oil until you are sure it has cooled sufficiently to avoid scalding you.

DON'T grasp any part of the engine, exhaust or catalytic converter without first ascertaining that it is sufficiently cool to avoid burning you.

DON'T allow brake fluid or antifreeze to contact vehicle paintwork.

DON'T syphon toxic liquids such as fuel, brake fluid or antifreeze by mouth, or allow them to remain on your skin.

DON'T inhale dust – it may be injurious to health (see *Asbestos* below).

DON'T allow any spilt oil or grease to remain on the floor – wipe it up straight away, before someone slips on it.

DON'T use ill-fitting spanners or other tools which may slip and cause injury.

DON'T attempt to lift a heavy component which may be beyond your capability – get assistance.

DON'T rush to finish a job, or take unverified short cuts.

DON'T allow children or animals in or around an unattended vehicle.

DO wear eye protection when using power tools such as drill, sander, bench grinder etc, and when working under the vehicle.

DO use a barrier cream on your hands prior to undertaking dirty jobs – it will protect your skin from infection as well as making the dirt easier to remove afterwards; but make sure your hands aren't left slippery.

DO keep loose clothing (cuffs, tie etc) and long hair well out of the way of moving mechanical parts.

DO remove rings, wristwatch etc, before working on the vehicle – especially the electrical system.

DO ensure that any lifting tackle used has a safe working load rating adequate for the job.

DO keep your work area tidy – it is only too easy to fall over articles left lying around.

DO get someone to check periodically that all is well, when working alone on the vehicle.

DO carry out work in a logical sequence and check that everything is correctly assembled and tightened afterwards.

DO remember that your vehicle's safety affects that of yourself and others. If in doubt on any point, get specialist advice.

IF, in spite of following these precautions, you are unfortunate enough to injure yourself, seek medical attention as soon as possible.

Asbestos

Certain friction, insulating, sealing, and other products – such as brake linings, brake bands, clutch linings, torque converters, gaskets, etc – contain asbestos. *Extreme care must be taken to avoid inhalation of dust from such products since it is hazardous to health.* If in doubt, assume that they *do* contain asbestos.

Fire

Remember at all times that petrol (gasoline) is highly flammable. Never smoke, or have any kind of naked flame around, when working on the vehicle. But the risk does not end there – a spark caused by an electrical short-circuit, by two metal surfaces contacting each other, by careless use of tools, or even by static electricity built up in your body under certain conditions, can ignite petrol vapour, which in a confined space is highly explosive.

Always disconnect the battery earth (ground) terminal before working on any part of the fuel or electrical system, and never risk spilling fuel on to a hot engine or exhaust.

It is recommended that a fire extinguisher of a type suitable for fuel and electrical fires is kept handy in the garage or workplace at all times. Never try to extinguish a fuel or electrical fire with water.

Fumes

Certain fumes are highly toxic and can quickly cause unconsciousness and even death if inhaled to any extent. Petrol (gasoline) vapour comes into this category, as do the vapours from certain solvents such as trichloroethylene. Any draining or pouring of such volatile fluids should be done in a well ventilated area.

When using cleaning fluids and solvents, read the instructions carefully. Never use materials from unmarked containers – they may give off poisonous vapours.

Never run the engine of a motor vehicle in an enclosed space such as a garage. Exhaust fumes contain carbon monoxide which is extremely poisonous; if you need to run the engine, always do so in the open air or at least have the rear of the vehicle outside the workplace.

If you are fortunate enough to have the use of an inspection pit, never drain or pour petrol, and never run the engine, while the vehicle is standing over it; the fumes, being heavier than air, will concentrate in the pit with possibly lethal results.

The battery

Never cause a spark, or allow a naked light, near the vehicle's battery. It will normally be giving off a certain amount of hydrogen gas, which is highly explosive.

Always disconnect the battery earth (ground) terminal before working on the fuel or electrical systems.

If possible, loosen the filler plugs or cover when charging the battery from an external source. Do not charge at an excessive rate or the battery may burst.

Take care when topping up and when carrying the battery. The acid electrolyte, even when diluted, is very corrosive and should not be allowed to contact the eyes or skin.

If you ever need to prepare electrolyte yourself, always add the acid slowly to the water, and never the other way round. Protect against splashes by wearing rubber gloves and goggles.

When jump starting a car using a booster battery, for negative earth (ground) vehicles, connect the jump leads in the following sequence: First connect one jump lead between the positive (+) terminals of the two batteries. Then connect the other jump lead first to the negative (–) terminal of the booster battery, and then to a good earthing (ground) point on the vehicle to be started, at least 18 in (45 cm) from the battery if possible. Ensure that hands and jump leads are clear of any moving parts, and that the two vehicles do not touch. Disconnect the leads in the reverse order.

Mains electricity

When using an electric power tool, inspection light etc, which works from the mains, always ensure that the appliance is correctly connected to its plug and that, where necessary, it is properly earthed (grounded). Do not use such appliances in damp conditions and, again, beware of creating a spark or applying excessive heat in the vicinity of fuel or fuel vapour.

Ignition HT voltage

A severe electric shock can result from touching certain parts of the ignition system, such as the HT leads, when the engine is running or being cranked, particularly if components are damp or the insulation is defective. Where an electronic ignition system is fitted, the HT voltage is much higher and could prove fatal.

LUBRICATION CHART

EXPLANATION OF SYMBOLS

CASTROL GTX.
An ultra high performance motor oil, recommended for the engine summer and winter.

CASTROL HYPOY LIGHT GEAR OIL.
A powerful, extreme pressure lubricant recommended for the transmission and steering gear.

CASTROL LM GREASE.
A high melting point lithium base grease recommended for wheel hub and steering lubrication.

EVERY 250 MILES

ENGINE
Check oil level and, if necessary, replenish to correct level with **Castrol GTX.**

EVERY 30,000 MILES Including 250 & 5,000 mile services

FRONT WHEEL HUBS
Dismantle, thoroughly clean out and repack with fresh **Castrol LM Grease.**

REAR WHEEL HUBS
Remove hub disc, if any evidence of grease leaking past retaining seals, your Dealer should be notified immediately. **Castrol LM Grease** should be used when repacking the hub.

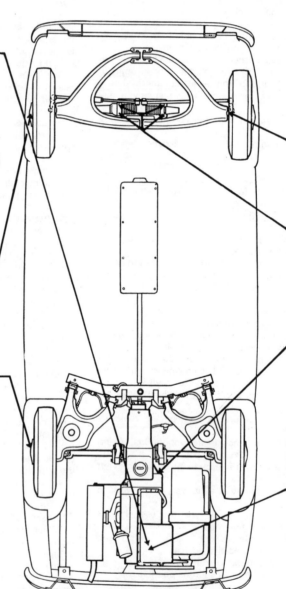

EVERY 5,000 MILES Including 250 mile service

FRONT STUB AXLES
Some later models are fitted with a grease nipple. Apply **Castrol LM Grease** with the grease gun.

STEERING UNIT
Examine rack unit carefully for leaks. If any evidence of leakage your Dealer should be notified immediately. **Castrol Hypoy Light Gear Oil** should be used for replenishing. Capacity—$\frac{1}{4}$ pint.

TRANSMISSION
Check oil level and, if necessary, top up to just below the level of the filler plug hole with **Castrol Hypoy Light Gear Oil.** After the first 500 miles, and thereafter every 15,000 miles, drain off the old oil while warm and refill with fresh **Castrol Hypoy Light Gear Oil.** The filler plug should be removed before drain plug in order to release pressure.

Capacity—$4\frac{1}{2}$ pints.

ENGINE
After the first 500 miles, and thereafter every 5,000 miles, drain off the old oil while warm and refill with fresh **Castrol GTX.**

Note:—Owners are reminded that in the car maker's handbook, more frequent sump draining periods are recommended if the operation of the car involves:—

(1) Frequent stop/start driving.
(2) Operation during cold weather, especially when appreciable engine idling is involved.
(3) Where much driving is done under dusty conditions.

Capacity—$5\frac{1}{4}$ pints (including filter).

OVERSEAS

Use **Castrolite** in all climatic conditions.

NOTE:—Whilst the diagram depicts the underside of the chassis the arrows are directed to the exact locations inside the engine compartment.

RECOMMENDED LUBRICANTS

COMPONENT	TYPE OF LUBRICANT OR FLUID	CORRECT CASTROL PRODUCTS
ENGINE	Multi-grade engine oil	Castrol GTX
TRANSMISSION UNIT	Gear oil of SAE 80EP standard	Castrol Hypoy Light Gear Oil
STEERING UNIT...	Gear oil of SAE 80EP standard	Castrol Hypoy Light Gear Oil
FRONT WHEEL BEARINGS & FRONT STUB AXLES	Medium Grade multi-purpose grease	Castrol L.M. Grease
REAR WHEEL BEARINGS & REAR DRIVESHAFT UNIVERSAL JOINTS	Medium Grade multi-purpose grease	Castrol L.M.Grease
DISTRIBUTOR & GENERATOR BEARINGS...	Engine or light oil	Castrol GTX
CONTACT BREAKER CAM	Medium Grade multi-purpose grease	Castrol L.M.Grease
BATTERY TERMINALS	Petroleum jelly	
CARBURETTER DASHPOT	Light engine oil	Castrolite
UPPER CYLINDER LUBRICANT..	... ...	Castrollo
BRAKE & CLUTCH MASTER CYLINDERS	Hydraulic fluid	Castrol/Girling Crimson

Additionally Castrol GTX can be used to lubricate door locks, strikers and hinges; bonnet and engine compartment locks, hinges and catches; rear screen locks and hinges.

Ordering Spare Parts

Always Order Genuine Chrysler United Kingdom spare parts from your nearest authorised dealer or local garage. Authorised dealers carry a comprehensive stock of GENUINE PARTS and can supply most items over the counter.

When ordering new parts it is essential to give full details of your car to the storeman. He will want to know the model type, e.g. Sunbeam Sport, and the full chassis number, including the prefix and suffix letters. These details are given on a plate fixed to the left hand side panel in the engine compartment.

The engine number will be found on the left hand side of the cylinder block immediately above the oil pressure switch.

If you want to retouch the paintwork, you can obtain an exact match (providing the original paint has not faded) by quoting the paint code number in conjunction with the chassis number.

Makers Identification Plate

Chapter 1/Engine

Contents

Engine Specification & Data

Engine — General

Type	4 cylinder, in line, single O.H.C.
Cubic capacity:	
Standard	875 c.c.
Rallye	998 c.c.
Compression ratio:	
High	10.1
Low	8.1
Compression pressure:	
H.C.	185/200 lbs/sq.in. (13/14 Kg.cm^2)
L.C.	175/190 lbs/sq.in. (12/13 Kg.cm^2)
Petrol octane requirement:	
H.C.	95/97 (Three star)

L.C.	85/87 (Two star)
Bore:	
Grade 'A'	2.6769–2.6766 (67.99/67.98 mm)
Grade 'B'	2.6772–2.6769 (68.00/67.99 mm)
Grade 'C'	2.6775–2.6772 (68.01/68.00 mm)
Rallye	2.86 (72.8 mm)

	lbs.ft.	R.P.M.
Torque maximum (Net):		
H.C.	52	2,800
L.C.	49	2,800
Sport	52	4,300
Rallye	62	3,200
B.H.P. (Net):		
H.C.	39	5,000
L.C.	34	4,900
Sport	51	6,100
Rallye	65	6,200

Firing order	1, 3, 4, 2.
Location of No. 1 Cylinder	Next to crankshaft pulley

Camshaft

Type	Overhead, running in three replaceable bearings
Camshaft drive	From crankshaft by single roller endless chain
Camshaft journal diameter	.9375/.9370 in. (23.81/23.79 mm)
Camshaft bearings internal diameter	.9395/.9375 in. (23.86/23.81 mm)
Camshaft to bearing running clearance	.002/.0005 in. (.05/.01 mm)
Camshaft bearing material	Steel shell, white metal lined
Camshaft endfloat	.007/.002 in. (.17/.05 mm)

Connecting Rods & Big & Little End Bearings

Connecting rod, type	'H' section
Connecting rod material	Steel forging
Big end bearing, type	Shell
Big end bearing material	Steel shell, lead bronze, lead indium overlay
Little end, type	Bush type, plain bearing
Big end bore (without bearings)	1.771/1.7705 in. (44.98/44.97 mm)
Big end, end float	.005 in. (.12 mm) Minimum
Big end to crankshaft, running clearance	.0027/.001 in. (.067/.025 mm)
Big end undersize bearings available	.020/.040 in. (.50/1.01 mm)
Little end bore:	
High grade	.6252/.6251 in. (15.880/15.877 mm)
Low grade	.6251/.6250 in. (15.877/15.875 mm)

Crankshaft & Main Bearings

Crankshaft, type	3 bearing, balanced
Main bearing, type	Steel shell, lead bronze, lead indium overlay
Crankshaft balance	By integrally forged counterweights
Crankshaft main bearing, journal diameter	1.875 in. (47.62 mm)
Crankshaft big end, journal diameter	1.625 in. (41.27 mm)
Crankshaft end thrust	Provided by thrust washers either side of the centre main bearing
Crankshaft, thrust washer oversize available	+.005 (.12 mm)
Crankshaft end float	.002/.001 in. (.05/.025 mm)
Main bearings, undersizes available	.020/.040 in. (.50/1.01 mm)
Main bearing to crankshaft running clearance	.0027/.001 in. (.067/.025 mm)

Cylinder Block

Material	Aluminium with fixed iron cylinder liners
Maximum oversize	.030 in. (.76 mm)

Cylinder Head

Material	Aluminium
Valve seat inserts interference fit	.0025/.0045 in. (.063/.114 mm)
Gasket, type	Composite

Gudgeon Pin

Type	Floating
Location	By circlips
Diameter:	
High grade	.6250/.6249 in. (15.88/15.87 mm)
Low grade	.6249/.6248 in. (15.87/15.86 mm)

Type of fit ... ...   Hand push at 20ºC (68ºF)

Lubrication System
Type ... ...   Pressure by oil pump
Oil ... ...   Multi-grade
Filter type ... ...   Full flow
Oil cooler (if fitted) ... ...   Clayton, tubular

Pistons
Type:

H.C.	Solid skirt, flat top
L.C.	Solid skirt, dished top

Material ... ...   LO-EX Aluminium alloy
Length:

Standard	2.054 in. (52.20 mm)
Sport	2.059 in. (52.32 mm)

Maximum weight variation per set ... ...   4 drams (7 grms)
Diameter (Standard):

Grade 'A'	2.6758/2.6755 in. (67.965/67.957 mm)
Grade 'B'	2.6761/2.6758 in. (67.972/67.965 mm)
Grade 'C'	2.6764/2.6761 in. (67.980/67.972 mm)
Grade 'D' (service only)	2.6767/2.6764 in. (67.987/67.980 mm)
Oversize available	.015 in. (.38 mm) & .030 in. (.76 mm)

Diameter (Sport saloons):

Grade 'A'	2.6752/2.6749 in. (67.950/67.942 mm)
Grade 'B'	2.6755/2.6752 in. (67.958/67.950 mm)
Grade 'C'	2.6758/2.6755 in. (67.965/67.958 mm)
Grade 'D' (service only)	2.6761/2.6758 in. (67.972/67.965 mm)
Oversize available	.015 in. (.38 mm) & .030 in. (.76 mm)

Diameter:

Grade 'A1'...	2.6755/2.6752 in. (67.958/67.950 mm)
Grade 'B1'...	2.6758/2.6755 in. (67.965/67.958 mm)
Grade 'C1'	2.6761/2.6758 in. (67.973/67.965 mm)
Grade 'D1' (service only)	2.6764/2.6761 in. (67.981/67.973 mm)
Oversizes available	+.015 in. (.38mm) .030 in. (.76 mm)

Skirt clearance (measured at 90º to gudgeon pin hole) grades A, B, C, D:

Standard	.0014/.0008 in. (.035/.020 mm)
Sport	.0020/.0014 in. (.050/.035 mm)

Skirt clearance (measured at 90º to gudgeon pin hole) grades A1,B1,C1,D1 ... .0017/.0011 in. (.043/.027 mm)

Piston Rings
Number ... ...   3 per piston
Types... ... ...   2 compression, 1 scraper
Clearance (vertical in groove) ... ...   .0035/.0015 (.088/.037 mm)
Ring gap (fitted) 'A' grade bore... ... ...   .013/.008 in. (.33/.20 mm)

Timing Chain
Type ... ...   Single row, roller
Width ... ...   .225 in. (5.71 mm)
Roller diameter ... ...   .25 in. (6.3 mm)
Pitch ... ...   .375 in. (9.5 mm)
Number of links   82
Tensioning ... ...   Automatic, by spring loaded tensioner

Valves
Operation ... ...   By overhead camshaft
Length ... ...   3.194 (81.12 mm)
Angle of seats and faces 45º
Stem clearance in guide ... ...   .002/.003 in. (.05/.07 mm)
Stem diameter ... ...   .2780/.2775 in. (7.06/7.05 mm)
Head diameter (Imp/Chamois Mk. 1):

Inlet	1.066/1.062 in. (27.07/26.97 mm)
Exhaust	1.012/1.008 in. (25.70/25.60 mm)

Head diameter (Imp/Chamois Mk. II):

Inlet	1.204/1.200 in. (30.58/30.48 mm)
Exhaust	1.066/1.062 in. (27.07/26.97 mm)

Head diameter (Sport saloon):

Inlet	1.278/1.274 in. (32.46/32.35 mm)
Exhaust	1.066/1.062 in. (27.07/26.97 mm)

Valve timing:

	Standard	Sport
Inlet opens	6º B.T.D.C.	23º B.T.D.C.
Inlet closes	46º A.B.D.C.	53º A.B.D.C.
Exhaust opens	46º B.B.D.C.	61º B.B.D.C.
Exhaust closes	6º A.T.D.C.	15º A.T.D.C.

Tappet clearance (cold):

	Inlet	Exhaust
Standard (Mk. I)...	.004/.006 (.10/.15 mm)	.006/.008 in. (.15/.20 mm)
Standard (Mk. II)	.004/.006 in. (.10/.15 mm)	.010/.012 in. (.25/.30 mm)
Sport saloon	.006/.008 in. (.15/.20 mm)	.013/.015 in. (.33/.38 mm)
Rallye saloon	.012 in. (.30 mm)	.014 in. (.35 mm)

Valve Guides

Outside diameter	.502/.501 in. (12.75/12.72 mm)
Interference fit	.002/.0008 in. (.05/.02 mm)

Fitted height above head:

Inlet	.39 in. (9.9 mm)
Exhaust	.45 in. (11.4 mm)

Length (Standard):

Inlet	1.463 in. (37.16 mm)
Exhaust	1.525 in. (38.72 mm)
Length (Sport) inlet & exhaust	1.463 in. (37.16 mm)

Valve Springs

Type	Single coil

Fitted length:

Saloon	1.18 in. (29.9 mm)
Sport	1.180 in. (29.97 mm)

Fitted load:

Standard	31 lbs. (14 Kgs.)
Sport (inner)	16.5 lbs. (7.5 Kg.)
Sport (outer)	32.6/29.4 lbs. (14.8/13.3 Kg.)
Retention	By cup and split cotters

Torque Wrench Settings

Cylinder head bolts (cold)	36 lb ft (5Kg m)
Crankshaft main bearing bolts	41 lb ft (5.6 Kg m)
Connecting rod big end bolts	18 lb ft (2.4 Kg m)
Camshaft bearing cap nuts	6 lb ft (0.8 Kg m)
Camshaft sprocket setscrew	19 lb ft (2.6 Kg m)
Crankshaft pulley bolt	60 lb ft (8 Kg m)
Bellhousing studs (engine to transaxle)	9 lb ft (1.2 Kg m)
Flywheel to crankshaft	32 lb ft (4.4 Kg m)
Rear engine mounting to rubber bush	43 lb ft (5.9 Kg m)
Sparking plugs	14 lb ft (1.9 Kg m)
Temperature switch body	20 lb ft (2.7 Kg m)

All stud nuts:

1/4 in. U.N.F.	6 lbs.ft. (.8 Kg.m)
5/16 in. U.N.F.	15 lbs.ft. (2.0 Kg.m)

1. General Description

1. The engine is of the four cylinder in line type with an overhead camshaft. The unit is supported on rubber mountings in the interest of silence and lack of vibration. Two valves per cylinder are mounted in an inclined position in the cylinder head. The inlet and exhaust valves are placed alternately throughout the length of the head to allow for even dispersion of heat. Vlave clearance is obtained by the use of shims in piston type tappets below the single overhead camshaft. The camshaft is rotated by the crankshaft by means of a single row endless timing chain. The oil pump and distributor, both running at half crankshaft speed are also driven from the crankshaft, but this time drive is by means of a skew gear located on the front end of the crankshaft (i.e. nearest fan belt pulley).

2. The crankshaft is of the forged steel type running in three thinwall steel backed bearings of the replaceable type, endfloat being controlled by two thrust washers mounted on the centre main bearing. Bolted to the transaxle end of the crankshaft is a flywheel and in turn bolted to the flywheel is a hydraulically operated diaphragm type clutch.

3. Located on the crankpins are H section connecting rods, running on replaceable shell bearings of a similar type to the mains. The connecting rod big end caps are serrated to facilitate correct replacement and are fixed to the connecting rods by two setscrews. At the small end of the connecting rods running in lead bronze bushes are the gudgeon pins to which are attached the pistons. The gudgeon pins are located in the piston bosses by circlips.

4. The pistons are of the solid skirt type and are fabricated from aluminium alloy. There are three piston rings located above the gudgeon pin, two compression and one oil control.

5. All the reciprocating parts are contained in a low pressure die-cast block. The cylinder liners are of centrifugally cast iron and are secured in the block by a spiral groove around their exteriors. The cylinder head, cambox and timing cover are also of die-cast aluminium in the interest of weight saving and fast heat dissipation. Attached to the base of the block is a pressed steel sump. The whole engine is supported in the car at an angle of 45º to allow a low centre of gravity and a lower overall height.

2. Routine Maintenance

1. Every 250 miles, or once a week, whichever is sooner, check the engine oil level which should be at the maximum mark on the dipstick. Top up the oil in the sump with the recommended grade (see page 10 for details). On no account should the oil be allowed to fall below the minimum mark.

2. Every 5,000 miles run the engine until it is hot; place a container with a capacity of at least 6 pints under the drain plug in the sump; undo and remove the drain plug and allow the oil to drain for at least 10 minutes. While the oil is draining wash the oil filler cap gauze in petrol, shake dry and re-oil.

3. Clean the drain plug, ensure the washer is in place and return the plug to the sump, tightening it firmly. Re-fill the sump with the recommended quantity and grade of oil as shown on page 10.

4. Also remove the oil filter and renew the filter element as described in Section 24. Examine the engine for oil leaks and rectify as necessary.

5. Every 10,000 miles renew the crankcase breather element. To do this remove the central setscrew, take off the breather assembly and discard the old element.

6. When refitting the new element should be stuck to the cover inside bottom face with quick setting jointing compound to keep it in place during its replacement. Note that the breather outlet pipe should always point upwards. Where a sealed breather system is fitted no maintenance is required.

7. Every 30,000 miles check the engine mounting rubbers for any signs of deterioration or damage and replace them as necessary.

3. Major Operations with Engine in Place

The following major operations can be carried out on the engine with it in place in the body frame:-

1. Removal and replacement of the cylinder head assembly.
2. Removal and replacement of the sump.
3. Removal and replacement of the big end bearings.
4. Removal and replacement of the pistons and connecting rods.
5. Removal and replacement of the timing chain and gears and the timing cover oil seal.
6. Removal and replacement of the camshaft.
7. Removal and replacement of the oil pump.

4. Major Operations with Engine Removed

The following major operations can be carried out with the engine out of the body frame and on the bench or floor:-

1. Removal and replacement of the main bearings.
2. Removal and replacement of the crankshaft.
3. Removal and replacement of the flywheel.

5. Methods of Engine Removal

There are two methods of engine removal. The engine can either be removed alone after being detached from the transaxle at the bellhousing, or both the engine and trans-axle can be removed as a unit. Both methods are described in the following paragraphs. However, the author feels that

Fig. 1.1. EXPLODED VIEW OF THE STATIC ENGINE COMPONENTS

1 Crankcase casting	25 Hose elbow	37 Hose connection union	47 'O' ring	72 Oil seal	86 Oil filler
2 Plug	26 Gasket	38 Lifting eye	48 Cylinder head gasket	74 Plug	87 Hose
3 Sealing washer	27 Stud	39 Banjo	49 Stud	78 Cambox cover	88 Filler tube
4 Plug	28 Cylinder head	40 Large washer	63 Stud	79 Gasket	89 Hose clip
5 Plug	29 Plug	41 Small washer	64 Special nut	80 Stud	90 Oil filler cap
6 Sealing ring	30 Dowel	42 Drain pipe union	67 Timing cover	81 Sump	92 Thermostat
7 Plug	31 Plug for temperature switch tapping	43 Sealing washer	68 Gasket	82 Oil filler	93 Water outlet elbow
8 Main bearing cap bolt	32 Sealing ring	44 Drain pipe	69 Tappet block	83 Gasket	94 Gasket
9 Tab washer	33 Welch plug	45 Bolt	70 Stud	84 Oil filler cap	95 Plug
10 Main bearing cap sealing strip		46 Sealing washers	71 'O' ring	85 Oil filler cap - sealed type	96 Washer

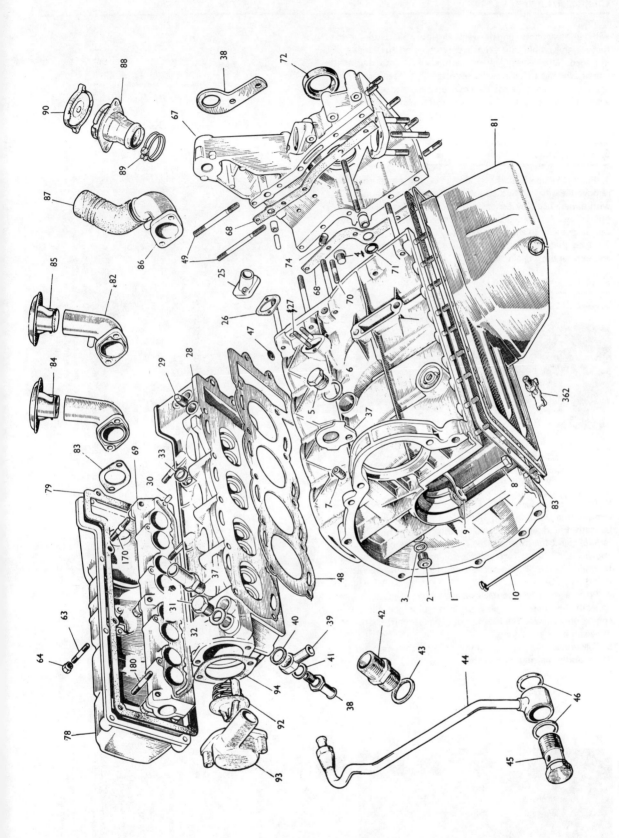

with this particular engine/transaxle layout it is easier to remove the whole unit even if only work on the engine is intended. The decision must eventually rest with the individual, who has to balance the advantages of ease of removal and replacement, against weight and bulk and equipment available. Note that on vans and estate cars the engine/transaxle unit should ALWAYS be removed as one unit.

6. Engine Removal without Transaxle

1. Practical experience has shown that the engine can be removed easily by two people in about three hours (less with experience), by adhering to the following sequence of operations. The sequence may be varied slightly but should not be changed to any great extent.

2. Open the engine cover (it is not necessary to remove it) and expose the engine.

6.2

3. Put the heater lever in the fascia to the red (hot) position, remove the radiator cap and place suitable receptacles beneath the drain taps, one on the bottom edge of the radiator, and the other on the right hand side of the block above the oil filter. Turn the taps on and allow the coolant to drain. NOTE: If the coolant contains anti-freeze retain it and it can be used again.

4. Place a suitable receptacle able to hold at least 6 pints beneath the sump drain plug, undo the plug and allow the engine oil to drain. Replace the plug and discard the oil, to use again is false economy.

5. Disconnect the battery, removing its earth terminal first. Then undo the retaining clamp nuts (photo) and remove the battery from the car.

6.5

Fig. 1.2. EXPLODED VIEW OF THE RECIPROCATING ENGINE COMPONENTS

14 Piston	64 Screw
15 Compression ring	65 Plain washer
16 Compression ring	66 Nyloc nut
17 Scraper ring	75 Oil pump
18 Gudgeon pin	76 Pump driving spindle
19 Circlip	77 Cover and filter unit
20 Connecting rod	78 Pin
21 Small end bush	79 Gasket
22 Special bolt	134 Valve guide - exhaust
23 Tabwasher	135 Valve guide - inlet
24 Bearing shell	136 Circlip
25 Bearing shell	152 Inlet valve (All models except Mk.I, Sport & Stiletto)
26 Thrust washer	153 Exhaust valve (All models
27 Crankshaft	except Mk.I, Sport & Stiletto)
28 Oil pump/distributor drive skew gear	154 Inlet valve (Sport & Stiletto)
29 Crankshaft sprocket	155 Exhaust valve(Sport & Stiletto)
30 Dowel	156 Valve spring
31 Crankshaft pulley	157 Cup-inlet valve
32 Woodruff key	158 Gasket
33 Bolt	159 Seal
34 Starting dog	160 Cup
35 Special washer	11 Valve spring collar
36 Tabwasher	162 Cotters
46 Flywheel and ring gear	163 Inner and outer springs - Sport & Stiletto
47 Ring gear	164 Cup
48 Bolt	165 Collar
49 Lockplate	167 Bucket tappet
50 Timing chain	168 Tappet shim
51 Bracket	171 Camshaft bearings
52 Pin	172 Camshaft
53 Stud	173 Camshaft sprocket
54 Tabwasher	174 Dowel
55 Nut	175 Washer
56 Chain tensioner blade	176 Tabwasher
57 Spring	177 Bolt
58 Shoe	
59 Damper	
60 Screw	
61 Plain washer	
62 Locknut	
63 Shoe runner	

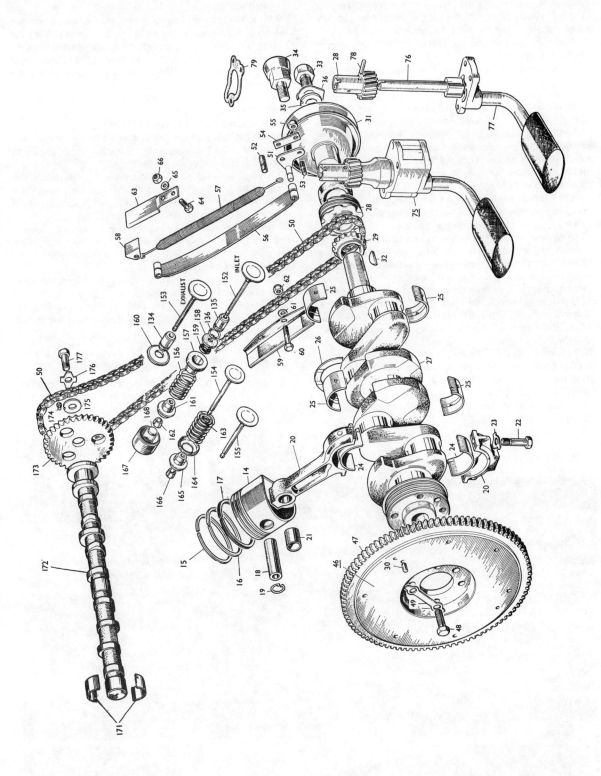

6. Undo the bolt on the silencer rear strap (photo A), remove the nut holding the silencer to the front triangular support bracket (photo B), loosen the silencer to manifold clamp (photo C) and remove the silencer (photo D).

7. Undo the two rear bumper retaining bolts and remove the bumper (photo).

8. Undo the screws holding the engine stoneguard in place (arrowed in photo's A and B) and remove the guard (photo C).

9. Now place a jack beneath the centre of the engine, raise the jack until it is in contact with the engine. The jack should have a wooden block interposed between it and the engine and should bear on the block casting at the point where it meets the sump flange. If it is possible to obtain and use a trolley jack for this purpose, do so as it will facilitate simply wheeling the engine out of the car, rather than lifting it as is the case with a stationary jack.

10 Undo and remove the four bolts retaining the rear engine mounting to the rear crossmember (photo).

11 Undo and remove the two nuts and four bolts holding the rear crossmember. The two nuts, one either side, are situated directly behind each of the rear reflectors (photo A) whilst two bolts are screwed into each end of the crossmember (photo B). Remove the rear crossmember (photo C).

12 Undo and remove the nut from the starter motor terminal and pull off the feed cable (photo).

13 Using a socket spanner and a long extension undo and remove the nuts holding the clutch slave cylinder to the bellhousing (photo A). Once the nuts are removed pull the slave cylinder away from the bellhousing (photo B) and tie it to the bulkhead out of the way. Remove the two bolts left protruding through the bellhousing.

14 Unscrew and remove the H.T. lead from the centre of the coil (photo).

15 Pull off the two lucar terminals from the rear of the dynamo (photo).

16 Now pull off the lucar connector on the low oil pressure warning switch (photo), at the same time remove the lucar connector from the temperature gauge sender unit (if fitted). This is located at the very rear of the cylinder head (i.e. furthest end from the crankshaft pulley) behind the top hose.

17 Remove the L.T. circuit lucar connector from the distributor (photo).

18 Loosen the clip and pull the feed pipe from the input side of the fuel pump (photo) and tie it out of the way. Note that if the fuel tank is very full it may be necessary to clamp this pipe with a mole wrench.

19 If your car is fitted with a pneumatic throttle remove the air pipe from the carburettor; if cable operated loosen the cable clamp on the throttle arm (arrowed) and withdraw the throttle cable from the carburettor (photo).

20 Now loosen the choke cable clamp (if manual choke is fitted) (arrowed) (photo A) and remove the outer cable retaining clip (arrowed) (photo B); withdraw the choke cable from the carburettor.

21 Loosen the clip and pull the bottom hose from its union on the base of the radiator (photo).

22 Loosen the clip (photo) and pull the heater hose from its union just in front of the top hose elbow at the rear end of the cylinder head.

23 Loosen the clip arrowed in the photo and pull the top hose from its elbow at the rear of the cylinder head.

24 Loosen the clip and pull the heater hose from its union (photo) on the bleed valve (if fitted in position shown), if not loosen the clip at the water pump union and pull the hose off from there.

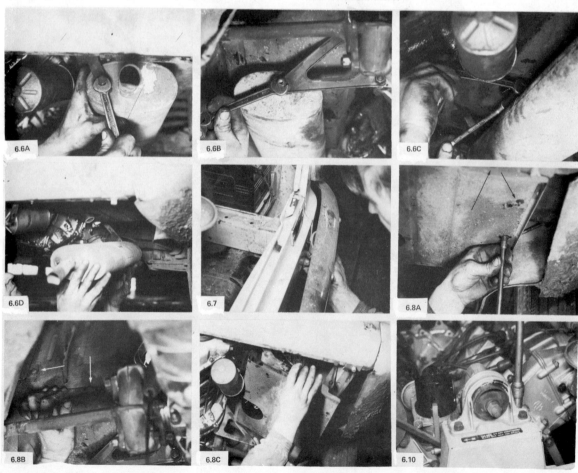

6.6A   6.6B   6.6C

6.6D   6.7   6.8A

6.8B   6.8C   6.10

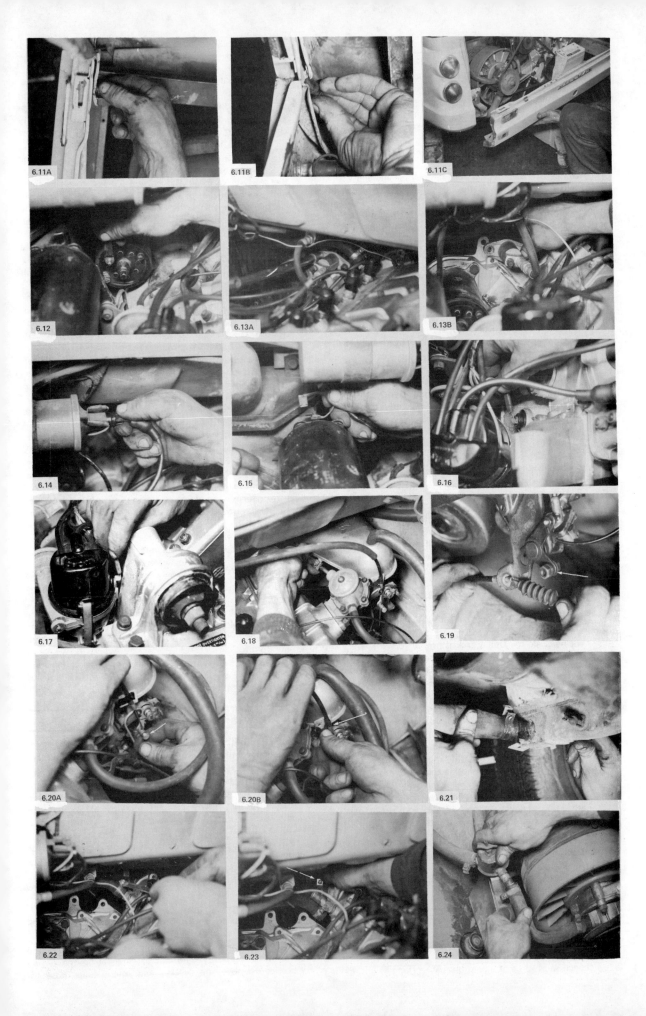

6.11A

6.11B

6.11C

6.12

6.13A

6.13B

6.14

6.15

6.16

6.17

6.18

6.19

6.20A

6.20B

6.21

6.22

6.23

6.24

25 Loosen the tensioning band around the rubber shroud (photo A), slide the band backwards and gently lever the shroud from the fan cowling (photo B).

26 Now from beneath the vehicle undo and remove all the nuts around the periphery of the bellhousing, except the bottom one.

27 Place a wooden support block underneath the transaxle unit and ensure that the handbrake is on.

28 Remove the last nut from the bellhousing and with the help of a friend, pull the engine backwards about three inches and then lift it clear of the car. If the engine is supported on a trolley jack, get a friend to hold the engine steady as it is pulled straight out from the rear of the car.

7. Engine Removal - With Transaxle

1. To remove the engine and transaxle as a unit follow the instructions in Section 6 up to and including paragraph 24.

2. From beneath the car remove the three nuts from the driveshaft spider arms (photo).

3. Using a soft drift knock the bolts from which the nuts were taken, far enough back through the rubber coupling to facilitate freeing the driveshaft spider from the coupling (photo A). This done, pull the spider end of the driveshaft downwards away from the coupling. Repeat this process on the other driveshaft. NOTE: If it is found to be difficult to push the bolts back through the coupling, it may help to lever the coupling downwards as shown in photo B.

4. Working through the hole in the chassis member, with a small chisel knock back the locking tab retaining the bolt on the remote gear change shaft. This done unscrew and remove the bolt (photo).

5. Unscrew and remove the nut retaining the earthing strap (arrowed) to the rear of the transaxle (photo). Once the earth strap is removed replace and lightly tighten the nut to prevent distortion of the transaxle cover.

6. At this stage with the jack still in position supporting the weight of the engine, place an additional sturdy support beneath the centre of the transaxle, and also beneath the exhaust manifold flange. The latter is to prevent the unit toppling sideways. If a trolley jack is being used, it will now be necessary to move it forward so that it is supporting the engine/transaxle unit beneath the bellhousing. This can be done by using a temporary jack to take the weight of the engine while the trolley jack is moved forward. The temporary jack should be left in place at the front of the engine until engine removal takes place. Using this method it will again be necessary to place a support beneath the exhaust manifold flange to stop the unit from toppling sideways.

7. Remove the two bolts (arrowed) and washers from the transaxle mounting rubbers (photo), one either side of the unit.

8. With a friend to hold the unit steady, slowly push the car forward leaving the transaxle engine unit behind (photo).

9. If the trolley jack method is being used, two people will be needed, one to hold the engine and prevent it from toppling, whilst the temporary jack and manifold support are being removed (photo A) and another to draw the trolley jack and engine/transaxle unit from the car (photo B).

Note: Unless it is known that the differential shafts on the transaxle are of the early type which cannot be pulled out, tie the two shafts together, over or under the transaxle to prevent them inadvertently falling out and causing damage to the splines.

8. Dismantling the Engine - General

1. It is best to mount the engine on a dismantling stand but if one is not available then stand the engine on a strong bench so as to be at a comfortable working height. Failing this, the engine can be stripped down on the floor.

2. During the dismantling process the greatest care should be taken to keep the exposed parts free from dirt. As an aid to achieving this, it is a sound scheme to thoroughly clean down the outside of the engine, removing all traces of oil and congealed dirt.

3. Use paraffin or good grease solvent such as 'Gunk'. The latter compound will make the job much easier, as, after the solvent has been applied and allowed to stand for a time, a vigorous jet of water will wash off the solvent and all the grease and filth. If the dirt is thick and deeply embedded, work the solvent into it with a hard bristled paintbrush.

4. Finally, wipe down the exterior of the engine with a rag and only then, when it is quite clean, should the dismantling process begin. As the engine is stripped, clean each part in a bath of paraffin or petrol.

5. Never immerse parts with oilways in paraffin, i.e. the crankshaft, but to clean wipe down carefully with a petrol dampened rag. Oilways can be cleaned out with pipe cleaners. If an air line is present all parts can be blown dry and the oilways blown through as an added precaution.

6. Re-use of old engine gaskets is a false economy and can give rise to oil and water leaks, if nothing worse. To avoid the possibility of trouble after the engine has been reassembled always use new gaskets throughout.

7. Do not throw the old gaskets away as it sometimes happens that an immediate replacement cannot be bought and the old gasket is then very useful as a template. Hang up the old gaskets as they are removed on a suitable hook or nail.

8. To strip the engine it is best to work from the top downwards. However, because of the unusual sump shape it will be necessary to use blocks to keep the engine upright. When the stage where the sump must be removed is reached the engine can be turned on its side and all other work carried out with it in this position.

9. Wherever possible, replace nuts, bolts and washers finger-tight from wherever they were removed. This helps avoid later loss and muddle. If they cannot be replaced then lay them out in such a fashion that it is clear from where they came, or alternatively place them in labelled jars.

10 If the engine was removed with the transaxle separate them by undoing the nuts and bolts, including those holding the starter motor, which hold the bellhousing to the endplate (photo).

11 Lift off the starter motor and place on one side (photo).

12 Carefully pull the transaxle complete with bellhousing off the engine (photo).

9. Removing Ancillary Engine Components

1. Before basic engine dismantling begins the engine should be stripped of all its ancillary components. These items should also be removed if a factory exchange reconditioned unit is being purchased. The items comprise:- Dynamo and dynamo brackets; water pump and thermostat housing; starter motor; distributor and sparking plugs; inlet and exhaust manifold and carburettors; fuel pump and fuel pipes; oil filter and dipstick; oil filler cap; breather pipe.

2. Without exception all these items can be removed with the engine in the car if it is merely an individual item which requires attention.

3. Starting work on the left-hand side of the engine, unscrew and remove the three dynamo retaining bolts. Take off the fan belt and remove the dynamo.

4. Loosen its clip and pull the intermediate hose from its union at the block.

5. Unscrew and withdraw the three through bolts holding the water pump/dynamo support bracket to the engine bosses. Remove the bracket and intermediate hose to-

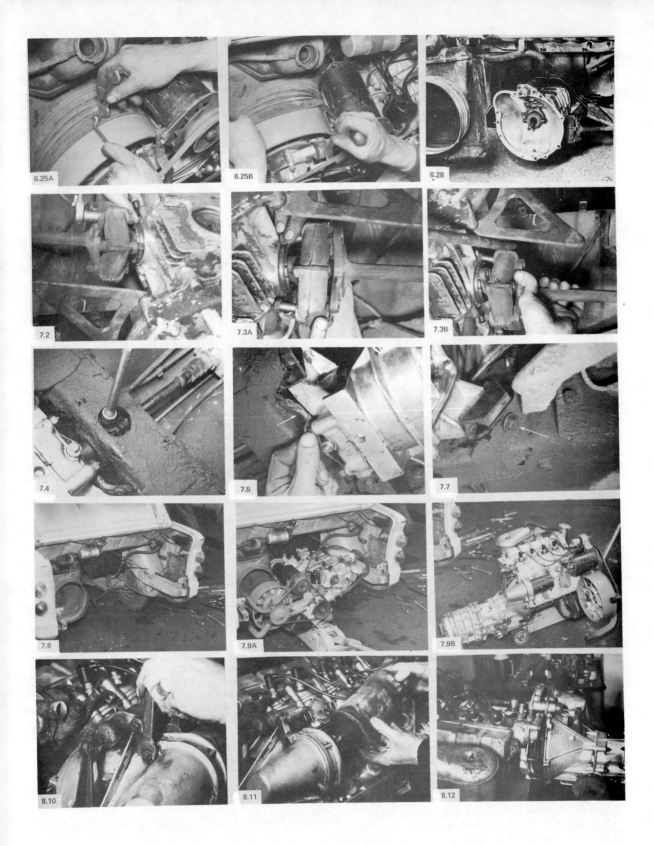

gether, retain any spacers that were removed and also the triangular plate which indicates TDC on the crankshaft pulley. Make a note of where the spacers (if any) were fitted.

6. Remove the distributor assembly complete with H.T. leads and plug caps after undoing the two nuts and washers which hold the bottom flange of the distributor to the cylinder block studs (photo). Do not loosen the square nut on the clamp at the base of the distributor body or the static timing will be lost.

7. Unscrew and remove the two retaining nuts and washers which hold the intermediate hose elbow to the cylinder block and lift away the hose (photo).

8. Remove the breather pipe from the base of the cylinder block by undoing the single retaining bolt.

9. Remove the thermostat housing/water outlet elbow (photo) after undoing its two retaining nuts and washers. If it is stiff soak the studs in penetrating oil and gently tap it off with a non-metallic hammer. On no account insert a screwdriver at the joint and try to lever it off. Remove the thermostat.

10 Remove the dipstick.

11 Loosen the retaining clip, and pull the petrol feed pipe from the outlet side of the fuel pump.

12 Using a suitable spanner unscrew and remove the temperature sensor/switch unit from the cylinder block (photo) where fitted.

13 Moving to the right-hand side of the engine, unscrew and remove the nuts retaining the manifolds to the cylinder head (a socket spanner and extension are best to reach the recessed nuts (photo). Remove the manifolds, carburettor/s and air filter as a unit (photo).

14 Undo and remove the domed nut above the filter body. Remove the filter casing and element from the oil filter body.

15 Unscrew and remove the three nuts and washers (photo) holding the oil filter body to the cylinder block. Remove the oil filter body.

16 Undo the two nuts holding the fuel pump to the cambox cover. Remove the pump (photo) and note the number of gaskets between the pump and cover as the thickness of these gaskets controls pump output pressure. The engine is now stripped of ancillary components and ready for major dismantling to begin.

10. Cylinder Head Removal - Engine on Bench

1. Undo and remove all the nuts around the periphery of the cambox cover, a box spanner will probably be found to be the best tool for this purpose. Lift off the cambox cover (photo).

2. The camshaft, driving sprocket, and timing chain will now be exposed. Knock back the tabs on the tab washer and unscrew the bolt holding the sprocket to the camshaft. To prevent the engine from turning wedge a screwdriver between a bellhousing stud and the starter ring teeth (photo). Remove the sprocket and hang the timing chain over the edge of its casing. Remove the dowel peg from the camshaft flange to avoid any possibility of it falling down into the engine.

3. Working in a diagonal sequence, and unscrewing the nuts and washers half a turn at a time to prevent distortion, (photo A) remove the eight nuts holding the camshaft/ tappet carrier to the cylinder head. Very gently lift the carrier from the cylinder head inverting it as you do so. Several things may happen at this stage. The tappet shims may be left in the top of the valves or in the tappet pistons, or pistons containing the shims may stay on top of the valves as shown in photo B. However, whatever does

happen it is essential that the tappet/pistons are replaced in the bore of the camshaft carrier from which they came. Any shims left on top of the valves must also be replaced in the tappet/piston from which they came. If this is not done it will be necessary to reset all the clearances as described in Sections 54 and 55.

4. Undo the 10 cylinder head bolts half a turn at a time in the sequence shown in Fig. 1.3. Undo and remove nuts 'A' and 'B' first of all.

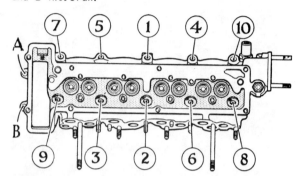

Fig. 1.3. Cylinder head bolt tightening sequence.

5. The cylinder head can now be removed by lifting it upwards. If the head is jammed, try to rock it to break the seal. Under no circumstances try to prise it apart from the block with a screwdriver or cold chisel as damage may be done to the faces of the head or block. If the head will not readily free, turn the engine over by the flywheel as the compression in the cylinders will often break the cylinder head joint. If this fails to work strike the head sharply with a non-metallic hammer or with a metal hammer with an interposed piece of wood to cushion the blows. Under no circumstances hit the head directly with a metal hammer as this may cause the casting to fracture. Several sharp taps with the hammer at the same time pulling upwards should free the head. Lift the head off and place on one side (photo).

11. Cylinder Head Removal - Engine in Car

1. Disconnect the battery by removing the lead from the positive terminal (negative on later models).

2. Remove the radiator cap. Place suitable receptacles under each drain tap (one at the base of the radiator and the other just above the oil filter on the right-hand side of the engine). Open the taps and drain the coolant.

3. Remove the air filter as described in Chapter 3.

4. Loosen the retaining clip and remove the carburettor feed pipe from the fuel pump.

5. Undo the two retaining nuts and washers and remove the fuel pump from the cambox cover; tie it up out of the way. Note the number of gaskets between the pump and cover as the thickness of these gaskets govern output pressure.

6. Pull the vacuum advance pipe from its connection on the carburettor and unbolt its retaining clip from the front of the cambox cover.

7 Later models have a breather pipe connected to the oil filter tube. Remove this pipe if fitted.

8 On some models cylinder head removal will be made easier if the carburettor is removed first.

9 From this point procedure is the same as that described in Section 10.

12. Valve Removal

1. Compress each spring in turn with a valve spring compressor (photo) until the two halves of the collets can be removed. Release the compressor and remove the spring, shroud and valve.) Great care must be taken not to

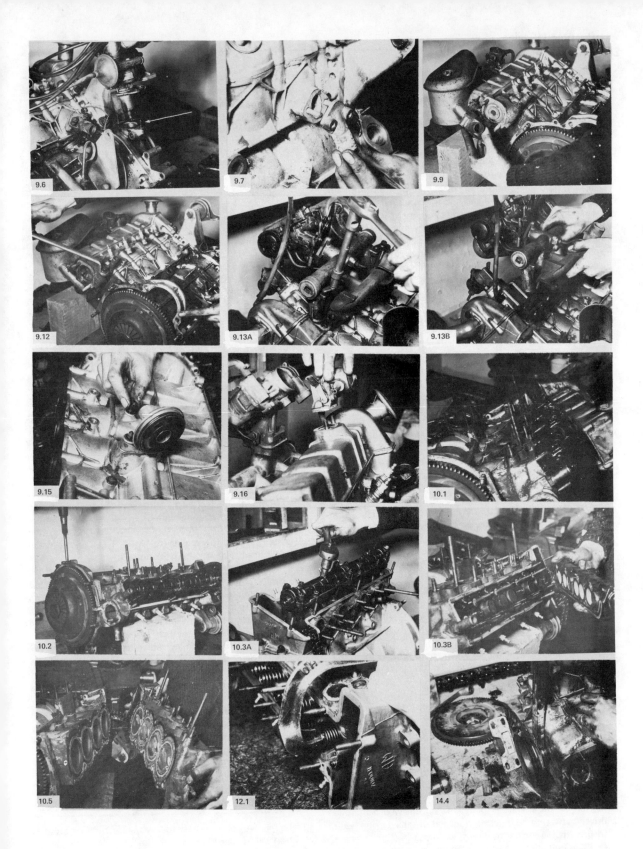

over compress the springs on inlet valves, otherwise the oil seal retaining cap at the base of the spring will be damaged.

2. If when the valve spring compressor is screwed down the valve spring retaining cap refuses to free and expose the split collet, do not continue to screw down on the compressor as there is a likelihood of damaging it.

3. Gently tap the top of the tool directly over the cap with a light hammer. This will free the cap. To avoid the compressor jumping off the valve spring retaining cap when it is tapped hold the compressor firmly in position with one hand. Drop each valve out through the combustion chamber.

4. It is essential that the valves are kept in their correct sequence unless they are so badly worn that they are to be renewed. If they are going to be kept and used again, place them in a sheet of card having eight holes numbered 1 to 8 corresponding with the relative positions the valves were in when fitted. Also keep the valve springs, washers, etc., in the correct order.

14.6

13. Valve Guide - Removal and Replacement

1. This is really a job for your local Rootes dealer or engineering works, as the head must be uniformly heated to 200°C (390°F) for 30 minutes. This would be very difficult to do without the correct facilities, and under no circumstances must the guides be driven out cold.

2. However, if the facilities are available proceed as follows: Remove the thermostat and uniformally heat the head to 200°C (390°F) for 30 minutes.

3. The guide is then driven out with a brass drift (Churchill tool RG 357). The drift is located on the combustion chamber end of the guide.

4. The new guide is then drifted in from the valve spring side of the cylinder head. The guide is correctly in position when its surrounding circlip contacts the casting.

14. Timing Chain Cover, Sprockets, Chain and Chain Tensioner - Removal - Engine on Bench

1. After turning the engine to No. 1 T.D.C. remove the cylinder head as described in Section 10.

2. Undo the nuts and washers around the periphery of the sump. Remove the sump.

3. If it is still fitted it will be necessary to remove the water pump/dynamo support bracket. To do this proceed as follows:-

a) Loosen the retaining clip and pull the intermediate hose from its union on the cylinder block.

b) Undo and remove the dynamo retaining bolts. Remove the dynamo and fan belt.

c) Undo and withdraw the three through bolts retaining the water pump support bracket to the timing cover bosses.

The bracket can now be removed.

4. Remove the crankshaft pulley. To do this wedge a screwdriver between a bellhousing stud and the starter ring teeth to prevent the engine from turning. Knock back the staking tabs and undo the bolt holding the pulley to the crankshaft. Lever off the pulley with a block of wood (photo) or if available draw it off with a puller.

5. Undo half a turn at a time to prevent distortion, the nuts around the periphery of the timing chain cover.

6. Remove the cap from the distributor (if still fitted) so that the rotor arm is in view. Pull the timing chain cover off and as this is done note that the distributor rotor turns from the four o'clock to the three o'clock position. If the **cover proves** stubborn to remove, gently knock it off

with a hammer and an interposed piece of wood (photo).

7. The timing chain is now simply lifted off the teeth on the crankshaft sprocket and removed from the engine.

8. The timing chain tensioner is easily removed by pushing downwards on the tensioner spring until the spring eye is freed from its groove on the bottom tensioner mounting. This done it is slid off the bottom mounting and removed.

9. The crankshaft sprocket can now be withdrawn using a suitable puller.

15. Timing Chain Cover, Sprockets, Chain and Chain Tensioner - Removal - Engine in Car

1. After turning the engine to No. 1 T.D.C. remove the cylinder head as described in Section 11.

2. Place a suitable receptacle beneath the sump plug, remove the drain plug and allow the oil to drain for at least ten minutes. Replace the sump plug. Undo the nuts and washers around the periphery of the sump. Remove the sump.

3. Place a jack beneath the engine and as near to the timing cover as possible without actually being on it.

4. Undo the two retaining bolts and remove the rear bumper. Then remove the rear crossmember as described in Section 6/10-11.

5. Next remove the water pump/dynamo support bracket as described in Chapter 2, Section 8/1-7.

6. The procedure is now the same as Section 14, paragraph 4 onwards, except that now it will be necessary to put the car in gear and apply the handbrake to prevent the engine from turning as the crankshaft pulley bolt is unscrewed.

16. Camshaft - Removal - Engine on Bench

1. To remove the camshaft follow the instructions given in Section 10/1-2, and then as follows:-

2. Mark the three camshaft bearing caps, so that they can be refitted in exactly the same position from which they were removed.

3. Undo the six camshaft bearing caps, retaining nuts and washers half a turn at a time. Gently remove the three caps and ensure that the bearings do not fall out as they are lifted.

4. Lift the camshaft from its carrier and withdraw it from the engine, ensuring that none of the shell bearings are adhering to its bearing surfaces.

17. Camshaft Removal – Engine in Car

1. To remove the camshaft follow the instructions given in Section 11/1-6 and then the instructions given in Section 16/1-4.

18. Sump, Piston, Connecting Rod and Big End Removal

1. The sump, pistons and connecting rods can be removed with the engine still in the car or with the engine on the bench. If in the car, proceed as for removing the cylinder head with the engine in the car, as described in Section 11. If on the bench proceed as for removing the cylinder head with th engine in this position, as described in Section 10. The pistons and connecting rods are drawn up out of the top of the cylinder bores.

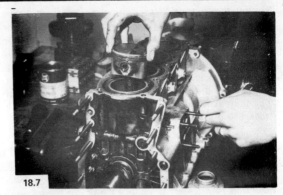

18.7

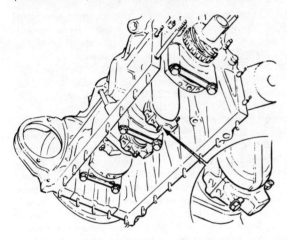

Fig. 1.4. Figure shows tab washers correctly fitted to main bearings and big ends. Insert shows conn-rod and cap identification numbers.

2. Remove the nuts and washers holding the sump in position. Remove the sump and the sump gasket.
3. Remove the self-locking nuts from the big end bearing caps. On early models, a conventional nut and bolt were used, locked with a tab washer (see Fig.1.4). Knock back the tab washers with a cold chisel to remove the bolts.
4. Remove the big end caps one at a time, taking care to keep them in the right order and the correct way round. Also ensure that the shell bearings are kept with their correct connecting rods and caps unless they are to be renewed. Normally, the numbers 1 to 4 are stamped on adjacent sides of the big end caps and connecting rods, indicating which cap fits on which rod and which way round the cap fits. If no numbers or lines can be found then with a sharp screwdriver or file scratch mating marks across the joint from the rod to the cap. One line for connecting rod No. 1, two for connecting rod No. 2, and so on. This will ensure there is no confusion later. It is most important that the caps go back in the correct position on the connecting rods from which they were removed.
5. If the big end caps are difficult to remove they may be gently tapped with a soft hammer.
6. To remove the shell bearing press the bearing opposite the groove in both the connecting rod and the connecting rod caps and the bearings will slide out easily.
7. Withdraw the pistons and connecting rods upwards (photo) and ensure they are kept in the correct order for replacement in the same bore. Refit the connecting rod caps and bearings to the rods if the bearings do not require renewal. This is to minimise the risk of getting the caps

and rods muddled. NOTE: If it proves difficult to push the pistons up past the wear ridge at the top of the bore place a length of wood against the base of the connecting rod and gently tap the wood with a hammer. This will force the piston rings past the ridge.

19. Gudgeon Pin – Removal

1. To remove the gudgeon pin to free the piston from the connecting rod remove one of the circlips at either end of the pin with a pair of circlip pliers.
2. Press out the pin from the rod and piston with your finger.
3. If the pin shows reluctance to move, then on no account force it out as this could damage the piston. Immerse the piston in a pan of boiling water, or better still, oil, for three minutes. On removal the expansion of the aluminium should allow the gudgeon pin to slide out easily.
4. Make sure the pins are kept with the same piston for ease of refitting.

20. Piston Rings – Removal

1. To remove the piston rings slide them carefully over the top of the piston, taking care not to scratch the aluminium alloy. Never slide them off over the bottom of the piston skirt. It is very easy to break the iron piston rings if they are pulled off roughly so this operation should be done with extreme caution. It is helpful to make use of an old hacksaw blade, or better still, an old .020 in. feeler gauge.
2. Lift one end of the piston ring to be removed out of its groove and insert the end of the feeler gauge under it.
3. Turn the feeler gauge slowly round the piston and as the ring comes out of its groove apply slight upward pressure so that it rests on the land above. It can then be eased off the piston with the feeler gauge stopping it from slipping into any empty groove if it is any but the top piston ring that is being removed.

21. Flywheel – Removal

Having removed the clutch (see Chapter 5) the flywheel can be removed. It is only possible for this operation to be carried out with the engine out of the car.
1. Bend back the locking tabs from the four bolts which hold the flywheel to the flywheel flange on the rear of the crankshaft.
2. Unscrew the bolts and remove them complete with the locking plates.

3. Lift the flywheel away from the crankshaft flange. NOTE: Some difficulty may be experienced in removing the bolts caused by the rotation of the crankshaft every time pressure is put on the spanner. To lock the crankshaft in position while the bolts are removed, use a screwdriver as a wedge between a bellhousing stud and the ring gear. Alternatively a wooden wedge can be inserted between the crankshaft and the side of the block inside the crankcase if the sump is off.

22. Crankshaft and Main Bearing – Removal

With the engine out of the car, remove the cylinder head (this is necessary to remove the timing chain cover), sump, timing chain cover, timing chain and chain tensioner, pistons and connecting rods, clutch and flywheel, as has already been described in Sections 10, 14, 18 and 21. Removal of the crankshaft can only be attempted with the engine on the bench or floor.

1. Remove the self-locking nuts, unscrewing them half a turn at a time. Early models may be fitted with conventional bolts, locked by tab washers. In this case, knock back the tab washers with a cold chisel to remove the bolts and washers together.

2. Remove the main bearing caps and the bottom half of each bearing shell, taking care to keep the bearing shells in the right caps. NOTE: The rear main bearing cap (i.e. nearest to the flywheel end of the crankshaft) is almost an interference fit in the crankcase casting. If for this reason it proves difficult to remove, place a block of wood against the top lip and gently tap the wood with a hammer until the cap frees itself from the casting.

3. Remove the crankshaft by lifting it away from the crankcase.

4. Remove the remaining shell bearings and lay them with their counterparts. Note the semi-circular thrust washers on either side of the centre main bearing. Remove them and lay them with the centre main bearing along the correct sides.

23. Lubrication and Crankcase Ventilation Systems – Description

1. Oil pressure is provided by a pump driven at half crankshaft speed from a skew gear on the nose of the crankshaft, just behind the pulley wheel. Oil pressure is controlled by a pressure relief valve in the body of the full flow oil filter unit. This unit returns excess oil supplied by the pump directly to the sump.

2. Filtration is provided by a full flow oil filter with a replaceable type element, mounted on the right-hand side of the engine. Oil comes directly from the pump and passes into compartment 'A' of the filter body (see Fig. 1.5.). When excess oil pressure develops in compartment 'A' it lifts the piston in the relief valve, this exposes a drilling into compartment 'C' via which excess oil returns directly to the sump. However, when pressure is normal, the oil from the pump via compartment 'A' surrounds the exterior of the paper filter element. Therefore, to gain access to compartment 'B' it must pass through the element. During the passage through the element all foreign bodies are removed from the oil, so clean oil is fed via compartment 'B' to all bearing surfaces in the engine.

3. Oil is drawn from the sump into the pump via a submerged gauze filter pick-up pipe. Oil is then fed under pressure from the pump to the full flow oil filer. From the filter the lubricant passes into the main oil gallery, from which the three main bearings are fed. Oil then passes from the main bearings through drillings in the crankshaft to the big end bearings. The camshaft and valve gear are lubricated **by another drilling from the main oil gallery.**

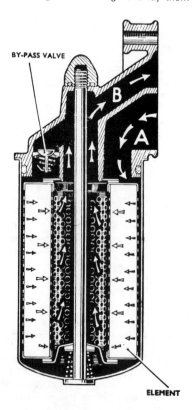 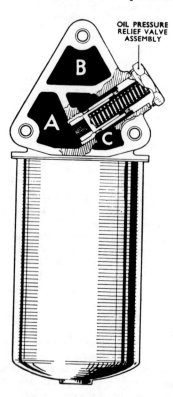

Fig. 1.5. Sectional views of the oil filter showing oil pressure relief valve and by-pass valve

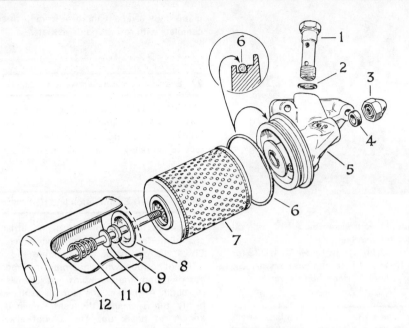

Fig. 1.6. EXPLODED VIEW OF THE OIL FILTER

1 Relief valve assembly	4 Rubber sealing washer used	7 Filter Element	11 Element support spring
2 Relief valve joint	under nut	8 Element support plate	12 Filter case
3 Filter case retaining	5 Filter main body	9 Felt washer	
nut	6 Filter case 'O' ring	10 Steel washer	

by another drilling from the main oil gallery.

4. Pistons and small ends are lubricated by oil exuding from the big end bearings and being thrown up the bores by the movement of the crankshaft, while the timing chain and its sprockets are lubricated by oil draining from the valve gear back into the sump via the timing chain compartment.

5. On early models excess crankcase pressure is ejected directly into the atmosphere via a breather pipe on the left of the engine at the base of the crankcase and a perforated oil filler tube cap. Later models are fitted with a semi-closed circuit which means that crankcase fumes are fed through a tube from the oil filter tube into the carburettor/s via which the fumes are passed into the combustion chambers and burnt. With this type of system the filter cap is no longer perforated.

24. Oil Filter - Removal and Replacement - Engine in Car

All numbers relate to Fig. 1.6.

1. To remove the element undo the domed nut (3) and pull the casing (12) from the filter body (5). Have a suitable receptacle handy to catch the oil that will spill.

2. Invert the casing and allow the paper element (7) to fall out. Thoroughly wash out the interior of the casing with paraffin until all traces of sludge are removed.

3. With a pin prise the rubber seal (4) from the groove in the lip of the filter body (photo A) and also the groove in the domed nut (photo B). Then push a new sealing ring (4) into the domed nut (3) and also ease a new sealing ring into the vacant groove in the filter body (5) lip; it should rest in the groove as shown in the inset.

4. Soak the new element (7) in fresh oil, place it over the casing (12) through bolt (photo), and ensure that it is centralised on its seating plate (8).

5. To replace the oil filter pass the through bolt through the centre of the oil filter body (5). With one hand hold the casing (12) in place against the filter body (5) and with the other screw the domed nut (3) finger tight onto the threads of the through bolt (photo), which should be protruding through the filter body (5). With a suitable spanner lightly tighten the domed nut (3).

24.3A

24.3B

24.4

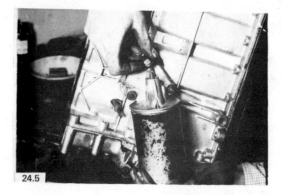

24.5

6. Pour into the engine the equivalent amount of fresh oil as that wasted when the filter was removed.

7. Start the engine but do not rev it, rather let it idle for two or three minutes first. This is to minimise any damage that may occur through a short period of oil starvation.

25. Oil Pressure Relief Valve - Removal and Replacement

1. To prevent excessive oil pressure, for example when the engine is cold, an oil pressure relief valve is incorporated in the lubrication system. This valve is screwed into the top of the oil filter body.

2. To remove the valve simply unscrew it with a 15/16 in. A.F. spanner. The valve should occasionally be removed, washed in paraffin and blown dry.

3. This unit should always be renewed at a major overhaul.

4. To replace the relief valve screw it back into its orifice on the top of the filter body. The valve sealing ring should be renewed whenever the relief valve is removed.

26. Oil Pump - Removal and Dismantling

1. Remove the sump.

2. Unscrew and remove the three nuts and washers and one cheese headed screw retaining the base plate. This done the base plate and pickup filter can be removed as a unit. Take care to ensure that neither of the rotors fall out at this stage. Replace the cheesehead screw in the oil pump body, with a large washer under its head. This will retain the two rotors. NOTE: No attempt should be made to remove the oil filter/pickup from the pump base.

3. The pump body will now be retained in place only by the seal between it and the crankcase. To break the seal place a block of wood against the pump body and gently tap the wood with a hammer (photo). Once the seal is broken the

26.3

pump body can be withdrawn from its three retaining studs complete with rotors and drive shaft.

27. Examination and Renovation - General

With the engine stripped down and all parts thoroughly cleaned it is now time to examine everything for wear. The following items should be checked and where necessary renewed or renovated as described in the following sections.

28. Crankshaft Examination and Renovation

Examine the crankpin and main journal surfaces on the crankshaft for scoring or scratches which may be present. Check the ovality of the crankpins and main journals at different positions with a micrometer. If more than 0.001 in. out of round, the crankpins and journals will have to be reground. Also check the journals in the same fashion. On highly tuned engines the centre main bearing has been known to break up. This is not always immediately apparent, but slight vibration in an otherwise normally smooth engine and a very slight drop in oil pressure under normal conditions are clues. If the centre main bearing is suspected of failure it should be immediately investigated by dropping the sump and removing the centre main bearing cap. Failure to do this will result in a badly scored centre main journal. If it is necessary to regrind the crankshaft and fit new bearings your local Chrysler garage or engineering works will be able to decide how much metal to grind off and the correct undersize shells to fit.

29. Big End & Main Bearing - Examination & Renovation

Big end bearing failure is accompanied by a noisy knocking from the crankcase and a slight drop in oil pressure. Main bearing failure is accompanied by vibration which can be quite severe as the engine speed rises and falls and a drop in oil pressure.

Bearings which have not broken up, but are badly worn, will give rise to low oil pressure and some vibration. Inspect the big ends, main bearings and thrust washers for signs of general wear, scoring, pitting and scratches. The bearing should be matt grey in colour. With lead bronze bearings should a trace of copper colour be noticed the bearings are badly worn as the lead bearing material has worn away to expose the indium underlay. Renew the bearings if they are in this condition or if there is any sign of scoring or pitting. If you are not sure how worn the bearings are take them to the stores at your local garage and compare them with new ones.

The undersizes available are designed to correspond with the regrind sizes, i.e. .010 in. bearings are correct for a crankshaft reground - .010 in. undersize. The bearings are in fact slightly more than the stated undersize as running clearances have been allowed for during their manufacture.

Very long engine life can be achieved by changing big end bearings at intervals of 30,000 miles and main bearings at intervals of 50,000 miles, irrespective of bearing wear. Normally, crankshaft wear is infinitesimal and a change of bearings will ensure mileages of up to 100,000 miles before crankshafts normally have to be reground because of scoring due to bearing failure.

30. Cylinder Bores - Examination and Renovation

1. The cylinder bores must be examined for taper, ovality, scoring and scratches. Start by carefully examining the top of each bore. If they are at all worn a very slight ridge will be found on the thrust side. This marks the top of the piston ring travel. The owner will have a good indication of bore wear prior to dismantling the engine or removing the cylinder head. Excessive oil consumption accompanied by blue smoke from the exhaust is a sure sign of worn cylinder bores and piston rings.

2. Measure the bore diameter just under the ridge with a micrometer and compare it with the diameter at the bottom of the bore, which is not subject to wear. If the difference between the two measurements is more than .006 in. then it will be necessary to fit special pistons and rings or to have the cylinders rebored and fit oversize pistons. If no micrometer is available remove the rings from a piston and place in each bore in turn about ¾ in. below the top of the bore. If a feeler gauge of dimensions greater than .0014 in. (A, B, C, D grade pistons) or .0017 in. (A1, B1, C1, D1 grade pistons) can be slid between the piston skirt and cylinder bore on the thrust side of the piston then remedial action should be taken.

3. Pistons are available of oversize dimensions of + .015 ins. (.38 mm) and + .030 ins. (.76 mm). However, the company that rebores the cylinder bores will be able to advise the exact grade and oversize of piston and rings needed.

4. If the bores are slightly worn but not so badly worn as to justify reboring them, then special oil control rings and pistons can be fitted which will restore compression and stop the engine burning oil. Several different types are available and the manufacturer's instructions concerning their fitting must be followed closely.

5. If new pistons or rings are being fitted and the bores have not been reground, it is essential to slightly roughen the hard glaze on the sides of the bores. This process is called 'glazebusting'. With a partly worn piece of No. 1 or 1½ grade emery paper, gently rub the interior of the bore working up and down and rotating one way and then the other. Spend about three minutes on each bore until the entire cylinder wall is criss-crossed with abrasions.

6. An easier way to carry out this task is to make a mandrel about 10 inches long with a slot two inches long in one end, form a piece of welding rod or similar of approximately 3/16 in. thickness. Mount a piece of emery paper (1 to 1½ grade) slightly wider than the bore in the mandrel slot. Place the unslotted end of the mandrel in the chuck of an electric drill and work up and down each bore with the emery paper for about two minutes.

31. Pistons and Piston Rings - Examination and Renovation

If the old pistons are to be refitted, carefully remove the piston rings and then thoroughly clean them. Take particular care to clean out the piston ring grooves. At the same time do not scratch the aluminium in any way. If new rings are to be fitted to the old pistons then the top ring should be stepped so as to clear the ridge left above the previous top ring. If a normal but oversize new ring is fitted, it will hit the ridge and break because the new ring will not have worn in the same way as the old, which will have worn in unison with the ridge.

Before fitting the rings on the pistons each should be inserted approximately 2¼ ins. down the cylinder bore and the gap measured with a feeler gauge. This should be between .008 ins. and .013 ins. It is essential that the gap

should be measured at the bottom of the ring travel, as if it is measured at the top of a worn bore and gives a perfect fit, it could easily seize at the bottom. If the ring gap is too small rub down the ends of the ring with a very fine file until the gap, when fitted, is correct. To keep the rings square in the bore for measurement line each up in turn by inserting an old piston in the bore upside down and use the piston to push the ring down about 2¼ in. Remove the piston and measure the piston ring gap.

When fitting new pistons and rings to a rebored engine the piston ring gap can be measured at the top of the bore as the bore will not now taper. It is not necessary to measure the side clearance in the piston ring grooves with the rings fitted as the groove dimensions are accurately machined during manufacture. When fitting new oil control rings to pistons it may be necessary to have the grooves widened by machining to accept the new wider rings. In this instance the manufacturers representative will make this quite clear, and will supply the address to which the pistons must be sent for machining.

32. Camshaft and Camshaft Bearings - Examination and Renovation

1. The camshaft bearings are not subject to heavy wear and it is, therefore, difficult to tell when they should be replaced. However, it is a good idea to replace them as a matter of course on a major overhaul.

2. The camshaft bearings are replaceable in pairs like the other plain bearings in the engine. They require no special fitting and are therefore new bearings simply substituted for the old ones. NOTE: Bearing caps or shells should not be filed.

3. The camshaft itself should show no signs of wear but if very slight scoring on the cams is noticed, the score can be removed by very gentle rubbing down with a very fine emery cloth. The greatest care should be taken to keep the cam profiles smooth and not to break through the case hardening. If the cam lobes are worn it is more satisfactory to buy a new camshaft.

33. Valves and Valve Seats - Examination and Renovation

1. Examine the heads of the valve for pitting and burning, especially the heads of the exhaust valves. The valve seatings should be examined at the same time. If the pitting on valve and seat is very slight the marks can be removed by grinding the seats and valves together with coarse, and then fine, valve grinding paste. Where bad pitting has occured to the valve seats it will be necessary to recut them and fit new valves. If the valve seats are so worn that they cannot be recut, then it will be necessary to fit new valve seats inserts. These latter two jobs should be entrusted to the local Chrysler agent or engineering works. In practice it is very seldom that the seats are so badly worn that they require renewal. Normally, it is the exhaust valve that is too badly worn for replacement and the owner can easily purchase a new set of valves and match them to the seats by valve grinding.

2. Valve grinding is carried out as follows:-

Smear a trace of coarse carborundum paste on the seat face and apply a suction grinder tool to the valve head. With a semi-rotary motion, grind the valve head to its seat, lifting the valve occasionally to redistribute the grinding paste. When a dull matt even surface finish is produced on both the valve seat and the valve, wipe off the paste and repeat the process with fine carborundum paste, lifting and turning the valve to redistribute the paste as before. A light spring placed under the valve head will greatly ease the operation. When a smooth unbroken ring of light grey matt finish is produced on both valve and valve seat faces, the grinding operation is completed.

3. Scrape away all carbon from the valve head and the valve stem. Carefully clean away every trace of grinding compound, taking great care to leave none in the ports or in the valve guides. Clean the valves and valve seats with a paraffin soaked rag, then with a clean rag, and finally, if an air line is available, blow the valves, valve guides and valve ports clean.

34. Timing Gears and Chain - Examination and Renovation

Examine the teeth on both the crankshaft sprocket and the camshaft sprocket for wear. Each tooth forms an inverted 'V' with the gearwheel periphery and if worn the side of each tooth under tension will be slightly concave in shape when compared with the other side of the tooth, i.e. one side of the inverted 'V' will be concave when compared with the other. If any sign of wear is present the gearwheels must be renewed.

Examine the links of the chain for side slackness by bending the chain sideways. If excessive slackness is noticeable the chain should be renewed. It is a sensible precaution to renew the chain at about 30,000 miles and at lesser mileage if the engine is stripped down for a major overhaul. The actual rollers on a very badly worn chain may be slightly grooved.

35. Timing Chain Tensioner - Examination and Renovation

1. If the timing chain is badly worn it is more than likely that the tensioner will be too.
2. Examine the side of the tensioner which bears against the chain and renew it if it is grooved or ridged.

36. Tappets - Examination and Renovation

Examine the bearing surface of the tappets which lie beneath the camshaft. Any indentation in this surface or any cracks indicate serious wear and the tappets should be renewed. It is most unlikely that the sides of the tappets will prove worn but if they are a very loose fit in their bores and can readily be rocked, they should be exchanged for new units. It is very unusual to find any wear in the tappets and any wear present is likely to occur only at very high mileages.

37. Flywheel Starter Ring - Examination, Renovation, Removal and Replacement

1. If the teeth on the flywheel starter ring are badly worn, or if some are missing, then it will be necessary to remove the ring. This is achieved by splitting the ring with a cold chisel. After drilling a hole as large as possible between the base of two teeth, this hole should almost penetrate to the flywheel.
2. The new ring together with a thermometer should be suspended by wire into a bath of clean oil (see Fig. 1.7.). It is important that neither the ring nor the thermometer should touch the sides or base of the bath otherwise false readings will result.

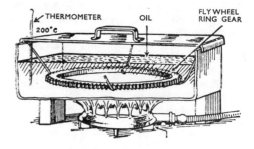

Fig.1.7. Heating the starter ring gear.

3. The oil should now be heated to a temperature of 200ºC (392ºF). NOTE: If an open flame is being used to heat the oil the bath should have a well fitting cover over it to prevent the oil from igniting.
4. Remove the ring from the oil and quickly wipe away any surplus oil with non-fluffy rag. Place the ring on the flywheel with the chamfered sides of its teeth facing the clutch side of the flywheel. Gently tap the ring into place against its locating face on the flywheel. As the ring cools it will contract until it gets a firm and permanent grip on the flywheel. NOTE: No attempt should be made to try and heat the starter ring gear with a naked flame.

38. Oil Pump - Examination and Renovation

An oil pump in really good condition is at the heart of a soundly rebuilt engine. The pump should therefore be checked very carefully for wear and a replacement fitted if in any doubt. To check the rotor endfloat and lobe clearances proceed in the following manner.

NOTE: If the pump is out of the engine invert it to

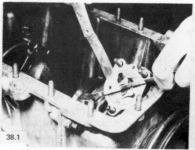

measure the clearances (i.e. pump to base joint face upwards).

1. To check the clearance between the rotors and base plate, place a straight rule across the joint face and measure the clearance between the rule and the rotors with a feeler gauge (photo). The maximum and minimum clearances are .003 in. (.076 mm) and .001 in. (.025 mm) respectively.

2. With the apex of one of the inner rotor lobes in line with the apex of one of the outer rotor lobes, check the clearance by pushing a feeler gauge between the two (photo). The maximum and minimum clearances are .006 in. (.152 mm) and .001 in. (.025 mm) respectively.

3. To check rotor to body clearance, push a feeler gauge between the outer rotor and pump body (photo). The maximum and minimum clearances are .008 in. (.20 mm) and .005 in. (.127 mm) respectively.

4. If any of these clearances are exceeded then the pump should be exchanged for a rebuilt unit.

39. Cylinder Head - Decarbonisation

This can be carried out with the engine either in or out of the car. With the cylinder head off carefully remove with a wire brush and blunt scraper all traces of carbon deposits from the combustion spaces and ports. The valve head stems and valve guides should also be freed of any carbon deposits. Wash the combustion spaces and ports down with petrol and scrape the cylinder head surface free of any foreign matter with a brass scraper, or one made of a similar soft metal.

Clean the pistons and top of the cylinder bores. If the pistons are still in the block then it is essential that great care is taken to ensure that no carbon gets into the cylinder bores as this could scratch the cylinder walls or cause damage to the piston and rings. To ensure this does not happen, first turn the crankshaft so that two of the pistons are at the top of their bores. Stuff rag into the other two bores or seal them off with paper and masking tape. The waterways should also be covered with small pieces of masking tape to prevent particles of carbon entering the cooling system and damaging the water pump.

There are two schools of thought as to how much carbon should be removed from the piston crown. One school recommends that a ring of carbon should be left round the edge of the piston and on the cylinder bore wall as an aid to low oil consumption. Although this is probably true for early engines with worn bores, on later engines the thought of the second school can be applied; which is that for effective decarbonisation all traces of carbon should be removed.

If all traces of carbon are to be removed, press a little grease into the gap between the cylinder walls and the two pistons which are to be worked on. With a blunt scraper carefully scrape away the carbon from the piston crown, taking great care not to scratch the aluminium. Also scrape away the carbon from the surrounding lip of the cylinder wall. When all carbon has been removed, scrape away the grease which will now be contaminated with carbon particles, taking care not to press any into the bores. To assist prevention of carbon build-up the piston crown can be polished with a metal polish such as Brasso. Remove the rags or masking tape from the other two cylinders and turn the crankshaft so that the two pistons which were at the bottom are now at the top. Place rag or masking tape in the cylinders which have been decarbonised and proceed as just described.

If a ring of carbon is going to be left round the piston then this can be helped by inserting an old piston ring into

the top of the bore to rest on the piston and ensure that carbon is not accidentally removed. Check that there are no particles of carbon in the cylinder bores. Decarbonising is now complete.

40. Valve Guides - Examination and Renovation

Examine the valve guides internally for wear. If the valves are a very loose fit in the guides and there is the slightest suspicion of lateral rocking using a new valve, then new guides will have to be fitted. If the valve guides have been removed compare them internally by visual inspection with a new guide as well as testing them for rocking with a new valve. If new valve guides are needed this is a job for your Chrysler garage or engineering works.

41. Sump - Renovation

1. It is essential to thoroughly wash out the sump with petrol.
2. Scrape all traces of the old sump gasket from the flange.
3. Renew the sump drainplug gasket.

42. Engine Reassembly - General

1. To ensure maximum life with minimum trouble from a rebuilt engine, not only must everything be correctly assembled, but all the parts must be spotlessly clean, all the oilways must be clear, locking washers and spring washers must always be fitted where indicated and all bearing and other working surfaces must be thoroughly lubricated during assembly. Before assembly begins renew any bolts or studs, the threads of which are in any way damaged, and whenever possible use new spring washers.

2. Apart from your normal tools, a supply of clean rag, an oil can filled with engine oil (an empty plastic detergent bottle thoroughly cleaned and washed out will invariably do just as well) a new supply of assorted spring washers and a set of new gaskets should be gathered together. A torque wrench is essential as the Imp engine is largely made from aluminium. If a torque wrench cannot be bought then one must be borrowed as if one is not used, then it is almost a certainty that trouble will be experienced after a few thousand miles through aluminium components distorting.

43. Crankshaft - Replacement

Ensure that the crankcase is thoroughly clean and that all oilways are clear. A thin-twist drill or a pipe cleaner is useful for cleaning them out. If possible, blow them out with compressed air.

Treat the crankshaft in the same fashion and then inject engine oil into the crankshaft oilways.

Commence work on rebuilding the engine by replacing the crankshaft and main bearings.

1. Note that at the back of each bearing is a tab which engages in locating grooves in either the crankcase of the main bearing cap housings.

2. If new bearings are being fitted, carefully clean away all traces of the protective grease with which they are coated.

3. If the old main bearing shells are to be re-used (a false economy, unless they are virtually as new) fit the three upper halves (i.e. those in the actual cylinder block casting) of the main bearing shells to their location in the crankcase, after wiping the locations clean (photo).

4. With the three upper bearing shells securely in place,

wipe the lower bearing cap housings (photo) and fit the three lower shell bearings to their caps ensuring that the right shell goes into the right cap if the old bearings are being refitted.

5. Wipe the recesses either side of the centre main bearing which locate the thrust washers.

6. Generously lubricate the crankshaft journals and the upper and lower main bearing shells (photo A) and carefully lower the crankshaft into place (photo B).

7. Rotating the crankshaft in the direction towards the main bearing tabs (so that the main bearing shells do not slide out). Feed the thrust washers into their locations with their oil grooves outwards away from the bearing.

9. The next task is to fit the rear main bearing cap by the following method. New 'club footed' rubber side joints must be fitted as shown in photo A. This done 'Hylomar' jointing compound should be very sparingly applied to the joint faces in the positions shown in Fig. 1.8. (photo B) and

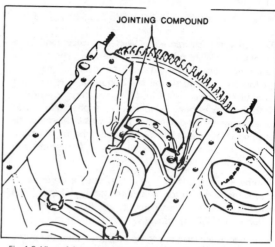

Fig. 1.8. View of the rear main bearing cap showing correct position of 'clubfoot' oil seals. Jointing compound should be sparingly applied where indicated.

models, new tab washers will be needed to lock the conventional bolts provided. Alternatively, replace the conventional bolts and tab washers with self-locking bolts. Tighten the bolts to a torque of 41 lb ft (photo A). Bend the locking tabs up against the bolt heads, if these are fitted (photo B).

12 Test the crankshaft for freedom of rotation; should it be very stiff to turn or possess high spots a most careful inspection must be made, preferably by a qualified mechanic with a micrometer to get to the root of the trouble. It is very seldom that any trouble of this nature will be experienced when fitting the crankshaft.

13 Check the crankshaft endfloat with a feeler gauge measuring the longitudinal movement between the crankshaft and a thrust washer. (Photo. Note that the crankshaft main bearing cap is not shown in the interest of clarity.) Endfloat should be between .002 in. and .01 in. If endfloat is excessive oversize thrust washers can be fitted.

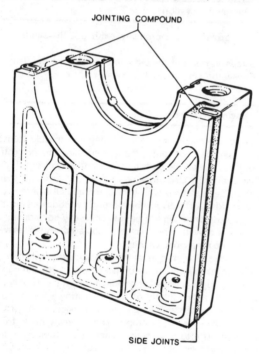

Fig. 1.9. Before refitting the rear main bearing cap, apply jointing compound in the positions shown.

also to the block in the position indicated in Fig. 1.9. It is extremely important that the jointing compound should only be applied sparingly, otherwise it may exude from the joint faces and block the scroll type oil seal on the crankshaft. Place the main bearing cap into position (photo C) and tap it home with a non-metallic hammer. NOTE: If the cap is of the type that is not located by dowels it will be necessary to check the scroll bore alignment. This can be done by sliding a feeler gauge around the circumference of the crankshaft scroll in the space between the scroll and the main bearing cap/cylinder block. The clearance must be consistent for the whole circumference.

10 Fit the other two main bearing caps in position (photo) ensuring they locate properly. The mating surfaces must be spotlessly clean or the caps will not seat correctly. As the bearing caps were assembled to the cylinder block and then line bored during manufacture, it is essential that they are returned to the same positions from which they were removed.

11 Refit the self-locking bearing cap bolts. On early

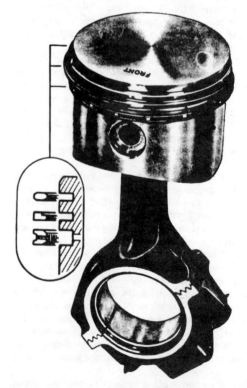

Fig. 1.10. Piston rings and piston and connecting rod correctly assembled

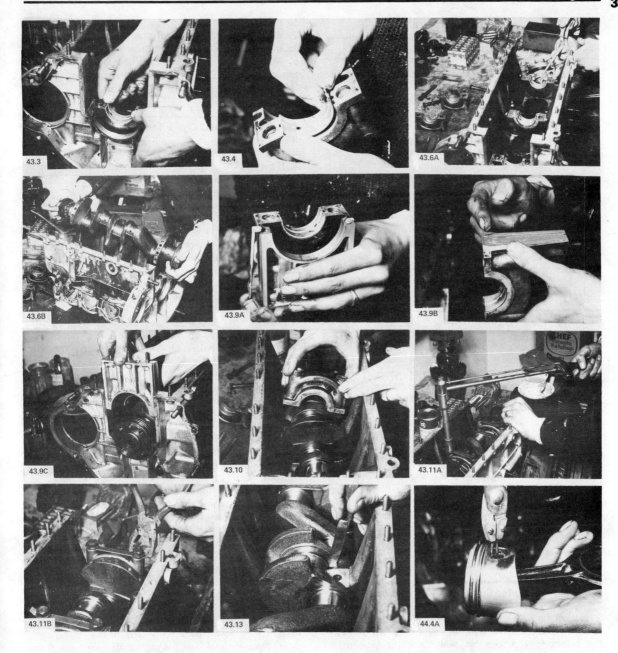

43.3 43.4 43.6A

43.6B 43.9A 43.9B

43.9C 43.10 43.11A

43.11B 43.13 44.4A

44. Piston and Connecting Rod Assembly

1. If the same pistons are being used, then they must be mated to the same connecting rod with the same gudgeon pin. If new pistons are being fitted it does not matter which connecting rod they are used with, but the gudgeon pins should be fitted on the basis of selective assembly.

2. Lay the correct piston adjacent to each connecting rod and remember that the same rod and piston must go back into the same bore. If new pistons are being used it is only necessary to ensure that the right connecting rod is placed in each bore.

3. Fit a gudgeon pin circlip in position at one end of the gudgeon pin hole in the piston.

4. Place one piston in boiling water for a few minutes. Remove it from the water and quickly wipe away any excess oil or water with a non-fluffy rag. Take care not to burn yourself during this process.

5. Hold the connecting rod in position inside the piston. Push the gudgeon pin through the piston and connecting rod small end until it contacts the fitted circlip. Fit the remaining circlip in its groove (photo A). NOTE: It is essential that the piston is assembled to the connecting rod as shown in Fig. 1.10. (i.e. when the side of the piston marked 'FRONT' (photo) is facing you, the connecting rod offset should be to the right.) Repeat this process with the other three pistons and connecting rods.

6. When all four pistons are assembled to their connecting rods, the following items should be checked:-

a) When the piston and connecting rod assembly is held horizontal, the connecting rod should be free to fall by its own weight.

b) Gripping the piston firmly with one hand and the connecting rod with the other, ensure that the connecting rod cannot be rocked from side to side on the gudgeon pin. NOTE: It is normal for there to be a sliding movement from one side to the other.

c) Check that all the gudgeon pin retaining circlips are firmly seated in their grooves. NOTE: It is essential that new circlips are used.

45. Piston Ring - Replacement

1. Check that the piston ring grooves and oilways are thoroughly clean and unblocked. Piston rings must always be fitted over the head of the piston and never from the bottom.
2. The easiest method to use when fitting rings is to wrap a .020 feeler gauge round the top of the piston and place the rings one at a time, starting with the bottom oil control ring, over the feeler gauge.
3. The feeler gauge, complete with ring, can then be slid down the piston over the other piston ring grooves until the correct groove is reached. The piston ring is then slid gently off the feeler gauge into the groove.
4. An alternative method is to fit the rings by holding them slightly open with the thumbs and both of your index fingers. This method requires a steady hand and great care as it is easy to open the ring too much and break it.

46. Piston/Connecting Rod - Replacement

The pistons, complete with connecting rods, can be fitted to the cylinder bores in the following sequence. NOTE: It is essential that the piston/connecting rod assembly should be replaced in the bore from which it was removed.
1. With a wad of clean rag wipe the cylinder bores clean. Next coat the interior of each bore with a thin smear of clean engine oil.
2. Push the piston/connecting rod assembly into its bore until the first piston ring is resting on the top edge of the bore. It will now be necessary to compress the piston rings with a piston ring compressor. If a proper piston ring compressor is not available, a large jubilee clip will do the job admirably (photo A). Gently tap the piston into the bore with a non-metallic hammer or with the handle of a metal hammer (photo B.). The piston MUST be fitted into the bore with the side marked 'FRONT' facing the crankshaft pulley wheel end of the engine.

47. Connecting Rod to Crankshaft - Reassembly

During the following procedures it is essential that the utmost cleanliness is observed as any dirt caught between the crankpins and bearings will score the crankshaft journals and will thus lead to early bearing failure.
1. Wipe the connecting rod half of the big end bearing cap and the underside of the shell bearing clean, and fit the shell bearing in position with its locating tongue groove engaged with the corresponding rod.
1. If the old bearings are nearly new and are being refitted, then ensure they are replaced in their correct locations on the correct rods.
3. Generously lubricate the crankpin journals with engine oil and turn the crankshaft so that the crankpin is in the most advantageous position for the connecting rod to be drawn onto it (photo).
4. Wipe the connecting rod bearing cap and back of the shell bearing clean and fit the shell bearing in position ensuring that the locating tongue (arrowed) at the back of the bearing engages with the locating groove in the connecting rod cap (photo).
5. Generously lubricate the shell bearing and offer up the connecting rod bearing cap to the connecting rod.
6. Fit the connecting rod bolts with the locking tabs under them (photo A) and tighten the bolts with a torque spanner to 18 lb.ft. (photo B).
7. With a hammer or pair of pliers knock up the locking tabs against the bolt head (photo).
8. When all the connecting rods have been fitted, rotate the crankshaft to check that everything is free, and that there are no high spots causing binding.

48. Timing Chain, Chain Tensioner and Chain Cover - Replacement

1. If the crankshaft sprocket was removed, it can be replaced by using a suitable hollow drift to push it back into position.
2. Place the timing chain over the crankshaft sprocket and refit the chain tensioner by pushing downwards on its tensioner spring, at the same time pushing the tensioner onto its bottom mounting peg (photo). When the spring eye locates into the mounting peg groove the tensioner is correctly replaced.
3. Ensure that the joint faces both on the cylinder block and timing chain cover are clean and that all traces of old gasket are removed.
4. Prise out the 'O' ring oil seal (photo) surrounding the oil passage, half way up the right-hand side of the cylinder block joint face (looking at the engine from the crankshaft pulley end). Place a new 'O' ring in the vacant groove. This is extremely important.
5. If jointing compound is to be used, spread a thin smear over all the joint faces. Place the two paper gaskets over the studs and on to the cylinder block joint faces.
6. Locate the timing chain over the teeth of the crankshaft sprocket and arrange the chain so that the free end is dropped over the timing chain case top.
7. If the timing chain cover crankshaft oil seal is to be replaced, gently lever the old seal out of the chain cover with a screwdriver (photo). Great care should be taken not to damage the timing chain cover in the process. The new seal will be fitted when the timing chain cover is in position.
8. If the oil pump and distributor are still fitted in the timing chain cover, turn the distributor rotor to the three o'clock position. As the cover is replaced the rotor should rotate until it is in the four o'clock position. Gently lower the cover over the cylinder block studs until the two joint faces meet (photo).
9. Replace all the nuts and washers and tighten them finger tight.
10 Next fit a new crankshaft oil seal in the timing chain cover. Place the seal over the crankshaft nose (photo) and tap it evenly into position with a hide faced hammer. If using a steel hammer a block of wood should be interposed between the hammer and the seal. NOTE: The seal should be fitted so that its contacting spring is facing away from the outside of the timing chain cover.
11 Place the crankshaft pulley wheel over the crankshaft nose and tap it firmly into its sealing taper with a block of wood and a hammer (photo). Place a new tab washer and the 'D' shaped spacer, respectively, onto the pulley retaining bolt or starter dog. Screw the bolt or dog into the end of the crankshaft. Tighten the bolt or dog to the specified torque. To prevent the engine from turning, place a piece of wood between a crankpin and the crankcase. With the pulley in position rotate the crankshaft once or twice to centralise the chain cover and then tighten the retaining nuts to the correct torque. As an alternative the bolt or dog can be left finger tight until the flywheel is reassembled to the crankshaft. The engine can then be prevented from turning by wedging a screwdriver between the teeth of the starter ring gear and a bellhousing stud.
12 Using a cold chisel or a small hammer knock one of the

44.4B

46.2A

46.2B

47.3

47.4

47.6A

47.6B

47.7

48.2

48.4

48.7

48.8

48.10

48.11

49.3

tabs on the locking washer over the flat of the 'D' shaped spacer and a second tab over one of the flats on the bolt or dog hexagon.

49. Oil Pump - Replacement

It is essential to get the oil pump into correct mesh with the crankshaft skew gear as the distributor is driven from a dog on the oil pump spindle and therefore ignition timing depends on the oil pump being fitted correctly.

1. Turn the engine to No. 1 T.D.C. This can be achieved by rotating the engine until No. 1 piston (i.e. piston nearest crankshaft pulley) is at the very top of its stroke.
2. Place a new gasket over the three studs which hold the oil pump body in place.
3. Replacing the oil pump correctly is largely a matter of trial and error, although once close to the correct setting the oil pump can be carefully withdrawn, and the spindle turned one or two teeth either way, until the correct mesh with the crankshaft is obtained. Pump replacement is correct when the offset slot in the oil pump spindle makes an angle of 55° (on engines fitted with a dynamo) or $77\frac{1}{2}^{\circ}$ (on engines which are fitted with an alternator) with an imaginary line drawn through the centres of the distributor retaining studs as shown in Fig.1.11. The best way to determine this on the engine is to cut a piece of cardboard with an apex angle of 55° (for engines with dynamos) or $77\frac{1}{2}^{\circ}$ (for engines with alternators) and to hold this card over the distributor slot (as shown in photo). Alter the oil pump mesh until the distributor drive slot is seen to be parallel with the side of the cardboard triangle that bisects the straight line between the two studs. Ensure that the largest segment of the offset distributor drive is nearest to the cylinder block as shown in Fig. 1.11 and not 180° out.

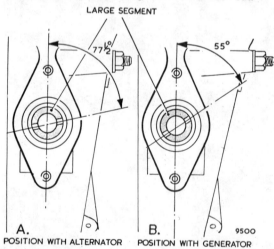

LARGE SEGMENT

$77\frac{1}{2}^{\circ}$ 55°

A. POSITION WITH ALTERNATOR   B. POSITION WITH GENERATOR   9500

Fig.1.11. Position of the oil pump drive for No.1. T.D.C.

4. Once the oil pump is correctly meshed invert the engine so that the sump is facing upwards. If a cheeseheaded screw and a large washer were screwed into the pump body to retain the pump rotors, during dismantling, now is the time to remove them.
5. Prime the pump with new engine oil (photo) to preclude any possibility of oil starvation when the engine starts.
6. Replace the pump base plate and intake filter assembly. Replace the three retaining nuts and washers and tighten them to the specified torque (photo). Lastly, replace the cheeseheaded screw and tighten it firmly. NOTE: There is

NO gasket between the pump body and base plate. Oil pump replacement is now complete.

50. Sump - Replacement

1. After the sump has been thoroughly cleaned, scrape all traces of the oil sump gasket from the sump and crankcase flanges, fit a new gasket in place (photo A) and then refit the sump (photo B).
2. Replace the sump retaining nuts and washers and tighten them down securely (photo).

51. Flywheel - Replacement

1. Make certain that the flange on the crankshaft, and the face of the flywheel are perfectly clean and offer up the flywheel to the end of the crankshaft (photo A). Ensure that the dowel (arrowed) enters into the special hole in the flywheel. The engine should now be prevented from turning by wedging a screwdriver between the starter ring teeth and a bellhousing stud (photo B). Fit new tab washers, tighten down the four retaining bolts and turn up the lock tabs (photo C).
2. Smear the crankshaft spigot bush with a small quantity of zinc oxide grease.

52. Valve and Valve Spring - Reassembly.

Before the valves and valve springs are replaced the inlet valve oil seals and joint rings should be renewed. To do this proceed as follows:-

a) Remove the four caps from above the inlet valve guides, Discard the old rubber oil seals and joint rings.
b) Place the four new joint rings over the valve guides and position the new rubber oil seals inside the caps. Replace the caps over the valve guides. Correct reassembly is shown in Fig. 1.12. To refit the valves and valve springs to the cylinder head, proceed as follows:-

1. Rest the cylinder head on its side.
2. Fit each valve in turn, wiping down and lubricating each valve stem as it is inserted into the same valve guide from which it was removed (photo).
3. Build up each valve assembly by first fitting the valve spring and then the valve spring shroud (photo).
4. With the base of the valve compressor on the valve head, compress the valve spring until the cotters can be slipped into place in the cotter grooves (photo). Gently release the compressor. NOTE: Great care should be taken not to compress the inlet valve springs any more than is necessary to replace the cotters, otherwise valve seals will be damaged.
5. Repeat this procedure until all eight valves and valve springs are fitted.

53. Cylinder Head - Replacement

1. Thoroughly clean the cylinder block top face and also the cylinder head face, ensuring that all traces of old gasket are removed.
2. Purchase two of the longer type cylinder head bolts and cut them off just below the head. Saw a groove in the top of each of them wide enough to take a screwdriver blade. Screw one of these dummy studs into a cylinder head bolt hole at each end of the head. If it is wished, jointing compound can be sparingly applied to the block face (photo).

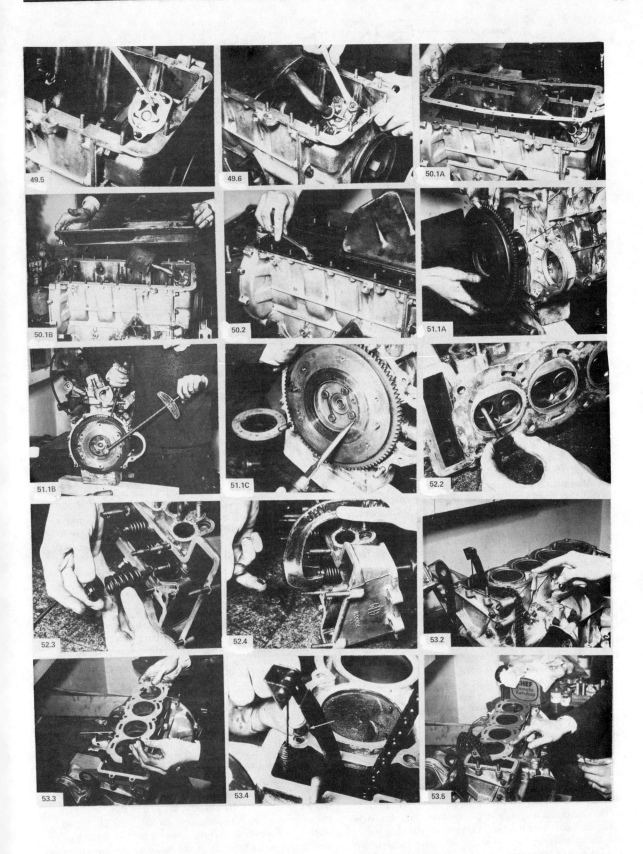

49.5   49.6   50.1A

50.1B   50.2   51.1A

51.1B   51.1C   52.2

52.3   52.4   53.2

53.3   53.4   53.5

3. Place the new gasket over the dummy studs and on to the cylinder block top face (photo). If the new gasket is marked 'Top' on one side, then this side should be facing upwards.

4. Place the new rubber sealing ring for the oilway to the camshaft bearings in position as shown in the photo. (Note: gasket now shown for clarity.)

5. If jointing compound is being used it should now be sparingly applied to the top face of the gasket (photo).

6. Generously lubricate each cylinder with engine oil.

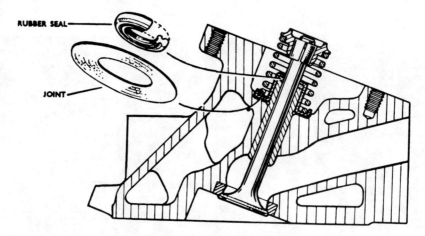

RUBBER SEAL

JOINT

Fig. 1.12. Inlet valve guide oil seal details

7.   Ensure that the cylinder head face is perfectly clean and then lower the cylinder head into place over the dummy studs and at the same time draw the timing chain through the orifice at the end of the head with a wire hook or similar (photo). Once the head is in place the chain should be attached to a weight hung down the side of the engine to prevent it falling to the bottom of the crankcase.
8.   Replace two of the cylinder head bolts and screw them down finger tight. Unscrew and remove the two dummy studs. Replace the remainder of the head bolts. NOTE: Before fitting the bolts they should be dipped in Shell Enis 256 oil. Tighten the bolts to a torque of 36 lb. ft. (photo A) in the order shown in Fig. 1.3. The nuts 'A' and 'B' in Fig. 1.3 should be tightened down last of all to a torque of 15 lb.ft. (photo B).
9.   After the car has travelled two to three hundred miles, the cylinder head bolt tightness should be checked. This task will be made a great deal easier if Churchill tool No. RG 355 can be borrowed from your local Chrysler garage or dealer. This tool allows the bolt tightness to be checked without removing the camshaft and tappet housing. Note the following:-
a) Bolt tightness should be checked when the engine is cold.
b) Before attempting to tighten the bolts they should be slackened off a little and then tightened to the correct torque, ONE at a time. If this is not done the initial effort required to move the bolts will cause the torque wrench to give a false reading.
10 Ensure that the engine is turned to No 1 TDC with the distributor rotor indicating No 1 cylinder firing.
11 Remove the tappet shims from the tappet pistons, one at a time and place them in their corresponding valve cap. This is very important and great care should be taken.
12 Turn the camshaft until the lobes for the inlet and exhaust valve of No. 1 cylinder are pointing slightly upwards and are equalistant from the camshaft carrier face. In this position the lobes controlling the valve in No. 4 cylinder will be holding their valves slightly open when the carrier is refitted. This done gently lower the camshaft carrier into position over its retaining studs. Care should be taken to ensure that the tappet pistons do not slide out of the carrier and also that the shims are not dislodged from the valve caps. Ensure that the camshaft is in the position described earlier (photo).
13 Replace the right camshaft carrier retaining nuts and washers. Working in a diagonal sequence, evenly tighten the nuts to the specified torque.

14 Before refitting the camshaft sprocket it will be necessary to compress the timing chain tensioner. This can be done in the following manner:-

a) Depress the 'bow' in the centre of the tensioner towards the side of the timing chain case. As this is done you will notice that the slide at the top end of the tensioner will move up to the top edge of the timing chain case.
b) When the slide reaches to top of the case hold it in position by clamping it with 'mole grips' preferably, or alternatively, pliers. The tensioner will now be in a state of compression.

15 Detach the timing chain from the weight holding it over the side of the timing chain case.
16 Place the camshaft sprocket into the chain and move it one tooth at a time in the appropriate direction until the line on the outer face of the sprocket is parallel with the top edge of the timing chain case as shown in the photo. It is imperative that the camshaft is still in the correct position and also that the engine is at No. 1 T.D.C.
17 If the dowel was removed from the sprocket flange on the camshaft it should now be replaced. Taking great care not to drop it into the engine.
18 Refit the sprocket to the camshaft. NOTE: The hole in the sprocket and the dowel in the camshaft flange should be in alignment and if more than a fractional rotation of the camshaft or sprocket is needed to refit the sprocket to the camshaft then either the camshaft is in the wrong position or the sprocket is incorrectly meshed with the timing chain.
19 Refit the sprocket centre bolt, together with the thick 'D' washer and a new tab washer. Note that the thick 'D' washer goes on first, the semi-circular niche on its circumference locating on the dowel protruding through the sprocket, followed by the tab washer and then the bolt. Release the timing chain tensioner.
20 Tighten the bolt to the specified torque (photo). Note that the tab washer has four tabs, two wide and two narrow. The tab washer is correctly positioned when one of the wider tabs is partly covering the end of the dowel and the other wide tab is overhanging the flat of the 'D' shaped washer. It is essential that the dowel is held in position by one of the wider tabs. Bend the tab over the flat of the washer and the other two narrow tabs up over the flats of the bolt head with a cold chisel (photo B). The tab covering the dowel MUST be left flat.
21 Check the valve clearances as described in Section 4.
22 Ensure that the joint faces of the cylinder head and

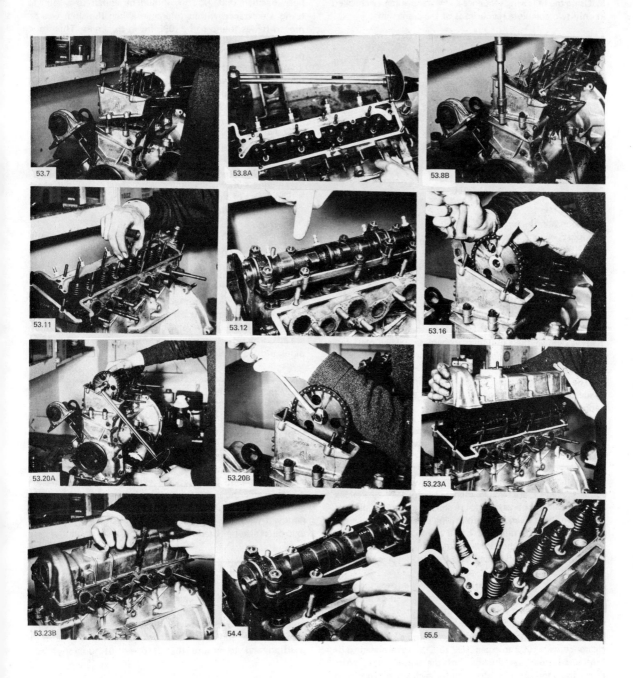

53.7   53.8A   53.8B

53.11   53.12   53.16

53.20A   53.20B   53.23A

53.23B   54.4   55.5

cambox cover are clean and free of any traces of old gasket. Slide a new gasket carefully down over the studs onto the cylinder head tab joint face. Liberally oil the timing chain camshaft and valvegear with clean engine oil.

23 Refit the cambox cover (photo A). Replace the nuts and washers around its periphery and working in a diagonal sequence tighten them to the specified torque (photo B).

54. Valve/Camshaft Clearance - Checking

1. The valve adjustment MUST be made with the engine cold. The importance of correct camshaft/valve stem clearances cannot be overstressed as they vitally affect the performance of the engine.

2. If the clearances are set too open, the efficiency of the engine is reduced as the valves open late and close earlier than was intended. If, on the other hand the clearances are set too close there is a danger that the stems will expand upon heating and not allow the valves to close properly which will cause burning of the valve head and seat and possible warping.

3. To check valve clearances it will be necessary to remove the cambox cover. If the engine is in the car this can be done by disconnecting the fuel pump, unscrewing and removing the nuts around the periphery of the cambox cover and lifting the cover and its gasket.

4. Clearances are checked with a feeler gauge between the tappet flat face and the heel of the cam (opposite side of the cam to the peak) when the cam peak is pointing toward the centre of the valve cover (if it were fitted). See photo.

5. Using the following sequence all clearances can be checked in only two complete revolutions of the crankshaft:-

Valve	Cam
No. 1 Cyl. Exhaust valve	No. 2
No. 2 Cyl. Inlet valve	No. 3
No. 3 Cyl. Exhaust valve	No. 6
No. 1 Cyl. Inlet valve	No. 1
No. 4 Cyl. Exhaust valve	No. 8
No. 3 Cyl. Inlet valve	No. 5
No. 2 Cyl. Exhaust valve	No. 4
No. 4 Cyl. Inlet valve	No. 7

Correct clearances are:-

	Inlet	Exhaust
Saloon Mk. I ...	.004/.006 in.	.006/.008 in.
Saloon Mk. II ...	.004/.006 in.	.010/.012 in.
'Sport' saloon ...	.006/.008 in.	.013/.015 in.
Rallye	.012 in.	.014 in.

6. The engine may be rotated by using a suitable spanner on the camcase pulley bolt head. NOTE: If for some reason the valve clearances are being checked when the timing chain is disconnected, then the camshaft can be turned by temporary refitment of the camshaft sprocket. However, it is extremely important that all pistons are half-way down their cylinders, otherwise a valve may contact a piston. To accomplish this, turn the engine 90° either way from T.D.C.

7. The clearance is measured by sliding a feeler gauge blade between the heel of the camshaft and the top of the tappet piston.

55. Tappet Pistons - Re-Shiming to Obtain Correct Valve/Camshaft Clearance

If it is found when checking the valve clearances that some exceed or are smaller than the permitted clearances, then it will be necessary to re-shim the tappet pistons. Instructions are given in the following paragraphs.

1. Write down the numbers 1 to 8 across the top of a sheet of paper. Measure the clearance of each valve and write it down under its number, i.e. .006 for No. 1 valve, .009 for No. 2 and so on.

2. Next work out what should be added or subtracted from each clearance to bring it within tolerance. For example on the Mk. I saloon, an inlet valve with a clearance of .008 in. will need .002 or .003 in. added to the tappet shim to bring it back to the correct clearance. Similarly, if the valve clearance were .003 in. then .002 to .003 would need to be subtracted from the thickness of the tappet shim. Write down the addition or subtraction for each valve beneath its number.

3. Undo and remove the nuts retaining the camshaft carrier. If the timing chain is still connected to the camshaft it will be necessary to remove the camshaft sprocket as described in Section 10.

4. Carefully lift the camshaft carrier off of its studs and out of the engine compartment. After reading the notes on carrier removal in Section 10, paragraphs 2 and 3.

5. When the camshaft carrier is removed, carefully lift the shims out of each tappet piston (photo) working numerically from tappets 1 to 8. As each shim is lifted out record its thickness (engraved on one of its two faces) beneath its relative number. Great care must be taken not to mix up the shims at this stage.

6. When the thickness of every shim has been recorded, add or subtract the thickness needed to bring the clearance for each shim within tolerance. For example, it has already

been decided that .003 in. should be added to a shim to bring a clearance within tolerance. When the shim was removed it was found to be .095 in. in thickness. Therefore, the shim needed to obtain the correct clearance for this particular valve is one of .098 in. thickness.

7. When the correct thickness of the shim has been determined for each valve, the correct shims can be purchased from your Chrysler dealer. Beneath is an example of what your calculations should look like for one valve.

Valve No. 1 Inlet (correct clearance .004 to .006 in.)	
Existing clearance	.010 in.
Thickness to be added to tappet shim to bring clearance within tolerance	.005 in.
Thickness of existing shim	.093 in.
Thickness of shim required to bring clearance within tolerance	.098 in.

In this case a shim of .098 in. thickness should be substituted for the existing shim.

8. When the new shims have been obtained, place them in their correct tappet pistons. Take great care to ensure that they do go into the correct tappet pistons because if they are incorrectly fitted your work will be nullified.

9. Replace the camshaft carrier in position as described in Section 53. Recheck the valve clearances to ensure that they are all correct. Replace the camshaft sprocket, cambox, fuel pipes, etc., as necessary.

56. Final Assembly

1. Fit new sparking plugs. Reconnect the ancillary components to the engine in the reverse order to which they were removed.

2. It should be noted that in all cases it is best to reassemble the engine as far as possible before refitting it to the car. This means that the inlet and exhaust manifolds, starter motor, water thermostat, oil filter, distributor, carburettors and dynamo should all be in position. If the engine was removed with the gearbox, the clutch assembly and transaxle must also be fitted together with the slave cylinder.

57. Engine Replacement

Although the engine can be replaced with one man and a suitable trolley or trolley jack, it is easier if two are present. One to manoeuvre the engine into the engine compartment and the other to guide the engine into position and to ensure that it does not foul anything.

57.4

Generally speaking, engine replacement is a reversal of the procedures used when removing the engine, (see Sections 6 and 7) but one or two added tips may come in useful.

1. Ensure all the loose leads, cables, etc., are tucked out of the way. If not it is easy to trap one and so cause much additional work after the engine is replaced.

2. Fit the starter motor and oil filter before moving the engine and transaxle into place.

3. After the dynamo has been replaced it is advisable to fit a new fan belt.

4. Carefully manoeuvre the engine into position (photo), and then refit the following:-

a) Transaxle mounting bolts and washers (if the engine was removed without the transaxle unit).

b) Rear crossmember and engine mounting.

c) Drive shafts to transaxle unit.

d) Reconnect the clutch pipe to the slave cylinder.

e) Remote control linkage to transaxle.

f) Gearchange remote control.

g) Oil pressure switch.

h) Rev counter drive (if fitted).

i) Wires to coil, distributor and dynamo.

j) Carburettor controls.

k) Fuel pipe to pump and carburettors.

l) Air cleaner/s.

m) Exhaust manifold to pipe and bracket.

n) Earth and starter motor cables.

o) Radiator and hoses and any items hung on radiator attachment bolts.

p) Heater hoses.

q) Water temperature cable.

r) Vacuum advance and retard pipe.

s) Battery.

5. Finally, check that the drain taps are closed and refill the cooling system with water and the engine and transaxle with the correct grade of oil. Prime the carburettor by working the fuel pump manually, pull out the choke, and start the engine. (If you are lucky it will fire first time.) Carefully check for oil or water leaks. There should be no oil or water leaks if the engine has been reassembled carefully, all nuts and bolts tightened down correctly, and new gaskets and joints used throughout.

6. After 300 miles check the tightness of the cylinder head nuts with a torque wrench and change the oil and the filter.

The cylinder head tightness check should be done when the engine is cold. It is important that each bolt is slackened slightly and retightened to the correct torque (one bolt at a time) in the order shown in Fig. 1.3. Nuts 'A' and 'B' are to be tightened last of all. The torque value for the nuts is 15 Ib f ft and for the cylinder head bolts is 36 Ib f ft.

Note: Unless you can obtain a cranked torque spanner (see Fig. 1.13), you will have to remove the camshaft to gain access to the bolts.

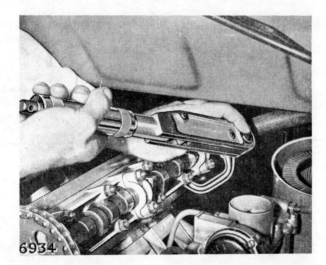

Fig. 1.13. Using a cranked torque spanner to check the tightness of the cylinder head bolts with the camshaft in position.

Cause	Trouble	Remedy
SYMPTOM: ENGINE FAILS TO TURN OVER WHEN STARTER IS OPERATED		
No current at starter motor	Flat or defective battery	Charge or replace battery. Push-start car.
	Loose battery leads	Earth end of earth lead.
	Defective starter solenoid or switch or broken wiring	Run a wire direct from the battery to the starter motor to by-pass the solenoid.
	Engine earth strap disconnected	Check and retighten strap.
Current at starter motor	Jammed starter motor drive pinion	Place car in gear and rock backwards and forwards. Alternatively, turn exposed square end of shaft with a spanner.
	Defective starter motor	Remove and recondition.
SYMPTOM: ENGINE TURNS OVER BUT WILL NOT START		
No spark at sparking plug	Ignition damp or wet	Wipe dry the distributor cap and ignition leads.
	Ignition leads to spark plugs loose	Check to ensure that HT leads are properly connected at both ends.
	Shorted or disconnected low tension leads	Check the wiring on the CB and SW terminals of the coil and to the distributor.
	Dirty, incorrectly set, or pitted contact breaker points	Clean, file smooth, and adjust.
	Fault condenser	Check contact breaker points for arcing. Renew condenser if necessary.
	Defective ignition switch	By-pass switch with wire.
	Ignition leads connected in wrong order to plugs	Remove and replace leads to spark plugs in correct order.
	Faulty coil	Remove and fit new coil.
	Contact breaker point spring earthed or broken	Check spring is not touching metal part of distributor. Check insulator washers are correctly placed. Renew points if the spring is broken.
No fuel at carburettor float chamber or at jets	No petrol in petrol tank	Refill tank!
	Vapour lock in fuel line (In hot conditions or at high altitude)	Blow into petrol tank, allow engine to cool, or apply a cold wet rag to the fuel line.
	Blocked float chamber needle valve	Remove, clean, and replace.
	Fuel pump filter blocked	Remove, clean, and replace.
	Choked or blocked carburettor jets	Dismantle and clean.
	Faulty fuel pump	Remove, overhaul and replace.
Excess of petrol in cylinder or carburettor flooding	Too much choke allowing too rich a mixture to wet plugs	Remove and dry sparking plugs or, with wide open throttle, push-start the car.
	Float damaged or leaking or needle not seating	Remove, examine, clean and replace float and needle valve as necessary.
	Float lever incorrectly adjusted.	Remove and adjust correctly.
SYMPTOM: ENGINE STALLS AND WILL NOT START		
No spark at sparking plug	Ignition failure - sudden	Check over low and high tension circuits for breaks in wiring.
	Ignition failure - Misfiring precludes total stoppage	Check contact breaker points, clean and adjust. Renew condenser if faulty.
	Ignition failure - In severe rain or after traversing water splash	Dry out ignition leads and distributor cap.
No fuel at jets	Sudden obstruction in carburettor(s)	Check jets, filter, and needle valve in float chamber for blockage.
	Water in fuel system	Drain tank, fuel pump and carburettor/s. Blow out fuel lines.
SYMPTOM: ENGINE MISFIRES OR IDLES UNEVENLY		
Intermittent sparking at sparking plug	Ignition leads loose	Check and secure as necessary at spark plug and distributor cap ends.
	Battery leads loose on terminals	Check and tighten terminal leads.
	Battery earth strap loose on body attachment point	Check and tighten earth lead to body attachment point.
	Transaxle earth lead loose	Tighten lead.

Cause	Trouble	Remedy
	Low tension leads to SW and CB terminals on coil loose.	Check and secure leads if found loose.
	Low tension lead from CB terminal side to distributor loose	Check and secure if found loose.
	Dirty, or incorrectly gapped plugs	Remove, clean, and regap.
	Dirty, incorrectly set, or pitted contact breaker points	Clean, file smooth, and adjust.
	Tracking across inside of distributor cover.	Remove and fit new cover.
	Ignition too retarded	Check and adjust ignition timing.
	Faulty coil	Remove and fit new coil.
Fuel shortage at engine	Mixture too weak	Check jets, float chamber needle valve, and filters for obstruction. Clean as necessary. Carburettor(s) incorrectly adjusted.
	Air leak in carburettor(s)	Remove and overhaul carburettor.
	Air leak at inlet manifold to cylinder head, or inlet manifold to carburettor	Test by pouring oil along joints. Bubbles indicate leak. Renew manifold gasket as appropriate.
Mechanical wear	Incorrect valve tappet/camshaft clearance	Re-shim valve tappets to compensate for wear.
	Burnt out exhaust valves	Remove cylinder head and renew defective valves.
	Sticking or leaking valves	Remove cylinder head, clean, check and renew valves as necessary.
	Weak or broken valve springs	Check and renew as necessary.
	Worn valve guides or stems	Renew valve guides and valves.
	Worn pistons and piston rings	Dismantle engine, renew pistons and rings.

SYMPTOM: LACK OF POWER & POOR COMPRESSION

Cause	Trouble	Remedy
Fuel/air mixture leaking from cylinder	Burnt out exhaust valves	Remove cylinder head, renew or re-grind defective valves, as necessary.
	Sticking or leaking valves	Remove cylinder head, clean, check, and renew valves as necessary.
	Worn valve guides and stems	Remove cylinder head and renew valves and valve guides.
	Weak or broken valve springs	Remove cylinder head, renew defective springs.
	Blown cylinder head gasket (Accompanied by noise and signs of oil and bubbles in the cooling system and/or water in the sump. The latter will be indicated by a rise in the level shown on the dipstick.	Remove cylinder head and fit new gasket.
	Worn pistons and piston rings	Dismantle engine, renew pistons and rings.
	Worn or scored cylinder bores	Dismantle engine, rebore, renew pistons and rings.
Incorrect Adjustments	Ignition timing wrongly set. Too advanced or retarded	Check and reset ignition timing.
	Contact breaker points incorrectly gapped	Check and reset contact breaker points.
	Incorrect valve tappet/camshaft clearance	Re-shim valve tappets to compensate for wear.
	Incorrectly set sparking plugs	Remove, clean and regap.
	Carburation too rich or too weak	Tune carburettor(s) for optimum performance.
Carburation and ignition faults	Dirty contact breaker points	Remove, clean and replace.
	Fuel filters blocked causing top end fuel starvation	Dismantle, inspect, clean, and replace all fuel filters.
	Distributor automatic balance weights or vacuum advance and retard mechanisms not functioning correctly	Overhaul distributor.
	Faulty fuel pump giving top end fuel starvation	Remove, overhaul, or fit exchange reconditioned fuel pump.

Cause	Trouble	Remedy
SYMPTOM: EXCESSIVE OIL CONSUMPTION		
Large amount of oil being burned by the engine (blue exhaust smoke)	Badly worn, perished or missing valve stem oil seals	Remove, fit new oil seals to valve stems
	Excessively worn valve stems and valve guides	Remove cylinder head and fit new valves and valve guides.
	Worn piston rings	Fit oil control rings to existing pistons or purchase new pistons.
	Worn pistons and cylinder bores	Fit new pistons and rings, rebore cylinders.
	Excessive piston ring gap allowing blow-by	Fit new piston rings and set gap correctly.
	Piston oil return holes choked	Decarbonise engine and pistons.
Oil being lost due to leaks	Leaking oil filter gasket	Inspect & fit new gasket as necessary.
	Leaking cambox gasket	Inspect & fit new gasket as necessary.
	Leaking oil filter body gasket	Inspect & fit new gasket as necessary.
	Leaking timing chain case gasket	Inspect & fit new gasket as necessary.
	Leaking sump gasket	Inspect & fit new gasket as necessary.
	Loose sump plug	Tighten, fit new gasket if necessary.
Excessive amount of oil being ejected by breather valve	Excessive crankcase pressure causing oil to be ejected from breather valve	Blocked oil filler cap vent.
SYMPTOM: UNUSUAL NOISES FROM THE ENGINE		
Excessive clearances due to mechanical wear.	Incorrect valve tappet to camshaft clearance (noisy tapping from cambox)	Re-shim valve tappets and examine tappets and camshaft for wear. Renew as necessary.
	Worn big end bearing/s (regular heavy knocking.	Remove sump and bearing caps. Inspect crankshaft and oil pump for wear, regrind crankshaft and fit exchange pump if necessary. Renew bearing shells.
	Worn timing chain and/or sprockets (light metallic rattle as revs are increased)	Remove cylinder head and timing chain case cover. Inspect chain and sprockets for wear. Renew as necessary.
	Worn main bearing/s (rumbling and vibrations, particularly on initial starting)	As for big end bearings. Note: some main bearing caps cannot be removed with engine 'in-situ'. See relevant text for details.

Chapter 2/Cooling System

Contents

Specifications

Type of System	Pressurised, centrifugal pump, fan assisted.
Thermostat starts to open	77ºC to 80ºC (170ºF to 179ºF)
Fan blades	9 blades
Fan diameter	9.94 ins. (25.2 cm)
Fan belt - depth	.325 ins. (8.25 mm)
Fan belt - width	.375 ins. (9.5 mm)
Fan belt angle of 'V'	40º
Fan belt - outside length...	43.62 in. (110.8 cm)
Fan belt - tension	1″ free play midway between the water pump and dynamo

NOTE: The fan belt of the 'Sport' is of the same dimensions, but is made of different material. It is characterised by
   a green flash on its outside edge.

Water pump - type	Centrifugal
Water pump - drive	Belt from crankshaft pulley

Drain tap location:
Radiator	In bottom water tank
Block	On right-hand side above oil filter

Torque Wrench Settings

Fan cowl to water pump body	11 lbs.ft. (1.5Kg.m)
Fan to shaft and pulley to shaft nuts	20 lbs.ft. (2.7 Kg.m)
Fan centre attachment bolts..	7 lbs.ft. (2.1 Kg.m)

1. General Description

The engine cooling water is circulated by a thermo-siphon, water pump assisted system. The radiator cap is pressurised and increases the temperature that the water can attain before boiling. If the water reaches boiling point it will increase the pressure in the cooling system to more than 7 lbs.in. This pressure will lift the internal part of the cap off its seat, thus exposing the overflow pipe down which the steam from the boiling water escapes. In this way the cap acts as a safety valve and relieves excess pressure in the cooling system.

It is, therefore, important to check that the radiator cap is in good condition and that the spring behind the sealing washer has not weakened. Most garages have a special machine in which radiator caps can be tested.

The cooling system comprises the radiator, top, bottom and intermediate hoses, heater hoses (if a heater and demister are fitted), the impellor water pump which has the unusual feature of being mounted remote from the engine, the thermostat, the two drain taps, and a bleed valve mounted behind the trim in the boot (early models) or adjacent to the water pump (later models). The last item is a nine bladed cooling fan mounted on the water pump spindle.

The system functions in the following fashion. Cold water in the bottom of the radiator circulates up the lower radiator hose to the water pump where it is pushed round the water passages in the cylinder block, helping to keep the cylinder bore and pistons cool.

The water then travels up into the cylinder head and circulates round the combustion spaces and valve seats absorbing more heat, and then, when the engine is at its proper operating temperatures, travels out of the cylinder head, past the open thermostat into the upper radiator hose and so into the radiator header tank.

The water travels down the radiator where it is rapidly cooled by the in-rush of cold air through the radiator core, which is created by both the fan and the motion of the car. The water, now cold, reaches the bottom of the radiator, whereupon the cycle is repeated.

When the engine is cold the thermostat (which is a valve which opens and closes according to the temperature of the water) maintains the circulation of the same water in the engine.

Only when the correct minimum operating temperature has been reached, as shown in the specification, does the thermostat begin to open, allowing water to return to the radiator.

2. Routine Maintenance

1. Once a week check the level of coolant in the radiator, and top up as necessary. Every 5,000 miles check the fan belt tension. If the belt requires adjustment details are given in Section 12.
2. Once a year or at 10,000 mile intervals, drain the radiator and refill with fresh coolant. If anti-freeze is not being used it will be necessary to add $1/3$ pint of Chrysler coolant inhibitor (Geigy 'C') to the cooling water. Details are given in Section 5. Details of the anti-freeze mixture are given in Section 10.
3. Periodically check the exterior of the radiator core and ensure that it is not chocked with debris, also check all hoses and connections for chafing, cracking and leakage. Renew or repair as necessary.

3. Cooling System - Draining

1. With the car on level ground drain the system as follows:-
2. If the engine is cold remove the filler cap from the radiator by turning the cap anti-clockwise. If the engine is hot, having just been run, then turn the filler cap very slightly until the pressure in the system has had time to disperse. Use a rag over the cap to protect your hand from escaping steam. If, with the engine very hot, the cap is released suddenly, the drop in pressure can result in the water boiling. With the pressure released the cap can be removed.
3. If anti-freeze is in the radiator drain it into a clean bucket or bowl for re-use.
4. Move the heater lever on the fascia to the red (hot) position.
5. Place a suitable receptacle under each tap and open the two drain taps. The radiator drain tap is on the bottom radiator tank, and the engine drain tap is situated on the right-hand side of the cylinder block above the oil filter. A short length of rubber tubing over the radiator drain tap nozzle will assist draining the coolant into a container without splashing.
6. When the water has finished running, probe the drain tap orifices with a short piece of wire to dislodge any particles of rust or sediment which may be blocking the taps and preventing all the water draining out. NOTE: that opening only the radiator tap will not drain the cylinder block.

4. Cooling System - Flushing

1. With time the cooling system will gradually lose its efficiency as the radiator becomes choked with rust scales, deposits from the water and other sediment. To clean the system out, remove the radiator cap and the drain tap and leave a hose running in the radiator cap orifice for ten to fifteen minutes.

2. In very bad cases the radiator should be reverse flushed. This can be done with the radiator in position. The cylinder block tap is closed and a hose placed over the open radiator drain tap. Water, under pressure, is then forced up through the radiator and out of the header tank filler orifice.
3. The hose is then removed and placed in the filler orifice and the radiator washed out in the usual fashion.

5. Cooling System - Filling

1. If no anti-freeze is to be added to the cooling water then it will be necessary to add $1/3$ pint of Chrysler coolant inhibitor. This special inhibitor prevents corrosion which would build up very quickly in the aluminium water-ways and eventually lead to serious overheating.
2. Proceed to fill the radiator, slowly, to the base of the filler neck, after closing the two drain taps. It is preferable to use the softest water available, rain water is ideal.

Fig.2.1. By-pass junction and method of bleeding the system.

3. If your car is fitted with a heater it will now be necessary to bleed the cooling system of air. To do this proceed as follows:-

a) On early models the bleed valve is situated in the boot on the bulkhead directly in front of the heater unit. To reach it, bend up the five clips retaining the hardboard skin at the rear of the boot and fold it forward until the valve is accessible. On later models the valve is much easier to get at, being adjacent to the water pump in the engine compartment.

A length of transparent bleeding tube will now be necessary, of the following dimensions:-

Early models .. .. .. Dia-inside .. .. $3/16$ in. (4.8mm)
                        Length .. .. .. 14 ft. (4.25 m)
Later models .. .. .. Dia-inside .. .. $3/16$ in. (4.8mm)
                        Length .. .. .. 2 ft. (60 cm)

b) Bleeding should be carried out with the engine cold to take advantage of the closed thermostat. The bleeding procedure is identical for all models. Fit one end of the tube over the bleed valve nozzle and immerse the other end in the header tank, fully open the bleed valve.
c) Move the heater control lever on the fascia to the red (hot)

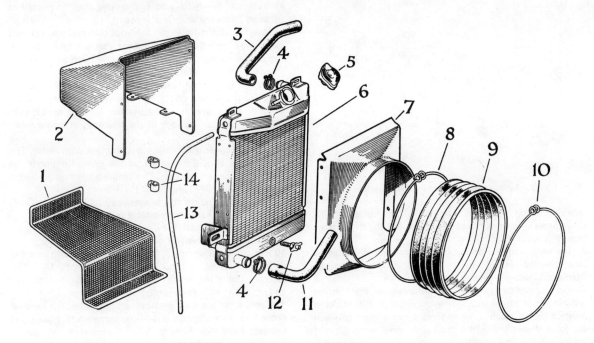

Fig. 2.2. EXPLODED VIEW OF THE RADIATOR ASSEMBLY

1 Stone guard	5 Radiator filler cap	9 Rubber shroud
2 Rear cowl	6 Radiator	10 Rubber shroud clip
3 Return hose	7 Front cowl	11 Radiator to pump hose
4 Hose clip	8 Rubber shroud clip	12 Radiator drain tap

13 Overflow pipe
14 Overflow pipe retaining
clips

position.

d) Start the engine and turn in the idling speed adjustment screw until the engine is turning at approximately 2000 r.p.m.

e) Watch the level of the coolant in the header tank and top it up as it decreases, in this way maintaining the level. Continue this procedure until no more air bubbles are seen to emerge from the bleed tube.

f) Momentarily rev the engine to expel any trapped air, then close the bleed valve.

g) Switch off the engine after returning the idling screw to its original position. Ensure that the coolant level is correct, and replace the radiator pressure cap. Bleeding is now complete.

h) If bleeding is not successful, the following should be checked: all hose clips for tightness and hoses for kinking; check that the heater control is operating its valve correctly and that the thermostat is of the correct type and working properly. Bleed the system again when the engine has cooled and all should be well.

---

6. Radiator Removal, Inspection, Cleaning and Replacement

1. To remove the radiator first drain the cooling system as described in Section 3.

2. Pull the top and bottom hoses off at their radiator unions after loosening their securing clips.

3. Now by loosening its tensioning nut and bolt slacken the wire bond that secures the rubber shroud to the radiator cowling. Gently ease both clip and throud off of the cowling.

4. From underneath the car unscrew and remove the three crosshead screws that retain the radiator stone guard to the adjacent vertical panel.

5. Unscrew and remove the three radiator retaining bolts, one either side of the header tank and the other on the left-

and side of the radiator at its base.

6. The radiator can now be withdrawn from beneath the car. NOTE: If the radiator is to be stored for any length of time, it should be in the upright position, otherwise sediment may block the narrow vertical cooling tubes.

7. With the radiator out of the car any leaks can be soldered up or repaired with a substance such as 'cataloy'. Clean out the inside of the radiator by flushing as detailed in the section before last. When the radiator is out of the car it is advantageous to turn it upside down for reverse flushing. Clean the exterior of the radiator by hosing down the radiator matrix with a strong jet of water to clear away road dirt, dead flies, etc. If the matrix is badly congested, it is best to completely immerse it in a bath of very hot water containing a mild detergent. Once immersed it should be vigorously scrubbed using a stiff bristle brush, on no account use a wire brush. Once all dirt and grease are removed, rinse the radiator in clean water.

8. Inspect the radiator hoses for cracks, internal or external perishing, and damage caused by overtightening of the securing clips. Replace the hoses as necessary. Examine the radiator hose securing clips and renew them if they are rusted or distorted. The drain taps should be renewed if leaking, but ensure the leak is not because of a faulty washer behind the tap. If the tap is suspected try a new washer first to see if this clears the trouble.

8. Replacement is a straightforward reversal of the removal procedure.

---

7. Thermostat Removal, Testing and Replacement

1. To remove the thermostat drain the cooling system as described in Section 3.

2. From beneath the car (it may be necessary to raise the rear of the car to gain access) unscrew and remove the five

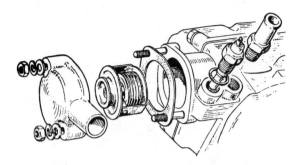

Fig.2.3. Bellows type thermostat and thermostat housing.

retaining screws from the periphery of the upright stone-shield panel in front of the cambox. Remove the shield from beneath the car.

3. The water outlet elbow/thermostat housing will now be visible on the rear end of the cylinder head (i.e. furthest from crankshaft pulley).

4. Remove the two nuts and all washers from the housing retaining studs. Remove the housing (photo). If it sticks in position on no account try to force a screwdriver between the joint. Instead soak the studs with penetrating oil, and gently tap the housing with a non-metallic hammer until it becomes loose.

7.4

5. Remove the thermostat (photo) which will now be visible.

7.5

6. Testing procedure is the same for both the wax and bellows type of thermostat.

a) Examine the thermostat and ensure that no riveted or soldered joints are broken or loose.

b) Check that the jiggle pin is in position and free to float.

c) On wax type thermostats ensure that the rubber seal on top of the element is not cracked or perished and also that there is no wax exuding from beneath it.

7. To test for correct opening on both types of thermostat, hang the thermostat and a thermometer by separate pieces of string in a saucepan of cold water. Neither items should touch the side or bottom of the saucepan or an incorrect reading will result.

8. Heat the water gently stirring with the thermometer. The temperature should be taken at the precise moment the thermostat begins to open. The temperature should be between 77ºC (170ºF) and 80ºC (179ºF).

9. As a further guide at a temperature of 98.9ºC to 100ºC (210º to 212ºF) the thermostat should be open ¼ in. approximately. Whilst the valve is open ensure there is no dirt or foreign matter around its seat.

10 Remove the thermostat from the hot water and immerse it in cold water, it should close itself within 15 to 20 seconds. If the thermostat fails any of these tests discard it, and replace it with a new unit.

11 Replacement is a straightforward reversal of the removal procedure. However, do not forget to renew the gasket. If the two joint faces have minor corrosion smear the gasket with jointing compound such as 'Hermetite'. If the water outlet elbow/thermostat housing unit is badly corroded it will be necessary to renew it.

8. Water Pump - Removal and Replacement

1. To remove the pump drain the cooling system as described in Section 3.

2. Slacken the two dynamo holding bolts and the bolt through the adjusting strap, swing the dynamo downwards and remove the now slack fan belt.

3. Loosen the nut and bolt tensioning the rubber shroud retaining band and gently ease both the band and shroud off the plastic fan cowling.

4. Disconnect the battery by loosening and removing the leads from its two terminal posts.

5. Pull the two wires with their lucar connectors from their terminals on the rear of the dynamo. Remove the already slack dynamo retaining bolts and take the dynamo from the engine compartment.

6. Loosen their clips and remove the intermediate hose from its union on the block; the bottom hose from its union on the radiator; and the heater hose from its union on the pump body.

7. Undo their nuts and remove the three long bolts which retain the water pump/fan assembly holding bracket to the cylinder block mounting bosses. Note the position of any spacers and washers before removing them. The fan pump and bracket assembly can now be lifted from the engine compartment.

8. To detach the cooling fan from the pump unscrew and remove the three retaining bolts. Note the positions of any spacers and ensure that they are correctly replaced on reassembly.

9. To remove the fan cowl undo and withdraw the four long bolts which pass through the inlet and outlet bodies of the water pump. The water pump is now devoid of ancillary components and is in the correct form to be exchanged if a new pump is to be fitted.

10 Replacement is a straightforward reversal of the removal procedure.

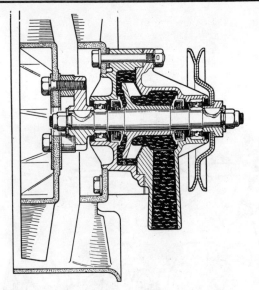

Fig.2.4. Sectioned view of the water pump and fan assembly (early models)

9. Water Pump - Dismantling and Reassembly

1. Although there are three different types of water pump fitted to the Imp the difference between them lies mainly in the type of seals and therefore the dismantling and re-assembly procedure is common to all. If it is wished to re-pair the pump, before starting first ascertain that spare parts are available. It appears that very few dealers stock spare parts as opposed to exchange rebuilt pump units.

2. To dismantle the pump proceed as follows. Using a puller draw off the tri-angular driving member and driving pulley, having first unscrewed and removed the large nuts at each end of the impellor spindle.

3. Hold one half of the pump body steady and turn the other half to break the seal between the two.

4. Using a non-metallic hammer drive the pump spindle out of the bearing at the fan end of the pump body.

5. Press the shaft or shaft and bearing out of the pump outer housing. If for some reason a bearing stays on the shaft, draw it off using a puller.

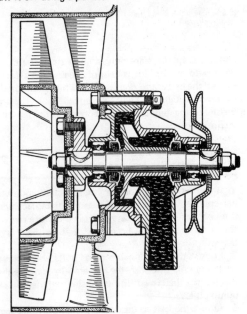

Fig.2.5. Sectioned view of the water pump and fan assembly (later models)

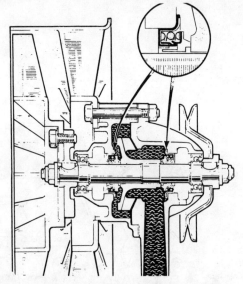

Fig.2.6. The later type of water pump with pressure balanced type seals - inset shows a seal in dry state

6. Press the other bearing out of its housing, after removing its retaining circlip, the circlip position is shown in Figs. 2.4, 2.5 and 2.6.

7. Remove the seals, noting carefully their type and fitted attitude. This is to ensure that the new seals are fitted properly and are of the correct type when the pump is re-assembled. Note: on some pumps thrower abutment washers are fitted behind the seals. No attempt should be made to remove the impellor from its spindle.

8. If either the impellor or its spindle are worn a new shaft assembly should be fitted.

9. New bearings, seals and gasket should always be fitted on reassembly.

10 Reassembling is a straightforward reversal of the removal procedure but note the following. When refitting the bear-ings, the arbor should press on both bearing races at the same time, whilst the other bearing is also supported on both of its tracks. When jointing the two halves of the pump together the jointing faces of each should be coated with Shell Ensis Fluid 256 to prevent corrosion and to help the joint to separate on future dismantling.

10. Anti-Freeze Mixture

1. With the Imp's aluminium engine, it is essential to use anti-freeze during the colder months of the year. The fluid can be of any make which conforms to B.S. 3150 specifica-tions.

2. Before filling the cooling system with an anti-freeze solution it is necessary to drain and flush the system as des-cribed in Sections 3 and 4. Also check all hoses for cracks or any signs of perishing. If either of these are apparent the defective hoses should be replaced. Check and if necessary tighten all hose connections.

3 Use 2¾ pints of Castrol antifreeze with 8½ pints of water in cooling system to give protection down to -12°C (10°F).

11. High Temperature Warning Light - Sender Unit Removal and Replacement

1. The sender unit (where fitted) is located in the cylinder head adjacent to the thermostat housing. Unfortunately the sender unit cannot be repaired and if faulty must be re-placed.

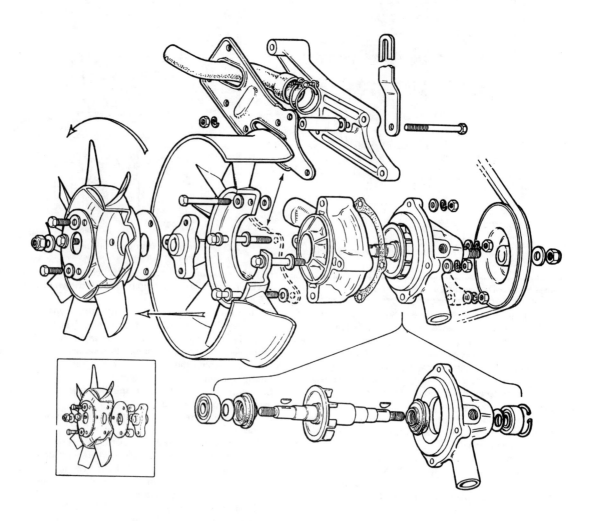

Fig. 2.7. Exploded view of water pump and fan assembly (inset shows the
early fan unit)

2. To remove the unit simply unscrew it from the block,
with a spanner, after partially draining the cooling system.
3. Replacement is a straightforward reversal of the removal
sequence. If the unit is fitted with a fibre washer remember
to replace it.

12. Fan Belt - Adjustment

1. It is important to keep the fan belt correctly adjusted
and although not listed by the manufacturer, it is considered that this should be a regular maintenance task per-
formed every 5,000 miles.
2. If the belt is too loose it will slip, wear rapidly, and
cause the dynamo and water pump to mal-function. If the
belt is too tight the dynamo and water pump bearings will
wear rapidly causing premature failure of these components.
3. Fan belt tension is correct when there is 1 inch of free
movement on its longest run (i.e. between the crankshaft
and water pump pulleys).
4. To adjust the fan belt, slightly slacken the two dynamo
securing bolts and the bolts on either end of the adjustment

strap. As the bolts are only slightly slack the dynamo will
be stiff to move. This is helpful because the effort required
to hold the belt at the right tension while the top adjustment
strap bolt is tightened will be reduced.
5. Check the tension and if correct, retighten all dynamo
securing bolts.

13. Fan Belt - Removal and Replacement

1. If the fan belt is worn or has stretched unduly it should
be replaced. The most usual reason for replacement is that
the belt has broken in service. It is therefore recommended
that a spare belt is always carried. Replacement is described
below.
2. Loosen the two dynamo pivot bolts and the nut on the
adjusting link and push the dynamo in towards the engine.
3. Slip the belt over the crankshaft, dynamo, and water
pump pulleys.
4. Adjust the belt as described in the previous section and
tighten the dynamo mounting nuts. NOTE: After fitting a
new belt it will require adjustment 250 miles later.

Cause	Trouble	Remedy
SYMPTOM: OVERHEATING Heat generated in cylinder not being successfully disposed of by radiator	Insufficient water in cooling system	Top up radiator.
	Fan belt slipping (Accompanied by a shrieking noise on rapid engine acceleration)	Tighten fan belt to recommended tension or replace if worn.
	Radiator core blocked or radiator grill restricted	Reverse flush radiator, remove obstructions.
	Bottom water hose collapsed, impeding flow	Remove and fit new hose.
	Thermostat not opening properly	Remove and fit new thermostat.
	Ignition advance and retard incorrectly set (Accompanied by loss of power, and perhaps, misfiring)	Check and reset ignition timing.
	Carburettor(s) incorrectly adjusted	Tune carburettor(s).
	Exhaust system partially blocked	Check exhaust pipe for constrictive dents and blockages.
	Oil level in sump too low	Top up sump to full mark on dipstick.
	Blown cylinder head gasket (Water/steam being forced down the radiator overflow pipe under pressure)	Remove cylinder head, fit new gasket.
	Engine not yet run-in	Run-in slowly and carefully.
	Brakes binding	Check and adjust brakes if necessary.
SYMPTOM: UNDERHEATING Too much heat being dispersed by radiator	Thermostat jammed open	Remove and renew thermostat.
	Incorrect grade of thermostat fitted allowing premature opening of valve	Remove and replace with new thermostat which opens at a higher temperature.
	Thermostat missing	Check and fit correct thermostat.
	Ignition timing incorrectly set (accompanied by loss of power and perhaps misfiring)	Check and reset ignition timing.
	Carburettor/s incorrectly adjusted	Tune carburettor/s.
SYMPTOM: LOSS OF COOLING WATER Leaks in system	Loose clips on water hoses	Check and tighten clips if necessary.
	Top, bottom, or by-pass water hoses perished and leaking	Check and replace any faulty hoses.
	Radiator core leaking	Remove radiator and repair.
	Thermostat gasket leaking	Inspect and renew gasket.
	Radiator pressure cap spring worn or seal ineffective	Renew radiator pressure cap.
	Blown cylinder head gasket (Pressure in system forcing water/steam down overflow pipe)	Remove cylinder head and fit new gasket.
	Cylinder wall or head cracked	Dismantle engine, dispatch to engineering works for repair.

Chapter 3/Fuel System and Carburation

Contents

Specifications

Fuel Pump:

Make and type...	A.C. mechanically operated diaphragm
Location	Top of cambox
Operation	Lever by eccentric on camshaft
Pump pressure	1¼ to 2 lbs. sq. in. (.08 to .14 Kg.cm^2)

Fuel Tank:

Location	Base of front luggage compartment
Capacity	6 gallons (7.2 U.S. gallons, 27.2 Litres)

Carburettors:

Type, Earlier single carburettor models	Solex, B.30 P.I.H.T., B.30 P.I.H.T.-2, B.30 P.I.H.T.-3, or B.30 P.I.H.-5.
Type, Later models and earlier twin carburettor models	Stromberg 125 CD

Air Cleaners:

Single carburettor models	Single paper element
Certain single carburettor models	Oil bath and steel gauze
Twin carburettor models	Twin paper element

Solex Carburetters - Settings up to 4,000 ft. (1200 m.)

	B30. P.I.H.T.	B30. P.I.H.T-2	B30. P.I.H.T-3	Mk.1 30.P.I.H-5	Mk.II 30.P.I.H-5
Choke	22 mm	20 mm	20 mm	20 mm	22 mm
Air Correction	160	150	150	150 H.C. 175 L.C.	190
Pilot Jet Air Bleed	100	90	140	140	140
Pilot Jet (Slow Running) ...	45	40	40	40	45
Econostat Jet	60	80	80	80 H.C. 70 L.C.	125
Main Jet	112.5	102 or 105	102	102	115
Progression Holes	1x1.2	2x1.2	1x1.2&1x0.9	1x1.2&1x0.9	1x1.2&1x0.9
Needle Valve Seat	1.3 with 1mm washer	1.6 with 1 mm washer	1.6 with 1 mm washer	1.6 with 1 mm washer	1.6 with 1 mm washer
Strangler Control	Automatic	Automatic	Automatic	Manual	Manual

Stromberg Carburettors - Settings up to 5,000 ft (1500 m)

Metering Needle	6K (B 173512)
Damper Spring	.032
Fast Idle Gap (At Throttle)...	0.9/1.0 mm
Slow Running Speed...	1000 R.P.M.
Strangler Control	Manual

1. General Description

On all models a six gallon fuel tank is mounted at the front of the car in the bottom of the luggage compartment. The fuel is pumped from the tank to the carburettor, which may be either a Solex or a Stromberg, by an A.C. mechanical fuel pump mounted centrally on the top of the cambox. This pump is actuated by an eccentric on the camshaft.

A fuel contents gauge is fitted to all models.

2. Routine Maintenance

1. Every 5,000 miles remove the air cleaner element and clean it thoroughly. Removal and cleaning are described in Sections 3 to 5.
2. Also if necessary, adjust the carburettor slow running. Details are given in Section 15 for Solex carburettors and Section 17 for the Stromberg 125 CD.
3. Check and clean if necessary the fuel pump filter gauze. Details are given in the following paragraphs.

a) Undo and remove the bolt in the centre of the pump cover and lift off the cover. Inspect the filter gauze for sediment. Lift it out and clean it with petrol and a soft brush if dirty.
b) Check the condition of the cork gasket, renew if it has hardened or broken. Replacement is a straightforward reversal of the removal sequence - do not forget to refit the fibre washer under the head of the retaining bolt and tighten the bolt just enough for the cover to make a leak-proof joint with the gasket.

4. Every 15,000 miles check the manifold and carburettor retaining bolts for tightness.
5. Also renew the filter element of the paper element type air cleaner/s. Details are given in Sections 4 and 5.
6. Stromberg carburettors incorporate a cold start device. Every winter when the air temperature is very cold areas such as North America drops to 28ºC (-20ºF) the setting of this device should be altered as described in Section 20.
7. Solex carburettors incorporate an accelerator pump, for which a longer actuating arm is available from Chrysler. The longer arm will help the carburettor provide a slightly richer mixture for winter motoring. Fitment is simply a matter of removing the retaining clips and spring from the existing arm, withdrawing it and putting the new arm in its place. Then refit the spring and clips. Keep the old arm and it can be refitted when the weather becomes warmer.

3. Air Cleaner - Oil Bath Type - Inspection, Cleaning and Oil Replenishment

1. Referring to Fig. 3.1. detach the oil tray from the base of the cleaner unit by releasing the three quick action retaining clips. Withdraw the tray from the engine compartment. (It will probably be necessary to remove the battery).
2. Inspect the condition of the oil in the tray and also note how much sediment has collected in its base.

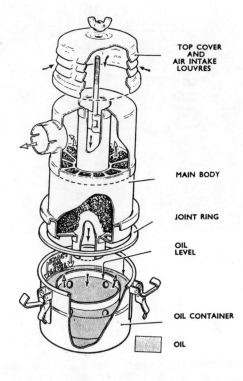

TOP COVER AND AIR INTAKE LOUVRES

MAIN BODY

JOINT RING

OIL LEVEL

OIL CONTAINER

OIL

Fig.3.1. Exploded view of the oil bath type air cleaner.

3. If the oil is dirty or there is a lot of sediment present, then the old oil should be discarded and the tray cleaned thoroughly with paraffin. Fill the tray to the level indicated with new multigrade engine oil.
4. Before refitting the oil tray to the base of the air cleaner unit, inspect the condition of the steel gauze above the oil tray; this can be done with a mirror.
5. If the gauze appears dirty then it should be removed and washed in paraffin or petrol and allowed to drain dry before refitment. It is a good idea to carry out this task twice yearly as a matter of course.
6. After refitting the steel gauze the oil tray can be re-placed. Whenever possible a new sealing ring should be used between the oil tray and filter unit.
7. Next inspect the condition of the louvres in the air intake at the top of the filter unit. Should these louvres be blocked by dirt or debris, the intake should be removed for cleaning.
8. To remove the intake unscrew the winged nut in its centre, lift the intake off the through bolt, and withdraw it from the engine compartment.
9. Thoroughly wash the air intake in paraffin. Ensure that the louvres are clear by poking them through if necessary. Replacing the air intake is a reversal of the removal procedure.

4. Air Cleaner - Dry Element Type Removal, Inspection, Cleaning and Replacement

1. Referring to Fig. 3.2. slacken the clip securing the air filter intake to the carburettor orifice. Remove the nut and washer retaining the air cleaner base bracket to the lug on the inlet manifold.

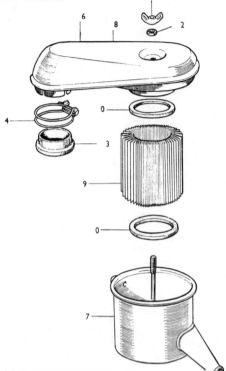

Fig.3.2. EXPLODED VIEW OF THE DRY ELEMENT TYPE AIR CLEANER

1. Wing nut	7. Air cleaner body
2. Washer	8. Top cover
3. Flexible seal	9. Element
4. Clip	0. Seals
6. Top cover	

2. Lift the air cleaner and move it into a position which will allow the wing nut retaining the air cleaner top to be removed, followed by the air cleaner top.
3. Lift the air filter element out of the air cleaner body and withdraw it from the engine compartment.
4. Inspect the element for dirt and debris. If the element is badly blocked then it should be removed. However, if there are only light deposits, these can probably be shaken free by gently tapping the element on a solid object.

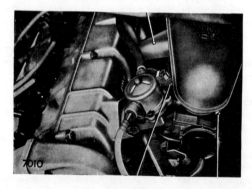

Fig.3.3. The air cleaner top cover must always be replaced so that the air intake is in the position shown

5. The element can now be replaced in the cleaner body, the top cover replaced and the bottom mounting strap fixed to the inlet manifold. Finally secure the cleaner intake to the carburettor body.
6. If it is wished to remove the complete air cleaner unit, follow the instructions given in paragraphs 1 and 2. Remove the battery, disconnecting the earth lead first.
7. The lower half of the cleaner body can now be withdrawn by easing it around the outside of the carburettor and over the vacant battery tray. Replacement is a reversal of the removal procedure. Ensure that the air cleaner top cover is replaced in the position shown in Fig. 3.3.

5. Air Cleaner - Twin Carburettor Dry Element Type - Removal, Inspection, Cleaning and Replacement

1. Referring to Fig. 3.4. slacken the clip securing the flame trap hose to the cleaner tap cover and pull the hose off the union on the cover.

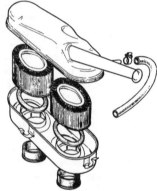

Fig.3.4. The air cleaner used with twin Stromberg 125 CD carburetters

trap hose to the cleaner tap cover and pull the hose off the union on the cover.
2. Release the clips securing the top cover to the cleaner body and lift the cover off. The two elements can now be removed.
3. Inspect the elements for dirt and debris. If the element is badly blocked then it should be renewed. However, if there are only light deposits, these can probably be shaken free by gently tapping the elements on a solid object.
4. The elements can now be replaced. Ensure that they are correctly seated on their sealing rings before replacing the top cover and flame trap.
5. If it is wished to remove the complete air cleaner unit, this can be done by releasing the flame trap hose and slackening the clips retaining the unit to the carburettor orifices. Lift the unit upwards and then withdraw it from the engine compartment. Replacement is a reversal of the removal procedure.

6. A.C. Fuel Pump - Description

The mechanically operated A.C. fuel pump is actuated through a spring loaded rocker arm. One arm of the rocker (8) bears against an eccentric on the camshaft and the other arm operates a diaphragm pull rod. (11) NOTE all references in brackets should be co-related with Fig.3.4.

As the engine camshaft rotates, the eccentric moves the pivoted rocker arm outwards which in turn pulls the diaphragm pull rod (11) and the diaphragm (16) down against the pressure of the diaphragm spring (15).

This creates sufficient vacuum in the pump chamber to

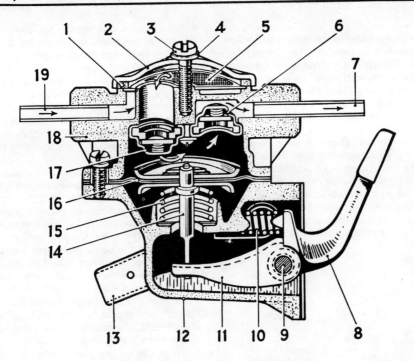

Fig. 3.5. SECTIONED VIEW THROUGH THE FUEL PUMP AND FILTER

1 Cover sealing washer	6 Non-return outlet valve	11 Diaphragm operating arm	16 Diaphragm
2 Cover	7 Outlet	12 Fuel pump body	17 Non-return valve
3 Bolt	8 Rocker	13 Hand priming lever	18 Pump body
4 Washer	9 Diaphragm operating arm	14 Diaphragm pull rod	19 Inlet
5 Filter gauze	10 Anti-rattle spring	15 Diaphragm spring	

draw in fuel from the tank through the fuel filter gauze (5), and non-return valve (17).

The rocker arm is held in constant contact with the eccentric by an anti-rattle spring (10), and as the engine camshaft continues to rotate the eccentric allows the rocker arm to move inwards. The diaphragm spring (15) is thus free to push the diaphragm (16) upwards forcing the fuel in the pump chamber out to the carburettor through the non-return outlet valve (6).

When the float chamber in the carburettor is full the float chamber needle valve will close so preventing further flow from the fuel pump.

The pressure in the delivery line will hold the diaphragm downwards against the pressure of the diaphragm spring, and it will remain in this position until the needle valve in the float chamber opens to admit more petrol.

7.2

7. A.C. Fuel Pump - Removal and Replacement

1. Slacken the clips and pull the petrol inlet and outlet pipes off the pump unions. Seal off the ends of the pipes to prevent the ingress of foreign matter and the leakage of petrol.
2. Remove the two nuts and washers retaining the fuel pump to the cambox (photo). Lift the pump and gaskets away. Note the number of gaskets as the thickness of these controls pump output pressure.
3. Replacement is a reversal of tne removal procedure. However, note the following:-

a) New gaskets should be used and they should be of the same number as those removed.
b) Ensure that the pump actuating lever is seated on the top of the camshaft eccentric and not beneath it.
c) Check that the nut with the slot in its head is replaced on the stud nearest the centre of the cambox cover.

8. A.C. Fuel Pump - Testing

1. Presuming that the fuel lines and unions are in good condition and that there are no leaks anywhere, check the performance of the fuel pump in the following manner. Disconnect the fuel pipe at the carburettor inlet union, and the high tension lead to the coil, and with a suitable container or a large rag in position to catch the ejected fuel, turn the engine over on the starter motor solenoid. A good spurt of petrol should emerge from the end of the pipe every second revolution.

9. A.C. Fuel Pump - Dismantling

1. Unscrew the securing bolt from the centre of the cover and lift the cover away. NOTE the fibre washer under the head of the bolt.
2. Remove the cork sealing washer and the fine mesh

filter gauze.

3. If the condition of the diaphragm is suspect or for any other reason it is wished to dismantle the pump fully, proceed as follows:- Mark the upper and lower flanges of pump that are adjacent to each other. Unscrew the five screws and spring washers which hold the two halves of the pump body together. Separate the two halves with great care, ensuring that the diaphragm does not stick to either of the two flanges.

4. Unscrew the screws which retain the valve plate and remove the plate and gasket together with the inlet and outlet valves. (Some later pumps have a simplified valve plate arrangement which is released by one screw.)

5. The latest type of pump has no valve retaining plate. Instead the valves are held in position by staking of the pump body. This being the case the staking can be tapped back with a hammer and centre punch (see photo). The valves can then be removed.

6. Press down and rotate the diaphragm a quarter of a turn (in either direction) to release the pull rod from the operating lever, and lift away the diaphragm and pull rod (which is securely fixed to the diaphragm and cannot be removed from it). Remove the diaphragm spring and the metal and fibre washer underneath it.

7. If it is necessary to dismantle the rocker arm assembly, remove the retaining circlips and washer from the rocker arm pivot rod and slide out the rod which will then free the rocker arm, operating rod, and anti-rattle spring.

10. A.C. Fuel Pump - Examination and Reassembly

1. Check the condition of the cork cover sealing washer, and if it is hardened or broken it must be replaced. The diaphragm should be checked similarly and replaced if faulty. Clean the pump thoroughly and agitate the valves in paraffin to clean them out. This will also improve the contact between the valve seat and the valve. It is unlikely that the pump body will be damaged, but check for fractures and cracks. Renew the cover if distorted by over-tightening. It should be noted that fuel pump service kits are available. These contain new valves, a diaphragm and the necessary gaskets and sealing rings.

2. To reassemble the pump proceed as follows:- Replace the rocker arm assembly comprising the operating link, rocker arm, anti-rattle spring and washer in their relative positions in the pump body. Align the holes in the operating link, rocker arm, and washers with the holes in the body and insert the pivot pin.

3. Refit the circlips to the grooves in each end of the pivot pin.

4. Earlier pumps used valves which had to be built up, while later versions used ready assembled valves which are

9.5

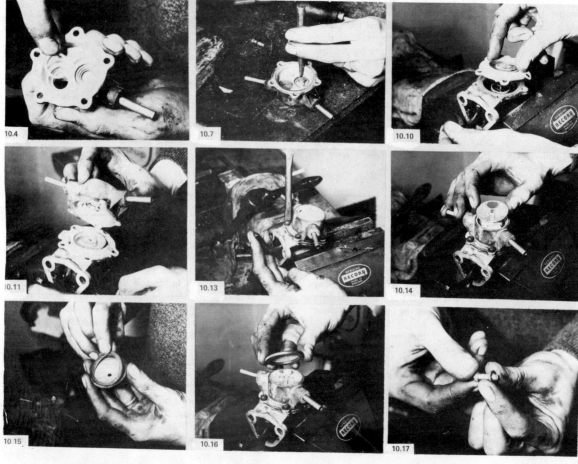

10.4   10.7   10.10

10.11   10.13   10.14

10.15   10.16   10.17

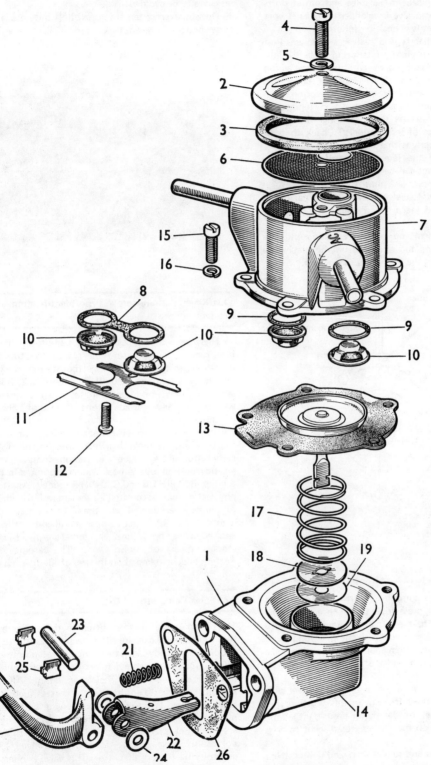

Fig. 3.6. EXPLODED VIEW OF THE A.C. FUEL PUMP

1 Pump lower body	8 Gasket *	15 Screw	22 Link
2 Filter cover	9 Gaskets *	16 Spring washer	23 Swivel pin
3 Sealing ring *	10 Valves *	17 Spring	24 Washers
4 Screw	11 Valve retaining plate	18 Oil seal washer	25 Pin retainers
5 Sealing washer *	12 Screw	19 Washer	26 Gasket *
6 Filter element	13 Diaphragm assembly *	20 Rocker arm	
7 Pump upper body	14 Lower body	21 Rocker arm return spring	

* All these parts comprise the pump overhaul kit

merely dropped into place in the inlet and outlet ports. Ensure that the correct valve is dropped into each port, also that the valve gasket is in position (photo).

5. Reassemble the earlier type of valve as follows:- Position the delivery valve in place on its spring. Place the inlet valve in position in the pump body and then fit the spring. Place the small four legged inlet valve spring retainer over the spring with the legs positioned towards the spring.

6. Place the valve retaining gasket in position, replace the plate, and tighten down the three securing screws. (Or single screw in the case of later models.) Check that the valves are working properly with a suitable piece of wire.

7. If the pump is of the latest type and there is no retaining plate the valves can be staked into position with a centre punch and hammer (see photo).

8. Position the fibre and steel washer in that order in the base of the pump and place the diaphragm spring over them.

9. Replace the diaphragm and pull rod assembly with the pull rod downwards and the small tab on the diaphragm adjacent to the centre of the flange and rocker arm.

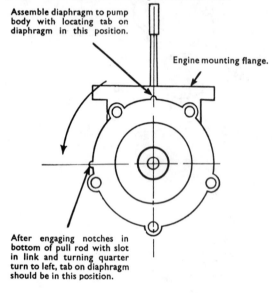

Assemble diaphragm to pump body with locating tab on diaphragm in this position.

Engine mounting flange.

After engaging notches in bottom of pull rod with slot in link and turning quarter turn to left, tab on diaphragm should be in this position.

Fig.3.7. Fitting the fuel pump diaphragm assembly

10 With the body of the pump held so that the rocker arm is facing away from one, press down the diaphragm, turning it a quarter of a turn to the left at the same time. This engages the slot on the pull rod with the operating lever. The small tab on the diaphragm should now be at an angle of 90° to the rocker arm and the diaphragm should be firmly located (photo).

11 Move the rocker arm until the diaphragm is level with the body flanges and hold the arm in this position. Reassemble the two halves of the pump ensuring that the previously made marks on the flanges are adjacent to each other (photo).

12 Insert the five screws and lockwashers and tighten them down finger tight.

13 Move the rocker arm up and down several times to centralise the diaphragm, and then with the arm held down, tighten the screws securely in a diagonal sequence (photo).

14 Replace the gauze filter in position (photo).

15 Fit the cork or rubber sealing washer to the cover (photo).

16 Then fit the cover in place over the top of the pump (photo).

17 Fit a new fibre or rubber washer under the head of the cover securing screw/bolt (photo). This is essential if petrol

leaks are to be avoided.

18 Do not overtighten the screw/bolt but ensure that it is tight enough to prevent leaks.

10.18

11. Solex Carburettors - Type Identification and Modifications

There were four types of Solex carburettor fitted to the Imp range of cars before the switch to Stromberg carburettors was made. The Solex carburettor can be identified by the type numbers B30-PIHT, B30-PIHT-2, B30-PIHT-3 and B30-PIH-5. Modifications made to these carburettors were slight. The major alteration consisted of a change from an automatic choke to manual on the B30-PIH-5 carburettor. Further modifications consisted of the discontinuation of the main well ball valve on the B30-PIHT-2 carburettor and subsequent alterations to the air correction jet and emulsion tube. A beak was incorporated in the choke tube on B30-PIHT-3 and B30-PIH-5 models. Apart from the physical differences created by the alteration in the method of choke operation all the Solex carburettors listed are identical for all practical purposes. All dismantling, setting and adjusting procedures are therefore the same for all models, unless otherwise stated. The carburettor identification code is stamped on the top of the float chamber.

12. Solex Carburettors - General Description

1. The Solex carburettors fitted to the earlier models of the Imp range of cars are all of the semi-downdraught type, and have the following systems incorporated in their design. Idling circuit, main spraying circuit; econostat circuit and a mechanically operated accelerator pump. All of these systems combine to ensure that the correct fuel/air mixture is administered to the engine under any given condition. All numerical references in this section are to Fig. 3.8. A constant fuel level is maintained in the float chamber by a non-return valve, known as a needle valve (17) which controls the in-flow of petrol. This valve is operated by a float (29). As the float sinks with the fuel level it operates the needle valve which then opens and allows fuel to flow into the chamber. As the fuel level in the chamber rises so does the float until it again operates the needle valve which stops the in-flow of fuel. Thus the fuel level is constantly maintained.

2. Idling Circuit - The mixture required for idling when the engine is worn is supplied through the orifice (34). Additionally the idling circuit provides the mixture for initial throttle opening which passes into the venturi through the by-pass orifice (35) located just above the throttle

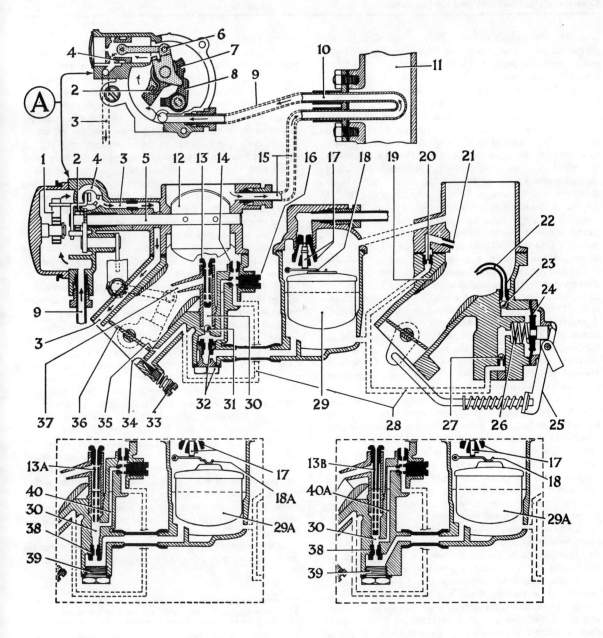

Fig. 3.8. SCHEMATIC SECTIONAL VIEW OF THE SOLEX CARBURETTOR

Lower insets show modification differences: 'A' Is a cross sectioned and end view of the auto-choke mechanism. Arrows show cold air flow into 'U' tube (10) and hot air flow from 'U' tube through the auto-choke mechanism into inlet manifold.

1 Bi-metal spring - large - operating choke valve
2 Bi-metal spring - small - operating stepped cam (7)
3 Vacuum feed passage - through which heated air from 'U' tube (10) is drawn
4 Vacuum kick piston
5 Choke valve spindle
6 Link and lever - connecting vacuum kick piston (4) and choke valve spindle (5)
7 Stepped cam
8 Lever - used to open throttle to fast idle, or to open choke valve, when partly closed, if accelerator pedal is moved half way or beyond
9 Hot air feed pipe from 'U' tube (10)
10 'U' tube - heated by exhaust gases

11 Exhaust manifold
12 Choke (strangler) valve
13 Air correction jet and emulsion tube B30 PIHT
13a Air correction jet and emulsion tube B30 PIHT-2
13b Air correction jet and emulsion tube B30 PIHT-3 and B30 PIH-5
14 Slow running jet air bleed
15 Cold air feed to 'U' tube (10)
16 Slow running (pilot) jet
17 Float needle valve and seating
18 Float lever arm - all carburettors except B30 PIHT
18a Float lever arm - B30 PIHT-2 only
19 Choke tube (Venturi) B30 PIHT and B30 PIHT-2 only
10 'U' tube - heated by exhaust gases

20 Econostat jet
21 Econostat discharge tube
22 Accelerator pump injector tube
23 Accelerator pump discharge valve - also called anti-reversal valve
24 Accelerator pump diaphragm and plunger
25 Accelerator pump operating lever
26 Diaphragm return spring
27 Accelerator pump non-return valve
28 Internal passages in carburettor body
29 Float - B30 PIHT
29a Float - all carburettors except B30 PIHT
30 Main well
31 Main well ball valve - B30 PIHT only

32 Main jet and holder
33 Slow running mixture volume control screw
34 Slow running mixture outlet
35 By-pass orifice (progression hole)
36 Throttle
37 Main spraying orifice
38 Main jet - all carburettors except B30 PIHT
39 Main jet cover plug
40 Slow running (pilot) jet feed B30 PIHT and B30 PIHT-2
40a Slow running (pilot) jet feed B30 PIHT-3 and B30 PIH-5

butterfly. The by-pass orifice is only in operation during the period when engine revs rise above idling speed until enough manifold depression is produced to draw fuel from the main spraying orifice (37). The fuel circuit in use during idling is as follows. Fuel is drawn from the well above the main jet (32) and passes through the pilot jet (16) where it is accurately metered. At the same time the mixture is emulsified by air from the pilot jet air bleed (14). During idling additional air is drawn into the venturi (choke tube) through the by-pass orifice (35). This would weaken the idling mixture, so to prevent this from happening a tapered screw known as the volume control screw (33) protrudes into the orifice. Thus by regulating the size of the orifice this screw controls the mixture volume (fuel/air ratio). Once the mixture has passed into the venturi it is further emulsified by the turbulent air passing the throttle butterfly (36) which is held partly open by an adjustment screw. As the throttle is progressively opened and the engine revs rise, the depression (vacuum) formed below the choke butterfly (12) is gradually increased until it becomes sufficient to suck fuel from the beak of the main discharge orifice (37). The main spraying system is then in operation.

3. Main Spraying System - When the main spraying system comes into operation as described above the circuit is as follows. Fuel is drawn from the float chamber to the main discharge orifice (37) via the main jet (32) where it is metered into the main spraying well (30). Here it combines with air metered through the air correction jet (13). This air enters the fuel through a series of holes in the emulsion tube located beneath the air correction jet (13). The emulsified mixture then passes from the main spraying well directly to the main discharge tube and thence into the venturi. The volume of air in the mixture is controlled by the fuel level in the main spraying well. As the fuel level in the well drops it uncovers more holes in the emulsion tube and thus more air mixes with the fuel providing a weaker mixture. In this way the correct mixture is supplied to the engine according to speed and load.

4. Econostat Circuit - The 'Econostat' device is non-mechanical in operation and is designed to permit maximum fuel economy to be maintained over the cruising range of the vehicle. It also accurately meters fuel under full throttle conditions. The 'Econostat' circuit works in the following manner. Once cruising speed has been reached there is sufficient manifold depression to draw fuel up to the inner end of the discharge tube (21) and thence into the venturi. Fuel is initially drawn from the float chamber. It passes through a jet (20) which controls the rate at which the fuel is supplied and from this jet the fuel travels directly to the discharge tube (21) from which it is passed into the venturi in the manner described earlier.

5. Accelerator Pump - The accelerator pump is a mechanical device linked to the throttle mechanism of the carburettor. Its main components are a pump diaphragm (24), pump spring (26) and an actuating lever (25). The pump operates in the following manner. Fuel enters the chamber on the inner side of the pump diaphragm. A non-return ball valve ensures that this fuel cannot return to the float chamber from where it was drawn. When the throttle is opened the accelerator actuating rod is operated by means of a lever. The pump diaphragm is then moved inwards. This action causes the fuel in the inner chamber to be forced through a drilling, past a ball valve (23) (which prevents the entry of air) into the calibrated injector tube (22) from which it is squirted directly into the venturi. By this action the accelerator pump ensures that under acceleration condition and rich mixture is fed to the engine, thus ensuring that acceleration is smooth and rapid.

6. Chokes - Two types of choke were fitted. The first three Solex carburettors incorporated an automatic choke, whilst on the fourth Solex, the B30-PIH-5, a manual choke was fitted in favour of the automatic which sometimes caused starting problems. The automatic choke is operated by a bimetalic 'clock' spring (1). Basically air is drawn from the exhaust manifold and passed over the bimetalic spring. When the engine is first started this air is cold and thus the spring is contracted, bringing the choke into operation. As the air in the exhaust manifold becomes warmer the spring progressively uncurls, causing the choke butterfly (12) to open. When the engine reaches normal operating temperature the spring has opened sufficiently to render the choke inoperative. The automatic choke also incorporates a stepped cam (8) which causes the engine idling speed to increase, dependant upon the amount of choke applied. This device is also rendered inoperative when the engine reaches normal operating temperature. When starting a car fitted with an automatic choke (cold engine) the correct technique is as follows. The accelerator pedal should be pressed right down to the floor and released just ONCE and should not be touched again until the engine is running. Operate the starter and the engine should fire first time. It is best then to drive the car away as quickly as possible as this will assist in a quick engine warm-up. When starting in very cold weather depress the clutch. This will reduce oil drag in the transaxle. The trouble with an automatic choke of this nature is that should the engine flood when starting from cold there is no way of permanently opening the choke, as its operation is totally dependant on exhaust manifold temperature. The choke can be temporarily opened by fully depressing the accelerator. The manual choke is entirely conventional and is cable operated from a small lever in front of the gear lever. When the operating lever is pulled it causes the choke butterfly (12) on the carburettor to close, thus bringing the choke into operation. The correct procedure for starting a car (cold engine) fitted with a manual choke is as follows. The choke lever should be pulled right the way back and the accelerator pedal should not be touched. Operate the starter and the engine should fire first time. Drive the car away as quickly as possible to assist in a quick warm-up. If the weather is very cold depress the clutch on starting to reduce oil drag in the transaxle.

---

13. Solex Carburettors - Removal and Replacement

1. Remove the air cleaner as described in Section 2 or 3. Slacken the retaining clip and pull the carburettor fuel feed pipe off the output side of the fuel pump.

2. If a pneumatic throttle is fitted pull the air pipe off its union on the throttle operating unit. Where the throttle is cable operated, disconnect the throttle cable from the throttle operating lever.

3. Pull the vacuum advance pipe off the union at the base of the carburettor.

4. Unscrew and remove the three nuts and washers which retain the carburettor to the manifold flange.

5. The carburettor can now be lifted off the manifold flange studs and withdrawn from the engine compartment. Note the number of gaskets fitted and their thickness.

6. Replacement is a reversal of the removal procedure but note the following:-

a) New gaskets should be used and they should be of the same number and thickness as those which were removed.

b) The gasket sealing faces of the carburettor and manifold flanges should be thoroughly cleaned with petrol and all traces of old gasket removed.

c) Jointing compound must NOT be used. Take care not to overtighten the carburettor retaining nuts.

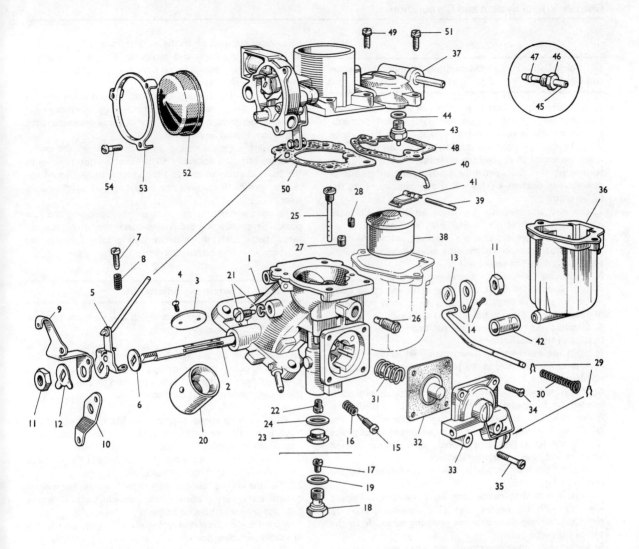

Fig. 3.9. EXPLODED VIEW OF THE SOLEX CARBURETTOR - AUTOMATIC CHOKE

1 Carburettor body
2 Throttle spindle
3 Butterfly
4 Screw
5 Lever & inter-connecting rod
6 Distance washer
7 Slow running adjustment screw
8 Spring
9 Throttle lever
10 Throttle lever
11 Spindle end nut
12 Lockwasher
14 Pump control rod
   assembly
15 Volume control screw

16 Spring
17 Main jet
18 Main jet holder
19 Washer
20 Choke tube
21 Washer and screw
22 Main jet
23 Plug
24 Washer
25 Emulsion tube and air
   correction jet
26 Auxiliary slow running jet
27 Auxiliary air bleed jet
28 Econostat jet
29 Circlip

30 Spring
31 Pump spring
32 Pump diaphragm assembly
33 Pump cover assembly
34 Screw
35 Screw
37 Float chamber cover and
   auto-choke body
38 Float
39 Float spindle
40 Clip
41 Float arm
42 Fuel connection pipe
43 Needle valve - size 1.6mm
44 Needle valve washer

45 Fuel inlet tube
46 Nut
47 Olive
48 Gasket
49 Screw
50 Gasket
51 Screw
52 Bimetalic coil and cover
   assembly
53 Cover collar
54 Screw

14. Solex Carburettors - Dismantling, Cleaning, Inspection and Reassembly

1. With time fine sediment deposits will accumulate in the float chamber, drillings and jets, giving rise to poor performance and possible heavy fuel consumption. At intervals of 20,000 miles it is beneficial to clean out the carburettor. It is not necessary to remove the carburettor from the car to accomplish this task. Begin by removing the air cleaner as described in Section 4. This will allow easier access to the carburettor.

2. Unscrew and remove the main jet holder (32) (all numerical references are to Fig. 3.8.) and main jet cover plug. Once the jet and plug are removed, petrol will drain from the float chamber and the slow running system passageway out through the vacant orifice.

3. A priming lever will be found on the fuel pump. This should be operated for a short time. This will cause clean petrol to wash through the float chamber and associated drillings and out through the main jet orifice.

4. Unscrew and remove the slow running jet (16) from the outside of the carburettor body.

5. Wash the main jet and slow running jet in clean petrol. Peer through the holes in the jets to ensure that there are no obstructions.

6. If it is desired the jets can be blown through with compressed air to ensure that they are free from blockages. Failing this they can be poked through with a nylon bristle. NOTE: It is imperative that wire is not poked through the hole in the jet as jets are extremely accurately calibrated and wire will have a detrimental effect.

7. Replace the main jet and its holder (32) followed by the slow running jet (16).

8. If it is wished to remove the float chamber to inspect the float (29) the needle valve (17) condition, start by removing the two float chamber retaining screws from the top of the carburettor.

9. Move the chamber downwards and forwards to disengage it from the plastic tube joining it to the main body of the carburettor. Withdraw the chamber and float from the engine compartment.

10 Lift out the float lever arm (18) and its spindle. Check the areas where it bears against the float (20) and on the opposite side the needle valve (17). If any signs of wear are apparent the arm should be renewed.

11 Remove the float (29) and shake it near your ear. If petrol can be heard splashing within the float then it is leaking and should be renewed.

12 With a finger press up the valve button of the needle valve (17) and at the same time operate the hand primer on the fuel pump. If petrol passes the valve when the button is held up then it is faulty and should be renewed.

13 Thoroughly wash the float, lever arm and interior of the float chamber with petrol. Also clean the gasket faces of the chamber and the carburettor top.

14 Replace the float in the float chamber, followed by the lever arm with the side marked top facing upwards. Place a new gasket on top of the float chamber.

15 Offer the float chamber up into position and replace the two retaining screws, taking care not to overtighten them.

16 If it is wished to inspect the accelerator pump for wear, proceed as follows. Release the circlip or pin on the end of the pump actuating rod.

17 Pull the actuating rod out of the pump lever (25), draw the spring off the actuating rod and put it where it will not be lost.

18 Unscrew and remove the four screws holding the accelerator pump cover to the carburettor body.

19 Lift away the cover and withdraw the pump diaphragm (24) and spring (26). As this is done fuel will drain from the inner chamber of the pump.

20 Wash all parts thoroughly in petrol, also clean out the interior of the pump chambers. Inspect the diaphragm for cracking, perishing or tears. If any of these are present the diaphragm should be renewed.

21 Install the return spring and diaphragm in the pump housing, refit the assembly to the carburettor body with the four retaining screws and then check the action of the return spring. Re-connect the actuating rod to the pump lever.

22 Prime the carburettor by manually operating the fuel pump. Before starting the engine check the carburettor for leaks, particularly the interconnecting tube between the float chamber and carburettor body.

15. Solex Carburettors - Adjustments

There are two adjustments which can be made to these carburettors. They are:-

a) Adjustment of the slow running speed and mixture strength to obtain correct idling.

b) Adjustment of the fast idling position on the throttle to allow easy starting under cold conditions.

1. Slow running speed adjustment: Start the engine and leave it running or better still go for a short drive until normal engine operating temperature is obtained.

2. Screw in the slow running speed adjustment screw until the engine is idling at approximately 750 r.p.m.

3. With the engine idling at this speed unscrew the volume control screw very gradually in an anti-clockwise direction until the engine just begins to 'hunt'.

4. Very slowly screw the volume control screw back in in a clockwise direction until the engine runs smoothly.

5. The engine speed may have altered during this operation but if it is still turning at a speed above 750 r.p.m. the idling adjustment screw should be unscrewed until an engine idling speed of approximately 500 r.p.m. is obtained. This may cause the engine to hunt slightly. If this is the case, slowly screw in the volume control screw until idling is once again smooth. Slow running adjustment is now complete.

6. Fast idling speed adjustment: It is very important that this adjustment is very carefully made, as initially it was set by coldroom test.

7. To make this adjustment to a car with an automatic choke it is necessary to remove the carburettor from the engine as described in Section 13.

8. Unscrew and remove the three screws retaining the black plastic cover to the choke heat chamber. Open the throttle so that the stepped cam (7) (all references to Fig. 3.8.) can be moved until its highest step is on operation. Hold it in this position with a small rubber band.

9. Slacken off the fast idle adjustment screw shown in Fig. 3.11. Find a drill with a thickness of .7 to .8 mm.

10 Open the throttle butterfly enough for the drill to be inserted between the throttle edge and the throttle bore at a right angle to the centre of the throttle spindle. Close the throttle butterfly as far as it will go with the drill in this position.

11 Check that the highest step of the stepped cam is still in position and then retighten the fast idle adjustment screw. Remove the drill and operate the throttle a few times. Replace the drill to check that the setting is still correct.

12 When replacing the black plastic cap containing the bi-

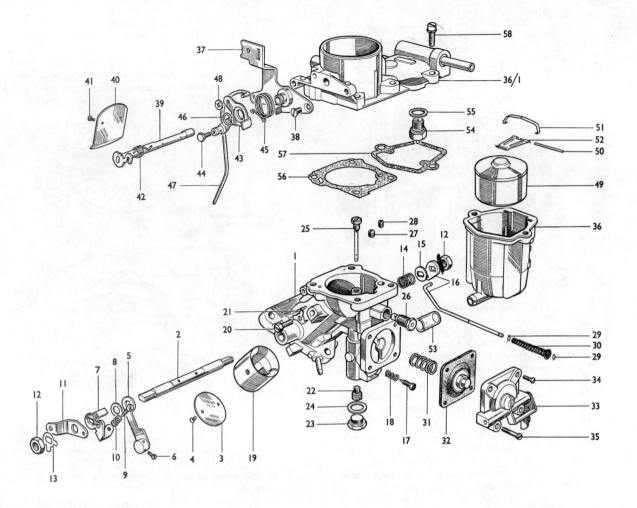

Fig. 3.10. EXPLODED VIEW OF THE SOLEX CARBURETTOR - MANUAL CHOKE

1 Main body	16 Pump control rod	30 Spring
2 Throttle spindle	17 Volume control screw	31 Pump spring
3 Throttle butterfly	18 Spring	32 Pump diaphragm assembly
4 Screw	19 Choke tube	33 Pump cover assembly
5 Lever	20 Screw	34 Screw
6 Swivel screw	21 Lockwasher	35 Screw
7 Abutment plate	22 Main jet	36 Float chamber
8 Distance washer	23 Plug	37 Cable abutment bracket
9 Slow running screw	24 Washer	38 Screw
10 Spring	25 Emulsion tube and air	39 Choke spindle assembly
11 Throttle lever	correction jet	40 Choke butterfly
12 Spindle end nut	26 Slow running auxiliary jet	41 Screw
13 Lockwasher	27 Air bleed auxiliary jet	42 Automatic spring
14 Throttle spindle spring	28 Econostat jet	43 Lever
15 Distance washer	29 Control rod circlip	44 Screw

45 Spring
46 Circlip
47 Inter-connecting rod
48 Lockwasher
49 Float
50 Spindle
51 Clip
52 Cloat arm
53 Fuel connection pipe
54 Needle valve
55 Valve washer
56 Gasket
57 Gasket
58 Screw

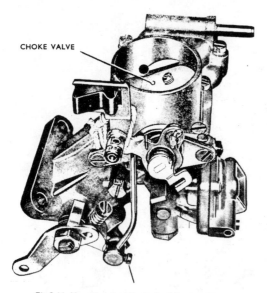

CHOKE VALVE

Fig.3.11. Manual choke valve in the fully closed position

metalic spring on to the automatic choke heat chamber note that two different types of outer end were incorporated in the bimetalic spring design as shown in Fig. 3.12. Determine which type is fitted to your vehicle.

13 If your carburettor is fitted with the unlooped ended spring, as shown in the top right hand inset of Fig. 3.12., the following instructions apply. The cover for this type of spring should be fitted to the carburettor so that the white line on its circumference is at the nine o'clock position and then turned in a clockwise direction until the white mark is in the position shown in Fig. 3.13. The cover fixing screws should then be replaced and tightened.

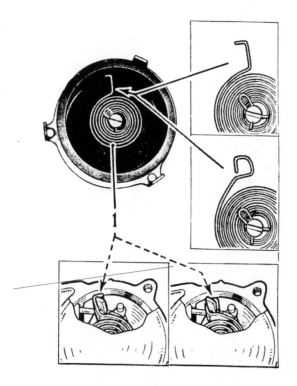

Fig.3.12. The different types of bi-metal springs fitted to the automatic choke

14 If your carburettor is fitted with the loop ended spring, as shown in the centre right hand inset of Fig. 3.12 different instructions apply. The cover for this type of bimetalic spring must be replaced so that the looped end of the spring fits over the lever on the end of the choke butterfly spindle and then turned in a clockwise direction to the position shown in Fig. 3.12. Replace the cover retaining screws.

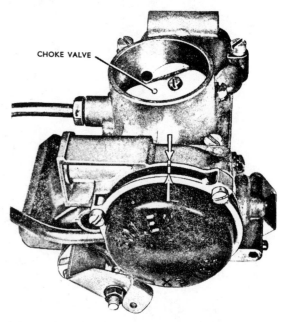

CHOKE VALVE

Fig.3.13. The automatic choke cover correctly replaced and the choke valve in the cold starting position

15 Adjustment of the automatic choke fast idling is now complete.

16 Adjustment of fast idling with manual choke Solex carburettors is as follows. Remove the carburettor from the car as described in Section 13.

17 Move the choke valve operating lever so that it has moved to the full extent of its travel and tie it in this position with a piece of string as shown in Fig. 3.11.

18 From this stage follow the instructions given in Section 15, paragraphs 9 and 10.

19 Ensure that the choke valve operating lever has not moved and then retighten the fast idle adjustment screw. Remove the drill, operate the throttle butterfly a few times and then replace the drill to check that the setting is still correct.

20 Fast idling adjustment is now complete and the carburettor can be replaced in the car.

16. Stromberg 125 CD Carburettors - General Description

Stromberg 125 CD 1¼ in constant depression carburettors are fitted to all twin-carburettor cars and also to later single carburettor models.

When starting from cold pulling the choke out rotates a lever and bar (all references are to Fig.3.14) which lifts the piston type air valve and needle (9, 21). On no account should the accelerator be pressed before the engine fires. The metering needle tapers slightly and fits into the jet orifice (24). The higher the needle is raised the richer the mixture becomes because of the increased discharge area available at the mouth of the jet.

At the same time as the choke is pulled out a cam on the lever opens the throttle beyond its normal idling position, the extent to which the throttle is opened, depending on

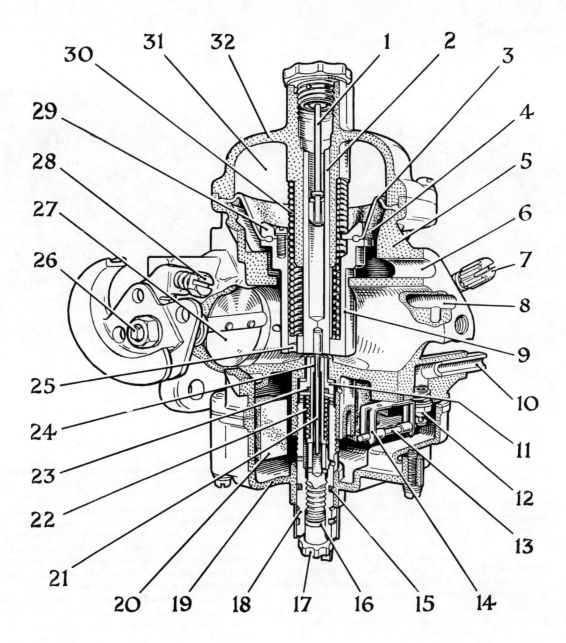

Fig. 3.14. SECTIONED VIEW OF THE STROMBERG 125 CD CARBURETTOR

1 Air valve piston hydraulic damper
2 Guide on air valve piston
3 Diaphragm
4 Air chamber below diaphragm
5 Carburettor body
6 Air feed hole to 4
7 Starter assembly travel adjustment
8 Air feed to float chamber
9 Air valve piston
10 Fuel inlet connection
11 Jet centralising bush
12 Float needle valve & seating
13 Float fulcrum pin
14 Float fulcrum
15 'O' ring
16 'O' ring
17 Jet adjustment
18 Jet bush retaining screw
19 Float chamber
20 Float
21 Metering needle
22 Jet spring
23 'O' ring
24 Jet
25 Depression transfer hole (one shown)
26 Throttle spindle
27 Throttle valve
28 Slow running speed adjustment screw
29 Retaining ring for diaphragm
30 Air valve piston return spring
31 Depression chamber above diaphragm
32 Depression chamber cover

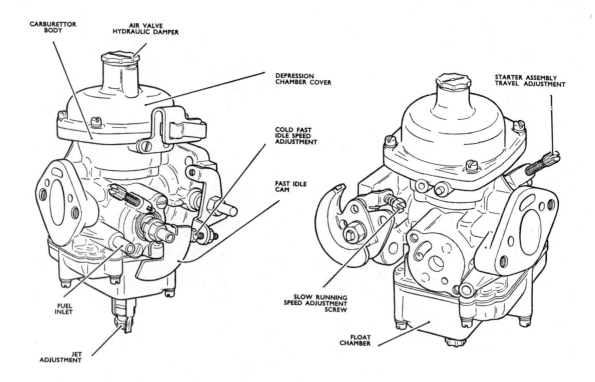

CARBURETTOR BODY

AIR VALVE HYDRAULIC DAMPER

DEPRESSION CHAMBER COVER

COLD FAST IDLE SPEED ADJUSTMENT

FAST IDLE CAM

SLOW RUNNING SPEED ADJUSTMENT SCREW

FUEL INLET

JET ADJUSTMENT

STARTER ASSEMBLY TRAVEL ADJUSTMENT

FLOAT CHAMBER

Fig. 3.15. External views of the Stromberg 125 CD Carburettor

the setting of the fast idle screw.

As soon as the engine starts, increased vacuum in the inlet manifold lifts the piston (9), so weakening the mixture to prevent the engine stalling because of over-richness. As the engine warms up the choke is pushed in gradually until the lever is back in its normal position.

When the throttle is opened the decrease in pressure in the induction manifold is also felt in the suction chamber (31) above the piston (9) because of the drilling (25) in the piston base. Because the suction chamber is sealed from the main body (5) by means of a diaphragm (3) pressure above the piston is decreased and the piston lifts. As this happens, the choke area is increased and the depression above the piston is reduced. In this way the pressure drop across the jet orifice and air velocity remains virtually constant at all speeds irrespective of throttle opening. Thus the piston rises and falls, and the choke area varies as the engine's demands alter. The tapered needle protruding from the base of the piston moves up and down in the jet, and the space between the needle and the jet increases and decreases as the piston rises and falls.

This of course, varies the mixture strength and accounts for the influence of needle shape on engine performance.

Snap acceleration requires a richer mixture. The Stromberg is now faced with an additional difficulty. Sudden throttle opening could increase suction over the piston to such an extent that the piston would rise very rapidly to the top of the chamber. This would lower the depression in the jet and cause a weakening of the mixture just when it should be enriched. In fact, this difficulty is avoided by the inclusion of a piston damper in the design. The oil well in the middle of the piston rod has a spindle in it which is attached to the screw cap. On the end of the spindle is a sleeve which provides opposition to the oil flow as the piston rises, but not when it falls. This obstruction decreases

the speed of the piston's rise and thus increases mixture strength when the throttle is opened suddenly.

17. Stromberg 125 CD Carburettors - Adjustments

1. As there is no separate idling jet, the mixture for all conditions is supplied by the main jet and variable choke. Thus the strength of the mixture throughout the range depends on the height of the jet in the carburettor body and when the idling mixture is correct, the mixture will be correct throughout the range. A slotted nut (17) at the base of the carburettor increases or decreases the strength of the mixture. Turning the nut clockwise raises the jet and weakens the mixture. Turning the jet anti-clockwise enriches the mixture. The idling speed is controlled by the throttle stop screw (28).

2. To adjust a Stromberg 125 CD carburettor from scratch, run the engine until it is at its normal working temperature and then remove the air cleaner and damper and cap assembly. Press and hold the piston down with a length of wire held in the oil well so the underside of the piston rests on the bridge of the choke. With a coin screw up clockwise the slotted jet adjustment nut (17) until the head of the jet can be felt to just touch the underside of the piston.

3. Then, from the position referred to in the previous paragraph turn the jet screw anti-clockwise three full turns. This will give an approximate setting. Start the engine and adjust the idle stop screw (28) so the engine runs fairly slowly and smoothly (about 600/650 r.p.m.) without rocking on its mountings. To get the engine to run smoothly at this speed it may be necessary to turn the jet adjuster nut a small amount in either direction.

4. To test if the correct setting has been found lift the piston 1/32 in. through the air intake with an electrical

spanner or wire spoke. This is a very small amount and care should be taken to lift the piston only fractionally. If the engine speed rises the mixture is too rich and if it hesitates or stalls it is too weak. Re-adjust the jet adjusting nut and re-check. All is correct when the engine speed does not increase when the piston is lifted the requisite amount.

18. Stromberg 125 CD Carburettors - Float Chamber Fuel Level Adjustment

1. Take off the air cleaner and then remove the carburettor from the engine as described in Section 4.
2. Undo the five small screws which hold the float chamber to the base of the carburettor body.
3. Turn the carburettor body upside down and accurately measure the highest point of the floats which should be 16 mm. above the flange normally adjacent to the float chamber (see Fig.3.16). During this operation ensure that the needle is against its seating. To reset the level carefully bend the tag which bears against the end of the needle, or alternatively, for small adjustments thin washers can be placed beneath the needle valve.

19. Stromberg 125 CD Carburettors - Fast Idle Speed (For Cold Starting) Adjustment

This adjustment will ensure that the engine runs at a suitable speed when the engine is initially started with the choke pulled out.

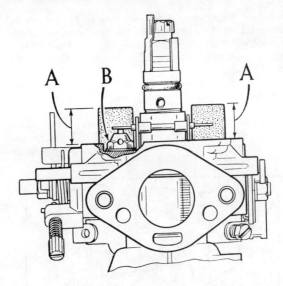

A = 16 mm.
B FLOAT NEEDLE VALVE ASSEMBLY

1. Remove the air cleaner/s assembly from the carburettor. If an oil cooler is fitted unscrew and remove the unit retaining bolts. Move the unit out of the way without disconnecting the two flexible pipes.

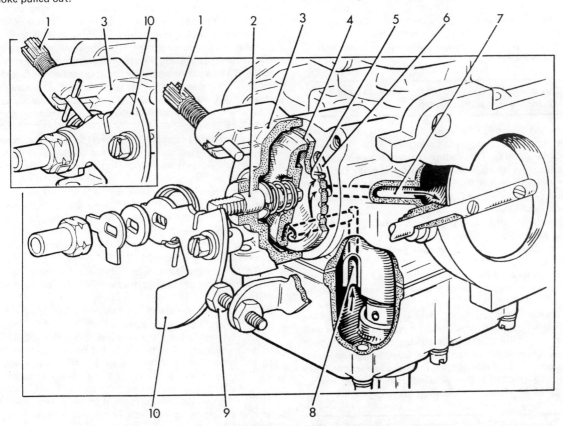

Fig. 3.17. STROMBERG 125 CD CARBURETTORS - STARTING OPERATION

1	Starter assembly travel adjuster	4	Starter assembly disc valve	7	Fuel feed from port (6) to throttle bore
2	Starter assembly disc valve spindle	5	Metering holes in disc valve	8	Fuel supply drilling to starter assembly
3	Starter assembly outer housing	6	Port feed by metering holes in disc valve	9	Fast idle speed adjustment
				10	Fast idle cam

The Inset shows the normal position of the stop (1).

2. If twin carburettors are fitted it is only necessary to adjust the inner carburettor as the two carburettors are interconnected. However, before starting, it is essential that twin carburettors are correctly synchronised. (See Section 23 for details.)

3. Ensure that the carburettor slow running speed is set correctly, with the choke control pushed fully down. (See Section 27 for details.)

4. With the choke control in the fully down position adjust the bolt stop (40) (all references to Fig. 3.18.) until a clearance of .012 ins. (.3 mm) measured with a feeler gauge exists between the bolt head (40) and the cam (41).

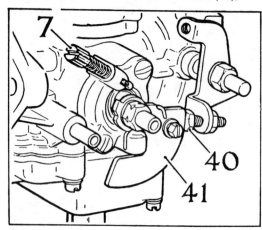

Fig. 3.18. Setting the throttle gap for cold starting

5. When this clearance is obtained tighten the locknut in the adjustment bolts and recheck the clearance.

6. Adjustment is now complete. Refit the oil cooler unit (if fitted) and the air cleaner/s.

20. Stromberg 125 CD Carburettors - Summer and Winter Settings for the Fast Idle Cam Stop

1. The Stromberg 125 CD carburettor/s fitted to some early models and all later ones incorporates a cold starting device. This device ensures the mixture entering the choke during initial starting is rich enough to fire the engine. The maximum amount of fuel metered into the choke by the cold starting device is governed by the fast idle cam 'stop' shown as item 7 in Fig. 3.17.

2. There are two possible positions for this stop. The usual operating position is shown in the inset of Fig. 3.17., whilst the position for very cold weather is shown in the main diagram.

3. The position of the stop should be altered to that shown in the main diagram when the air temperature falls to around −28ºC (20ºF).

4. To alter the stop position push it in towards the cold start device housing, then turn the stop 90º. Let it out again and ensure that the bar passing through the stop is firmly located in the correct groove. Do not forget to return the stop to its normal position once the temperature rises above -28ºC (20ºF). Over-richness when starting may be due to the stop being in the wrong position.

21. Stromberg 125 CD Carburettors - Jet Re-centralisation

It is very rarely that the jet needs to be re-centralised during normal service. However, if the jet is removed from the carburettor for any reason, it will be necessary to re-centralise the jet on its replacement. It is easiest to re-

centralise the jet with the carburettor in position.

1. Remove the air cleaner/s. Check that the shoulder of the jet is flush with the base of the air valve piston.

2. Slacken the jet bushing retaining screw three flats (half a complete revolution) using a ¾ in. A.F. spanner.

3. Screw up the jet adjustment screw as far as it will go. Tap the retaining screw sharply on one of its hexagon sides. This will assist the jet and its bushing to centralise around the needle. This will usually allow the air valve piston to fall freely at the first attempt to position the jet. Tighten the jet retaining screw.

4. The jet adjustment should now be made so that the top of the jet is level with its bushing. The air valve piston should now fall freely when lifted and dropped.

5. When jet centralisation is completed the jet adjustment should be checked as described in Section 17 until smooth idling is obtained. Replace the air cleaner/s.

22. Stromberg 125 CD Carburettors - Dismantling and Reassembly

1. Remove the air cleaner/s, disconnect the choke and throttle cables at the carburettor/s and also the vacuum pipe from the distributor. Disconnect the fuel feed pipe at the fuel pump.

2. Unscrew and remove the nuts retaining the carburettor/s to the inlet manifold flange/s. Lift the carburettor off the studs and withdraw it from the engine compartment. If twin carburettors are fitted they can be lifted and withdrawn together.

3. Dismantling should be carried out on a bench covered with clean newspapers. Wash off any dirt clinging to the exterior of the carburettor with paraffin or petrol before commencing dismantling. If it is wished to separate twin carburettors for dismantling this can be done by slackening the clamp bolts (72 and 77) (all references in brackets are to Fig. 3.19.) and disconnecting the interconnecting linkage.

4. With the carburettor on the bench undo and remove the clamper cap and plunger (66). Then undo the four screws (65) which hold the suction chamber cover (64) in place and lift off the cover.

5. The piston (58) complete with needle (37) and diaphragm (59) is then lifted out. Handle the assembly with the greatest of care as it is very easy to knock the needle out of true.

6. The bottom of the float chamber (39) is removed by undoing the five screws (40, 41, etc.) and the spring and flat washers (43, 42, etc.) which hold it in place. Take out the pin (46) and remove the float assembly (45).

7. If wished the needle may be removed from the piston by undoing the grub screw (38).

8. To remove the diaphragm (59) from the piston simply undo the four screws and washers (62) which hold the diaphragm retaining ring (61) in place.

9. The jet (47) and associated parts are removed after the jet locking nut has been undone.

10 On reassembly there are several points which should be noted particularly. The first is that if fitting a new needle to the piston ensure it has the same markings as the old stamped on it and fit it so that the needle shoulder is perfectly flush with the base of the piston.

11 Thoroughly clean the piston and its cylinder in paraffin and when replacing the jet centralise it as described in Section 21.

12 Make sure that the holes in the diaphragm line up with the screw holes in the piston and retaining ring and that the diaphragm is correctly positioned. Reassembly is otherwise a straightforward reversal of the dismantling sequence.

13 When replacing the carburettor/s on to the inlet mani-

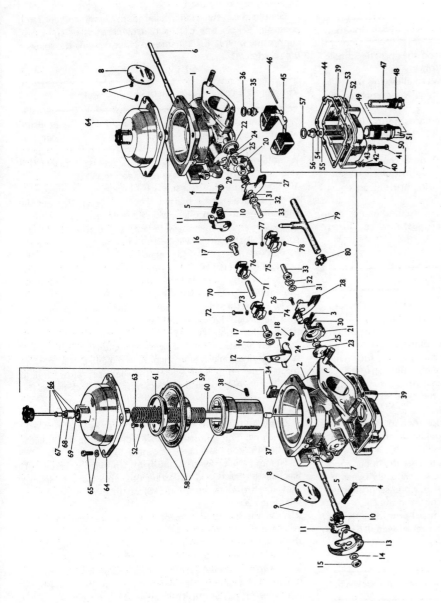

Fig. 3.19. EXPLODED VIEW OF THE TWIN STROMBERG 125 CD CARBURETTORS

1 Body	29 Return spring	57 Washer
2 Body	30 Spring	58 Diaphragm shaft and air
3 Plunger and spring	31 Spacing washer	valve assembly
4 Throttle stop screw	32 Tabwasher	59 Diaphragm
5 Spring	33 Extension nut	60 Shaft
6 Throttle spindle	34 Clip and bracket	61 Washer
7 Spindle	35 Needle valve 1.5 mm	62 Screw and washer
8 Butterfly	36 Washer	63 Air valve return spring
9 Screw	37 Metering needle	64 Suction chamber cover
10 Return spring	38 Locking screw	65 Screw and washer
11 Throttle stop	39 Float chamber	66 Damper assembly
12 Lever	40 Screw	67 Washer
13 Throttle lever	41 Screw	68 Bushing
14 Washer	42 Spring washer	69 Retaining ring
15 Nut	43 Plain washer	70 Throttle coupling spindle
16 Spindle tab washer	44 Gasket	71 Spindle coupling assembly
17 Extension nut	45 Rubber float	72 Bolt
18 Fast idler screw	46 Float pivot	73 Plain washer
19 Locknut	47 Screw	74 Nut
20 Starter cover	48 'O' ring	75 Starter coupling
21 Cover	49 'O' ring	76 Bolt
22 Spindle	50 'O' ring	77 Plain washer
23 Spindle	51 Locking clip	78 Nut
24 Spring	52 Orifice jet	79 'T' piece
25 'C' washer	53 Spring	80 Clip
26 Swivel screw	54 'O' ring	
27 Cam lever	55 Washer	
28 Cam lever assembly	56 Jet orifice bushing	

fold do not forget that new gaskets should be used. Also take care not to overtighten the carburettor/s retaining nuts.

14 If twin carburettors were separated for dismantling it will be necessary to re-synchronise them as described in the next section.

23. Twin Stromberg 125 CD Carburettors - Synchronisation

1. Slacken off the clamping bolts on the throttle spindle couplings between the two carburettors.

2. Unscrew both throttle stop screws to allow the throttles in each carburettor to close completely. Now retighten the clamping bolts.

3. Ensure that the screw (40) (all references are to Fig. 3.18) is adjusted to give a gap of .012 ins. (.3 mm) between it and the fast idle cam (41).

4. Screw in the throttle stop screws until they just make contact with the carburettor body. Then rotate each screw one complete turn thus opening both throttles an equal amount.

5. The two carburettors are now synchronised and tuning adjustments as detailed in Section 17 must now be carried out.

24. Fuel Tank - Removal and Replacement

When removing the fuel tank remember that there should be no naked flames or cigarettes in the vicinity.

1. Remove the spare wheel and any other equipment which may have accumulated in the luggage compartment.

2. Remove all the cardboard trim covering the fuel tank and wheel arches by bending back the retaining tabs.

3. Pull the lead off the lucar terminal of the fuel gauge sender unit, located on the top of the tank. Insulate the terminal end of the wire with tape.

4. Undo the screws around the periphery and remove the fuel gauge sender unit. Syphon the fuel left in the tank into a suitable container (preferably sealable). Release the filler hose at the filler end of the air vent hose at the upper end.

5. Unscrew the petrol pipe union situated centrally beneath the tank. Remove the five 7/16 in. A.F. bolts securing the tank to the body and withdraw the tank from the car.

6. Replacement is a reversal of the removal procedure. Note that the petrol pipe union should be reconnected before replacing the tank retaining bolts.

25. Pneumatic throttle control - Description and repair

Early models of the Imp were fitted with a pneumatic device, to operate the throttle. This device consists of two interconnected diaphragms - one beneath the throttle pedal,

and another attached to the carburettor. When the throttle pedal is depressed the diaphragm beneath it is compressed, this caused compressed air to feed along the connecting tubing to the carburettor diaphragm which is expanded by the incoming air, and this operates the throttle butterfly by means of a pushrod. The system works in reverse when the throttle pedal is released.

Should the system fail in operation, the most likely fault is an air leak in one of the two diaphragms or the interconnecting piping. For diaphragm failure, renew the suspect unit complete.

26. Throttle cable - Adjustment and Renewal

Cable adjustment: The cable should only be adjusted when the engine has reached its normal operating temperature. This ensures that the normal hot idling speed is obtained when the throttle pedal is released. All references in the following text are to Fig. 3.20.

1. First, ensure that the screw (6) attaching the inner cable to the throttle pedal shaft is securely tightened. Hold the cable trunnion with pliers whilst checking screw tightness.

2. Check and if necessary adjust the carburettor 'slow running'. Instructions will be found in Sections 15 and 17.

3. Slacken the screw (13) securing the inner cable to the cranked lever (10). Pull the inner cable backwards through the trunnion. Then holding the trunnion, retighten the cable retaining screw (13).

4. To check throttle for correct operation, fully depress the throttle pedal. The rod (9) between the cranked lever and throttle operating lever (8) should open the throttle fully and then expand. This rod (9) is spring loaded and acts as a safety device. Release the throttle pedal and check that the throttle operating lever (8) returns against its slow running stop screw. Also, ensure that there is some slackness in the cable.

Cable renewal: It is not advisable to renew the inner cable alone. The following instructions are for the replacement of the complete cable assembly.

1. Remove the cover over the front trunnion set screw (6). Slacken the screw and withdraw the cable from it. Release the cable from the trunnion (13) at the carburettor end in the same fashion.

2. With the car jacked up or on ramps, remove the cover plate from the centre tunnel beneath the floorpan. Release the cable from the securing clip (7) and the other fixing clips in the floor tunnel.

3. The complete cable can now be removed by withdrawing it from the front abutment mounting and from the body hole where it passes into the engine compartment.

4. Fitting the replacement cable is a reversal of the removal procedure. When the new cable is installed, adjust it as described in the previous paragraphs. Do not forget to replace the cable rubber boot at the carburettor end.

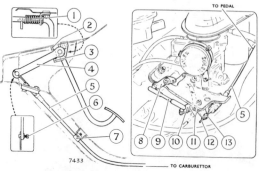

Fig. 3.20. Cable operated throttle

Cause	Trouble	Remedy
SYMPTOM: FUEL CONSUMPTION EXCESSIVE, BLACK DEPOSITS IN EXHAUST PIPE, DIFFICULT HOT STARTING		
Carburation and ignition faults	Air cleaner choked and dirty giving rich mixture	Remove, clean and replace air cleaner.
	Fuel leaking from carburettor(s), fuel pumps, of fuel lines	Check for and eliminate all fuel leaks. Tighten fuel line union nuts.
	Float chamber flooding	Check and adjust float level.
	Generally worn carburettor(s)	Remove, overhaul and replace.
	Distributor condenser faulty	Remove, and fit new unit.
	Balance weights or vacuum advance mechanism in distributor faulty	Remove, and overhaul distributor.
	Incorrect main jet fitted (calibre too large)	Check with specifications and renew as necessary.
incorrect adjustment	Carburettor/s incorrectly adjusted, mixture too rich	Tune and adjust carburettor/s.
	Idling speed too high	Adjust idling speed.
	Contact breaker gap incorrect	Check and reset gap.
	Valve clearances incorrect	Check rocker arm to valve stem clearances and adjust as necessary.
	Incorrectly set sparking plugs	Remove, clean, and regap.
	Tyres under-inflated	Check tyre pressures and inflate if necessary.
	Wrong sparking plugs fitted	Remove and replace with correct units.
	Brakes dragging	Check and adjust brakes.
SYMPTOM: LACK OF POWER, OVERHEATING, WHITE DEPOSITS IN EXHAUST PIPE OR DIFFICULT COLD STARTING		
Vacuum in fuel system	Petrol tank air vent restricted	Remove petrol cap, clean out air vent.
Dirt in system	Partially clogged filter in pump	Remove and clean filter.
	Dirt lodged in float chamber needle housing	Remove and clean out float chamber and needle valve assembly.
	Partially blocked jets	Remove jets, clear obstruction and replace.
Fuel pump faults	Debris preventing fuel pump valves from seating correctly	Remove, dismantle and clean out fuel pump.
	Fuel pump diaphragm leaking or damaged.	Remove, and overhaul fuel pump.
	Gasket in fuel pump damaged	Remove, and overhaul fuel pump.
	Fuel pump valves sticking due to petrol gumming	Remove, and thoroughly clean fuel pump.
Air entering system	Union joints on pipe connections loose	Tighten joints and check for air leaks.
	Split in fuel pipe on suction side of fuel pump	Examine, locate, and repair.
	Inlet manifold to block or inlet manifold to carburettor(s) gasket leaking	Test by pouring oil along joints - bubbles indicate leak. Renew gasket as appropriate.
	Fuel tank empty	Refill.
SYMPTOM: ENGINE WILL NOT IDLE		
Incorrect adjustment	Idling speed too low (Engine cuts out when revs drop) Note: Check ignition	Re-adjust idling speed.
	Incorrect fuel/air mixture	Re-adjust volume control screw.
Dirt in system	Idling jet blocked (Engine cuts out when revs drop) Note: Check ignition	Remove jet and clear obstruction.
SYMPTOM: 'FLAT SPOTS' OR HESITATION ON ACCELERATION		
Incorrect adjustment	Incorrect fuel/air mixture. Note: check ignition	Re-adjust volume control screw.
Accelerator pump (if fitted) not functioning correctly	Torn diaphragm or operating linkage faulty	Inspect pump and linkage. Renew or repair as necessary.
Mixture too rich or weak	Obstructions (weakness). Wear (Richness)	See earlier sections of Fault Finding Chart.

Chapter 4/Ignition System

Contents

Specifications

Type	Coil and distributor

Sparking Plugs

Make and type	Champion N9Y
Plug gap	.025 in. (.63 mm)
Firing order	1, 3, 4, 2

Coil

Make and type	Lucas H A.12 or 11.C.12 (BA.7 in certain export models)

Distributor

Make and type	25.D.4
Contact points gap setting	.015 in. (.38 mm)
Rotation of rotor	Anti-clockwise
Automatic advance	Centrifugal and vacuum
Drive	Offset from oil pump
Contact lever spring tension (measured at free contact)..	18 to 24 oz. (.51/.68 Kg.)
Firing angles	0º, 90º, 180º, 270º $\pm$ 1º
Cam dwell - closed...	60º $\pm$ 3º
Ignition Timing - static	3º - 5º (3 mm - 5 mm) B.T.D.C.

1. General Description

In order that the engine can run correctly it is necessary for an electrical spark to ignite the fuel/air mixture in the combustion chamber at exactly the right moment in relation to engine speed and load. The ignition system is based on feeding low tension voltage from the battery to the coil where it is converted to high tension voltage. The high tension voltage is powerful enough to jump the sparking plug gap in the cylinders many times a second under high compression pressures, providing that the system is in good condition and that all adjustments are correct.

The ignition system is divided into two circuits. The low tension circuit and the high tension circuit.

The low tension (sometimes known as the primary) circuit consists of the battery, lead to the control box, lead to the ignition switch, lead from the ignition switch to the low tension or primary coil windings (terminal SW), and the lead from the low tension coil windings (coil terminal CB) to the contact breaker points and condenser in the distributor.

The high tension circuit consists of the high tension or secondary coil windings, the heavy ignition lead from the centre of the coil to the centre of the distributor cap, the rotor arm, and the sparking plug leads and sparking plugs.

The system functions in the following manner:-

Low tension voltage is changed in the coil into high tension voltage by the opening and closing of the contact breaker points in the low tension circuit. High tension voltage is then fed via the carbon brush in the centre of the distributor cap to the rotor arm of the distributor. The rotor arm revolves inside the distributor cap, and each time it comes in line with one of the four metal segments in the cap, which are connected to the sparking plug leads, the opening and closing of the contact breaker points causes the high tension voltage to build up, jump the gap from the rotor arm to the appropriate metal segment and so via the sparking plug lead to the sparking plug, where it finally jumps the spark plug gap before going to earth.

The ignition is advanced and retarded automatically, to ensure the spark occurs at just the right instant for the particular load at the prevailing engine speed.

The ignition advance is controlled both mechanically and by a vacuum operated system. The mechanical governor mechanism comprises two lead weights, which move out from the distributor shaft as the engine speed rises due to centrifugal force. As they move outwards they rotate the cam relative to the distributor shaft, and so advance the spark. The weights are held in position by two light springs and it is the tension of the springs which is largely responsible for correct spark advancement.

The vacuum control consists of a diaphragm, one side of which is connected via a small bore tube to the carburettor, and the other side to the contact breaker plate. Depression in the inlet manifold and carburetter, which varies with engine speed and throttle opening, causes the diaphragm to move, so moving the contact breaker plate, and advancing or retarding the spark. A fine degree of control is achieved by a spring in the vacuum assembly.

2. Contact Breaker - Adjustment

1. To adjust the contact breaker points to the correct gap, first pull off the two clips securing the distributor cap to the distributor body, and lift away the cap. Clean the cap inside and out with a dry cloth. It is unlikely that the four segments will be badly burned or scored, but if they are the cap will have to be renewed.
2. Push in the carbon brush located in the top of the cap once or twice to make sure that it moves freely.
3. Gently prise the contact breaker points open to examine the condition of their faces. If they are rough, pitted, or dirty, it will be necessary to remove them for resurfacing, or for replacement points to be fitted.
4. Presuming the points are satisfactory, or that they have been cleaned and replaced, measure the gap between the points by turning the engine over until the contact breaker arm is on the peak of one of the four cam lobes.
5. A 0.015 in. feeler gauge should now just fit between the points.
6. If the gap varies from this amount, slacken the contact plate securing screw.
7. Adjust the contact gap by inserting a screwdriver in the notched hole at the end of the plate. Turning clockwise to decrease and anti-clockwise to increase the gap. Tighten the securing screw and check the gap again.

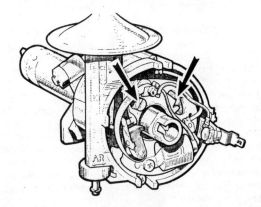

Fig.4.1. Loosen the screw (arrowed) and by means of a screwdriver placed between the notches (arrowed) the points can be adjusted

8. Replace the rotor arm and distributor cap and clip the spring blade retainers into position.

3. Removing and Replacing Contact Breaker Points

1. If the contact breaker points are burned, pitted or badly worn, they must be removed and either replaced, or their faces must be filed smooth.
2. To remove the points unscrew the terminal nut and remove it together with the steel washer under its head. Remove the flanged nylon bush and then the condenser lead and the low tension lead from the terminal pin. Lift off the contact breaker arm and then remove the large fibre washer from the terminal pin.
3. The adjustable contact breaker plate is removed by unscrewing the one holding down screw and removing it, complete with spring and flat washer.
4. To reface the points, rub their faces on a fine carborundum stone, or on fine emery paper. It is important that the faces are rubbed flat and parallel to each other so that there will be complete face to face contact when the points are closed. One of the points will be pitted and the other will have deposits on it.

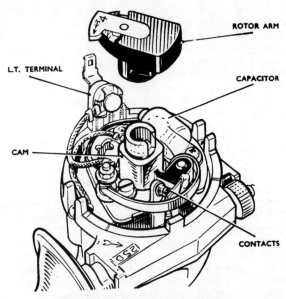

ROTOR ARM

L.T. TERMINAL

CAPACITOR

CAM

CONTACTS

Fig.4.2. The distributor assembly with the cover removed

5. It is necessary to completely remove the built-up deposits, but not necessary to rub the pitted point right down to the stage where all the pitting has disappeared, though obviously if this is done it will prolong the time before the operation or refacing the points has to be repeated.
6. To replace the points first position the adjustable contact breaker plate over the terminal pin.
7. Secure the contact plate by screwing in the screw which should have a spring and a flat washer under its head.
8. Then fit the fibre washer over the terminal pin.
9. Next fit the contact breaker arm complete with spring over the terminal pin.
10 Drop the fibre washer over the terminal bolt.
11 Then bend back the spring of the contact breaker arm and fit it over the terminal bolt.
12 Place the terminals of the low tension lead and the condenser over the terminal bolt.
13 Then fit the flanged nylon bush over the terminal bolt with the two leads immediately under its flange as shown.
14 Next fit a steel washer and then a 'star' washer over the nylon bush.
15 Then fit the nut over the terminal bolt and tighten it down as shown.

16 The points are now reassembled and the gap should be set as described in the previous section.

17 Finally replace the rotor arm and then the distributor cap.

4. Condenser Removal, Testing and Replacement

1. The purpose of the condenser, (sometimes known as a capacitor) is to ensure that when the contact breaker points open there is no sparking across them which would waste voltage and cause wear.

2. The condenser is fitted in parallel with the contact breaker points. If it develops a short circuit, it will cause ignition failure as the points will be prevented from interrupting the low tension circuit.

3. If the engine becomes very difficult to start or begins to miss after several miles running and the breaker points show signs of excessive burning, then the condition of the condenser must be suspect. A further test can be made by separating the points by hand with the ignition switched on. If this is accompanied by a flash it is indicative that the condenser has failed.

4. Without special test equipment the only sure way to diagnose condenser trouble is to replace a suspected unit with a new one and note if there is any improvement.

5. To remove the condenser from the distributor, remove the distributor cap and the rotor arm. Unscrew the contact breaker arm terminal nut, and remove the nut, washer, and flanged nylon bush and release the condenser lead from the bush. Unscrew the condenser retaining screw from the breaker plate and remove the condenser. Replacement of the condenser is simply a reversal of the removal process. Take particular care that the condenser lead does not short circuit against any portion of the breaker plate.

5. Distributor - Lubrication

1. It is important that the distributor cam is lubricated with petroleum jelly at the specified mileages, and that the breaker arm, governor weights, and cam spindle, are lubricated with engine oil once every 5,000 miles.

2. Great care should be taken not to use too much lubricant, as any excess that finds it way into the contact breaker points could cause burning and mis-firing.

3. To gain access to the cam spindle, lift away the rotor arm. Drop no more than two drops of engine oil onto the screw head. This will run down the spindle when the engine is hot and lubricate the bearings.

4. To lubricate the automatic timing control allow a few drops of oil to pass through the hole in the contact breaker base plate through which the four-sided cam emerges. Apply not more than one drop of oil to the pivot post and remove any excess.

6. Distributor - Removal and Replacement

1. To remove the distributor from the engine, start by pulling the terminals off each of the sparking plugs. Release the Lucar connector which holds the low tension lead to the terminal on the side of the distributor and unscrew the high tension lead retaining cap from the coil and remove the lead.

2. Pull the vacuum tube from the carburettor off its union on the distributor.

3. Remove the distributor body clamp bolts which hold the distributor clamp plate to the engine and remove the distributor (photo). NOTE if it is not wished to disturb the

6.3

timing then under no circumstances should the clamp pinch bolt, which secures the distributor in its relative position in the clamp, be loosened. Providing the distributor is removed without the clamp being loosened from the distributor body, the timing will not be lost.

4. Replacement is a reversal of the above process providing that the engine has not been turned in the meantime. If the engine has been turned it will be best to retime the ignition. This will also be necessary if the clamp pinch bolt has been loosened.

7. Distributor - Dismantling

1. With the distributor removed from the car and on the bench, remove the distributor cap and lift off the rotor arm. If very tight, lever it off gently with a screwdriver.

2. Remove the points from the distributor as described in Section 3.

3. Remove the condenser from the contact breaker plate by releasing its securing screw.

4. Unhook the vacuum unit spring from its mounting pin on the moving contact breaker plate.

5. Remove the contact breaker plate.

6. Unscrew the two screws and lockwashers which hold the contact breaker base plate in position and remove the earth lead from the relevant screw. Remember to replace this lead on reassembly.

7. Lift out the contact breaker base plate.

8. NOTE the position of the slot in the rotor arm drive in relation to the offset drive dog at the opposite end of the distributor. It is essential that this is reassembled correctly as otherwise the timing may be 180º out.

9. Unscrew the cam spindle retaining screw, which is located in the centre of the rotor arm drive, and remove the cam spindle.

10 Lift out the centrifugal weights together with their springs.

11 To remove the vacuum unit, spring off the small circlip which secures the advance adjustment nut which should then be unscrewed. With the micrometer adjusting nut removed, release the spring and the micrometer adjusting nut lock spring clip. This is the clip that is responsible for the 'clicks' when the micrometer adjuster is turned, and it is small and easily lost as is the circlip, so put them in a safe place. Do not forget to replace the lock spring clip on reassembly.

12 It is only necessary to remove the distributor drive shaft or spindle if it is thought to be excessively worn. With a thin punch drive out the retaining pin from the driving tongue collar on the bottom end of the distributor drive shaft. The shaft can then be removed. The distributor is now completely dismantled.

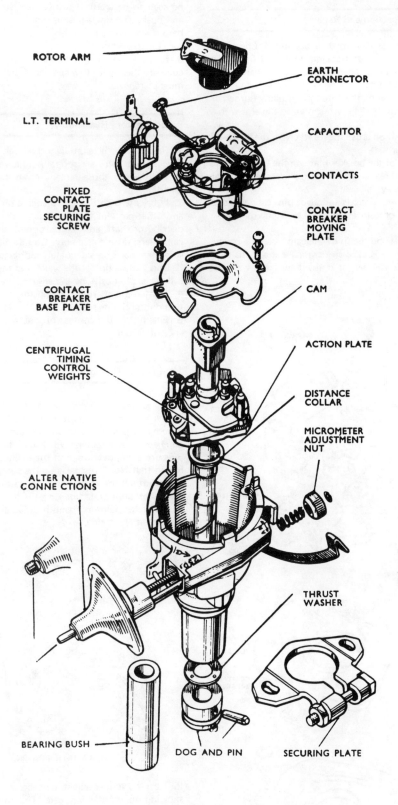

ROTOR ARM

EARTH CONNECTOR

L.T. TERMINAL

CAPACITOR

CONTACTS

FIXED CONTACT PLATE SECURING SCREW

CONTACT BREAKER MOVING PLATE

CONTACT BREAKER BASE PLATE

CAM

CENTRIFUGAL TIMING CONTROL WEIGHTS

ACTION PLATE

DISTANCE COLLAR

MICROMETER ADJUSTMENT NUT

ALTER NATIVE CONNE CTIONS

THRUST WASHER

BEARING BUSH

DOG AND PIN

SECURING PLATE

Fig. 4.3. Exploded view of the distributor

8. Distributor - Inspection and Repair

1. Check the points as described in Section 3. Check the distributor cap for signs of tracking, indicated by a thin black line between the segments. Replace the cap if any signs of tracking are found.

2. If the metal portion of the rotor arm is badly burned or loose, renew the arm. If slightly burnt clean the arm with a fine file.

3. Check that the carbon brush moves freely in the centre of the distributor cover.

4. Examine the fit of the breaker plate on the bearing plate and also check the breaker arm pivot for looseness or wear and renew as necessary.

5. Examine the balance weights and pivot pins for wear, and renew the weights or cam assembly if a degree of wear is found.

6. Examine the shaft and the fit of the cam assembly on the shaft. If the clearance is excessive compare the items with new units, and renew either, or both, if they show excessive wear.

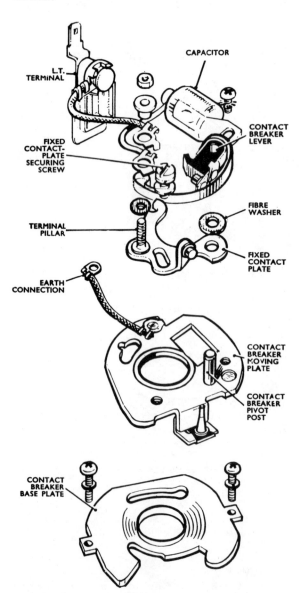

Fig.4.4. Exploded view of the contact breaker assembly

7. If the shaft is a loose fit in the distributor bush and can be seen to be worn, it will be necessary to fit a new shaft and bush. The single bush is simply pressed out. NOTE that before inserting a new bush, it should be stood in engine oil for at least 24 hours.

8. Examine the length of the balance weight springs and compare them with new springs. If they have stretched they must be renewed.

9. Distributor - Reassembly

1. Reassembly is a straight reversal of the dismantling process, but there are several points which should be noted in addition to those already given in the section on dismantling.

2. Lubricate with S.A.E. 20 engine oil the balance weights and other parts of the mechanical advance mechanism, the distributor shaft, and the portion of the shaft on which the cam bears, during assembly. Do not oil excessively but ensure these parts are adequately lubricated.

3. Check the action of the weights in the fully advanced and fully retarded positions and ensure they are not binding.

4. Tighten the micrometer adjusting nut to the middle position on the timing scale.

5. Finally, set the contact breaker gap to the correct clearance of .015 in.

10. Ignition Timing

1. To set the ignition timing proceed as follows: Turn the engine in its normal rotational direction until No. 1 piston is coming up to t.d.c. on the compression stroke. (This can be checked by removing No. 1 sparking plug and feeling the pressure being developed in the cylinder.) Once it is determined that No. 1 piston is on the compression stroke, continue turning the engine until the cut-out in the rim of the crankshaft pulley is in line with the triangular pointer bolted to the water pump/dynamo support bracket. The engine is now set at No. 1 t.d.c.

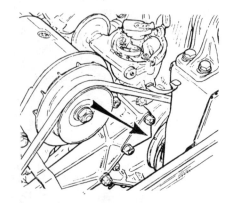

Fig.4.5. The ignition timing marks

2. Turn the vernier adjustment screw until two divisions are showing on the vernier scale. This means that the vernier adjustment is now set at its midpoint (neutral) position.

3. Open a pair of dividers to 4 mm. noting that 1 mm. at the periphery of the crankshaft pulley corresponds to 1º of crankshaft rotation. Measure off this distance in a clockwise direction (looking from the rear of car) from the t.d.c. cut-out on the crankshaft pulley. Mark the point arrived at with a spot of white paint.

4. Remove the distributor cap and connect a 12 volt bulb between the L.T. terminal of the distributor and a good earth. With the ignition switched on this bulb will light at the precise moment that the contact breaker points open.

5. Undo the distributor clamp bolt until the distributor is free to turn. Turn on the ignition. If the bulb lights turn the distributor body anti-clockwise until the bulb goes out.

6. Apply light pressure to the rotor arm with a finger in a clockwise direction. With this light pressure still applied to the rotor, turn the distributor body in a clockwise direction until the bulb just lights. Retighten the clamp bolt.

7. To check the setting, turn the engine two complete revolutions, until the bulb just lights. With the engine in this position check that the t.d.c. pointer and the new marking are in line; if they are all is correct. Should they not line up then repeat the timing process and check again.

8. Disconnect the bulb and replace the distributor cap. Static ignition timing is now complete.

9. It must be noted that to get the very best setting the final adjustment should be made on the road. The distributor vernier can be moved about ¼ of a division at a time until the best setting is obtained. The amount of wear in the engine, quality of petrol used, and amount of carbon in the combustion chambers all contribute to make the recommended settings no more than nominal ones. To obtain the best setting under running conditions first start the engine and allow it to warm up to normal temperature, and then accelerate in top gear from 30 to 50 m.p.h. listening for heavy pinking. If this occurs, the ignition needs to be retarded slightly until just the faintest trace of pinking can be heard under these operating conditions.

10 Since the ignition advance adjustment enables the firing point to be related correctly in relation to the grade of fuel used, the fullest advantage of any change of fuel will only be attained by re-adjustment of the ignition settings.

11. Sparking Plugs and Leads

1. The correct functioning of the sparking plugs is vital for the correct running and efficiency of the engine.

2. At intervals of 5,000 miles the plugs should be removed, examined, cleaned, and if worn excessively, replaced. The condition of the sparking plug will also tell much about the overall condition of the engine.

3. If the insulator nose of the sparking plug is clean and white, with no deposits, this is indicative of a weak mixture, or too hot a plug. (A hot plug transfers heat away from the electrode slowly - a cold plug transfers it away quickly.)

4. The plugs fitted as standard are the Champion N9Y type. If the top and insulator nose is covered with hard black looking deposits, then this is indicative that the mixture is too rich. Should the plug be black and oily, then it is likely that the engine is fairly worn, as well as the mixture being too rich.

5. If the insulator nose is covered with light tan to greyish brown deposits, then the mixture is correct and it is likely that the engine is in good condition.

6. If there are any traces of long brown tapering stains on the outside of the white portion of the plug, then the plug will have to be renewed, as this shows that there is a faulty joint between the plug body and the insulator, and compression is being allowed to leak away.

7. Plugs should be cleaned by a sand blasting machine, which will free them from carbon more thoroughly than cleaning by hand. The machine will also test the condition of the plugs under compression. Any plug that fails to spark at the recommended pressure should be renewed.

8. The sparking plug gap is of considerable importance, as, if it is too large or too small, the size of the spark and its efficiency will be seriously impaired. The sparking plug gap should be set to 0.025 in. for the best results.

9. To set it, measure the gap with a feeler gauge, and then bend open, or close, the outer plug electrode until the correct gap is achieved. The centre electrode should never be bent as this may crack the insulation and cause plug failure if nothing worse.

10 When replacing the plugs, remember to use new plug washers, and replace the leads from the distributor in the correct firing order, which is 1, 3, 4, 2, No. 1 cylinder being the one nearest the crankshaft pulley.

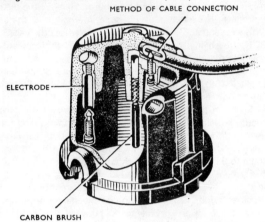

Fig.4.6. The distributor cover and H.T. leads

11 The plug leads require no routine attention other than being kept clean and wiped over regularly. Unfortunately if an H.T. lead is suspected of being faulty, it must be replaced with a complete new H.T. lead assembly which includes fitted connectors. The reason for this is that with the carbon granule suppressed type of H.T. lead fitted, it is not possible to fit a new cable to the old connectors as was the case with the old type of wire H.T. leads.

12. Ignition System - Fault Finding

By far the majority of breakdown and running troubles are caused by faults in the ignition system either in the low tension or high tension circuits.

13. Ignition System - Fault Symptoms

There are two main symptoms indicating ignition faults. Either the engine will not start or fire, or the engine is difficult to start and misfires. If it is a regular misfire, i.e. the engine is only running on two or three cylinders the fault is almost sure to be in the secondary, or high tension, circuit. If the misfiring is intermittent, the fault could be in either the high or low tension circuits. If the car stops suddenly, or will not start at all, it is likely that the fault is in the low tension circuit. Loss of power and overheating, apart from faulty carburation settings, are normally due to faults in the distributor or incorrect ignition timing.

14. Fault Diagnosis - Engine Fails to Start

1. If the engine fails to start and the car was running normally when it was last used, first check there is fuel in the petrol tank. If the engine turns over normally on the starter motor and the battery is evidently well charged, then the fault may be in either the high or low tension circuits.

First check the H.T. circuit. NOTE: If the battery is known to be fully charged; the ignition light comes on, and the starter motor fails to turn the engine CHECK THE TIGHTNESS OF THE LEADS ON THE BATTERY TERMINALS and also the secureness of the earth lead to its CONNECTION TO THE BODY. It is quite common for the leads to have worked loose, even if they look and feel secure. If one of the battery terminal posts gets very hot when trying to work the starter motor this is a sure indication of a faulty connection to that terminal.

2. One of the commonest reasons for bad starting is wet or damp sparking plug leads and distributor. Remove the distributor cap. If condensation is visible internally dry the cap with a rag and also wipe over the leads. Replace the cap.

3. If the engine still fails to start, check that current is reaching the plugs, by disconnecting each plug lead in turn at the sparking plug end, and hold the end of the cable about 3/16th inch away from the cylinder block. Spin the engine on the starter motor.

4. Sparking between the end of the cable and the block should be fairly strong with a regular blue spark. (Hold the lead with rubber to avoid electric shocks). If current is reaching the plugs, then remove them and clean and regap them to 0.025 in. The engine should now start.

5. If there is no spark at the plug leads take off the H.T. lead from the centre of the distributor cap and hold it to the block as before. Spin the engine on the starter once more. A rapid succession of blue sparks between the end of the lead and the block indicate that the coil is in order and that the distributor cap is cracked, the rotor arm faulty or the carbon brush in the top of the distributor cap is not making good contact with the rotor arm. Possibly the points are in bad condition. Clean and reset them as described in this chapter, sections 2 and 3.

6. If there are no sparks from the end of the lead from the coil check the connections at the coil end of the lead. If it is in order start checking the low tension circuit.

7. Use a 12v voltmeter on a 12v bulb and two lengths of wire. With the ignition switch on and the points open test between the low tension wire to the coil (it is marked S.W. or +) and earth. No reading indicates a break in the supply from the ignition switch. Check the connections at the switch to see if any are loose. Refit them and the engine should run. A reading shows a faulty coil or condenser or broken lead between the coil and the distributor.

8. Take the condenser wire off the points assembly and with the points open test between the moving point and earth. If there now is a reading then the fault is in the condenser. Fit a new one and fault is cleared.

9. With no reading from the moving point to earth, take a reading between earth and the CB or - terminal of the coil. A reading here shows a broken wire which will need to be replaced between the coil and distributor. No reading confirms that the coil has failed and must be replaced, after which the engine will run once more. Remember to refit the condenser wire to the points assembly. For these tests it is sufficient to separate the points with a piece of dry paper while testing with the points open.

15. Fault Diagnosis - Engine Misfires

1. If the engine misfires regularly run it at a fast idling speed. Pull off each of the plug caps in turn and listen to the note of the engine. Hold the plug cap in a dry cloth or with a rubber glove as additional protection against a shock from the H.T. supply.

2. No difference in engine running will be noticed when the lead from the defective circuit is removed. Removing the lead from one of the good cylinders will accentuate the misfire.

3. Remove the plug lead from the end of the defective plug and hold it about 3/16th inch away from the block. Restart the engine. If the sparking is fairly strong and regular the fault must lie in the sparking plug.

4. The plug may be loose, the insulation may be cracked, or the points may have burnt away giving too wide a gap for the spark to jump. Worse still, one of the points may have broken off. Either renew the plug, or clean it, reset the gap, and then test it.

5. If there is no spark at the end of the plug lead, or if it is weak and intermittent, check the ignition lead from the distributor to the plug. If the insulation is cracked or perished, renew the lead. Check the connections at the distributor cap.

6. If there is still no spark, examine the distributor cap carefully for tracking. This can be recognised by a very thin black line running between two or more electrodes, or between an electrode and some other part of the distributor. These lines are paths which now conduct electricity across the cap thus letting it run to earth. The only answer is a new distributor cap.

7. Apart from the ignition timing being incorrect, other causes of misfiring have already been dealt with under the section dealing with the failure of the engine to start. To recap - these are that:-

a) The coil may be faulty giving an intermittent misfire.
b) There may be a damaged wire or loose connection in the low tension circuit.
c) The condenser may be short circuiting.
d) There may be a mechanical fault in the distributor (broken driving spindle or contact breaker spring).

8. If the ignition timing is too far retarded, it should be noted that the engine will tend to overheat, and there will be a quite noticeable drop in power. If the engine is overheating and the power is down, and the ignition timing is correct, then the carburettor should be checked, as it is likely that this is where the fault lies.

Measuring plug gap. A feeler gauge of the correct size (see ignition system specifications) should have a slight 'drag' when slid between the electrodes. Adjust gap if necessary

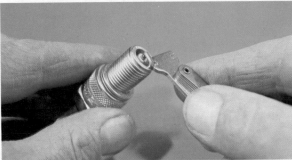

Adjusting plug gap. The plug gap is adjusted by bending the earth electrode inwards, or outwards, as necessary until the correct clearance is obtained. Note the use of the correct tool

Normal. Grey-brown deposits, lightly coated core nose. Gap increasing by around 0.001 in (0.025 mm) per 1000 miles (1600 km). Plugs ideally suited to engine, and engine in good condition

Carbon fouling. Dry, black, sooty deposits. Will cause weak spark and eventually misfire. Fault: over-rich fuel mixture. Check: carburettor mixture settings, float level and jet sizes; choke operation and cleanliness of air filter. Plugs can be re-used after cleaning

Oil fouling. Wet, oily deposits. Will cause weak spark and eventually misfire. Fault: worn bores/piston rings or valve guides; sometimes occurs (temporarily) during running-in period. Plugs can be re-used after thorough cleaning

Overheating. Electrodes have glazed appearance, core nose very white – few deposits. Fault: plug overheating. Check: plug value, ignition timing, fuel octane rating (too low) and fuel mixture (too weak). Discard plugs and cure fault immediately

Electrode damage. Electrodes burned away; core nose has burned, glazed appearance. Fault: pre-ignition. Check: as for 'Overheating' but may be more severe. Discard plugs and remedy fault before piston or valve damage occurs

Split core nose (may appear initially as a crack). Damage is self-evident, but cracks will only show after cleaning. Fault: pre-ignition or wrong gap-setting technique. Check: ignition timing, cooling system, fuel octane rating (too low) and fuel mixture (too weak). Discard plugs, rectify fault immediately

Chapter 5/Clutch and Actuating Mechanism

Contents

Specifications

Make and Type	Laycock diaphragm spring, hydraulically operated

Diameter - driven plate

Saloons, early	5½ in. (13.97 cm)
Saloons, late...	6¼ in. (15.9 cm)
Sport	6¼ in. (15.9 cm)
Van	6¼ in. (15.9 cm)
Driven plate - compressed thickness	0.298 to 0.282 in. (7.56/7. 16 mm)
Release bearing	Carbon ring
Actuating arm - free movement	None
Hydraulic fluid	Girling, Crimson

Torque Wrench Settings

Clutch to flywheel bolts (5½ in. dia.)	7 lbs.ft. (.9 Kg.m)
Clutch to flywheel bolts (6¼ in. dia.)	17 lbs.ft. (2.3 Kg.m)

1. General Description

A Laycock diaphragm clutch is fitted, the driven plate of which is either 5½ inches (early models) or 6¼ inches (later models) in diameter. The clutch is operated by a girling hydraulic system. The pendant clutch pedal is connected to the clutch master cylinder by a short actuating rod. The master cylinder is mounted directly behind the clutch pedal on the bulkhead beneath the petrol tank. An hydraulic fluid reservoir is mounted in the lip of the boot for easy access and feeds the master cylinder through a length of tubing. Depressing the clutch pedal moves the piston in the master cylinder forwards, so forcing hydraulic fluid through the clutch hydraulic pipe to the slave cylinder.

The piston in the slave cylinder moves forward on the entry of the fluid and actuates the clutch release arm by means of a short pushrod.

The release arm pushes the release bearing forwards to bear against the release plate, so moving the centre of the diaphragm spring inwards. The spring is sandwiched between two annular rings which act as fulcrum points. As the centre of the spring is pushed in the outside of the spring is pushed out, so moving the pressure plate backwards and disengaging the pressure plate from the clutch disc.

When the clutch pedal is released the diaphragm spring forces the pressure plate into contact with the high friction linings on the clutch disc and at the same time pushes the clutch disc a fraction of an inch forwards on its splines so engaging the clutch disc with the flywheel. The clutch disc is now firmly sandwiched between the pressure plate and the flywheel so the drive is taken up.

As the friction linings on the clutch disc wear the pressure plate automatically moves closer to the disc to compensate. There is therefore no need to adjust the clutch and neither is any means provided.

2. Routine Maintenance

1. Routine maintenance consists of checking the level of the hydraulic fluid in the master cylinder weekly. Top up with Lockheed or Girling hydraulic fluid if the level falls.
2. If it is noted that the level of the liquid has fallen then an immediate check should be made to determine the source of the leak.
3. Before checking the level of the fluid in the master cylinder reservoir, carefully clean the cap and body of the reservoir unit with clean rag so as to ensure that no dirt

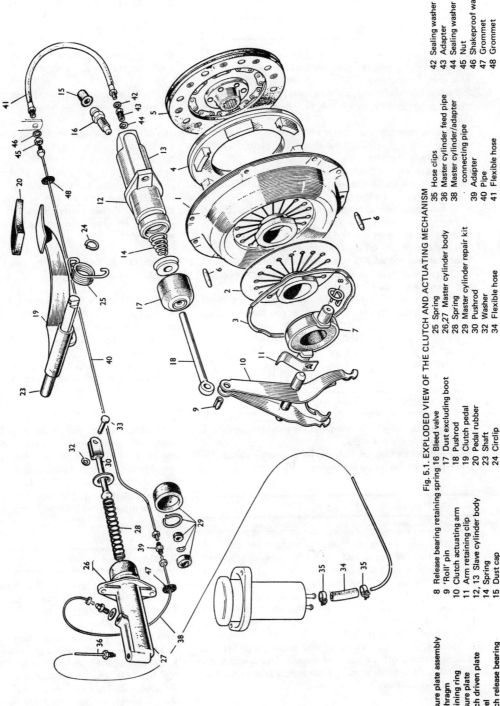

Fig. 5.1. EXPLODED VIEW OF THE CLUTCH AND ACTUATING MECHANISM

1	Pressure plate assembly	8	Release bearing retaining spring	16	Bleed valve	25	Spring
2	Diaphragm	9	'Roll' pin	17	Dust excluding boot	26,27	Master cylinder body
3	Retaining ring	10	Clutch actuating arm	18	Pushrod	28	Spring
4	Pressure plate	11	Arm retaining clip	19	Clutch pedal	29	Master cylinder repair kit
5	Clutch driven plate	12, 13	Slave cylinder body	20	Pedal rubber	30	Pushrod
6	Dowel	14	Spring	23	Shaft	32	Washer
7	Clutch release bearing	15	Dust cap	24	Circlip	34	Flexible hose

35	Hose clips	42	Sealing washer
36	Master cylinder feed pipe	43	Adapter
38	Master cylinder/adapter connecting pipe	44	Sealing washer
39	Adapter	45	Nut
40	Pipe	46	Shakeproof washer
41	Flexible hose	47	Grommet
		48	Grommet

enters the system when the cap is removed. On no account should paraffin or any other cleaning solvent be used in case the hydraulic fluid becomes contaminated.

4. Check that the level of the hydraulic fluid is up to the top of the reservoir separator.

3. Clutch System - Bleeding

1. Gather together a clean jam jar, length of rubber tubing which fits tightly over the bleed nipple in the slave cylinder, a tin of hydraulic brake fluid, and a friend to help.

2. Check that the master cylinder is full and if not fill it, and cover the bottom two inches of the jar with hydraulic fluid.

3. Remove the rubber dust cap from the bleed nipple on the slave cylinder and with a suitable spanner open the bleed nipple ½ to ¾ of a turn.

4. Place one end of the tube securely over the nipple and insert the other end in the jam jar so that the tube orifice is below the level of the fluid.

5. The assistant should now pump the clutch pedal using a sequence of 3 long and 3 short strokes until air bubbles cease to emerge from the end of the tubing. It is essential that the end of this tube should stay immersed at all times. Your assistant should also ensure that the fluid reservoir is kept topped up as if this empties, air will enter the system and it will be necessary to start again.

6. When no more air bubbles appear, tighten the bleed nipple on the downstroke. This done remove the bleed tube from the nipple and replace the rubber dust cap.

7. Allow the hydraulic fluid in the bleeding jar to stand for at least 24 hours before using it. This is to allow all minute air bubbles to escape.

4. Clutch Pedal - Removal and Replacement

1. The clutch pedal is removed and replaced in exactly the same way as the brake pedal.

2. A full description of how to remove and replace the brake pedal can be found in Chapter 8/15.

5. Clutch - Removal

1. To remove the clutch it is necessary to remove the engine from the car. To do this see the instructions given in Chapter 1/7. This done remove the bellhousing bolts and split the engine and transaxle.

2. Undo the six bolts holding the pressure plate to the flywheel, half a turn at a time, so as to prevent distortion of the pressure plate. Note that before removing the pressure plate from the flywheel, mark it and the flywheel so that the pressure plate can be replaced in the same position.

3. With all the bolts and spring washers removed lift the clutch assembly off the locating dowels. The driven plate will fall out at this stage as it is not attached to either the clutch cover assembly or the flywheel.

6. Clutch - Inspection

1. To check the condition of the clutch driven plate proceed as follows:-

a) Visually inspect the facing material. There should be no evidence of oil contamination, deep scoring, pitting or signs of uneven wear. Also ensure that there is at least 1/32 in. of lining material above the heads of the rivets. Glazing of

the lining material is acceptable as long as the lining material pattern can clearly be seen through the glaze.

b) Next check the centre plate for distortion. Note that this plate can easily be damaged by the transaxle input shaft when the engine and transaxle are mated. To test the plate for distortion, slide it onto the input shaft splines. Rotate the plate against a fixed object. Any distortion will become immediately apparent. Whilst the plate is on the input shaft, ensure that it runs up and down freely. Renew the driven plate if the splines are worn or if any of the previously described faults are in evidence.

2. The clutch pressure plate assembly can be checked in the following manner:-

a) Although blueing is acceptable there should be no actual burning or pitting of the diaphragm spring thrust pad.

b) Carefully check the condition of the contact area of the pressure plate, blueing outside of the actual contact area is alright. However, there should be no deep scoring or cracks on the bearing surface.

c) If any of these faults are present, or any other obvious faults when inspected visually, renew the pressure plate assembly.

3. The carbon release bearing has two main parts which should be inspected.

a) Carefully check the carbon ring for bad scoring, burning or excessive wear. Also check that the carbon ring has not been turning in its housing.

b) Examine the withdrawal fork for any cracks or other visual damage.

c) If either of these items are faulty renew them. If the driven plate is sufficiently worn to warrant renewal it is a false economy not to renew the carbon ring at the same time.

4. Visually inspect the condition of the input shaft spigot bush and ensure that it is not badly worn, cracked or scored. (The bush is located in the annulus in the centre of the flywheel.) If the condition of the bush is at all doubtful it should be renewed. NOTE: This bush can be responsible for very elusive squeaks and rattles that can sometimes develop in even the best maintained cars.

7. Clutch - Replacement

1. It is important that no oil or grease gets on the clutch disc friction linings, or the pressure plate and flywheel faces. It is advisable to replace the clutch with clean hands and to wipe down the pressure plate and flywheel faces with a clean dry rag before assembly begins.

2. Place the clutch disc against the flywheel with the longer end of the hub facing outwards (photo), away from the flywheel. On no account should the clutch disc be replaced with the longer end of the centre hub facing in to the flywheel as on reassembly it will be found quite impossible to operate the clutch with the friction disc in this position.

3. Replace the clutch cover assembly loosely on the dowels (photo). Replace the six bolts and spring washers and tighten them finger tight so that the clutch disc is gripped but can still be moved.

4. The clutch disc must now be centralised so that when the engine and gearbox are mated, the gearbox input shaft splines will pass through the splines in the centre of the driven plate hub.

7.2

7.3

7.7

5. Centralisation can be carried out quite easily by inserting a round bar or long screwdriver through the hole in the centre of the clutch, so that the end of the bar rests in the small hole in the end of the crankshaft containing the input shaft bearing bush. Ideally an old input shaft should be used.

6. Using the input shaft bearing bush as a fulcrum, moving the bar sideways or up and down will move the clutch disc in whichever direction is necessary to achieve centralisation.

7. Centralisation is easily judged by removing the bar and viewing the driven plate hub in relation to the hole in the release bearing. When the hub appears exactly in the centre of the release bearing hole all is correct (photo). Alternatively the dummy input shaft will fit the bush and centre of the clutch hub exactly, obviating the need for visual alignment.

8. Tighten the clutch bolts firmly in a diagonal sequence to ensure that the cover plate is pulled down evenly and without distortion of the flange. Note how the flywheel is prevented from turning by a screwdriver located between the teeth of the starter ring and a bellhousing stud (see Chapter 1, photo 51.1B).

9. Mate the engine and transaxle, bleed the slave cylinder if the pipe was disconnected and check the clutch for correct operation.

8. Clutch - Dismantling

It is not very often that it is necessary to dismantle the clutch cover assembly, and in the normal course of events clutch replacement is the term used for simply fitting a new clutch disc. Under no circumstances must the diaphragm clutch unit be dismantled. If a fault develops in the unit an exchange replacement assembly must be fitted.

9. Clutch Slave Cylinder - Removal, Dismantling, Examination and Reassembly

1. The clutch slave cylinder is positioned at the top of the bellhousing.

2. With a socket on a long extension, undo and remove the two nuts and bolts which hold the slave cylinder in place. Remove the cylinder. NOTE: Great care must be taken not to drop the nuts or bolts into the opening above the clutch, through which the actuating arm protrudes.

3. Before removing the slave cylinder take off the clutch reservoir cap and place a piece of thin polythene over the top of the reservoir. Screw the cap down tightly over the polythene. This will prevent hydraulic fluid from running out when the slave cylinder is removed.

4. Next unscrew the feed pipe from the rear of the slave cylinder. This done the cylinder can be removed from the engine compartment.

5. Before starting dismantling place clean newspaper on the bench at which you intend to work and clean off any dirt or grease adhering to the slave cylinder exterior. These precautions are necessary to preclude the chance of any foreign matter entering the hydraulic system.

6. Remove the rubber boot and using a thin nosed pair of pliers, remove the circlip from the cylinder barrel.

7. Invert the cylinder and tap it on the palm of the hand until the piston and spring are ejected.

8. Wash all parts in commercial alcohol (methylated spirits) and when dry inspect the assembly for the following:-

a) Bad scratching of the piston and cylinder bore.

b) Cracking, wear or perishing of the rubber seals. If the bore or piston are scratched it will be necessary to renew the whole unit as repairs are not practicable. If it is only the rubbers which are faulty a repair kit can be bought, containing a new piston seal and dust excluding boot.

9. To fit new seals use a pin to remove the old piston seal from its groove, first noting its fitted attitude. The new seal should then be carefully eased over the piston into the vacant groove.

10 To reassemble, first replace the spring into the barrel, largest coils first. Smear the piston assembly with hydraulic fluid and gently push it into the barrel after locating the piston pin into the end of the spring. Replace the circlip and ensure that it is firmly located in its groove. Replace the rubber dust cover.

11 Replacement of the slave cylinder in the car is simply a reversal of the removal procedure. When the cylinder is back in place bleed the system as instructed in Section 3.

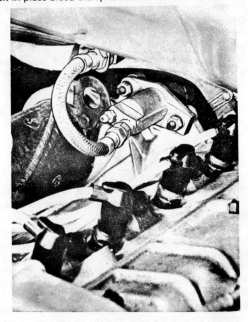

Fig.5.2. The clutch slave cylinder

10. Clutch Master Cylinder - Removal, Dismantling, Examination and Reassembly

1. To remove the clutch master cylinder it will first be necessary to remove the fuel tank. The procedure for this is described in Chapter 3/24.
2. Unscrew the cap from the hydraulic fluid reservoir and place a piece of thin polythene over the orifice, replace the cap and screw it down tightly. This is to prevent fluid running out when the hydraulic pipes are disconnected.
3. Unscrew and remove the input pipe union from the master cylinder, repeat the procedure with the outlet pipe and gently bend the pipes away.
4. From inside the car, remove the split pin from the clevis pin retaining the master cylinder actuating rod to the clutch pedal. Remove the retaining clevis pin from the clutch pedal.
5. Undo and remove the two master cylinder retaining bolts and remove the unit from the car.
6. Place clean newspaper over the bench at which you will be working, after thoroughly cleaning off any deposits of dirt and grease on the exterior of the master cylinder. These precautions are necessary to prevent the ingress of foreign matter into the hydraulic system.
7. Referring to Fig. 5.1. pull off the rubber boot (29) to expose the circlip which must be removed so the pushrod complete with metal retaining washer can be pulled out of the master cylinder.
8. With a small electrical screwdriver lift the tag on the spring retainer which engages against the shoulder on the front of the piston shank and separate the piston from the retainer.
9. To dismantle the valve assembly manoeuvre the flange on the valve shank stem through the eccentrically positioned hole in the end face of the spring retainer. The spring, distance piece and valve spring seal washer (29) can now be pulled off the valve shank stem.
10 Carefully ease the rubber seals from the valve stem and the piston respectively.
11 Clean and carefully examine all the parts, especially the piston cup and rubber washers, for signs of distortion, swelling, splitting, or other wear and check the piston and cylinder for wear and scoring. Replace any parts that are faulty.
12 During the inspection of the piston seal it has been found advisable to maintain the shape of this seal as regular as possible and for this reason do not turn it inside out as slight distortion may be caused.
13 Rebuild the piston and valve assembly in the following sequence:-

a) Fit the piston seal to the piston so the larger circumference of the rubber lip will enter the cylinder bore first.
b) Fit the valve seal to the valve in the same way.
c) Place the valve spring seal washer (29) so its convex face abuts the valve stem flange, and then fit the seat spacer and spring (28).
d) Fit the spring retainer to the spring (28) which must then be compressed so the valve stem can be reinserted in the retainer.
e) Replace the front of the piston in the retainer and then press down the retaining leg so it locates under the shoulder at the front of the piston shank.
f) Generously lubricate the assembly with hydraulic fluid and carefully replace it in the master cylinder taking great care not to damage the rubber seals as they are inserted into the cylinder bore.
g) Fit the pushrod and washer in place and secure with the

circlip. Replace the rubber boot (29).
14 Replacement of the unit in the car is a straightforward reversal of the removal sequence. Finally, bleed the system as described earlier in Section 3.

11. Clutch Release Bearing - Removal, Examination and Replacement

1. To remove the clutch release bearing it is necessary to split the engine and transaxle at the bellhousing. Removal of the bearing is achieved by simply levering the pins of the spring clip retainers out of the bearing trunnions (photo). A screwdriver may prove helpful.

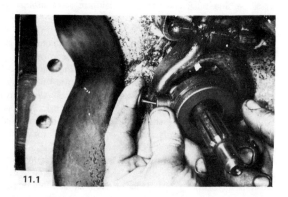

11.1

2. Examination: Inspect the carbon ring for cracking, pitting and general wear. If there is less than $1/32$ in. of carbon protruding above the metal body the bearing should be renewed.
3. Replacement: Place the clutch release bearing in its normal operating position (photo). Position one spring clip so that its hooked end is located in the cut-out at the rear of the clutch actuating arm and the pin end is ready to enter the hole in the bearing trunnion. Lever the pin into the trunnion with a screwdriver and repeat the process with the other securing clip. Replacement is now complete.

11.3

12. Clutch Faults

There are four main faults to which the clutch and release mechanism are prone. They may occur by themselves or in conjunction with any of the other faults. They are clutch squeal, slip, spin, and judder.

13. Clutch Squeal - Diagnosis and Cure

1. If on taking up the drive or when changing gear, the clutch squeals, this is a sure indication of a badly worn clutch release bearing.

2. As well as regular wear due to normal use, wear of the clutch release bearing is much accentuated if the clutch is ridden, or held down for long periods in gear, with the engine running. To minimise wear of this component the car should always be taken out of gear at traffic lights and for similar hold-ups.

3. The clutch release bearing is not an expensive item, but difficult to get at.

14. Clutch Slip - Diagnosis and Cure

1. Clutch slip is a self-evident condition which occurs when the clutch friction plate is badly worn, the release arm free travel is insufficient, oil or grease have got onto the flywheel or pressure plate faces, or the pressure plate itself is faulty.

2. The reason for clutch slip is that, due to one of the faults listed above, there is either insufficient pressure from the pressure plate, or insufficient friction from the friction plate to ensure solid drive.

3. If small amounts of oil get onto the clutch, they will be burnt off under the heat of clutch engagement, and in the process, gradually darkening the linings. Excessive oil on the clutch will burn off leaving a carbon deposit which can cause quite bad slip, or fierceness, spin and judder.

4. If clutch slip is suspected, and confirmation of this condition is required, there are several tests which can be made.

5. With the engine in second or third gear and pulling lightly up a moderate incline, sudden depression of the accelerator pedal may cause the engine to increase its speed without any increase in road speed. Easing off on the accelerator will then give a definite drop in engine speed without the car slowing.

6. In extreme cases of clutch slip the engine will race under normal acceleration conditions.

7. If slip is due to oil or grease on the linings a temporary cure can sometimes be effected by squirting carbon tetra-chloride into the clutch. The permanent cure is, of course, to renew the clutch driven plate and trace and rectify the oil leak.

15. Clutch Spring - Diagnosis and Cure

1. Clutch spring is a condition which occurs when there is a leak in the clutch hydraulic actuating mechanism, the release arm free travel is excessive, there is an obstruction in the clutch either on the primary gear splines, or in the operating lever itself, or the oil may have partially burnt off the clutch linings and have left a resinous deposit which is causing the clutch disc to stick to the pressure plate or flywheel.

2. The reason for clutch spin is that due to any, or a combination of, the faults just listed, the clutch pressure plate is not completely freeing from the centre plate even with the clutch pedal fully depressed.

3. If clutch spin is suspected, the condition can be confirmed by extreme difficulty in engaging first gear from rest, difficulty in changing gear, and very sudden take-up of the clutch drive at the fully depressed end of the clutch pedal travel as the clutch is released.

4. Check the clutch master and slave cylinders and the connecting hydraulic pipe for leaks. Fluid in one of the rubber boots fitted over the end of either the master of slave cylinders is a sure sign of a leaking piston seal.

5. If these points are checked and found to be in order then the fault lies internally in the clutch, and it will be necessary to remove the clutch for examination.

16. Clutch Judder - Diagnosis and Cure

1. Clutch judder is a self-evident condition which occurs when the gearbox or engine mountings are loose or too flexible, when there is oil on the faces of the clutch friction plate, or when the clutch pressure plate has been incorrectly adjusted.

2. The reason for clutch judder is that due to one of the faults just listed, the clutch pressure plate is not freeing smoothly from the friction disc, and is snatching.

3. Clutch judder normally occurs when the clutch pedal is released in first or reverse gears, and the whole car shudders as it moves backwards or forwards.

Chapter 6/Transmission Unit

Contents

Specifications

Transmission Unit

Number of gears	4 forward, 1 reverse
Synchromesh	On all forward gears
Oil Capacity	4½ pints (5.5 U.S. pints; 2.5 litres)
Filler/level plug location	Central, left-hand side
Oil type	Shell Spirax 80 E.P. (75 E.P. below - 15ºC (5ºF))

Gear Ratios:

First	3.417:1
Second	1.833:1
Third	1.174:1
Fourth	.852:1
Reverse	2.846:1

Overall Gear Ratios:

First	16.595:1
Second	8.905:1
Third	5.702:1
Fourth	4.138:1
Reverse	13.824:1

Final Drive

Type and ratio	Hypoid level 4.857:1 (34:7)

Adjustments

Output shaft and pinion...	Shims
Differential bearings	Screwed sleeves
Crown wheel backlash	Screwed sleeves .0055/.0035 in. (.139/.088 mm)

Bearing Types

Output shaft and pinion	Taper rollers
Input shaft	Front needle rollers: Rear, ball
Differential assembly	Taper rollers

Torque Wrench Settings

Drain and filler plugs...	35 lbs.ft. (4.8 Kg.m)
Output shaft	45 lbs.ft. (6.2 Kg.m)
Input shaft	45 lbs.ft. (6.2 Kg.m)
Bevel pinion bearing pre-load:	
New bearings	14/20 lbs.in. (.16/.23 Kg.m)

Old bearings	7/10 lbs.in. (.08/.11 Kg.m)
Casing nuts:	
1/4 in. U.N.F.	11 lbs.ft. (1.5 Kg.m)
5/16 in. U.N.F.	12 lbs.ft. (1.6 Kg.m)
Mounting cover bolts 5/16 in. U.N.C.	16 lbs.ft. (2.2 Kg.m)
Crown wheel to cage (bolts marked 'X' or '75')...	40 lbs.ft. (5.5 Kg.m)
Differential shaft locknuts	130 lbs.ft. (18.0 Kg.m)
Bellhousing nuts	25 lbs.ft. (3.5 Kg.m)
Clutch release lever nut	11 lbs.ft. (1.5 Kg.m)
Detent retaining plug	7 lbs.ft. (1.0 Kg.m)

1. General Description

The transmission unit fitted to all models contains four forward and one reverse gear, synchromesh being incorporated on all forward gears. The casing is made of aluminium alloy and can be separated into four parts, namely, the mounting cover, gearbox casing, hypoid casing and clutch housing. It is interesting to note that no gaskets are used in the joints of these parts, sealing being achieved by jointing compound only. The transmission unit also incorporates the differential assembly, sandwiched between the gearbox and engine/clutch assembly. Drive is transmitted to the crown wheel by a combined gearbox output shaft and crownwheel pinion.

Gear changing is achieved by a remote control system operated by a short floor mounted gear lever to the left of the driver (R.H.D.).
NOTE: Also refer to Chapter 12, Sections 1 and 2.

2. Routine Maintenance

1. Every 5,000 miles remove the filler/level plug and check the oil level. If the oil appears a little low top the unit up

2.1

with the recommended grade of oil (see page 10) (photo) until it runs back out of the filler/level hole. Wash the plug in petrol and check the washer. Replace the plug and tighten it firmly. Also visually inspect the transaxle for leaks and rectify as necessary.
2. Every 15,000 miles run the car until the engine is hot and then obtain a bowl or other container of at least 5 pints capacity. Remove the transmission unit drain plug and also the filler/level plug and allow the oil to drain for at least 10 minutes. While the oil is draining wash the plugs in petrol and check their washers.
3. Replace the drain plug, tightening it firmly. Refill the transaxle with the recommended oil until it flows back out of the filler plug (it should take 4½ pints). Replace the filler plug and tighten it firmly.
4. Visually inspect the rubber transmission unit mountings for deterioration or damage.
5. Clean and grease the gear control shaft as described in Section 12.

3. Transmission Unit - Removal and Replacement

1. Unfortunately the transmission unit cannot be removed by itself but must be removed as a unit with the engine. Details are given in Chapter 1, section 7.
NOTE: Also refer to Chapter 12, Section 1, paragraph 3.
2. When the transmission/engine unit has been removed the two units can be separated by undoing the nuts and bolts around the periphery of the bellhousing (photo) including those securing the starter motor (photo).
3. This done the units can be gently pulled apart (photo) and the transmission unit rested on a bench ready for dismantling to begin. It is a good idea to thoroughly wash the exterior of the transmission unit with paraffin or 'Gunk'. This will simplify dismantling considerably and also help to prevent the ingress of dirt into the internal working parts.

4. Transmission Unit - Dismantling

NOTE: Before commencing any dismantling operations refer to Chapter 12, Sections 1 and 2.
1. All numbers in brackets in this section refer to Fig. 6.1. Lift the sleeve off the end of the main selector shaft (49)

3.2A

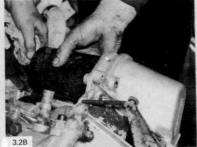

3.2B

3.3

protruding through the end cover (1) of the transmission unit (photo). Select second or fourth gear to fully extend the shaft and examine it for rust and burrs. Lightly dress, if necessary, to prevent damage to the end cover when it is removed.

2. Slacken the nuts and washers around the periphery of the end cover. Remove the two nuts securing the earth strap and detent plug retainer and then lift the retainer strap away (photo).

3. Unscrew and remove the detent plug. The detent spring and ball (50) will then fall out (photo). Remove the remaining nuts securing the end cover.

4. Lift the end cover (1) off its studs. The reverse gear selector mechanism will now be in view (photo).

5. Ease the small interlock plate dowel (47) out with a screwdriver (photo A). Next lift out the reverse plunger and its spring (78) (photo B).

6. The reverse gear pivot assembly (51) together with the reverse idler gear (52) can now be lifted upwards and removed (photo).

7. Lift and remove the interlock plate (47) (photo) followed by the reverse idler gear shaft.

8. Select a gear by manipulating the main selector shaft. Then using a small cold chisel or centre punch, knock back the staking on both the reverse gear wheel (45) and reverse pinion gearwheel (54) retaining nuts (46, 53) (photo).

9. The nuts can now be unscrewed by placing a chisel in the grooves in the sides of the nuts. Gently strike the chisel rotating the nuts until they become loose enough to unscrew with your fingers (photo).

10 Lift off the reverse gear wheel (54) (photo A) followed by the reverse pinion gear wheel (45) (photo B). Re-select neutral by turning the main selector.

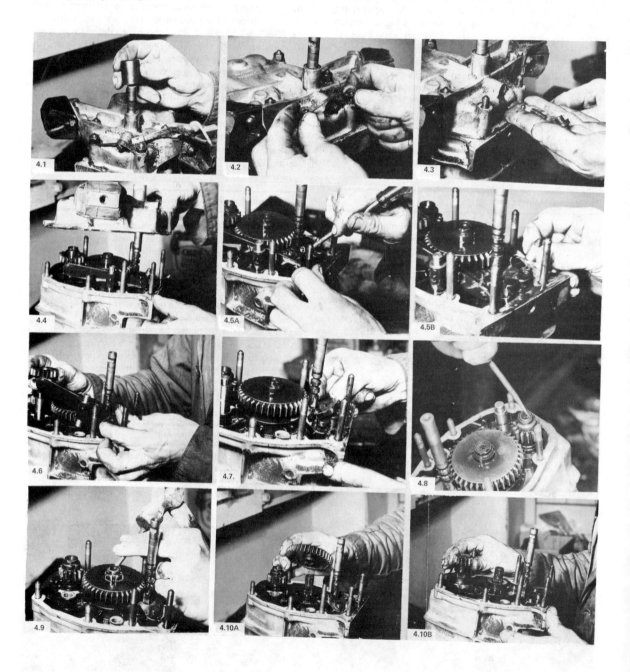

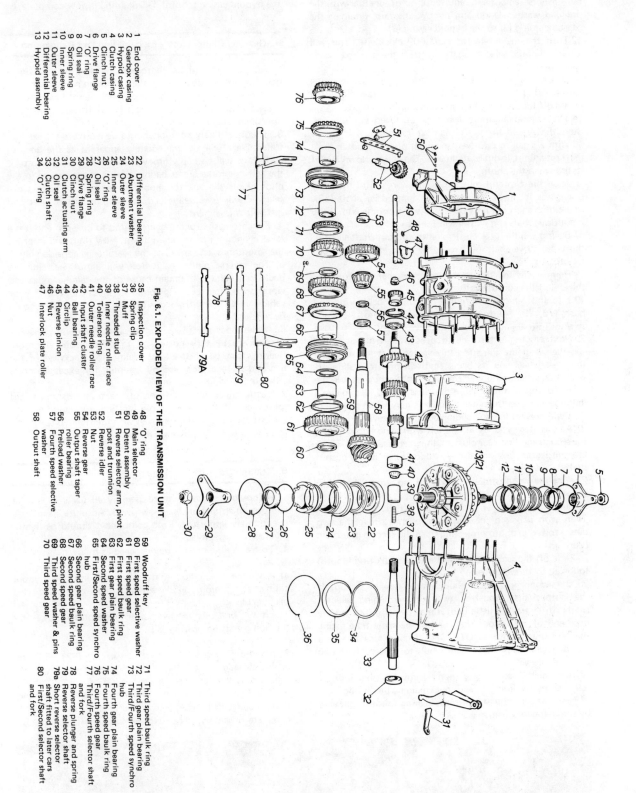

Fig. 6.1. EXPLODED VIEW OF THE TRANSMISSION UNIT

1 End cover
2 Gearbox casing
3 Hypoid casing
4 Clutch casing
5 Clinch nut
6 Drive flange
7 'O' ring
8 Oil seal
9 Spring ring
10 Inner sleeve
11 Outer sleeve
12 Differential bearing
13 Hypoid assembly

22 Differential bearing
23 Abutment washer
24 Outer sleeve
25 Inner sleeve
26 'O' ring
27 Oil seal
28 Spring ring
29 Drive flange
30 Clinch nut
31 Clutch actuating arm
32 Oil seal
33 Clutch shaft
34 'O' ring

35 Inspection cover
36 Spring clip
37 Muff
38 Threaded stud
39 Inner needle roller race
40 Outer needle roller race
41 Tolerance ring
42 Input shaft cluster
43 Ball bearing
44 Circlip
45 Reverse pinion
46 Nut
47 Interlock plate roller

48 'O' ring
49 Main selector
50 Detent assembly
51 Reverse selector arm, pivot
   post and trunnion
52 Reverse idler
53 Nut
54 Reverse gear
55 Output shaft taper
56 Preload washer
57 Fourth speed selective
   washer
58 Output shaft

59 Woodruff key
60 First speed selective washer
61 First speed gear
62 First speed baulk ring
63 First gear plain bearing
64 Second speed washer
65 First/Second speed synchro
   hub
66 Second gear plain bearing
67 Second speed baulk ring
68 Second speed gear
69 Third speed washer
70 Third speed gear

71 Third speed baulk ring
72 Third gear plain bearing
73 Third/Fourth speed synchro
   hub
74 Fourth gear plain bearing
75 Fourth speed baulk ring
76 Fourth speed gear
77 Third/Fourth selector shaft
   and fork
78 Reverse plunger and spring
79 Reverse selector shaft
79a Short reverse selector
   shaft fitted to later cars
80 First/Second selector shaft
   and fork

11 The output shaft end taper roller bearing (55) can now be gently prised out and removed (photo) together with the pre-load washer. Undo and remove the nuts retaining the gearbox casing (2) to the hypoid casing (3).

12 Turn the main selector shaft 90° clockwise. This will 'clear' all three selector shafts. Lift off the gearbox casing (photo).

13 Unscrew and remove the nuts and washers securing the clutch casing (4) to the hypoid casing (3). Draw the clutch casing off the studs in the hypoid casing (photo).

14 The hypoid assembly can now be lifted out (photo). Store the hypoid unit in a clean dust free place.

15 With a small screwdriver or similar prise the clutch shaft muff retaining clip out of its groove. The clip is shown out of its groove in the photo.

16 Slide the clip and muff (37) backwards until the muff disengages from the splines on the input drive shaft (33). The clutch shaft can now be unscrewed from the end of the input drive shaft and withdrawn (photo).

17 By moving the gear clusters on the output shaft slightly, the input drive shaft (42) can now be carefully lifted out (photo).

18 Remove the fourth speed selective washer (photo) from the end of the output shaft.

19 Lift and remove the fourth gearwheel, baulk ring and bush (76, 75, 74) together, arrowed in photo. Note the selector rods are not shown to improve clarity.

20 Next remove the third/fourth speed synchro hub assembly together with the third/fourth selector shaft (photo). The third gearwheel and its baulk ring will probably slide off with the synchro hub assembly. If not, they should be removed after the hub. Note that it is a good idea to clip a 'bulldog' clip over the synchro hub assembly when removing. This will prevent the hub sliding out of its sleeve.

21 At this stage you should be left with two selector forks, the second and first gear clusters, the plain bearing on which the third gear runs and also a woodruff key in the output shaft.

22 Prise the woodruff key (59) out of the output shaft (58) (photo).

23 Slide the third gear plain bearing off the output shaft. Then with a pair of needle nosed pliers remove the two pins arrowed in photo projecting from the second gear plain bearing.

24 Slide off the second gearwheel and its baulk ring (photo) followed by its plain bearing.

25 The second/first synchro hub unit can now be slid up off the output shaft together with the remaining selector shafts. If it proves a little tight it may be helpful to tap the nose end of the output shaft and at the same time lifting the hub unit (photo). NOTE: It is a good idea to clip a 'bulldog' clip over the synchro hub to prevent it sliding out of its sleeve.

26 Remove the second gear (non-selective) washer (photo) followed by the first gear and the remaining baulk ring.

27 Next lift off the first gear plain bearing (photo) followed by the first gear selective washer.

28 The pinion shaft can now be withdrawn from the rear of the hypoid casing (photo). Dismantling is now complete.

5. Gearbox Components - Examination and Renovation

1. All parts should be thoroughly washed in paraffin or petrol and then laid out on a sheet of clean newspaper.
2. Generally examine the gearwheels and bearings for excessive wear, distortion, slackness of fit and damage to machined faces and threads.
3. The most likely components to be worn are the selector forks. Wear will be immediately apparent as the ends of each fork will be badly grooved as shown in the photo. If the selector forks are as badly worn as those shown in the photograph, the selector should be renewed. A badly worn selector will eventually lead to jumping out of gear and difficult engagement.
4. Synchromesh baulk rings are bound to be worn and it is a false economy not to renew them. New rings will improve the smoothness and speed of the gearchange considerably.
5. The reverse pinion gearwheel will almost certainly be badly worn and is the main cause of the familiar buzz and vibration during reversing found in these models. If your vehicle is suffering from this malady the gearwheel should be renewed.
6. If the input shaft bearings are worn they will cause the gearbox to be very noisy and to suffer from vibration. Bearings can be checked by feeling for slackness of the bearings in races and also by listening for excessive noise when the bearings are spun.
7. Lastly check the condition of the transmission casings joint faces. If any traces of old jointing compound are still present they should be removed with methylated spirit and NOT scraped under any circumstances.

6. Transmission Unit - Reassembly

Before proceeding with reassembly all parts should be laid out on a sheet of clean newspaper. Absolute cleanliness is extremely important. Each component should be lightly oiled as it is assembled.

1. To reassemble the gearbox proceed as follows:-

a) Assemble the pinion shaft (58) back into the hypoid casing. The pinion can be supported on a 2 in. (5 cm) packing block.
b) Fit the first selective washer (60) (photo) followed by the first gear plain bearing (63).

2. Fit the first gear (61) and baulk ring (62) with the projecting edge of the baulk ring facing upwards (photo) followed by the non-selective washer (64).
3 The first/second synchro hub unit, together with the first/second and reverse selector shafts are fitted next as a complete assembly. The two selector shafts should be

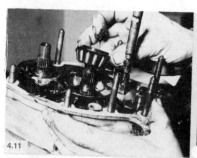
4.11

4.12

4.13

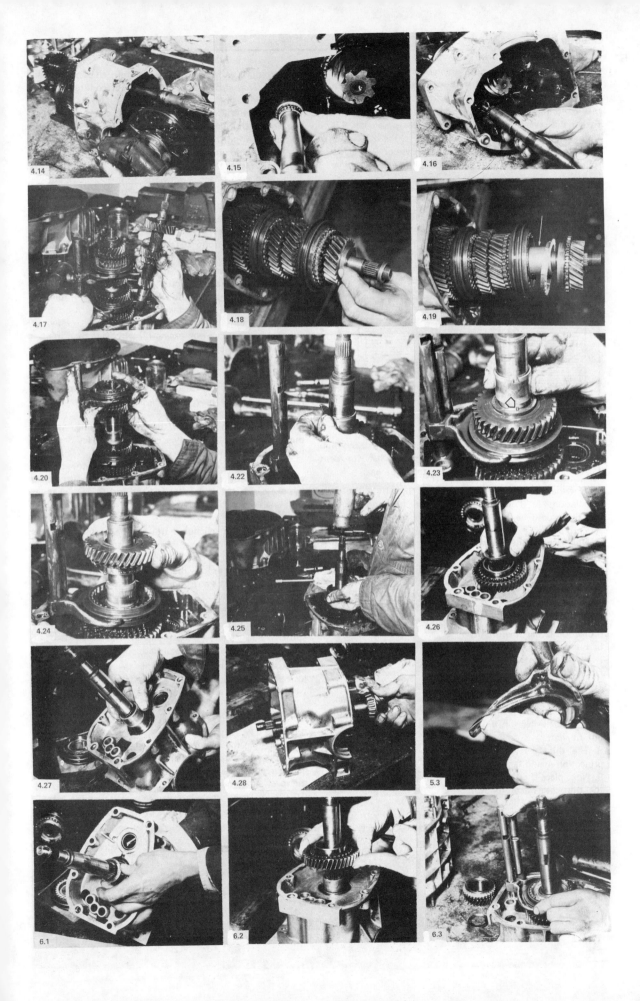

guided into their holes whilst sliding the hub unit down the input shaft. Where a short reverse selector shaft is fitted, care must be taken not to allow it to fall into the casing. It may be found preferable to assemble it immediately prior to fitting the reverse plunger and spring (see paragraph 22). **Note:** If the synchro hub being refitted is of the later spring ring type, it MUST be refitted with the wider face of the splined hub centre facing towards the pinion head. See 'A' in Fig. 6.2. Some hubs have an identification step in the

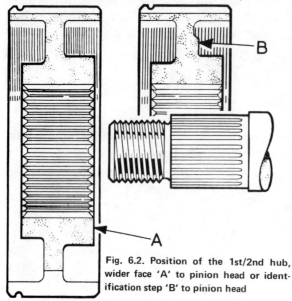

Fig. 6.2. Position of the 1st/2nd hub, wider face 'A' to pinion head or identification step 'B' to pinion head

root of the recess on the first speed side to assist in correct installation. See 'B' in Fig. 6.2. Ensure that the three lugs on the first speed baulk ring located into the slots in the synchro hub.

4. Next replace the second gear baulk ring (67) ensuring that its three lugs locate in the slots of the synchro hub, followed by the second gear bush (66) which should be fitted with the two small slots in the bush face upwards. One slot should be in line with the keyway in the output shaft.
5. Slide the second gearwheel (68) into position with the projection facing downwards.
6. Fit the third gear selective washer (69) and then refit the two small pegs into the slots in the second gear bush (photo. Note selector rods not shown in the interest of clarity).
7. Replace the third gear bush (72) locating the slots at its base on to the pegs protruding from the second gear bush. The large slot must be in line with the keyway in the output shaft. Fit the woodruff key (59) into its keyway in the output shaft.
8. The third gearwheel (70) can now be replaced. The projection should face upwards (photo).
9. Next place the third gear baulk ring (71) in position on the third gearwheel (photo). The projection should face upwards.
10 The third/fourth synchro hub (73) and the third/fourth

selector shaft and fork (77) are now refitted as an assembly (photo). The selector shaft should be guided into its hole in the hypoid casing as the hub is being slid down the output shaft. Ensure that the third gear baulk ring lugs engage with the slots in the synchro hub.
11 Slide the fourth gear bush (74) into position. The slot in its bore should locate on the woodruff key (59) (photo).
12 Replace the fourth gear baulk ring (75) (photo). Its projection should face downwards.
13 The fourth gearwheel can now be slid into position (photo) with the projecting side facing downwards.
14 At this stage the input shaft (42) should be replaced. This can quite simply be achieved by moving the gear clusters on the output shaft as shown in photos 'A' and 'B' and at the same time offering the input shaft into positojn, pushing it downwards into its roller bearings and turning it to engage the gears on the output shaft.
15 Fit the fourth gear selective washer (57) (photo), followed by the pre-load adjustment washer (56).
16 Smear the joint faces of both the hypoid casing (3) (photo) and the gearbox casing (2) with 'Hylomar' jointing compound (NO compound other than Hylomar should be used) applied sparingly.
17 Remove the main selector shaft (49) from the gearbox casing. Prise the old sealing ring out of its groove and replace it with a new one (photo). Replace the selector shaft in the gearbox casing.
18 Looking at the inside of the gearbox casing, turn the main selector until its finger is pointing away from the reverse plunger bore.
19 Refit the gearbox casing (photo). When the gearbox casing studs have passed through the stud holes in the hypoid casing, fit a plain washer and nut to each. Tighten the nuts evenly, finally tightening each nut to the specified torque.
20 Turn the main selector shaft until it engages the selector shafts within the gearbox. Place the output shaft end taper roller bearing into its race (photo).
21 Replace the interlock plate (47) first into the groove in the main selector shaft and then into the grooves of the other shafts (photo).
22 Fit the reverse plunger spring into its bore followed by the reverse plunger (78) (photo). If your gearbox has a short reverse selector shaft and it was not fitted at paragraph 3, it should now be fitted.
23 Next ease the small dowel (47) into the recess in the interlock plate (photo), whilst depressing the reverse plunger.
24 Refit the reverse gearwheel (54) over the splines on the end of the output shaft (photo).
25 Fit a new reverse gearwheel retaining nut (53) and screw it down finger tight (photo).
26 Tightening the nut further presents a problem as it is not of the hexagon variety. The nut cannot be tightened with a hammer and chisel as it is essential that it be tightened to the specified torque.
27 It was found that by placing a ball bearing from a discarded synchro hub into one of the grooves in the nut a

6.6

6.8

6.9

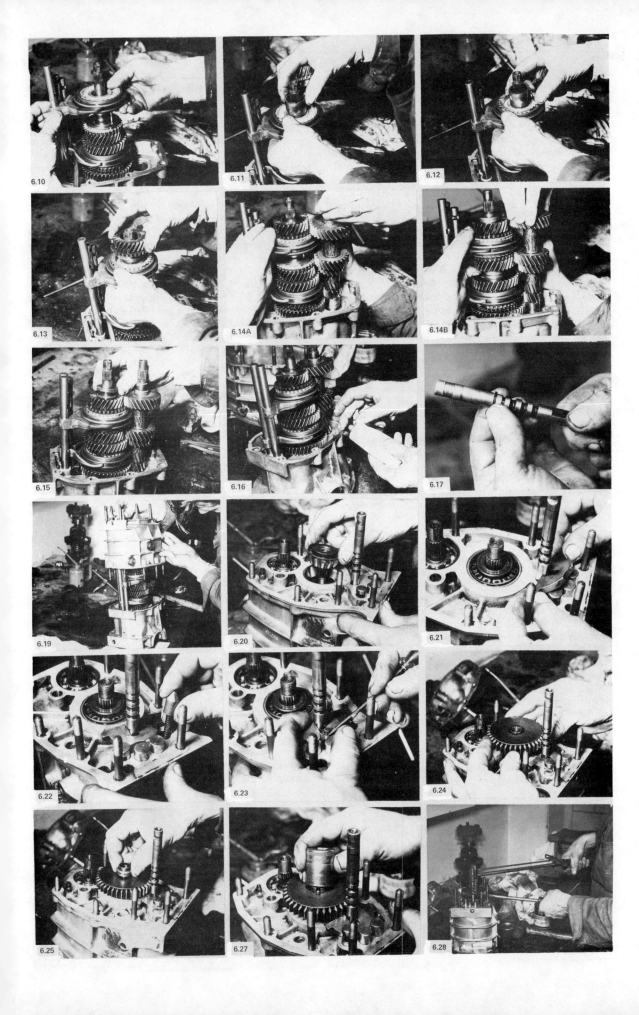

15/16 A.F. socket could be used to tighten the nut in the normal manner (photo).

28 Tighten the reverse gearwheel retaining nut to 45 lbs. ft. During tightening the output shaft should be turned at least three times. For final tightening the reverse gearwheel can be locked by wedging a screwdriver between a tooth and a gearbox casing stud (photo).

29 Replace the reverse idler shaft (52) into its bore (photo).

30 Fit the reverse pinion gearwheel (45) followed by its retaining nut (photo) and tighten it to its correct torque. The procedure is as detailed in paragraphs 26 up to and including 28.

31 Stake the reverse gearwheel and pinion gearwheel retaining nuts by knocking the nut rim into the grooves in the shafts with a chisel (photo).

32 The reverse gear pivot (51) and reverse idler gear (52) can now be fitted as an assembly. As the idler gear is lowered down its shaft, guide the pivot shaft into its bore and also the trunnion into the slot in the selector shaft. Photo A shows the assembly being lowered and photo B shows the trunnion (arrowed) correctly located in the selector shaft groove.

33 Ensure that there are no burrs on the end of the main selector shaft. Fit a new 'O' ring in the aperture in the end cover then sparingly apply Hylomar jointing compound to the joint faces of the cover and gearbox casing.

34 Lower the end casing into position over the gearbox casing studs (photo). Fit the retaining nuts and plain washers (except the two which hold the detent plug strap) tightening them evenly to the specified torque.

35 Refit the detent ball, spring and plug (photo). Tighten the plug to the specified torque.

36 Place a new retaining strap across the detent plug as shown in the photo. Replace the two nuts and washers and tighten them to the specified torque.

37 Slide a new tolerance ring (40) over the splines on the end of the input shaft. (If the roller bearing inner race has been renewed check that it is fitted with the two holes towards the clutch shaft end). Fit a new circlip and the splined muff on to the clutch shaft (photo).

38 Screw the clutch shaft fully into the end of the input shaft (photo) and then turn back one full spline.

39 Line up the splines of the two shafts and slide the muff into position. Fit the muff retaining circlip into its groove (photo) and ensure that it is securely located. Check that the clutch shaft has at least .10 in. (2.7 mm) free up and down movement at its free end. This is essential.

40 Sparingly smear the joint faces of the hypoid casing and clutch casing with Hylomar jointing compound.

41 Refit the hypoid assembly (photo) ensuring that the raised ring around the differential shaft sleeves (24) fits into the groove in the hypoid casing.

42 Replace the clutch casing (photo), fit the plain washers and nuts and tighten them evenly to the specified torque. Reassembly is now complete.

7. Synchromesh Hub (Early Type) Dismantling, Examination and Reassembly

1. To dismantle cover the complete hub assembly with a piece of cloth. Carefully slide the sleeve off the synchromesh hub. The cloth should retain the springs, caps, balls and plates which will be ejected. Collect the springs, caps, etc., and place them in a jar to ensure that they are not lost.

2. Before final reassembly temporarily assemble the synchro hub sleeve and shifting plates as shown in the photo.

3. Slide a feeler gauge between the hub and shifting plate (photo) to determine the clearance. Ensure that the gauge bridges the semi-circular groove in the hub beneath each plate.

4. It is essential that the clearance 'A' in Fig. 6.4. does not exceed .018 in. (.46 mm). If this clearance is exceeded the shifting plates may tilt and jam. NOTE: Before assembling the hub to check the above clearance carefully stone off any burrs in the hub cut-outs which locate the shifting plates. If this is not done a flase reading may result.

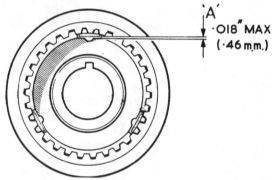

Fig.6.4. Checking the shifting plate clearance

5. Dismantle the hub. Wash all components thoroughly in paraffin in preparation for final reassembly.

6. Final reassembly: Slide the hub into the sleeve until the spring bores are just in view above the top edge of the sleeve.

7. Insert the three springs together with their caps into the three bores in the hub (photo).

8. The hub can now be slid further into the sleeve until its progress is arrested by the protruding caps contacting the top face of the sleeve.

9. Place a ball into the recess of each of the three shifting plates. The balls can be retained by a blob of grease.

10 One at a time fit each of the balls and shifting plate assemblies over a spring cap and between the hub and sleeve, a screwdriver may help (photo).

11 With one finger depressing each ball and plate assembly (photo A) the hub can be pushed into the sleeve (photo B).

Fig.6.3. Exploded view of the synchro hub

7.11A

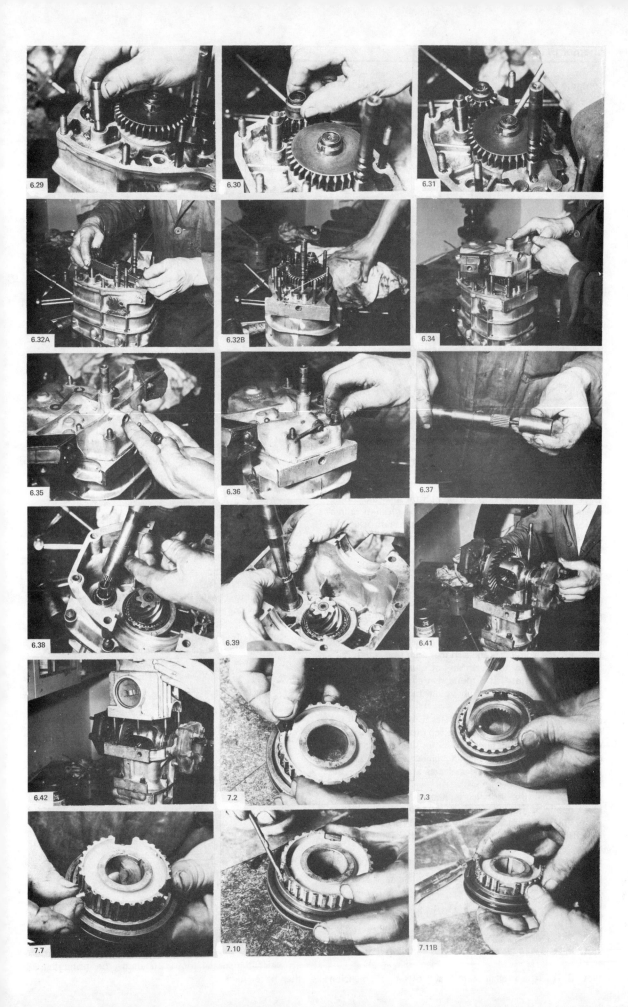

Continue to press the hub into the sleeve until the balls are felt to locate in the sliding sleeve groove.

12 Reassembly is now complete. Lightly oil the synchro hub assembly before refitting.

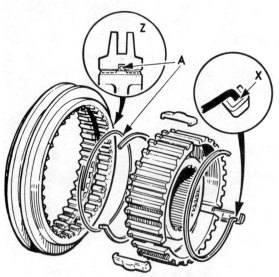

Fig.6.5. Synchro hub assembly

8. Synchromesh Hub (Later Spring Ring Type) - Dismantling, Examination and Reassembly

1. To dismantle smartly push the hub through the sliding sleeve. Collect the three shifting plates and place them in a jar for safe keeping. If more than one synchro hub assembly is being dismantled at the same time ensure that each synchro hub and sleeve are kept together as matched pairs. Thoroughly wash all components in paraffin or petrol.

2. Examine the hub components as follows:-

a) Ensure that the sliding sleeve moves freely over the splines of the hub and that it will not tilt when in its normal operating position.

b) Check that the chamfers on the sliding sleeve internal teeth are free from burrs and also that each face is flat.

c) Ensure that the hub teeth do not foul the roots of the sliding sleeve teeth. If it is found that contact is made the tops of the teeth on the hub should be carefully stoned until a clearance is obtained.

d) Compare the three shifting plates to ensure that all are the same length and have the same top profile.

e) Inspect the shifting plate circlips for signs of wear at the contact faces with the shifting plates and for general weakness. If either of these maladies are in evidence the circlips should be renewed.

f) Ensure that the short leg on the end of each shifting plate circlip is not butting on the base of the shifting plate. Where necessary, carefully grind off part of the short leg sufficient to ensure a small gap at position X in Fig. 6.9.

3. Before reassembly begins it will be necessary to make the special tool shown in Fig. 6.6. from a sheet of $1/16$ in. to $1/8$ in. mild steel. Dimensions:-

A $2^{3}/8$ in. (60.33 mm) E $13/16$ in. x $1/8$ in.
B 1½ in. (38.1 mm)   (20.64 x 3.18 mm)
C $2^{27}/32$ in. (72.23mm) F 1¼ in. (31.75 mm)
D $9/16$ in. (14.29 mm)

Slot 'E' is cut central in plate 1 and offset to dimension

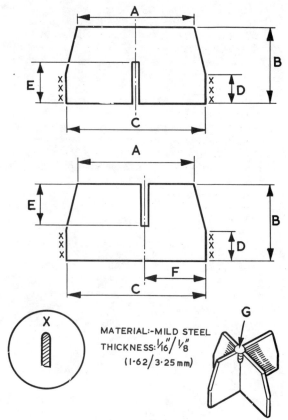

MATERIAL:-MILD STEEL
THICKNESS: $1/16 / 1/8$
(1·62 / 3·25 mm)

Fig.6.6. The template required for reassembly

'F' in plate 2. 'G' illustrates the plates slotted and tacked together with brace or weld. (Note: 'Araldite' or 'Plastic padding' will probably suffice in place of the brace or weld. When assembly of the special tool is completed slightly round off the vertical edges to locate easily in the root of the sliding sleeve teeth.

4. Reassembly: Use the first and second fingers of each hand to hold the ring in the sliding sleeve groove. Lower the two over the taper of the fixture so that the gap in the ring falls into one of the small quarters of the special tool, see Fig. 6.7. and the special tool locates in the teeth of the sleeve.

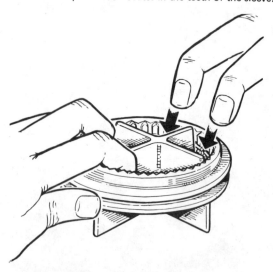

Fig.6.7. Engaging the spring ring into the sliding sleeve

5. Push the sliding sleeve down until it contacts the surface on which the special tool is standing. The spring ring will then be retained.

6. Position the sleeve and special tool together over the synchro hub with the teeth of both components lined up. Using an equal pressure on both the sleeve and special tool, carefully slide the sleeve off the special tool and on to the hub. It may be helpful to utilise a small screwdriver to ease the ends of the spring ring into the groove.

7. Place the shifting plates into the slots in the hub and refit both circlips, one on each side of the hub. The hook end of each being located in a different shifting plate and wrapped in opposite directions as shown in Fig. 6.5.

8. Reassembly is now complete. Lightly oil the unit and test it to ensure that the sleeve will slide across the hub and that the spring ring makes a positive engagement in the detent.

9. Input Shaft Ball Bearing - Removal, Examination and Replacement

1. With the gearbox casing removed and on a bench, remove the input shaft ball bearing retaining circlip using a pair of circlip pliers (photo).

9.1

2. Invert the casing. It will be noticed that a niche is provided in the casing on each side of the bearing. This is to allow access to the bearing outer race.

3. Using a suitable drift tap the bearing out. The drift should bear on the small portion of outer race exposed by the niche (photo). Move the drift from one side of the bearing to the other on alternate blows to ensure that the bearing is driven out 'squarely'.

4. Examination: Thoroughly wash the bearing in petrol or paraffin. Then examine it for looseness between the inner and outer races, general wear or noisy operation when the bearing is spun. Renew as necessary.

5. Replacement: Heat the gearbox casing in a domestic oven to approximately 200ºF (93ºC). NOTE: Do NOT place the casing in an oven already at this temperature, rather, place it in a cold oven and bring the temperature up to that required. At the same time place the bearing in a refrigerator.

6. When the casing has reached the required temperature, remove it from the oven and place it on a bench. Place the bearing squarely over its bore (photo).

7. Using a ¾ in. W socket as a drift, tap the bearing into its bore (photo) until it contacts the bore shoulder.

8. Replace the bearing retaining circlip with a pair of circlip pliers (photo). Ensure that the circlip is securely located in its groove.

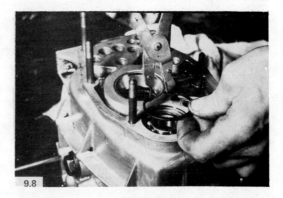

9.8

10. Control Shaft - Removal and Replacement

1. From inside the car, unscrew and remove the two small bolts situated just behind the base of the gear lever, after rolling back the carpets.

2. Jack up one side of the car until there is sufficient room to work underneath. Secure the car in this position by chocking the wheels and using axle stands or blocks for added support to the jack. Remove the large protective plate on the underside of the car by unscrewing the eight retaining bolts.

3. Disconnect the gear control shaft from the transaxle by turning back the locking tab (177). (All numerals refer to Fig. 6.9.) and removing the clamp bolt (176).

4. Pull the control shaft socket (170) off the ball on the base of the gear lever (155). The control shaft can now be pulled forward until the end of the control shaft has passed through the rear bearing (173 and 174) and withdrawn from the car.

5. Replacement is a reversal of the removal procedure. However, do not forget to stake the flexible coupling (175) clamp bolt (176) with its tab washer (177).

11. Gear Lever - Removal and Replacement

1. Roll back the carpets and remove the two small bolts situated just behind the base of the gear lever.

2. Jack up one side of the car and secure it as described in

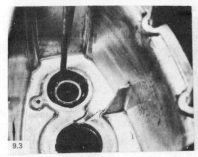

9.3

9.6

9.7

the previous section. Remove the large plate on the under-side of the car by unscrewing the eight retaining bolts.

3. Pull the control shaft socket (170) (all references to Fig. 6.9.) off the ball on the base of the gear lever.

4. Unscrew and remove the four bolts securing the gear lever assembly (165) to the floorpan of the car.

5. The gear lever assembly can now be pulled downwards and withdrawn from the car.

6. Replacement is generally a reversal of the removal procedure. However, note the following:-

a) The gear lever MUST be replaced with the spring loaded ball towards the front of the car.

b) Before fully tightening the four bolts securing the gear lever assembly to the floorpan, the gear lever setting must be adjusted. To achieve this select neutral and slide the gear lever assembly backwards or forwards until the gear lever is upright. With the lever in this position, tighten the four bolts.

c) Ensure that the protective rubber boot (166) is fitted securely to the flanges on the underside of the gear lever assembly.

d) The tongue on the large protective plate should be towards the front of the car.

12. Gear Control Shaft Rear Bush - Removal and Replacement

1. Jack up the car and secure it as described in Section 10.

2. Remove the two setscrews securing the rear bush bracket (173) (all references to Fig. 6.9.). Slide the bracket and bush rearwards to the flexible section of the control shaft (175).

3. Collapse the nylon bush and pull it out of its bracket.

4. Thoroughly clean the section of the control shaft adjacent to the normal operating position of the bush. Fit a new bush into the bracket and pack it with 'Shell Retinax 'A' grease.

5. Slide the bracket and bush back along the shaft to their normal position. Replace the two setscrews.

13. Control Shaft Felxible Coupling - Removal and Replacement

1. Remove the control shaft as described in Section 10.

2. Mount the control shaft in a vice and using a suitable drift, drive out the pin (X in Fig. 6.8) securing the flexible coupling to the control shaft.

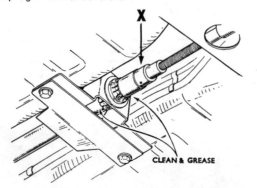

Fig.6.8. The flexible coupling on the gearchange control shaft

3. The flexible coupling can now be pulled out of the end of the control shaft.

4. Slide the new flexible coupling into the control shaft until the pin holes are aligned. Before refitting the pin ensure that the bolt side of the clamp is on the same side as

the niche in the main transaxle selector shaft.

5. Drive the pin through its bore and refit the gear control shaft to the car.

14. Gear Control Shaft - Maintenance

1. Jack up the car on one side and secure it with blocks or axle stands and check the wheels.

2. Clean the areas of the control shaft which pass through the front and rear nylon bearings. NOTE: It will be necessary to unslip the protective boot at the front end of the shaft.

3. Inspect the control shaft for excessive clearance in the rear bush as this can cause a vibrating noise at higher engine speeds. If necessary renew the rear bush as described in Section 12.

4. Liberally smear the bushes, control shaft and gear lever ball and socket with Shell Retinax 'A' grease. Re-secure the protective rubber boot and lower the car.

15. Hypoid Assembly - Removal, Inspection and Replacement

Note: Although it is difficult to assess the condition of the hypoid assembly, it can be viewed after removing the inspection cover in the base of the transaxle casing.

1. Remove the transmission unit from the engine as described in Section 3. With the transmission unit cleaned and on a bench remove the clutch release bearing as described in Chapter 5/11.

2. Unscrew and remove the ring of nuts and plain washers securing the clutch housing to the hypoid casing. The clutch housing can then be lifted off the hypoid casing studs.

3. The complete hypoid assembly will now be free and can be lifted out of the hypoid casing.

4. Thoroughly wash the hypoid assembly in a bowl of clean paraffin. NOTE: If the rubber drive couplings are still fitted to the differential shafts care should be taken to ensure that they are not accidentally contaminated with paraffin, as this will lead to rapid rubber deterioration.

5. When the unit has been cleaned inspect the teeth of the crown wheel and ensure that the wear markings are correct as shown in 'A' of Fig. 6.10.

6. If the wear markings are incorrect it will be necessary to re-adjust the crown wheel to pinion mesh setting. NOTE: This will also be necessary if a new hypoid assembly is being fitted. Incorrect meshing of the crown wheel and pinion will cause the hypoid assembly to be noisy and short lived.

7. Unfortunately this is not really a do-it-yourself task as a special tool is needed to turn the inner screwed sleeves of the pinion shafts, also a dial guage is required to check crown wheel run out.

8. If difficulty is encountered in determining the shape and position of the wear marks on the crown wheel teeth, paint the teeth with 'Engineers blue', (this can be obtained at most ironmongers) and temporarily reassemble the hypoid assembly to the transaxle.

9. This done manually rotate the hypoid assembly by turning the differential shaft flanges. Remove the hypoid from its casing. It will be found that the wear marks are now clearly shown, as the engineers blue will have been rubbed off on contact areas. Clean off all traces of the engineers blue.

10 Before reassembly starts, ensure that all traces of old jointing compound are removed from the joint faces of the clutch and hypoid casings. DO NOT scrape off the old jointing compound; instead use a piece of soft rag dampened with carbon tetrachloride. NOTE: This chemical should not be used in confined spaces or inhaled for long periods.

11 Replacement: Lightly smear the joint faces of the clutch and hypoid casings with Hylomar jointing compound.

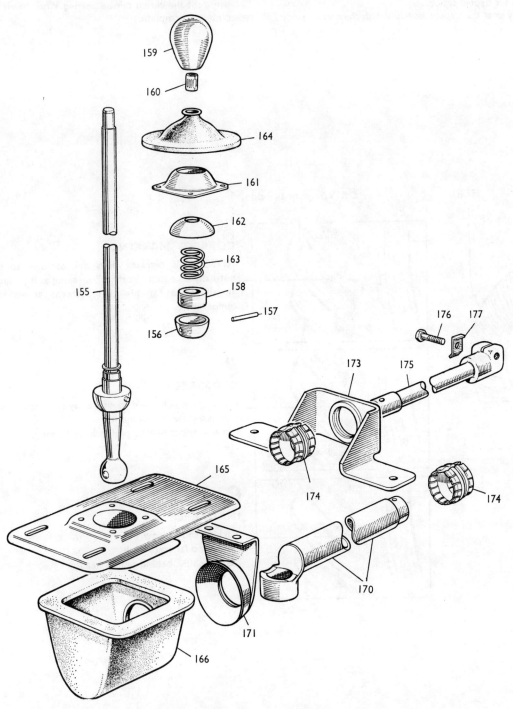

Fig. 6.9. EXPLODED VIEW OF THE GEARCHANGE MECHANISM

155 Gear lever	161 Lever mounting cap	170 Socket unit gear control shaft	175 Flexible coupling
156 Ball cup	162 Lever closing disc		176 Pinch bolt
157 Pin	163 Spring	171 Bearing bracket	177 Tab washer
158 Collar	164 Grommet	173 Rear support bracket and bearing	
159 Gear knob	165 Lever mounting plate		
160 Knob to lever clip	166 Dust excluding boot	174 Bearing grommet	

12 Lower the hypoid assembly into position in the hypoid casing. Ensure that the raised ring around the circumference of each of the differential shaft sleeves locates into its groove in the hypoid casing.

13 Lightly coat the hypoid assembly with the correct grade of oil.

14 Replace the clutch casing, fit the plain washers and nuts and tighten them evenly to the specified torque.

15 Lastly refit the clutch release bearing. When this is done replacement is complete.

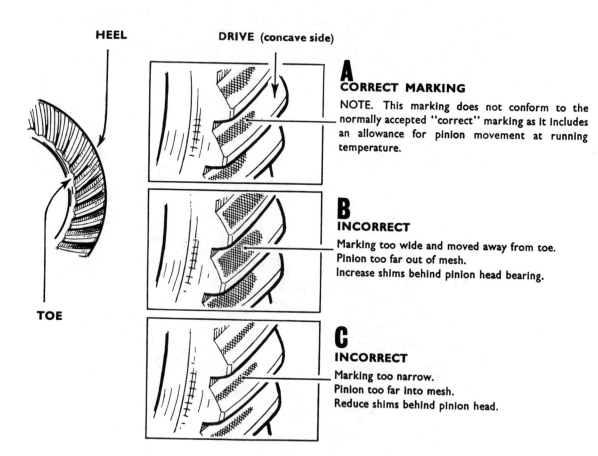

HEEL

DRIVE (concave side)

TOE

A
CORRECT MARKING

NOTE. This marking does not conform to the normally accepted "correct" marking as it includes an allowance for pinion movement at running temperature.

B
INCORRECT

Marking too wide and moved away from toe.
Pinion too far out of mesh.
Increase shims behind pinion head bearing.

C
INCORRECT

Marking too narrow.
Pinion too far into mesh.
Reduce shims behind pinion head.

Fig. 6.10. Crown wheel tooth markings

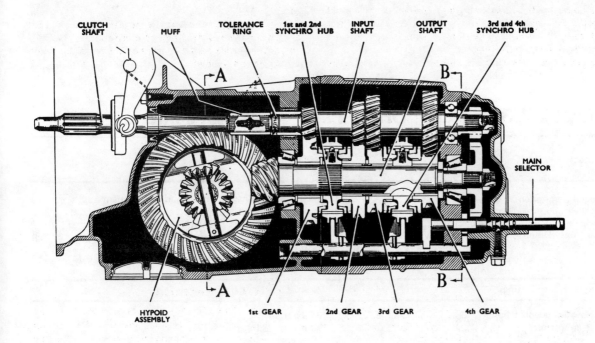

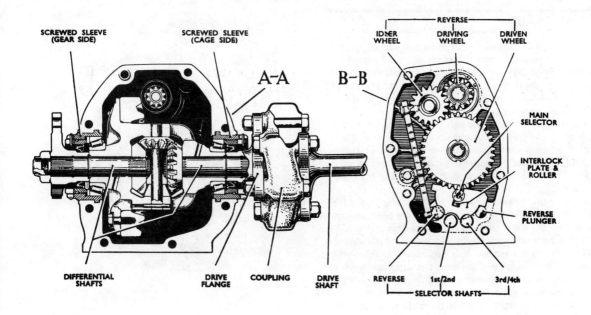

Fig. 6.11. General layout of the transaxle assembly

Chapter 7/Rear Hubs - Drive Shafts - Universal Joints

Contents

Torque Wrench Settings

Rotoflex coupling bolts	34 lbs.ft. (4.7 Kg.m)
Rear hub nuts	170 lbs.ft. (23.5 Kg.m)

1. General Description

Drive is transmitted from the differential unit to the rear wheels by means of open driveshaft of 7/8 in. or 1 in. diameter. These shafts incorporate two flexible joints. The joint nearest the differential unit is of the rubber rotoflex coupling type, whilst the other is a solid universal joint running on needle roller bearings.

The hub shaft runs in two ball bearings. The inner bearing is of smaller diameter than the outer bearing and is held in position by a shoulder on the hub shaft and a distance tube between it and the outer bearing. The outer bearing is retained by a shoulder in the shaft housing and the brake back plate.

An oil seal is located between the inner bearing and the hubshaft side of the solid universal joint. The hub is internally splined and slides over the external splines on the hubshaft; it is retained in this position by a nut and tab washer. NOTE: On Mark I models it is impossible to renew the driveshaft as a single item. Instead it is supplied together with a new hubshaft as one unit. This is because small dimensional modifications have been made and a new drive shaft will not pair satisfactorily with an old type hubshaft. This does not apply to later models. Also if the driveshafts are of 1 in. diameter rather than 7/8 in. then it is essential that they are not replaced by the 7/8 in. units. However, it is perfectly in order to replace the 7/8 in. unit with 1in. diameter shafts and may well be a good idea if the car is tuned or is subjected to any other unusually strenuous conditions.

2. Rotoflex Coupling - Removal and Replacement

It will be very much easier to remove and replace the rubber coupling which is fitted under compression if a compressor is available. The correct type of compressor is shown fitted in Fig. 7.1. However, if this is not available, jubilee clips joined end to end will serve the purpose equally well. NOTE: New couplings are usually supplied in a compressed state. If this is the case leave the compressing band in

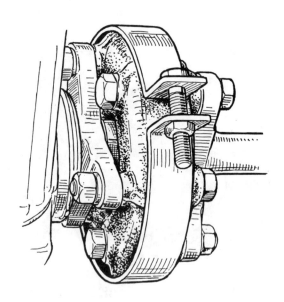

Fig.7.1. The drive shaft coupling compressor

position until the coupling has been fitted.

1. Fit the compressor around the circumference of the coupling and tighten it until it just begins to compress the coupling.

2. Jack up the roadwheel on the same side as the coupling which is being removed. Place the jack so that it bears on the suspension wishbone. This will allow the wheel to be rotated.

3. Loosen the six nuts on the coupling through bolts. Turn the roadwheel to bring each nut in turn within easy reach. Mark the coupling and both flanges to ensure that the coupling can be refitted in exactly the same position from which it was removed. If this is not done premature failure of the coupling will result.

4. Remove the six loose nuts and their spring washers and withdraw the through bolts, again turning the roadwheel to bring each within easy reach.

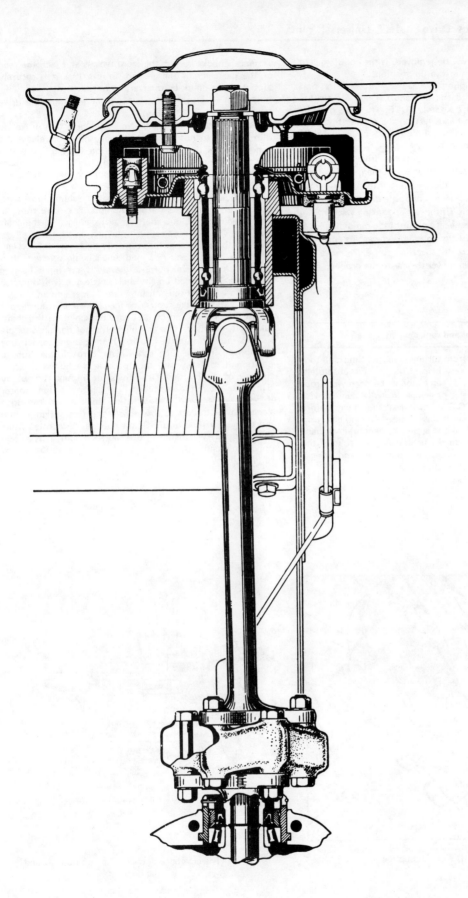

Fig. 7.2. Sectioned view of the rear hub and drive shaft assembly.

5. The coupling can now be removed. If the coupling is to be refitted leave the compressor in position.

6. To replace the coupling proceed as follows: First bolt the coupling back on to the driveshaft flange and tighten the nuts to 34 lb/ft (4.7 Kg.m.). NOTE: The bolts must be fitted so that the bolt heads rest on the smaller bosses of the coupling, i.e. on the opposite side of the coupling to the driveshaft flange, as shown in Fig. 7.3.

7 Smear the faces of the transaxle drive flange and coupling with a soap and water solution then, using a large tyre lever, carefully prise the coupling into position until one bolt can be installed in the opposite direction to those already installed. Loosely fit the nut and spring washer.

8 Rotate the wheel, as necessary, until the remaining holes are in alignment then fit the bolts, spring washers and nuts. Tighten all the nuts to the specified torque, remove the coupling compressor then lower the car to the ground.

3 Driveshafts - removal and replacement

To prevent the hub from turning a special Churchill tool No. RG188C/3 will be very helpful but it is not absolutely necessary. This special tool can probably be borrowed from your local Chrysler dealer or garage against a deposit. If a Churchill tool RG188C/3 is not available, then before starting work as described below, remove the hub cap from the wheel to be worked on and apply the handbrake as hard as possible. Also place chocks behind and in front of the wheel. This done, knock back the staking tabs and using a suitable spanner loosen the hub nut.

1 Place chocks against the front wheels and jack the rear of the car clear of the ground. Ensure that it is securely supported on stands before starting work.

2 Detach the rotoflex coupling from the transaxle drive flange (see previous Section).

3 Remove the rear wheel from the hub that is to be dismantled. Do not remove the brake drum or release the handbrake, as these provide a location for the hub which will simplify refitting of the driveshaft.

4 Remove the hub nut and tab washer previously loosened.

5 Using a large hammer and brass or aluminium drift, drive out the hub shaft from the hub. Take care that the end threads of the hub shaft are not damaged as the shaft may take some effort to start it moving.

6 With the shaft removed, carefully clean the splined end to ensure that it will not bind when being refitted, then apply a little general purpose grease. If the inner bearing and oil seal remained on the shaft as it was driven out, also clean and lubricate the housing in the suspension arm.

7 Installation is the reverse of the removal procedure, but where the bearing and oil seal have remained on the shaft, take care to ensure that the oil seal is not damaged as the shaft is inserted into the housing. If the bearing spacer tube has moved, pass a long screwdriver through the hub to position it centrally and then push in the hub shaft from the rear of the housing. Draw the shaft through the hub by tightening the nut; do not forget the tab washer (and spacer if one was removed). After fitting the shaft to the drive flange, lower the car to the ground and finally tighten hub nut to the specified torque. If the hub was dismantled while the driveshaft was removed (see next Section), it is a good policy to recheck the torque figure after about 500 miles of running.

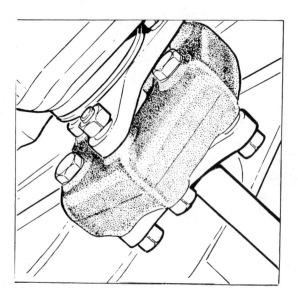

Fig.7.3. The drive coupling

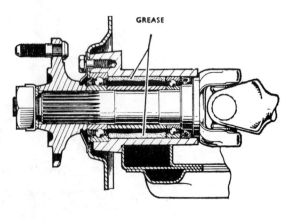

Fig.7.4. The clearance between the hub housing and the boss

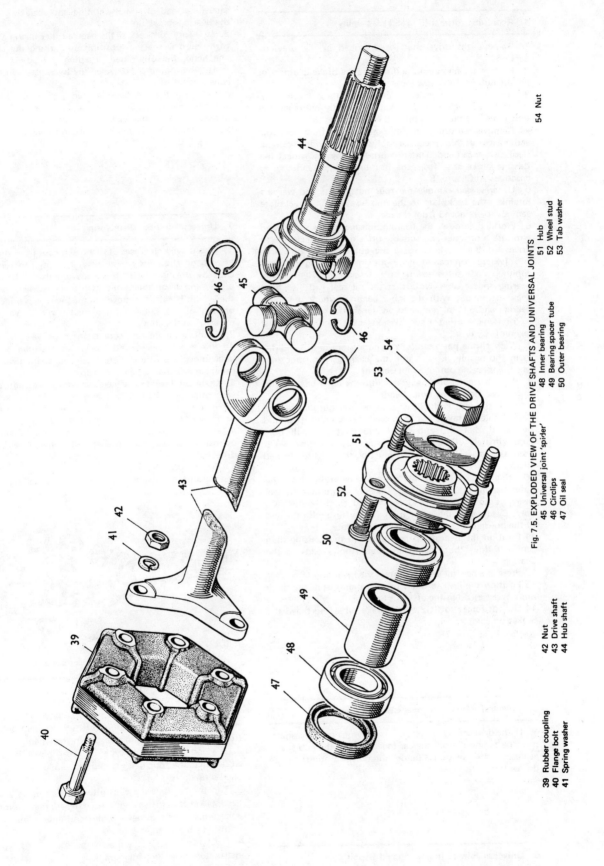

Fig. 7.5. EXPLODED VIEW OF THE DRIVE SHAFTS AND UNIVERSAL JOINTS

39 Rubber coupling
40 Flange bolt
41 Spring washer

42 Nut
43 Drive shaft
44 Hub shaft

45 Universal joint 'spider'
46 Circlips
47 Oil seal

48 Inner bearing
49 Bearing spacer tube
50 Outer bearing

51 Hub
52 Wheel stud
53 Tab washer

54 Nut

4   Rear hubs - dismantling and reassembly

1   Remove the drive shaft as described in the previous Section.

2   Release the handbrake and remove the brake drum; take off the hub which is now loose.

3   Disconnect the handbrake cable from the actuating arm in the brake backplate. This can be done by removing the split pin from the clevis pin and withdrawing the clevis pin.

4   Remove the cap from the brake/clutch fluid reservoir and place a thin piece of polythene over the orifice. Replace the cap and tighten it firmly. Now disconnect the flexible brake hose from the rear brake wheel cylinder as described in Chapter 8.

5   Unscrew and remove the four nuts, bolts and washers retaining the backplate to the hub housing. The backplate can now be removed from the car.

6   Working through the bearing housing in the suspension arm, use a hammer and suitable brass drift or steel tube to drive out the bearings. Drive the outer bearing outwards and (where applicable) drive the inner bearing inwards, applying loads to the bearing outer tracks only. Remove the bearing spacer tube. Note that the oil seal will also have been driven out with the inner bearing. Where the inner bearing and oil seal remained on the shaft, the bearing can be drawn off using a suitable extractor then the oil seal taken off by hand.

7   Wash all the parts carefully in paraffin or petrol and dry them thoroughly. Ensure that the bearings run smoothly; where applicable obtain a replacement.

8   Work a general purpose grease into the inner bearing and to the rear face of the outer bearing.

9   Pack the hub with 30 cc of a general purpose grease. Care should be taken not to exceed this amount. It should be noted that a front wheel hub dust cap will hold approximately 30 cc of grease. However, if a dust cap is used as a measuring vessel, it must be thoroughly cleaned first.

10 Using a tube of suitable diameter, carefully drive the outer bearing into the housing. Take great care that the seal casing is not damaged and apply load to the outer race only. Ensure that the outer track face is flush with the end of the housing, then refit the brake backplate.

11 Position the bearing spacer tube into the housing then carefully drive the inner bearing in. Apply loads to the bearing outer track only.

12 Press in a new oil seal to contact the bearing.

13 Position the hub to outer bearing then install the drive shaft as described in the previous Section.

14 Do not forget to fit the handbrake cable and bleed the brakes on completion.

5.   Universal Joints - Removal and Replacement

1.   If the driveshaft universal joints are worn the driveshafts must be removed from the car together with the hub shafts as described in Section 3 before the universal joints can be dismantled.

6.   Universal Joints - Inspection and Repair

1.   Wear in the needle roller bearings is characterised by vibration in the transmission, 'clonks' on taking up the drive, and in extreme cases of lack of lubrication, metallic squeaking, and ultimately grating and shrieking sounds as the bearings break up.

2.   It is easy to check if the needle roller bearings are worn with the driveshaft in position by turning the shaft with one hand, the other hand holding the yoke of the hub shaft. Any movement between the two parts is indicative of considerable wear.

3.   If worn, the old bearings and spiders will have to be discarded and a repair kit, comprising new universal joint spiders, bearings, oil seals, and retainers purchased. Check also by trying to lift the shaft and noticing any movement in the joints.

7.   Universal Joints - Dismantling

1.   Clean away all traces of dirt and grease from the circlips located on the ends of the bearing cups, and remove the clips by pressing their open ends together with a pair of pliers, and lever them out with a screwdriver. NOTE: If they are difficult to remove tap the bearing cup face resting on top of the spider with a mallet which will ease the pressure on the circlip.

2.   Remove the bearing cups from the drive shaft yoke. To do this select two sockets from a socket spanner set, one large enough to fit completely over the bearing cup and the other smaller than the bearing cup.

3.   Open the jaws of the vice and with the sockets opposite each other and the U.J. in between tighten the vice and so force the narrower socket to move the opposite cup partially out of the yoke into the larger socket.

4.   Remove the cup with a pair of pliers. Remove the opposite cup, and then free the hub shaft yoke from the driveshaft.

5.   To remove the remaining two cups now repeat the instructions in paragraph 3, or use a socket and hammer.

Fig.7.6. The universal joint components

8.   Universal Joints - Reassembly

1.   Place the new spider into the driveshaft yoke. It is essential that the grease nipple if fitted (see Section 9) faces towards the transaxle and away from the wheel.

2.   If a non-grease nipple type universal joint is being fitted ensure that the four bearing cups are about $1/3$ filled with Shell retinax 'A'.

3.   Tap the two bearing cups into position using a suitably sized socket as a drift. When both cups are right home in the yoke arms, refit two new circlips and ensure that they are firmly located in their grooves.

4.   Refit the hub shaft yoke to the spider and repeat the instructions given in paragraph 3.

5.   Ensure that the grease nipple (if fitted) is screwed into the spider firmly. Grease the joint well with Shell retinax 'A' by means of the grease nipple.

6.   Refit the driveshaft and hubshaft to the car.

9. Universal Joints - Modification

If a new universal joint fitted with a grease nipple is being fitted in place of sealed universal joint, then it will be necessary to modify the driveshaft yoke to prevent the nipple from binding. Instructions for this modification are given below. Both Chrysler and the Author recommend that sealed type universal joints are replaced by the type fitted with a grease nipple when and if renewal becomes necessary.

1. Using a 1 inch (25 mm) file, file a groove across the centre of the driveshaft yoke as shown in Fig. 7.7. until there is a gap of $^{13}/_{32}$ ins. (10.3 mm) between a straight edge passed through the bores and the bore of the groove (see 'A' Fig. 7.7.).

2. When the groove depth is correct the sides of the groove should be smoothly radiused and blended to avoid any stress joints, as shown in 'B' and 'C' in Fig. 7.7.

3. Modification is now complete and a grease nipple type spider can be fitted to the universal joint without fear of fouling.

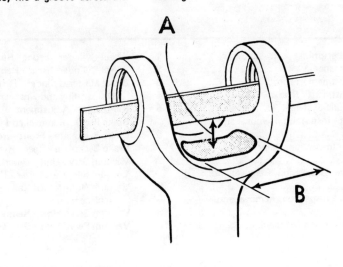

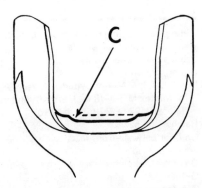

Fig 7.7. The modification to the drive shaft and the method of checking the clearance

Chapter 8/Braking System

Contents

Specifications

Make and type	Girling, twin leading shoe at front, 8 in. drums all round
Footbrake	Hydraulic on all four wheels
Handbrake	Cable, to rear wheels only
Brake fluid	Girling, crimson
Lining material	Don 202 (.7 in. Master Cylinder. No servo). Ferodo MS3 or Mintex M79 ($5/8$ in. Master Cylinder. No servo). Mintex M22 or M79 (With servo)
Handbrake type	Ratchet and pawl
Handbrake location	On floor between front seats
Brake adjusters type	Square headed
Brake adjusters location	On brake backplates
Servo unit (if fitted) type	Girling
Brake drum diameter	8 in. front and rear
Brake lining width	1.5 in (38.1 mm)
Brake lining total area	75 in.^{2} (483.8 cm.^{2})
Master cylinder bore:	
Early saloons and sport saloon	.7 in. (17.78 mm)
Later saloons	$5/8$ in. (15.875 mm)
Wheel cylinder bore - front	.7 in. (17.78 mm)
Wheel cylinder bore - rear	3/4 in. (19.05 mm)

Torque Wrench Settings

Backplate to stub axle	14 lbs.ft (1.9 Kg.m)
Wheel cylinder to backplate	6 lbs.ft (.8 Kg.m)
Bleed screws	5 lbs.ft. (1.7 Kg.m)
Union nuts (male)	7 lbs.ft. (.9 Kg.m)
Union nuts (female)	9 lbs.ft (1.2 Kg.m)

1. Brakes - General Description

The four wheel drum brakes fitted to all 'Imps' and variants are of the internal expanding type. The brakes are operated hydraulically by means of the brake pedal which is coupled to the brake master cylinder mounted on the bulkhead at the rear of the boot beneath the petrol tank.

The front brakes are of the twin leading shoe type with a separate cylinder for each shoe. Both cylinders are fixed to

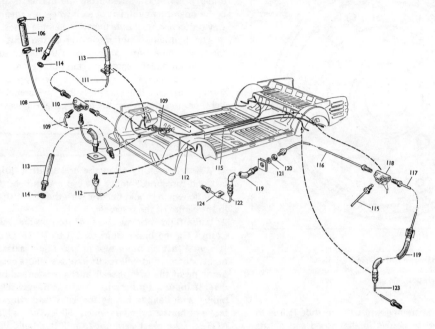

Fig. 8.1. DIAGRAMMATIC VIEW OF THE HYDRAULIC BRAKING SYSTEM - ALL MODELS
EXCEPT SPORT AND STILETTO

106 Flexible hose
107 Hose clips
108 Feed pipe to master
    cylinder
109 Male union
110 'T' union (4 way)
111 Flexible hose R.H./'T' union
    connecting pipe

112 Flexible hose L.H./'T' union
    connecting pipe
113 L.H. flexible hose
114 Sealing washer
115 Front & rear systems
    connecting pipe
116 'T' union/Rear R.H.
    flexible hose connecting pipe

117 'T' union/Rear L.H. flexible
    hose connecting pipe
118 Rear union
119 L.H. flexible hose
120 Nut
121 Washer
122 Flexible hose to slave
    cylinder connecting pipe

123 Flexible hose to slave
    cylinder connecting pipe
124 Bracket

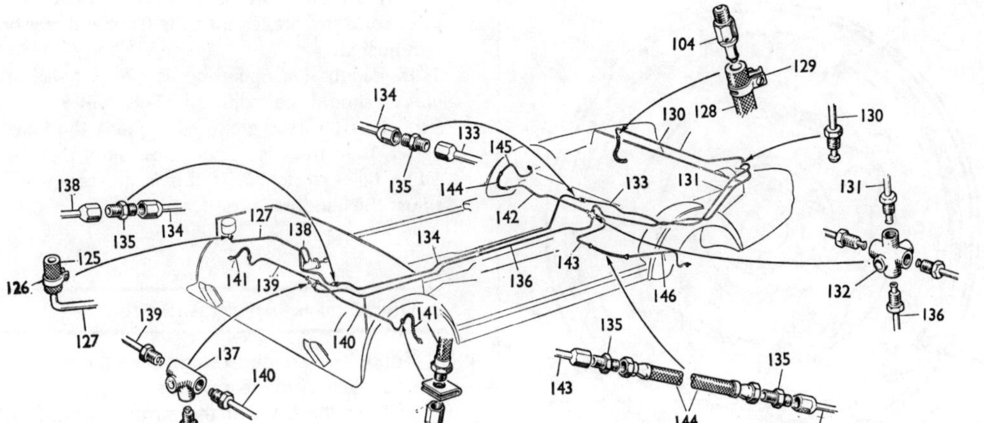

Fig. 8.2. DIAGRAMMATIC VIEW OF THE HYDRAULIC BRAKING SYSTEM - SPORT AND STILETTO

104 Adapter
125 Flexible hose
126 Hose clip
127 Master cylinder feed pipe
128 Flexible hose
129 Hose clip
130 Female union
131 Female union

132 Multi-way union
133 Master cylinder to servo
    unit pipe - rear section
134 Master cylinder to servo
    unit pipe - middle section
135 Male connector
136 Male union
137 'T' union

138 Master cylinder to servo
    unit pipe - front section
139 Union/R.H. flexible hose
    connecting pipe
140 Union/L.H. flexible hose
    connecting pipe
141 L.H. Flexible hose
142 Union/rear R.H. flexible

    hose connecting pipe
143 Union/rear L.H. flexible
    hose connecting pipe
144 L.H. flexible hose
145 Flexible hose/slave cylinder
    connecting pipe
146 Flexible hose/slave cylinder
    connecting pipe

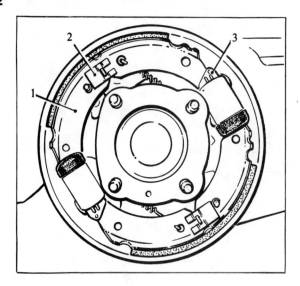

Fig.8.3. RIGHT-HAND FRONT BRAKE ASSEMBLY
1. Toe end of brake shoe   3. Angled abutment of wheel
2. Leaf spring of steady post   cylinder body

the backplate and the trailing end of each shoe is free to
slide laterally in a small groove in the closed end of the
brake cylinder, so ensuring automatic centralisation when
the brakes are applied.

The rear brakes are of the single leading shoe type, with
one brake cylinder per wheel for both shoes. The cylinder
is free to float on the backplate. Diametrically opposed to
each of the rear wheel operating cylinders is a mechanical
expander of the tapered screw type. This serves to adjust
the rear brakes.

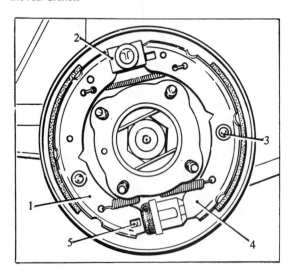

Fig.8.4. RIGHT-HAND REAR BRAKE ASSEMBLY
1. Leading brake shoe   4. Trailing brake shoe
2. Brake shoe adjuster   5. Tip of handbrake lever
3. Slotted washer of steady post

Drum brakes have to be adjusted periodically to compensate for wear in the linings. It is unusual to have to
adjust the handbrake system as the efficiency of this
system is largely dependent on the condition of the brake
linings and the adjustment of the brake shoes. The handbrake can, however, be adjusted separately to the footbrake
operated hydraulic system.

The hydraulic brake system functions in the following
manner:- On application of the brake pedal, hydraulic fluid
under pressure is pushed from the master cylinder to the
brake operating cylinders at each wheel, by means of a four
way union and steel pipe lines and flexible hoses.

The hydraulic fluid moves the pistons out so pushing
the brake shoes into contact with the brake drums. This
provides an equal degree of retardation on all four wheels
in direct proportion to the brake pedal pressure. Return
springs between the backplate and the brake shoes draw
the shoes together when the brake pedal is released.

2. Drum Brake - Maintenance

1. Weekly, carefully clean the brake/clutch fluid reservoir
cap and surround, remove the cap and inspect the level of
the fluid which should be level with the top of the separator
in the centre of the reservoir.
2. If the fluid is below this level, top up the reservoir with
Castrol Girling brake fluid of S.A.E. 7OR3 specifications.
It is vital that no other type of brake fluid is used. Use of a
non-standard fluid will result in brake failure caused by the
perishing of the special seals in the master and brake cylinders. If topping up becomes frequent then check the metal
piping and flexible hosing for leaks, and check for worn
brake or master cylinders which will also cause loss of fluid.
NOTE: Take great care not to spill hydraulic fluid on the
paintwork when topping up the reservoir, as the fluid will
damage any paintwork it comes into contact with.
3. Every 5,000 miles check the brake linings for wear. If
the surface of the lining is almost at rivet level, then the
linings must be replaced or damage to the drums will ensue.
However, if the linings are in good condition, take this
opportunity to brush and blow any dust off the linings,
backplate and drum. For this purpose use a clean brush and
if available a footpump or compressed air.
4. If it is found that excessive brake pedal travel is needed
to operate the brakes then the front and rear brakes should
be adjusted.
5. If handbrake operation is not satisfactory, the rear
brakes should be adjusted. This will normally effect a
cure. If after rear brake adjustment the handbrake is no
better, then there is a strong possibility that the handbrake
cables have stretched. If this is the case it is necessary to
adjust the handbrake itself.

3. Drum Brakes - Adjustment - Front

1. Apply the handbrake and place chocks behind and in
front of each of the rear wheels.
2. Jack up the front of the car until both front wheels are
clear of the ground.
3. Turn both adjusters on the backplate anti-clockwise until
they are fully retracted. (For adjuster positions see Fig.8.6.)
Now turn the adjusters, one at a time, clockwise (slowly
rotating the wheel at the same time) until the wheel just
locks. Turn back each adjuster two clicks. The wheel should
again be free to rotate. Spin the wheel and apply the brakes
hard to centralise the shoes. Recheck that it is not possible
to turn the adjuster further clockwise without locking the
wheel. NOTE: A rubbing noise when the wheel is spun is
usually due to dust in the brake drum. If there is no obvious
slowing of the wheel due to brake binding there is no need
to slacken off the adjusters until the noise disappears. Better
to remove the drum and blow out the dust.
4. Repeat this process with the other front wheel. Adjustment of the front brakes is now complete.

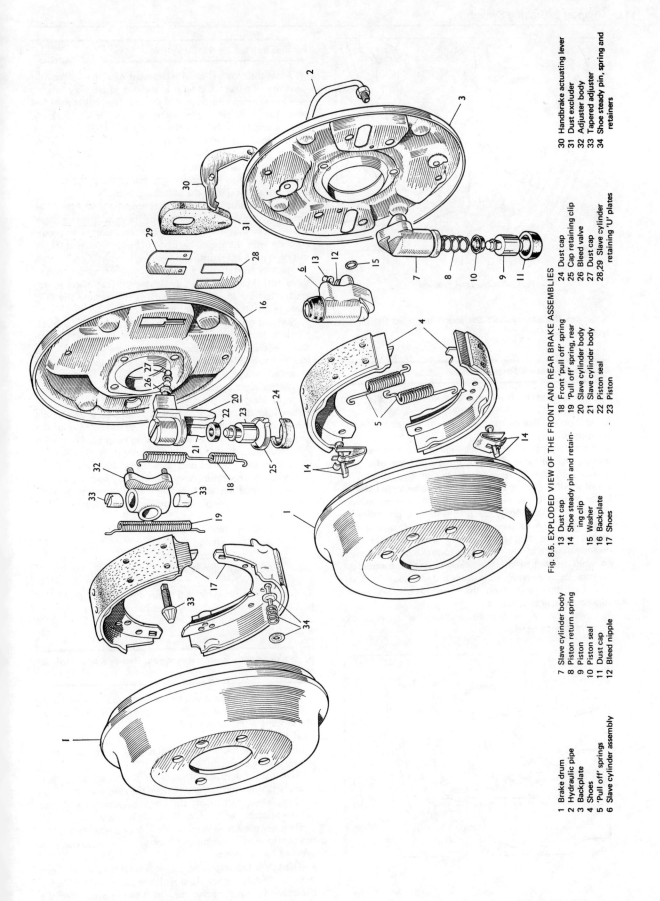

Fig. 8.5. EXPLODED VIEW OF THE FRONT AND REAR BRAKE ASSEMBLIES

1   Brake drum
2   Hydraulic pipe
3   Backplate
4   Shoes
5   'Pull off' springs
6   Slave cylinder assembly

7   Slave cylinder body
8   Piston return spring
9   Piston
10 Piston seal
11 Dust cap
12 Bleed nipple

13 Dust cap
14 Shoe steady pin and retain-
      ing clip
15 Washer
16 Backplate
17 Shoes

18 Front 'pull off' spring
19 'Pull off' spring, rear
20 Slave cylinder body
21 Slave cylinder body
22 Piston seal
23 Piston

24 Dust cap
25 Cap retaining clip
26 Bleed valve
27 Dust cap
28,29 Slave cylinder
      retaining 'U' plates

30 Handbrake actuating lever
31 Dust excluder
32 Adjuster body
33 Tapered adjuster
34 Shoe steady pin, spring and
      retainers

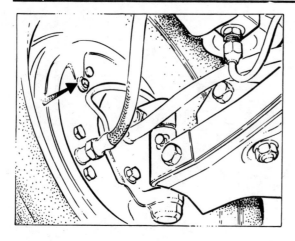

Fig.8.6. The front brake adjuster

5. Lower the car, remove the jack/s and also the chocks from the rear wheels.

4. Drum Brakes - Adjustment - Rear

1. Place chocks in front and behind each of the front wheels.
2. Jack up the rear of the car until both wheels are clear of the ground.
3. Turn the single adjuster (see Fig.8.7) clockwise (slowly turning the wheel at the same time) until the wheel just locks. Turn the adjuster anti-clockwise two clicks. The wheel should again be free to rotate. Recheck that the adjuster cannot be turned any further clockwise without locking the wheel. Apply the brakes hard to centralise the shoes. NOTE: A rubbing noise when the wheel is spun is usually due to dust in the brake drum. If there is no obvious slowing of the wheel due to brake binding there is no need to slacken off the adjusters until the noise disappears. Better to remove the drum and blow out the dust.
4. Repeat this process on the other wheel. Rear brake adjustment is now complete.
5. Lower the car, remove the jack/s and also the chocks from the front wheels.

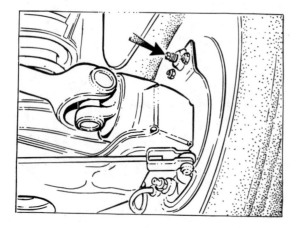

Fig.8.7. The rear brake adjuster

5. Bleeding the Hydraulic System

After the removal and replacement of some component or if the reservoir fluid level is allowed to fall very low, air will have entered the hydraulic system.. The brakes may feel very spongy or require pumping to make them work. To restore braking efficiency the system will have to be bled.
1. To bleed the system gather together a length of tubing (about 1½ feet) which is a tight fit over a bleed nipple and a glass jar containing about two inches of brake fluid. An assistant will also be necessary to pump the pedal and top up the reservoir during the bleeding process.
2. If a servo unit is fitted (Sports models) it will be necessary to pump the pedal for two or three minutes to dispel any vacuum that may be left in the servo unit. This should be done with the engine switched off and the engine should not be started again until the bleeding process is completed.
3. Slacken the adjusters on the front brakes by turning them anti-clockwise and fully tighten the rear wheel adjusters by turning them clockwise. This will reduce the fluid space in the wheel cylinder bodies.
4. Starting on the rear nearside wheel, unscrew the bleed nipple ½ to ¾ of a turn. Push one end of the bleed tube on the nipple and immerse the other end in the fluid in the jam jar. The tube MUST stay immersed in the fluid during the period when a nipple is open.
5. The assistant should now pump the pedal in a sequence of three long and three short strokes until bubbles stop issuing from the end of the immersed bleed tube. The nipple should then be tightened during a slow downstroke of the pedal. Remember that it is essential to keep the fluid reservoir topped up at all times. If this is not done air will enter the system and it will be necessary to start again.
6. Repeat the operation described in paragraphs 4 and 5 on the other three wheels. Bleeding is now complete. NOTE: The correct order for bleeding the brakes is as follows:-

> 1st Rear nearside wheel
> 2nd Rear offside wheel
> 3rd Front nearside wheel
> 4th Front offside wheel

7. Top up the reservoir and replace its cap. Replace any rubber dust covers that may have been removed from the bleed nipples. Readjust the brakes.

6. Brake Shoes - Front - Inspection, Removal and Replacement

After high mileages it will be necessary to fit replacement brake shoes with new linings. Refitting new brake linings to old shoes is not always satisfactory, but if the services of a local garage or workshop with brake lining equipment is available, then there is no reason why your own shoes should not be successfully relined.
1. Remove the hub cap, loosen off the wheel nuts, then securely jack up the car, and remove the road wheel.
2. Completely slacken off the brake adjustment and take out the setscrew which holds the drum in place.
3. Remove the brake drum. If it proves obstinate tap the rim gently with a soft headed hammer. The shoes are now exposed for inspection.
4. The brake linings should be renewed if they are so worn that the rivet heads are flush with the surface of the lining. If bonded linings are fitted they must be removed when the material has worn down to $1/32$ in. at its thinnest point. If the shoes are being removed to give access to the wheel cylinders, then cover the linings with masking tape to prevent any possibility of their becoming contaminated with

grease.

5. Remove the leaf springs and steady post from the brake shoe and backplate by holding the head of the post with a pair of pliers while compressing the leaf spring and sliding it sideways.

6. Detach the shoes and return springs by pulling one end of the shoes away from the slot in the closed end of one of the brake cylinders.

7. Disengage the brake shoe from the return spring carefully noting the holes into which the spring fits and then remove the remaining shoe in similar fashion. Place rubber bands over the wheel cylinders to prevent any possibility of the pistons dropping out.

8. Thoroughly clean all traces of dust from the shoes, backplates, and brake drums with a dry paint brush and compressed air, if available. Brake dust can cause squeal and judder and it is therefore important to clean out the brakes thoroughly.

9. Check that the pistons are free in their cylinders and that the rubber dust covers are undamaged and in position and that there are no hydraulic fluid leaks.

10 Prior to reassembly smear a trace of white brake grease to all sliding surfaces. The shoes should be quite free to slide on the closed end of the cylinder and the piston anchorage point. It is vital that no grease or oil comes in contact with the brake drums or the brake linings.

11 Replacement is a straightforward reversal of the removal procedure, but note the following points:-

a) Do not omit to replace the steady pins and their retaining springs.

b) Ensure that the return springs are in their correct holes both in the shoes and backplate.

c) When readjusting the brakes, if new shoes were fitted, back the adjusters off by three turns instead of the normal two. This is to allow for shoe expansion. After two or three hundred miles, readjust the brakes in the normal manner.

7. Brake Shoes - Rear - Inspection, Removal and Replacement

1. Follow the instructions given in Section 6, up to and including paragraph 4.

2. Press in each brake shoe steady pin securing washer against the pressure of its spring.

3. Turn the head of the washer 90º so the slot will clear the securing bar on the steady pin and remove the spring and washer.

4. Detach the shoes and return springs by pulling the heel of the rearmost shoe from the slot in the adjuster assembly. This done its toe can be released from the slave cylinder and handbrake lever. The other shoe will now be slack. Remove it by simply pulling it away from the back plate. Remove the two springs interconnecting the two shoes, after noting which holes each of the springs were clipped into.

5. Place a rubber band around the slave cylinder to prevent the piston from coming out.

6. Prior to reassembly, smear white brake grease over the tip of the handbrake lever, the steady post platforms and the slots in the wheel cylinder and adjuster links.

7. Replacement is a straightforward reversal of the removal procedure but note the following points:-

a) Do not omit to replace the steady pins and their retaining washers.

b) Ensure that the return springs are in their correct holes both in the shoes and backplate.

c) When readjusting the brakes, if new shoes were fitted, lock the adjusters off by three turns instead of the normal

two. This is to allow for shoe expansion. After two or three hundred miles readjust the brakes in the normal manner.

8. Flexible Hose - Front - Inspection, Removal and Replacement

Inspect the condition of the flexible hydraulic hoses leading from the chassis mounted metal pipes to the brake backplates. If any are swollen, damaged, cut, or chafed, they must be renewed.

1. Unscrew the cap from the hydraulic fluid reservoir, place a piece of thin polythene over the orifice, replace the cap and screw it down tightly. This will prevent fluid running out when the hose is disconnected.

2. Adjacent to the hose support bracket is the hexagon of the flexible hose. Grip this with a spanner and release the pressure pipe on the opposite side by unscrewing the union nut with a second spanner.

3. Continue to grip the hexagon with a spanner whilst undoing the nut and washer retaining the flexible hose union to the support bracket.

4. To remove the flexible hose from the rear of the slave cylinder, grip the hexagon with a suitable spanner and unscrew it allowing the hose to rotate.

5. Replacement is a reversal of the removal procedure.

6. Remember to bleed the brakes.

9. Flexible Hose - Rear - Inspection, Removal and Replacement

1. Follow the instructions given in Section 8 up to and including paragraph two. NOTE: The support bracket will be found on the main rear suspension crossbeam.

2. Repeat the previous operation on the second union, only this time the support bracket is mounted near the apex of the rear suspension wishbone.

3. Replacement is a reversal of the removal procedure.

4. Bleed the brakes.

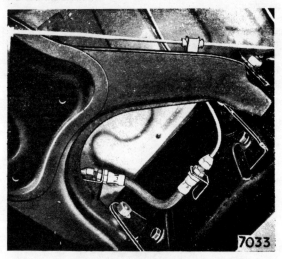

Fig.8.8. Location of rear flexible hose

10. Brake Seals - Inspection and Overhaul

If hydraulic fluid is leaking from one of the brake cylinders it will be necessary to dismantle the cylinder and replace the dust cover and piston sealing rubber. If brake fluid is found running down the side of the wheel, or it is noticed that a pool of liquid forms alongside one wheel in the master cylinder has dropped, and the hoses are all in good order, proceed as follows:-

1. Remove the brake drums and brake shoes as described in Section 6 or 7.
2. Ensure that all the other wheels, and all the other brake drums are in place. Remove piston sealing rubber and the spring from the leaking cylinder by applying gentle pressure to the footbrake. Place a quantity of rag under the backplate or a tray to catch the hydraulic fluid as it pours out of the cylinder.
3. Inspect the inside of the cylinder for score marks caused by impurities in the hydraulic fluid. If any are found the cylinder and piston will require renewal together as an exchange assembly.
4. If the cylinder is sound thoroughly clean it out with fresh hydraulic fluid.
5. The old rubber seal will probably be swollen and visibly worn. Smear the new rubber seal with hydraulic fluid and reassemble in the cylinder the spring, seal and piston, and then the rubber boot. The seal must be fitted with its lip towards the bottom of the cylinder.
6. Replenish the brake fluid, replace the brake shoes and brake drum, and bleed the hydraulic system as previously described.

11. Wheel Cylinder - Front - Removal and Replacement

1. Remove the brake shoes from the backplate as described in Section 6.
2. To remove the foremost wheel cylinder from the backplate, first unscrew the bridge pipe union from the rear of the cylinder. Then undo and remove the two retaining bolts and washers which hold the cylinder in place. The cylinder can now be withdrawn from the backplate.
3. If it is the rearmost cylinder being removed, the procedure is the same except that the flexible hose should also be removed as described in Section 8.
4. Replacement is a straightforward reversal of the removal procedure.

12. Wheel Cylinder - Rear - Removal and Replacement

1. Remove the left or right-hand brake drum and brake shoes as required, as described in Section 7. To avoid

having to drain the hydraulic system screw down the master cylinder reservoir cap tightly over a piece of cellophane.
2. Free the hydraulic pipe from the wheel cylinder at the union, and disconnect the handbrake cable clevis from its lever.
3. Take off the dust excluder, the retaining plate and the spring clip, and remove the cylinder from the backplate.
4. On replacement smear the slot in the backplate and the cylinder neck with Girling white brake grease. The rest of the replacement process is a straightforward reversal of the removal sequence. Bleed the brakes on completion of reassembly.

13. Brake Master Cylinder - Removal and Replacement, Dismantling and Reassembly

The removal procedure for the brake master cylinder is identical to that for clutch master cylinder. This is described in Chapter 5, section 10.

The dismantling and reassembly procedures are also exactly the same as for the clutch master cylinder. These too are described in Section 10 of Chapter 5.

14. Handbrake - Adjustment

The handbrake does not normally require adjustment as it is automatically adjusted when the rear brakes are taken up. If there is play in the handbrake mechanism proceed as follows:-

1. Place chocks in front and behind the front wheels. Jack up the rear of the car until the rear wheels are clear of the ground.
2. Turn the brake adjusters on both rear wheels clockwise until the wheels are locked. From beneath the car undo and remove the eight bolts and washers which hold the protective plate to the floorpan. This plate will be found directly beneath the handbrake lever, running almost the length of the central floor tunnel. The two handbrake adjusters will now be in view.
3. Take up the slack on each cable by turning the larger nut on the adjuster clockwise, at the same time gripping the smaller hexagon with a suitable spanner to prevent the threaded part of the adjuster from rotating. When the cable is just taut enough to remove any excessive slack, but not under any tension, handbrake adjustment is correct.

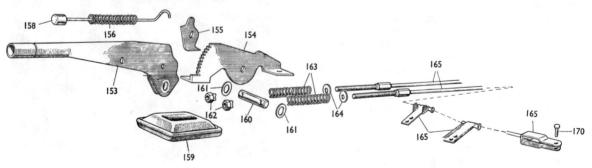

Fig. 8.9. EXPLODED VIEW OF THE HANDBRAKE MECHANISM

153 Handbrake handle	156 Spring	161 Washer	165 Handbrake cable and
154 Ratchet: stepped cam and	158 Pawl release rod	162 Cable adjusting nuts - special	clevis assembly
handbrake mounting bracket	159 Rubber gaitor	163 Springs	170 Clevis pin
155 Pawl	160 Cable cross bar	164 Washers	

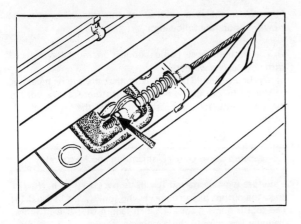

Fig.8.10. The handbrake adjuster

4. Replace the protective plate. The upturned tongue should be at the end nearest the front of the car.
5. Readjust the rear brakes as described in Section 4.
6. Lower the car and remove the chocks from the front wheels. Adjustment is now complete.

15. Brake Pedal - Removal and Replacement

1. Remove the circlip from the clevis pin retaining the master cylinder actuating rod to the pedal. Withdraw the clevis pin. Repeat this operation on the clutch pedal (it will be necessary to remove both pedals as they are retained by the same shaft).
2. Ease the inner leg of each tension spring off the pedals with a pair of pliers.
3. With a pair of circlip pliers release and remove the circlip from the left-hand end of the spindle. Draw the spindle out of the bracket from the right-hand side; as this is done both pedals will be released and can be removed from the car.
4. The spindle is fed back through the bracket, springs and pedals 'D' shaped end first, from the right-hand side. NOTE: The right-hand tension spring is fitted to the fulcrum of the brake pedal so that its outer end will hook around the right-hand flange of the bracket. The left-hand tension spring is fitted to the left-hand side of the clutch pedal in a similar fashion.
5. Replace the spindle retaining circlip and hook the tension springs around the pedals.
6. Push the clevis pins through the actuating arm ends and the two pedals. Refit the split pins to the clevis pins. Replacement is now complete.

16. Brake Backplate - Front - Removal and Replacement

1. Remove the wheel, drum and brake shoes as described in Section 6.
2. Disconnect the flexible hose as described in Section 8. NOTE: This is only necessary if the backplate is being removed from the car. If the backplate is only being removed from the stub axle, it can be tied up out of the way still connected to the flexible hose.
3. Remove the hub as described in Chapter 10/4. Undo and remove the three bolts and washers retaining the backplate to the stub axle. Remove the backplate.
5. Reassembly is a straightforward reversal of the removal procedure. If the flexible hose was disconnected bleed and readjust the brakes.

17. Brake Backplate - Rear - Removal and Replacement

1. Remove the wheel, drum and brake shoes as described in Section 7.
2. Remove the flexible hose to the wheel cylinder as described in Section 9.
3. Release the handbrake from the lever in the backplate by removing the split pin retaining the clevis pin. Withdraw the clevis pin.
4. Remove the hub as described in Chapter 7/3.
5. Undo and remove the four retaining bolts and washers which hold the backplate to the rear axle shaft. Remove the backplate.
6. Replacement is a reversal of the removal procedure. When replacement is complete, bleed and readjust the brakes.

18. Vacuum Servo Unit - Description

The servo unit is connected into the braking system so that the master cylinder outlet is connected to the servo inlet port (9) (all numbers refer to Fig. 8.12.) and all wheel cylinders are connected to the servo outlet port (14). When air at atmospheric pressure is required it enters the servo via the air filter (12). Constant vacuum is supplied (when the engine is running) to the servo via a pipe from the inlet manifold to the vacuum inlet port (19). This pipe line incorporates as safety features a non-return valve and a flame trap. The servo fitted works by the suspended vacuum method. In practice this means that the vacuum piston (5) is held in equilibrium by an equal vacuum on both its sides. The movement that is needed to multiply the drivers braking effort is obtained by venting the vacuum on one side of the piston to the atmosphere. Thus with an unequal pressure acting on the piston it slides towards the vacuum. This movement is used to increase hydraulic pressure at the wheel cylinders. Servo outlet pressure is controlled by the pressure in the master cylinder line and thus pressure applied at the wheel cylinders is directly proportional to the pressure applied to the pedal by the driver. The servo unit's design incorporates a fail safe system. In the event of vacuum cut-off (i.e. engine stalling) the brakes will still be servo assisted for two or three applications and even if the servo unit runs completely out of vacuum the brakes will still work although a greater pedal pressure will be required. The servo unit can be split into three major parts. These are vacuum piston and piston rod (5 and 15), hydraulic control piston, air and vacuum control valves (10, 30 and 20) and the output piston (25). These three parts operate simultaneously. With the engine running and the brakes not in use the hydraulic control piston is at rest, the air valve is closed and the vacuum valve on the thrust side of the piston is open. In this way equal vacuum is applied to both sides of the control piston. When the brakes are applied, the master cylinder pressure is applied to both sides (10 and 13) of the control piston. However, although equal pressure is exerted on both sides, the low pressure side of the control piston has a greater surface area and therefore the piston moves down the cylinder. This movement operates the 'T' lever (11) which in turn closes the vacuum valve (20) and opens the air valve (30). Air enters the thrust side of the vacuum piston through the transfer tube (16). The initial movement of the vacuum piston seats the nose of the piston rod (15) in the port of the output piston. This seals the output cylinder and the high pressure end of the control piston from the low pressure input side of the servo. The vacuum control piston continues to move, driving the output piston down its bore. This continues until the pressure on the high pressure end of the control piston (13) just overcomes the master cylinder pressure on the low pressure end of the control valve. This causes the control piston to move back again operating the 'T' lever which closes both the air and vacuum valves (30 and 20). The vacuum piston is then suspended in its cylinder and thus the pressure applied to the wheel cylinders is constant, until the driver increases or relieves the pressure on the brake pedal. When the pedal pressure is released, master cylinder line pressure collapses. The control piston is then driven back to the 'at rest' position by the hydraulic pressure on its high pressure end (13). This action causes the air valve (30) to close and the vacuum valve to open so that pressure and eventually vacuum equalises on both sides of the vacuum piston and return spring (6). Aided by hydraulic pressure, the output piston spring (25) returns the vacuum piston to its 'at rest' position. Movement of the output piston is halted by a circlip (24). The last movement of the vacuum piston is aided by its return spring (16) only. This opens the port in the output piston to the low pressure side of the servo which helps the servo to recuperate very quickly in preparation for its next operation.

19. Vacuum Servo Air Filter - Removal and Replacement

1. At intervals of 10,000 miles the servo cellular air filter element must be removed.
2. Unscrew and remove the centre screw from the filter top cover.
3. Lift off the filter cover, followed by the rubber washer. Remove the element and discard it.
4. Thoroughly clean the interior of the filter cover, the filter baseplate and also the rubber washer.
5. Place the new element and the rubber washer in position on the base plate. Replace the filter cover and tighten down the centre screw.

20. Vacuum Non-Return Valve - Removal and Replacement

The vacuum non-return valve is incorporated in the banjo connection on the top of the servo unit. This valve is not serviceable and in the event of failure must be renewed.
1. Unscrew and remove the banjo connection retaining bolt. Remove the banjo connection and its two sealing washers from the top of the servo unit.
2. Slacken the hose retaining clip and pull the banjo connection from the end of the vacuum hose.
3. Replacement of the new banjo connection is a reversal of the removal procedure. It is preferable to use new sealing washers on the banjo connection to preclude the possibility of a leakage through a fulty seal.

21. Vacuum Servo Unit - Removal and Replacement

1. Unscrew and remove the bolt retaining the banjo connection of the vacuum hose to the top of the servo unit. Remove the connection and its two sealing washers.
2. Remove the cap from the brake/clutch fluid reservoir. Place a piece of thin polythene over the orifice and replace the cap, screwing it down firmly. This will minimise hydraulic fluid loss when the inlet and outlet pipes are disconnected from the servo unit.
3. Disconnect the servo unit inlet and outlet hydraulic pipes from the servo by unscrewing their unions.
4. Unscrew and remove the three bolts and washers retaining the servo unit to its mounting bracket. Withdraw the servo unit from its mounting bracket.

5. Replacement is a reversal of the removal procedure. However, note the following:-

a) The vacuum hose banjo connection must be replaced with new sealing washers.
b) The brakes should be bled. Note that the engine must not be started before this is done, as once there is a vacuum in the servo unit, it is impossible to bleed the brakes effectively.

22. Vacuum Servo Unit - Dismantling and Reassembly

Before work is started it will be necessary to borrow or make the output piston compressing tool shewn in Fig.8.11. The tool is made from a 12 inch length of $^1/8$ in. (3 mm) diameter iron wire to the dimensions shewn.

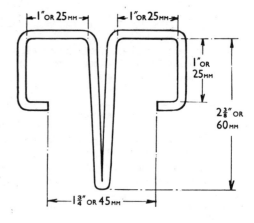

Fig.8.11. The output piston compression tool

1. Place the unit in a vice. The jaws should grip the unit by the two lower lugs in its cast body.
2. Remove the air filter as described in Section 19.
3. Remove the end cover (1) (all numerals refer to Fig.8.12) and remove the vacuum piston and spring. This can be done by unscrewing the seven nuts and bolts at the same time controlling the spring pressure on the end cover.
4. Remove the three bolts and washers and also the clamping plate retaining the vacuum cylinder (17) to the servo body. Ease the grommet in the flange of the cylinder from the transfer pipe. Remove the vacuum cylinder (17) and its gasket from the servo body (27).
5. Undo the four retaining screws and washers and remove the combined cover, transfer pipe and cork gasket from inside the valve chest.
6. Unscrew and remove the two screws retaining the valve retainer (26) and flat horseshoe spring (29). Remove the latter two components from inside the valve chest.
7. Now withdraw the valves (20 and 30) and the 'T' lever (11) complete from inside the valve chest. This can be done by applying light pressure to the plug (8).
8. Remove the body from the vice and shake the control piston assembly from the top bore by tapping the mounting flange of the body on a block of wood.
9. The control piston assembly can now be dismantled by compressing the piston spring, removing the circlip and taking off the spring and retainers.
10 Next remove the two seals from the control piston and one from the plug. It is preferable when removing the seals not to use metal tools as these may damage working surfaces. Better to use a piece of dirt free rag to grasp the

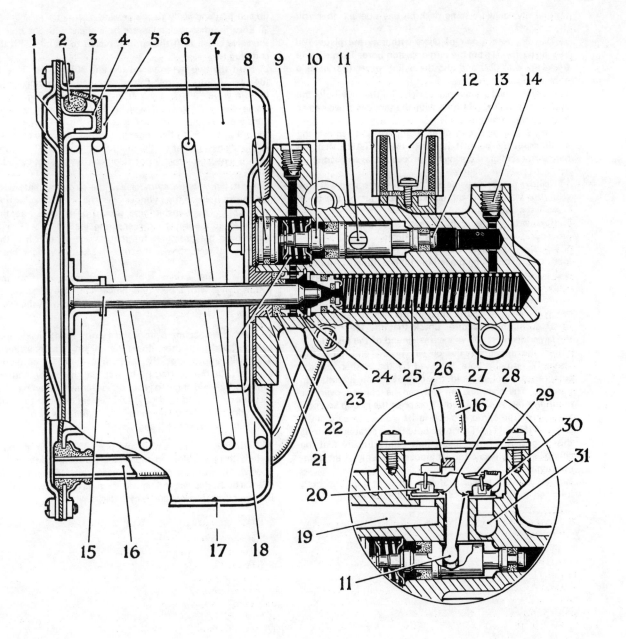

Fig. 8.12. SECTIONED VIEW OF GIRLING VACUUM SERVO IN 'AT REST' POSITION - BRAKES OFF

1 End cover and gasket
2 Vacuum piston backing ring
3 Vacuum piston seal
4 Vacuum piston seal retainer
5 Vacuum piston
6 Vacuum piston return spring
7 Constant vacuum chamber
8 End plug
9 Hydraulic inlet port (from master cylinder)
10 Control piston (low pressure end)
11 'T' lever
12 Air filter
13 High pressure end of control piston
14 Hydraulic outlet port (to wheel cylinders)
15 Piston rod
16 Vacuum transfer tube
17 Vacuum cylinder
18 Control piston spring
19 Vacuum inlet
20 Vacuum valve
21 Bearing bush
22 Gland seal
23 Nylon spacer
24 Output piston circlip
25 Output piston and spring
26 Valve retainer
27 Cast body
28 Valve springs
29 Flat horseshow shaped spring
30 Air valve
31 Air inlet, from air filter 12

seals firmly, draw up some slack on one side and then roll the seals off.

11 Twisting with a pair of pliers withdraw the piston rod bearing bush (21) from the output piston bore. Then remove the gland seal (22) and also the nylon spacer (23) using a hooked tool.

12 With the body mounted upright in the vice hold the output piston down its bore with the tool described earlier in this section (see Fig. 8.11).

13 With a pair of circlip pliers, compress and remove the circlip from the bore. It is MOST IMPORTANT that the bore is not scratched during this procedure, as any scratches may lead to brake failure.

14 Remove the compressing tool. The piston spring will now push the washer and the output piston out of the bore. Discard the output piston.

15 Reassembly is generally a reversal of the dismantling procedure, except for the following item.

16 All the seals must be renewed. New seals should be lubricated with Girling brake fluid before fitment. All bores and pistons should be sparingly lubricated with Girling red rubber grease.

17 Fit a new output piston. This is necessary as the piston rod seal which is incorporated in the piston can only be fitted during manufacture. Check that the taper seal has the larger diameter nearer the smaller end of the piston.

18 Fit the spring to the output piston and push this assembly into the bore, followed by the washer. Fit the compression tool to hold the output piston assembly in position. The compression tool can be clipped over the mounting flange of the body. Compress the circlip and pass it down the bore into position in its groove. Once again it is MOST IMPORTANT that the bore is not scratched during this procedure as brake failure may result. Ensure that the circlip is firmly located in its groove and remove the compressing tool.

19 Fit the nylon spacer (23) into the bore large end first, followed by the gland seal (22) which goes into the bore,

lip end first and lastly fit the bearing bush (21).

20 Ensuring that the transverse hole aligns with the hole in the valve chest, refit the control piston to its bore. Fit the end plug (8).

21 Refit the two nylon valves (20 and 30) and the 'T' lever together. Ensure that the horseshoe spring location above the air valve (30) is away from the two securing screws inside the valve chest. It will be found necessary to compress the end plug (8) to allow location of the 'T' lever in the control piston. Refit the horseshoe spring and valve retainer.

22 Place a new gasket on the mounting face of the body and also fit a new grommet in the flange of the vacuum cylinder (17).

23 Refit the vacuum cylinder and the clamping plate with the centre hole of the cylinder over the protruding bearing bush (21). The transfer pipe should be entered into the grommet at the same time ensuring that there will be a space over the grommet for the passage of air when the cover is refitted. Leave the three vacuum cylinder bolts slack.

24 Replace the sponge rubber backing ring (2) on the piston flange with a new one. Smear the leather seal (3) of the piston with the special lubricant, supplied with the overhaul kit.

25 Place the vacuum piston and return spring inside the cylinder, and push them down the full stroke several times. This will ensure that the vacuum cylinder is correctly aligned with the bearing bush. Remove the piston and return spring and tighten the three screws retaining the vacuum cylinder to the body, taking great care not to move the cylinder whilst doing so as if the cylinder is displaced it can cause the brakes to 'hang on'.

26 Refit the piston assembly and place the end cover complete with new gasket on top of the piston. Press the cover downwards ensuring that the piston rod (15) enters the bearing bush. Replace and tighten the nuts and bolts securing the end cover to the vacuum cylinder.

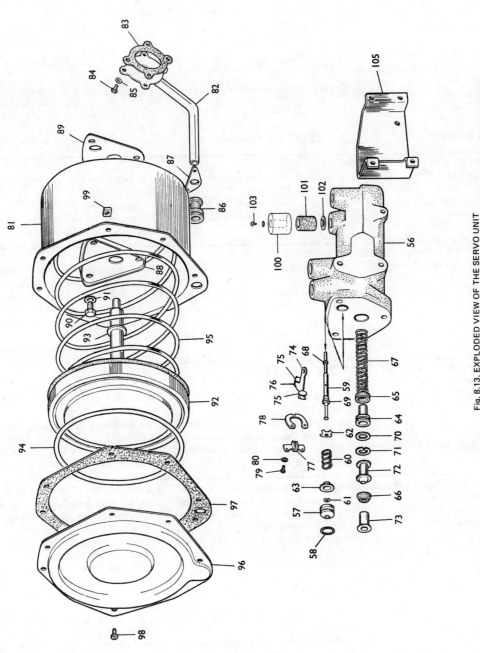

Fig. 8.13. EXPLODED VIEW OF THE SERVO UNIT

56 Body
57 Plug
58 Plug sealing ring
59 Valve operating piston
60 Piston spring
61 Piston circlip
62 Piston abutment
63 Piston retainer
64 Output piston

65 Output piston seal
66 Piston rod gland seal
67 Piston spring
68 Small piston seal
69 Large piston seal
70 Piston stop washer
71 Piston circlip
72 Seal spacer
73 Bush

74 Rocking lever
75 Pilot valve
76 Valve clip
77 Rocking lever guide
78 Valve spring
79 Rocking lever guide screw
80 Copper washer
81 Vacuum cylinder
82 Vacuum pipe

83 Gasket
84 Pipe to cylinder screw
85 Shakeproof washer
86 Vacuum pipe grommet
87 Grommet retaining plate
88 Servo clamping plate
89 Clamping plate gasket
90 Screw
91 Copper washer

92 Vacuum piston and rod
93 Nylon piston washer
94 Vacuum pirton seal locking ring
95 Vacuum piston return spring
96 Vacuum cylinder end and cover
97 Cover gasket
98 Screw
99 Nut (square)

100 Element cover
101 Filter element
102 Cover seal
103 Element screw
105 Servo mounting bracket

Cause	Trouble	Remedy
SYMPTOM: PEDAL TRAVELS ALMOST TO THE FLOOR BEFORE BRAKES OPERATE		
Leaks and air bubbles in hydraulic system	Brake fluid level too low	Top up master cylinder reservoir. Check for leaks.
	Wheel cylinder leaking	Dismantle wheel cylinder, clean, fit new rubbers and bleed brakes.
	Master cylinder leaking (Bubbles in master cylinder fluid)	Dismantle master cylinder, clean, and fit new rubbers. Bleed brakes.
	Brake flexible hose leaking	Examine and fit new hose if old hose leaking. Bleed brakes.
	Brake line fractured	Replace with new brake pipe. Bleed brakes.
	Brake system unions loose	Check all unions in brake system and tighten as necessary. Bleed brakes.
Normal wear	Linings over 75% worn	Fit replacement shoes and brake linings.
Incorrect adjustment	Brakes badly out of adjustment	Jack up car and adjust brakes.
SYMPTOM: BRAKE PEDAL FEELS SPRINGY		
Brake lining renewal	New linings not yet bedded-in	Use brakes gently until springy pedal feeling leaves.
Excessive wear or damage	Brake drums badly worn or cracked	Fit new brake drums.
Lack of maintenance	Master cylinder securing nuts loose	Tighten master cylinder securing nuts. Ensure spring washers are fitted.
SYMPTOM: BRAKE PEDAL FEELS SPONGY		
Leaks or bubbles in hydraulic system	Wheel cylinder leaking	Dismantle wheel cylinder, clean, fit new rubbers, and bleed brakes.
	Master cylinder leaking (Bubbles in master cylinder reservoir	Dismantle master cylinder, clean, and fit new rubbers and bleed brakes. Replace cylinder if internal walls scored.
	Brake pipe line or flexible hose leaking	Fit new pipeline or hose.
	Unions in brake system loose	Examine for leaks, tighten as necessary.
SYMPTOM: EXCESSIVE EFFORT REQUIRED TO STOP CAR		
Lining type or condition	Linings badly worn	Fit replacement brake shoes and linings.
	New linings recently fitted - not yet bedded-in	Use brakes gently until braking effort normal.
	Harder linings fitted than standard causing increase in pedal pressure	Remove linings and replace with normal units.
Oil or grease leaks	Linings and brake drums contaminated with oil grease, or hydraulic fluid	Rectify source of leak, clean brake drums, fit new linings.
SYMPTOM: BRAKES UNEVEN & PULLING TO ONE SIDE		
Oil or grease leaks	Linings and brake drums contaminated with oil, grease, or hydraulic fluid	Ascertain and rectify source of leak, clean brake drums, fit new linings.
Lack of maintenance	Tyre pressures unequal	Check and inflate as necessary.
	Radial ply tyres fitted at one end of car only	Fit radial ply tyres of the same make to all four wheels.
	Brake backplate loose	Tighten backplate securing nuts and bolts.
	Brake shoes fitted incorrectly	Remove and fit shoes correct way round.
	Different type of linings fitted at each wheel	Fit the linings specified by the manufacturers all round.
	Anchorages for front suspension or rear axle loose	Tighten front and rear suspension pick-up points including spring anchorage.
	Brake drums badly worn, cracked or distorted	Fit new brake drums.
Lack of maintenance	Wheel cylinder and piston seized	Remove cylinder and overhaul or replace as necessary.

Chapter 9/Electrical System

Contents

Specifications

Battery	... ...	Lead acid
Type:		
	Home market saloons	Lucas BHNH 7/9A
	Some export saloons	Lucas 9A
Capacity at 20 hr. rate:		
	Lucas BHNH 7/9A	32 amp. hr.
	Lucas 9A	38 amp. hr.

Polarity		
Mk. I Saloons		Positive earth
Mk. II Saloons, Sport Saloon		Negative earth

Voltage	... ...	12

Dynamo, Make	... ...	Lucas
Type	... ...	C40-I or C40-L
Maximum output:		
	C40-I	22 amp.) At 13.5 volts
	C40-L	25 amp.)
Number of brushes	... ...	2
Brush spring tension:		
	New brushes	30 oz. Maximum
	Worn brushes up to ¼ in.	15 oz. Maximum
Field resistance	... ...	5.9 ohms.

Cutting in speed	1350 R.P.M. Maximum at 13 volts
Minimum brush length	¼ in.

Starter Motor ... ... — Lucas M.35G

Number of brushes	4
Lock torque	7.7 lbs.ft. (1.06 Kg.m) 330/350 amps at 7.5/7.1 volts
Drive	Lucas 'SB'
Brush spring tension	30/34 oz. (.85/.96 Kg.)
Control type	Solenoid

Regulator/Control box ... ... — Lucas RB 340

Cut-in voltage	12.6 to 13.4 volts
Drop off voltage	9.3 to 11.2 volts
Open circuit settings	10°C (50°F) 14.9 to 15.5 volts
	20°C (68°F) 14.7 to 15.3 volts
	30°C (86°F) 14.5 to 15.1 volts
	40°C (104°F) 14.3 to 14.9 volts
Reverse current	3.0 to 5.0 amps.
Current regulator	25+ or -1½ amps.

Windscreen wiper, type	Lucas DR3A
	or Lucas 12W
	or Lucas 14W
Normal running current:	
Lucas DR3A	11.5 volts, 3.4 amps. maximum
Lucas 12W	11.5 volts, 1.4 amps. maximum
Lucas 14W	11.5 volts, 1.5 amps. maximum
Armature end play	

Horns, type ... ... — Lucas 9H or 6H

	or Clear Hooter F725
Operating current	3.5 to 4.0 amps.
Flasher unit, type	Lucas FL5 or 8FL

Bulbs

Head (RHD and Stiletto LHD inner)	Sealed beam unit
Head (LHD including stiletto outer)	Bulb 12v 45/40w
Head (North America)	Sealed beam unit
Side lamps	12v, 4 or 6w
Stop and tail lamps	12v, 21/6w
Front and rear flashing indicator bulbs	12v, 21w
Rear number plate bulb	12v, 6w
Interior lamp bulb	12v, 6w 'Festoon'
Panel lamp bulbs	12v, 2.2w
Headlamp main beam indicator bulb	12v, 2.2w
Ignition warning light bulb	12v, 2.2w
Flashing indicator warning light bulb	12v, 2.2w
Oil pressure warning light bulb	12v, 2.2w

Headlamps, type

All models except Stiletto	Two Lucas F700 Mk.10 units
Stiletto	Four Lucas F575 units

1. General Description

The electrical system fitted to all Imps and variants is of the 12-volt type and the major components comprise: a 12-volt battery with positive earth on early models. (Later Mk. II models have the negative lead earthed); a control box and cut-out; a Lucas C40/1 dynamo which is driven by the fan belt from the crankshaft pulley wheel; and a starter motor which is fitted to the engine/transaxle bellhousing on the left-hand side of the engine.

An unusual feature is that no fuses are fitted. The ignition system is also part of the electrical system but because of its importance and complexity is covered separately in Chapter 4.

On negative earth cars great care should be taken if fitting any electrical accessory containing silicon diodes or transistors that their polarity is correct. Serious damage may otherwise result to the components concerned.

Items such as radios, tape recorders, electronic ignition systems, electronic tachometers, automatic dipping, parking lamp and anti-dazzle mirrors should all be checked for correct polarity.

The twelve volt battery provides a steady supply of current for the ignition, lighting and other electrical circuits and provides a reserve of electricity when the current consumed by the electrical equipment exceeds that being produced by the dynamo.

The dynamo is of the two brush type and works in conjunction with the voltage regulator and cut-out. The dynamo is cooled by a multi-bladed fan mounted behind the dynamo pulley, and blows air through cooling holes in the dynamo end brackets. The output from the dynamo is controlled by the voltage regulator which ensures a high output if the battery is in a low state of charge or the demands from the electrical equipment high, and a low output if the battery is fully charged and there is little demand from the electrical equipment.

2. Battery - Removal and Replacement

1. The earthed battery terminal should always be removed first. Therefore on later negative earth cars remove the negative lead before the positive, and replace the negative lead last. On positive earth models disconnect the positive and then the negative leads from the battery terminals by slackening the retaining nuts and bolts, or by unscrewing the retaining screws if these are fitted.
2. Remove the battery clamp and carefully lift the battery out of its compartment. Hold the battery vertical to ensure that none of the electrolyte is spilled.
3. Replacement is a direct reversal of this procedure. NOTE: Replace the negative lead before the earth (positive) lead and smear the terminals with petroleum jelly (vaseline) to prevent corrosion. NEVER use an ordinary grease as applied to other parts of the car.

3. Battery - Maintenance and Inspection

1. Normal weekly battery maintenance consists of checking the electrolyte level of each cell to ensure that the separators are covered by ¼ in. of electrolyte. If the level has fallen top up the battery using distilled water only. Do not overfill. If a battery is overfilled or any electrolyte spilled, immediately wipe away the excess as electrolyte attacks and corrodes any metal it comes into contact with very rapidly.
2. As well as keeping the terminals clean and covered with petroleum jelly, the top of the battery, and especially the top of the cells, should be kept clean and dry. This helps prevent corrosion and ensures that the battery does not become partially discharged by leakage through dampness and dirt.
3. Once every three months remove the battery and inspect the battery securing bolts, the battery clamp plate, tray, and battery leads for corrosion (white fluffy deposits on the metal which are brittle to touch). If any corrosion is found clean off the deposits with ammonia and paint over the clean metal with an anti-rust/anti-acid paint.
4. At the same time inspect the battery case for cracks. If a crack is found, clean and plug it with one of the proprietary compounds marketed by firms such as Holts for this purpose. If leakage through the crack has been excessive then it will be necessary to refill the appropriate cell with fresh electrolyte as detailed later. Cracks are frequently caused to the top of the battery cases by pouring in distilled water in the middle of winter AFTER instead of BEFORE a run. This gives the water no chance to mix with the electrolyte and so the former freezes and splits the battery case.
5. If topping up the battery becomes excessive and the case has been inspected for cracks that could cause leakage, but none are found, the battery is being overcharged and the voltage regulator will have to be checked and reset.
6. With the battery on the bench at the three monthly interval check, measure its specific gravity with a hydrometer to determine the state of charge and condition of the electrolyte. There should be very little variation between the different cells and if a variation in excess of 0.025 is present it will be due to either:

a) Loss of electrolyte from the battery at some time caused

by spillage or a leak resulting in a drop in the specific gravity of the electrolyte, when the deficiency was replaced with distilled water instead of fresh electrolyte.
b) An internal short circuit caused by buckling of the plates or a similar malady pointing to the likelihood of total battery failure in the near future.

7. The specific gravity of the electrolyte for fully charged conditions at the electrolyte temperature indicated, is listed in Table A. The specific gravity of a fully discharged battery at different temperatures of the electrolyte is given in Table B.
8. Specific gravity is measured by drawing up into the body of a hydrometer sufficient electrolyte to allow the indicator to float freely (see Fig. 9.1.). The level at which the indicator floats indicates the specific gravity.

Table A
Climate ordinarily below 26.7ºC (80ºF)

Cell fully charged	1.270–1.290
Cell half charged	1.190–1.210
Cell fully discharged	1.110–1.130

Table B
Climate ordinarily above 26.7ºC (80ºF)

Cell fully charged	1.210–1.230
Cell half charged	1.130–1.150
Cell fully discharged	1.050–1.070

NOTE: Electrolyte specific gravity alters with its temperature. The figures quoted above are for an electrolyte temperature of 15.6ºC (60ºF). Therefore, if the electrolyte temperature is above 15.6ºC add .002 to the hydrometer reading for every additional 2.8ºC (5ºF) rise to obtain a true reading. Similarly, deduct .002 for every 2.8ºC below 15.6ºC.

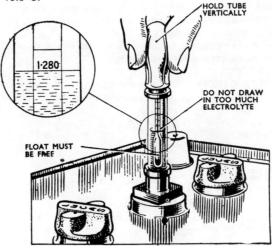

Fig. 9.1. Method of taking hydrometer readings. Take readings at eye level.

4. Electrolyte Replenishment

1. If the battery is in a fully charged state and one of the cells maintains a specific gravity reading which is 0.025 or more lower than the others, and a check of each cell has been made with a voltage meter to check for short circuits (a four to seven second test should give a steady reading of between 1.2 to 1.8 volts), then it is likely that electrolyte has been lost from the cell with the low reading at some time.
2. Top the cell up with a solution of 1 part sulphuric acid to

2.5 parts of water. If the cell is already fully topped up draw some electrolyte out of it with a pipette. The total capacity of each cell is as shown below:

Acid for one cell	Battert type
2/3 pint (380 cc)	BHNH7/9A
3/5 pint (340 cc)	BHNH9A
3/4 pint (400 cc)	D type

3. When mixing the sulphuric acid and water NEVER ADD WATER TO SULPHURIC ACID - always pour the acid slowly onto the water in a glass container. IF WATER IS ADDED TO SULPHURIC ACID IT WILL EXPLODE.

4. Continue to top up the cell with the freshly made electrolyte and then recharge the battery and check the hydrometer readings.

5. Battery Charging

1. In winter time when heavy demand is placed upon the battery, such as when starting from cold, and much electrical equipment is continually in use, it is a good idea to occasionally have the battery fully charged from an external source at the following rates:-

BHNH7/9A Batteries (32 amphere-hour) ...3 amp
BHNH9A Batteries (38 amphere-hour) ... ...3.5 amps
D type Batteries (32 amphere-hour) ... ...3 amps

2. Continue to charge the battery at this rate until no further rise in specific gravity is noted over a four hour period.

3. Alternatively, a trickle charger charging at the rate of 1.5 to 2 amps can be safely used overnight.

4. Specially rapid 'boost' charges which are claimed to restore the power of the battery in 1 to 2 hours are most dangerous as they can cause serious damage to the battery plates through over-heating.

5. While charging the battery note that the temperature of the electrolyte should never exceed:-

37.8°C (100°F)... ...   Climates below 26.7°C (80°F)
48.9°C (120°F)... ...   Climates below 48.9°C (120°F)

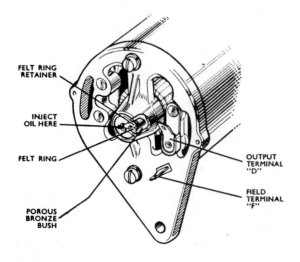

FELT RING RETAINER

INJECT OIL HERE

FELT RING

POROUS BRONZE BUSH

OUTPUT TERMINAL "D"

FIELD TERMINAL "F"

Fig. 9.2. Generator lubrication and terminal connections.

6. Dynamo - Routine Maintenance

1. Routine maintenance consists of checking the tension of the fan belt periodically and lubricating the dynamo rear bearing once every 5,000 miles.

2. The fan belt should be taut enough to ensure no slip between the belt and the dynamo pulley. If a shrieking noise comes from the engine when the unit is accelerated rapidly, it is likely that it is the fan belt slipping. On the other hand, the belt must not be too tight or the bearings will wear rapidly and cause dynamo failure or bearing seizure. Ideally 1 inch of free movement should be available in the centre of the longest run (between the crankshaft pulley and water pump).

3. To adjust the fan belt tension slightly slacken the three dynamo retaining bolts, and swing the dynamo on the upper two bolts outwards to increase the tension, and inwards to lower it.

4. It is best to leave the bolts fairly tight so that considerable effort has to be used to move the dynamo; otherwise it is difficult to get the correct setting. Retighten the dynamo bolts and check that the dynamo pulley is correctly aligned with the fan belt.

5. Lubrication of the dynamo consists of inserting three drops of S.A.E. 30 engine oil in the small oil hole in the centre of the commutator end bracket. This lubricates the rear bearing. The front bearing is pre-packed with grease and requires no attention.

7. Dynamo - Testing in Position

1. If, with the engine running no charge comes from the dynamo, or the charge is very low, first check that the fan belt is in place and is not slipping. Then check that the leads from the control box to the dynamo are firmly attached and that one has not come loose from its terminal.

2. The lead from the larger 'D' terminal on the dynamo should be connected to the 'D' terminal on the control box. Check that this is so and that the leads have not been incorrectly fitted. Ensure that a good connection exists to control box terminal 'E'.

3. Make sure none of the electrical equipment (such as the lights or radio) is on and then pull the leads off the dynamo terminals marked 'D' and 'F', join the terminals together with a short length of wire.

4. Attach to the centre of this length of wire the negative clip of a 0-20 volts voltmeter (reverse this if the vehicle is negative earth) and run the other clip to earth on the dynamo yoke. Start the engine and allow it to idle at approximately 1,000 r.p.m. At this speed the dynamo should give a reading of about 15 volts on the voltmeter. There is no point in raising the engine speed above a fast idle as the reading will then be inaccurate.

5. If no reading is recorded then check the brushes and brush connections. If a very low reading of approximately 1 volt is observed then the field winding may be suspect.

6. If a reading of between 4 to 6 volts is recorded it is likely that the armature winding is at fault.

7. If the voltmeter shows a good reading then with the temporary link still in position connect both leads from the control box to 'D' and 'F' on the dynamo ('D' to 'D' and 'F' to 'F'). Release the lead from the 'D' terminal at the control box end and clip one lead from the voltmeter to the end of the cable, and the other lead to a good earth. With the engine running at the same speed as previously, an identical voltage to that recorded at the dynamo should be noted on the voltmeter. If no voltage is recorded then there is a break in the wire. If the voltage is the same as

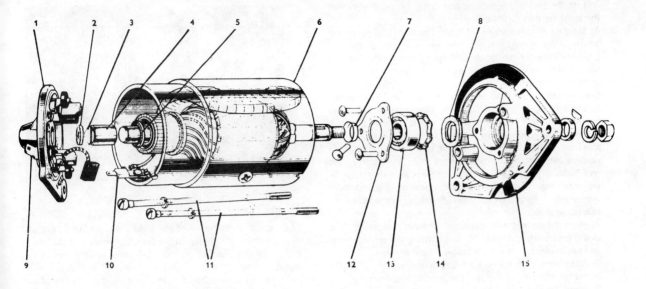

Fig. 9.3. EXPLODED VIEW OF THE DYNAMO

1 Commutator end bracket	5 Fibre washer	9 Terminal 'D'
2 Felt ring	6 Yoke	10 Terminal 'F'
3 Felt ring retainer	7 Retaining cup	11 Through bolts
4 Bronze bush	8 Felt ring	12 Bearing retainer

13 Drive-end bearing
14 Corrugated washer
15 Drive end bracket

recorded at the dynamo then check the 'F' lead in similar fashion. If both readings are the same as at the dynamo then it will be necessary to test the control box.

8. Dynamo - Removal and Replacement

1. Slacken the two dynamo retaining bolts, and the bolt on the sliding link, and move the dynamo in towards the engine so that the fan belt can be removed.
2. Disconnect the two leads from the dynamo terminals.
3. Remove the bolt from the sliding link, and remove the two upper bolts. The dynamo is then free to be lifted away from the engine.
4. Replacement is a reversal of the above procedure. Do not finally tighten the retaining bolt and the nut on the sliding

link until the fan belt has been tensioned correctly.

9. Dynamo - Dismantling and Inspection

1. Mount the dynamo in a vice and unscrew and remove the two through bolts from the commutator end bracket. (See photo.)
2. Mark the commutator end bracket and the dynamo casing so the end bracket can be replaced in its original position. Pull the end bracket off the armature shaft. NOTE some versions of the dynamo may have a raised pip on the end bracket which locates in a recess on the edge of the casing. If so, marking the end bracket and casing is not necessary. A pip may also be found on the drive end bracket at the opposite end of the casing. (See photo.)

9.1

9.2

3. Lift the two brush springs and draw the brushes out of the brush holders (arrowed).

4. Measure the brushes and if worn down to 9/32 in. or less unscrew the screws holding the brush leads to the end bracket. Take off the brushes complete with leads. Old and new brushes are compared in the photograph.

5. If no locating pip can be found, mark the drive end bracket and the dynamo casing so the drive end bracket can be replaced in its original position. Then pull the drive end bracket complete with armature out of the casing (photo).

6. Check the condition of the ball bearing in the drive end plate by firmly holding the plate and noting if there is visible side movement of the armature shaft in relation to the end plate. If play is present the armature assembly must be separated from the end plate. If the bearing is sound there is no need to carry out the work described in the following two paragraphs.

7. Hold the armature in one hand (mount it carefully in a vice if preferred) and undo the nut holding the pulley wheel and fan in place. Pull off the pulley wheel and fan.

8. Next remove the woodruff key (arrowed) from its slot in the armature shaft and also the bearing locating ring.

9. Place the drive end bracket across the open jaws of a vice with the armature downwards and gently tap the armature shaft from the bearing in the end plate with the aid of a suitable drift.

10 Carefully inspect the armature and check it for open or short circuited windings. It is a good indication of an open circuited armature when the commutator segments are burnt. If the armature has short circuited the commutator segments will be very badly burnt, and the overheated armature windings badly discoloured. If open or short circuits are suspected then test by substituting the suspect armature for a new one.

9.8

11 Check the resistance of the field coils. To do this, connect an ohmmeter between the field terminals and the yoke and note the reading on the ohmmeter which should be about 6 ohms. If the ohmmeter reading is infinity this indicates an open circuit in the field winding. If the ohmmeter reading is below 5 ohms this indicates that one of the field coils is faulty and must be replaced.

12 Field coil replacement involves the use of a wheel operated screwdriver, a soldering iron, caulking and riveting and this operation is considered to be beyond the scope of most owners. Therefore, if the field coils are at fault either purchase a rebuilt dynamo, or take the casing to a Chrysler dealer or electrical engineering works for new field coils to be fitted.

13 Next check the condition of the commutator (arrowed). If it is dirty and blackened as shown, clean it with a petrol dampened rag. If the commutator is in good condition the

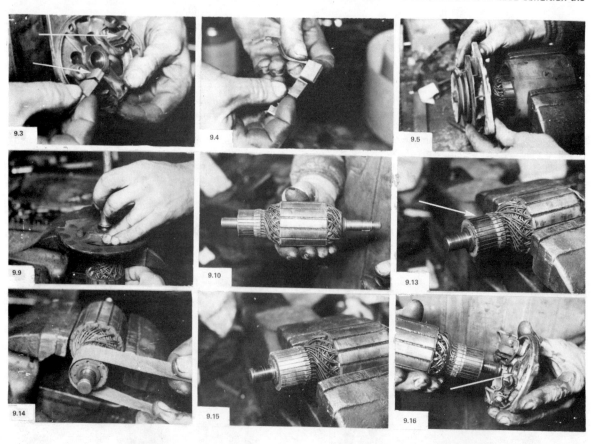

9.3

9.4

9.5

9.9

9.10

9.13

9.14

9.15

9.16

surface will be smooth and quite free from pits or burnt areas, and the insulated segments clearly defined.

14 If, after the commutator has been cleaned pits and burnt spots are still present, wrap a strip of glass paper round the commutator taking great care to move the commutator ¼ of a turn every ten rubs till it is thoroughly clean (photo).

15 In extreme cases of wear the commutator can be mounted in a lathe and with the lathe turning at high speed, a very fine cut may be taken off the commutator. Then polish the commutator with glass paper. If the commutator has worn so that the insulators between the segments are level with the top of the segments, then undercut the insulators to a depth of $^1/32$ in. (.8 mm). The best tool to use for this purpose is half a hacksaw blade ground to a thickness of the insulator, and with the handle end of the blade covered in insulating tape to make it comfortable to hold. This is the sort of finish the surface of the commutator should have when finished. (See photo.) NOTE: Although it is permissible to undercut the segment insulators on fabricated commutators, it is not permissible to do so on moulded commutators, both types being fitted to the C40/1 dynamo. Both types of commutator are easily identified. The moulded commutator is quite smooth on the exposed end, whereas the fabricated type has a metal roll-over and insulating cone protruding from its end. The difference is clearly shown in Fig.9.4. It should also be noted that a commutator of the moulded type cannot be skimmed below a minimum diameter of 1.43 inches (3.64 cm).

16 Check the bush bearing (arrowed) in the commutator end bracket for wear by noting if the armature spindle rocks when placed in it. If worn it must be renewed.

17 The bush bearing can be removed by a suitable extractor or by screwing a $^5/8$ in. tap four or five times into the bush. The tap complete with bush is then pulled out of the end bracket.

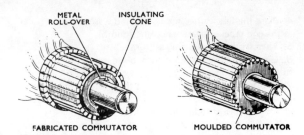

Fig. 9.4. Figure shows both the fabricated and moulded types of commutator.

18 NOTE before fitting the new bush bearing that it is of the porous bronze type, and it is essential that it is allowed to stand in S.A.E. 30 engine oil for at least 24 hours before fitment. In an emergency the bush can be immersed in hot oil 100ºC) for 2 hours.

19 Carefully fit the new bush into the end plate, pressing it in until the end of the bearing is flush with the inner side of the end plate. If available press the bush in with a smooth shouldered mandrel the same diameter as the armature shaft.

10. Dynamo - Repair and Reassembly

1. To renew the ball bearing fitted to the drive end bracket drill out the rivets which hold the bearing retainer plate to the end bracket and lift off the plate.

2. Press out the bearing from the end bracket and remove the corrugated and felt washers from the bearing housing.

3. Thoroughly clean the bearing housing, and the new bearing and pack with high melting-point grease.

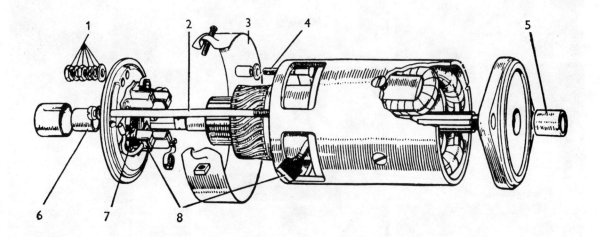

Fig. 9.5. EXPLODED VIEW OF THE STARTER MOTOR

1 Terminal nuts and washers	3 Cover band	5 Bearing bush (drive end)	7 Brush springs
2 Through bolt	4 Terminal post	6 Bearing bush (commutator end)	8 Brushes

4. Place the felt washer and corrugated washer in that order in the end bracket bearing housing (photo).

5. Then fit the new bearing as shown.

6. Gently tap the bearing into place with the aid of a suitable drift (photo).

7. Replace the bearing plate and fit three new rivets (photo).

8. Open up the rivets with the aid of a suitable cold chisel to secure the plate in place (photo).

9. Finally peen over the open end of the rivets with the aid of a ball hammer as illustrated.

10 Refit the drive end bracket to the armature shaft. Do not try and force the bracket on but with the aid of a suitable socket abutting the bearing tap the bearing in gently, so pulling the end bracket down with it (photo).

11 Slide the spacer up the shaft and refit the woodruff key (photo).

12 Replace the fan and pulley wheel and then fit the spring washer and nut and tighten the latter. The drive bracket end of the dynamo is now fully assembled as shown.

13 If the brushes are little worn and are to be used again then ensure that they are placed in the same holders from which they were removed. When refitting brushes, either new or old, check that they move freely in their holders. If either brush sticks, clean with a petrol moistened rag and if still stiff, lightly polish the sides of the brush with a very fine file until the brush moves quite freely in its holder.

14 Tighten the two retaining screws and washers which hold the wire leads to the brushes in place.

15 It is far easier to slip the end piece with brushes over the commutator if the brushes are raised in their holders as shown and held in this position by the pressure of the springs resting against their flanks (arrowed).

16 Refit the armature to the casing and then the commutator end plate and screw up the two through bolts.

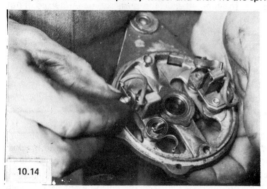
10.14

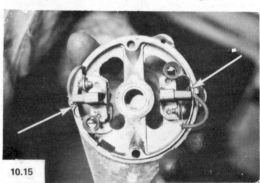
10.15

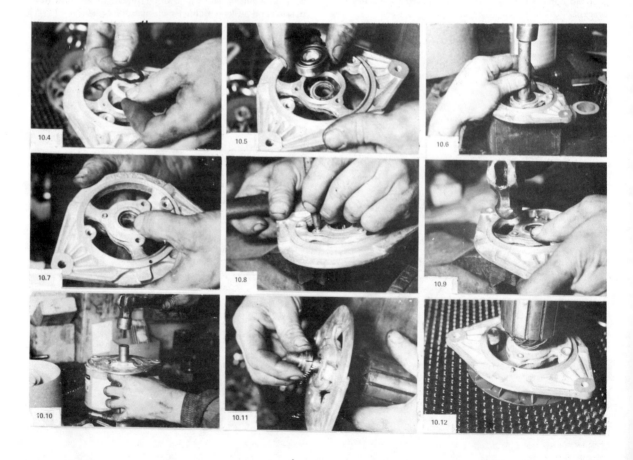
10.4
10.5
10.6
10.7
10.8
10.9
10.10
10.11
10.12

17 Finally, hook the ends of the two springs off the flanks of the brushes and onto their heads so the brushes are forced down into contact with the armature.

11. Starter Motor - General Description

The starter motor is mounted on the left hand side of the engine end plate, and is held in position by two bolts which also clamp the bellhousing flange. The motor is of the four field coil, four pole piece type, and utilises four spring-loaded commutator brushes. Two of these brushes are earthed, and the other two are insulated and attached to the field coil ends. (See Fig. 9.5. on page 129.)

12. Starter Motor - Testing in Engine

1. If the starter motor fails to operate then check the condition of the battery by turning on the headlamps. If they glow brightly for several seconds and then gradually dim, the battery is in an uncharged condition.
2. If the headlamps glow brightly and it is obvious that the battery is in good condition then check the tightness of the battery wiring connections (and in particular the earth lead from the battery terminal to its connection on the body-frame). Check the tightness of the connections at the relay switch and at the starter motor. Check the wiring with a voltmeter for breaks or shorts.
3. If the wiring is in order then check that the starter motor switch is operating. To do this press the rubber covered button in the centre of the starter solenoid on the bulkhead at the front of the engine compartment. If it is working the starter motor will be heard to 'click' as it tries to rotate. Alternatively check it with a voltmeter.
4. If the battery is fully charged, the wiring in order, and the switch working and the starter motor fails to operate then it will have to be removed from the car for examination. Before this is done, however, ensure that the starter pinion has not jammed in mesh with the flywheel. Check by turning the square end of armature shaft with a spanner. This will free the pinion if it is stuck in engagement with the flywheel teeth.

13. Starter Motor - Removal and Replacement

1. Disconnect the battery earth lead from the positive terminal (negative on later models).
2. Disconnect the heavy lead to the starter motor at the solenoid terminal. (This end is much more accessible than the end fitted to the starter motor.)
3. Undo and remove the two bolts which hold the starter motor in place and withdraw it upwards.
4. Generally replacement is a straightforward reversal of the removal sequence. Check that the electrical cable is firmly attached to the starter motor terminal before fitting the starter motor in place.

14. Starter Motor - Dismantling and Reassembly

1. With the starter motor on the bench, loosen the screw on the cover band and slip the cover band off. With a piece of wire bent into the shape of a hook, lift back each of the brush springs in turn and check the movement of the brushes in their holders by pulling on the flexible connectors. If the brushes are so worn that their faces do not rest against the commutator, or if the ends of the brush leads are exposed on their working face, they must be renewed.

2. If any of the brushes tend to stick in their holders then wash them with a petrol moistened cloth and, if necessary, lightly polish the sides of the brush with a very fine file, until the brushes move quite freely in their holders.
3. If the surface of the commutator is dirty or blackened, clean it with a petrol dampened rag. Secure the starter motor in a vice and check it by connecting a heavy gauge cable between the starter motor terminal and a 12-volt battery.
4. Connect the cable from the other battery terminal to earth in the starter motor body. If the motor turns at high speed it is in good order.
5. If the starter motor still fails to function or if it is wished to renew the brushes, then it is necessary to further dismantle the motor.
6. Lift the brush springs with the wire hook and lift all four brushes out of their holders one at a time.
7. Remove the terminal nuts and washers from the terminal post on the commutator end bracket.
8. Unscrew the two through bolts which hold the end plates together and pull off the commutator end bracket. Also remove the driving end bracket which will come away complete with the armature.
9. At this stage if the brushes are to be renewed, their flexible connectors must be unsoldered and the connectors of new brushes soldered in their place. Check that the new brushes move freely in their holders as detailed above. If cleaning the commutator with petrol fails to remove all the burnt areas and spots, then wrap a piece of glass paper round the commutator and rotate the armature.
10 If the commutator is very badly worn, remove the drive gear as detailed in the following section. Then mount the armature in a lathe and with the lathe turning at high speed, take a very fine cut out of the commutator and finish the surface by polishing with glass paper. DO NOT UNDERCUT THE MICA INSULATORS BETWEEN THE COMMUTATOR SEGMENTS.
11 With the starter motor dismantled, test the four field coils for an open circuit. Connect a 12-volt battery with a 12-volt bulb in one of the leads between the field terminal post and the tapping point of the field coils to which the brushes are connected. An open circuit is proved by the bulb not lighting.
12 If the bulb lights, it does not necessarily mean that the field coils are in order, as there is a possibility that one of the coils will be earthed to the starter yoke or pole shoes. To check this, remove the lead from the brush connector and place it against a clean portion of the starter yoke. If the bulb lights the field coils are earthing. Replacement of the field coils calls for the use of a wheel operated screw driver, a soldering iron, caulking and riveting operations and is beyond the scope of the majority of owners. The starter yoke should be taken to a reputable electrical engineering works for new field coils to be fitted. Alternatively, purchase an exchange Lucas starter motor.
13 If the armature is damaged this will be evident after visual inspection. Look for signs of burning, discolouration, and for conductors that have lifted away from the commutator. Reassembly is a straightforward reversal of the dismantling procedure.

15. Starter Motor Drive - General Description

1. The starter motor drive is of the outboard type. When the starter motor is operated the pinion moves into contact with the flywheel gear ring by moving in towards the starter motor.
2. If the engine kicks back, or the pinion fails to engage with the flywheel gear ring when the starter motor is

actuated no undue strain is placed on the armature shaft, as the pinion sleeve disengages from the pinion and turns independently.

3. Unfortunately the starter drive assembly cannot be dismantled. If and when necessary the complete barrel assembly and screwed sleeve must be renewed.

16. Starter Motor Bushes - Inspection, Removal and Replacement

1. With the starter motor stripped down check the condition of the bushes. They should be renewed when they are sufficiently worn to allow visible side movement of the armature shaft.

2. The old bushes are simply driven out with a suitable drift and the new bushes inserted by the same method. As the bearings are of the phospher bronze type it is essential that they are allowed to stand in S.A.E. 30 engine oil for at least 24 hours before fitment.

17. Control Box - General Description

The control box comprises the voltage regulator and the cut-out. The voltage regulator controls the output from the dynamo depending on the state of the battery and the demands of the electrical equipment and ensures that the battery is not overcharged. The cut-out is really an automatic switch and connects the dynamo to the battery when the dynamo is turning fast enough to produce a charge. Similarly it disconnects the battery from the dynamo when the engine is idling or stationary so that the battery does not discharge through the dynamo.

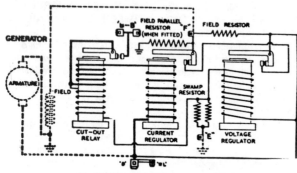

Fig. 9.6. Control box internal wiring diagram.

18. Cut-Out and Regulator Contacts - Maintenance

1. Every 10,000 miles check the cut-out and regulator contacts. If they are dirty or rough or burnt, place a piece of fine glass paper (DO NOT USE EMERY PAPER OR CARBORUNDUM PAPER) between the cut-out contacts, close them manually and draw the glass paper through several times.

2. Clean the regulator contacts in exactly the same way, but use emery or carborundum paper and not glass paper. Carefully clean both sets of contacts from all traces of dust with a rag moistened in methylated spirits.

19. Regulator Adjustment

1. If the battery is being undercharged check that the fan belt is not slipping and the dynamo is producing its correct output. Check the battery lead terminals for secureness on their posts. If the battery is being overcharged this points fairly definitely to an incorrectly set regulator.

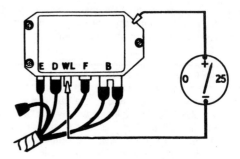

Fig. 9.7. Checking cut in voltage of the regulator.

2. Checking the action of the regulator and cut-out is not difficult but must be completed as quickly as possible (NOT more than 30 seconds for each test) to avoid errors caused by heat of the coils. Essential test equipment comprises a 0-20 volt voltmeter and a moving coil -40 to +40 amp ammeter and an air temperature gauge. Also required is a special adjusting tool illustrated in Fig. 9.8.

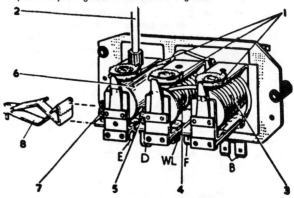

Fig. 9.8. THE LUCAS RB 340 CONTROL BOX
WITH THE COVER REMOVED

1 Adjustment cams	5 Current regulator contacts
2 Tool for setting adjustment	6 Voltage regulator
3 Cut-out relay	7 Voltage regulator contacts
4 Current regulator	8 Clip to close points manually

3. The regulator portion of the three bobbin type control box comprises the voltage regulator and the current regulator. The third bobbin at the 'B' terminal end is the cut-out.

4. To test the regulator take off the control box cover and slip a piece of thin card between the cut-out points. Connect the voltmeter between control box terminal 'D' and a good earth. Start and run the engine at about 3,000 r.p.m. When a steady reading on the voltmeter should be given as shown in Table A.

Table A

Air Temperature		Type RB 340 Open Circuit Voltage
10°C or 50°F	... ...	14.9 to 15.5
20°C or 68°F	... ...	14.7 to 15.3
30°C or 86°F	... ...	14.5 to 15.1
40°C or 104°F	... ...	14.3 to 14.9

5. If the reading fluctuates by more than 0.3 volts then it is likely that the contact points are dirty. If the reading is steady but incorrect turn the voltage adjustment cam clockwise with the special Lucas tool to increase the settings and anticlockwise to lower it.

6. Stop the engine and then restart it gradually increasing the speed. If the voltage continues to rise with a rise in engine speed this indicates short circuited or fused points or a faulty magnet coil. If this is the case the only remedy

is to fit an exchange control box.

7. The dynamo should be able to provide 22 amps at 4,500 r.p.m. irrespective of the state of the battery.

8. To test the dynamo output take off the control box cover, and short out the voltage regulator contacts by holding them together with a bulldog clip.

9. Pull off the Lucar connectors from the control box terminals 'B' and connect an ammeter reading to 40 amps to the two cables just disconnected and to ONE of the 'B' Lucar connectors.

10 Turn on all the lights and other electrical equipment and start the engine. At about 4,500 r.p.m the dynamo should be giving between 21 and 23 amps as recorded on the ammeter. If the ammeter needle flickers it is likely that the contact points are firty.

11 To increase the current turn the cam on top of the current regulator clockwise, and to lower it, anti-clockwise.

20. Cut-Out Adjustment

1. Check the voltage required to operate the cut-out by connecting a voltmeter between the control box terminal 'WL' and a good earth. Remove the control box cover, start the engine and gradually increase its speed until the cut-outs close. This should occur when the reading is between 12.7 to 13.3 volts.

2. If the reading is outside these limits turn the adjusting cam on the cut-out relay (see Fig. 9.9.) a fraction at a time clockwise to raise the voltage cut-in point and anti-clockwise to lower it.

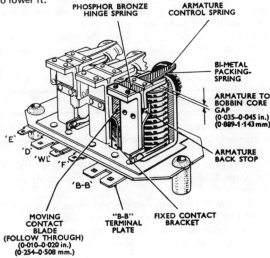

Fig. 9.9. Air gap (or mechanical settings) of cut-out relay.

3. To adjust the drop off voltage bend the fixed contact blade carefully. The adjustment to the cut-out should be completed within 30 seconds of starting the engine as otherwise heat build-up from the shunt coil will affect the readings.

4. If the cut-out fails to work, clean the contacts, and, if there is still no response, renew the cut-out and regulator unit.

21. Flasher Circuit - Fault Tracing and Rectification

1. The actual flasher unit consists of a small alloy cylindrical container positioned under the fascia.

2. If the flasher unit works twice as fast as usual when indicating either right or left this is a sure indication of a broken filament in the front or rear indicator bulb on the side operating too quickly.

3. If the external flashers are working but the internal flasher warning light has ceased to function check the filament of the warning bulb and replace as necessary.

4. With the aid of the wiring diagram check all the flasher circuit connections if a flasher bulb is sound but does not work.

5. With the ignition turned on check that current is reaching the flasher unit by connecting a voltmeter between the 'plus' or 'B' terminal and earth. If this test is positive connect the 'plus' or 'B' terminal and the 'L' terminal and operate the flasher switch. If the flasher bulb lights up the flasher unit itself is defective and must be replaced as it is not possible to dismantle and repair it.

22. Windscreen Wiper Mechanism - Maintenance

1. Renew the windscreen wiper blades at intervals of 10,000 miles, or more frequently if necessary.

2. The motor and drive assembly is packed with grease on assembly and requires no maintenance until a major overhaul takes place.

23. Windscreen Wiper Arms - Removal and Replacement

1. Before removing a wiper arm, turn the windscreen wiper switch on and off to ensure the arms are in their normal parked position parallel with the bottom of the windscreen.

2. Press the retaining clip (see Fig. 9.10.) and draw the arm off its driving spindle.

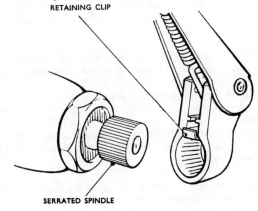

Fig. 9.10. Wiper blade and adjustment

3. When replacing an arm position it so it is in the correct relative parked position and then press the arm head onto the splined drive till the retaining clip clicks into place. NOTE: If it is wished to alter the arc of the wiper blades each serration on the wiper arm drive spindle equals 5°.

24. Windscreen Wiper Mechanism - Fault Diagnosis and Rectification

1. Should the windscreen wipers fail to park or park badly then check the limit switch on the gearbox cover.

2. Loosen the four screws which retain the gearbox cover and place the projection close to the rim of the limit switch in line with the groove in the gearbox cover.

3. Rotate the limit switch anti-clockwise 25° and tighten the four screws retaining the gearbox cover. If it is wished

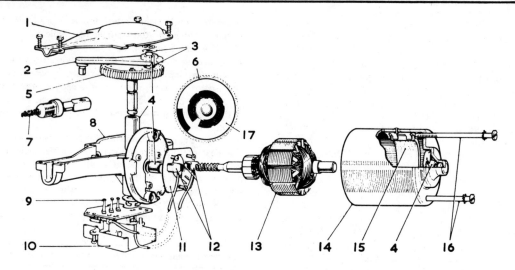

Fig. 9.11. EXPLODED VIEW OF THE 12 W WIPER MOTOR AND GEARBOX

1 Gearbox cover	6 Underside of 5	11 Brush box plate	16 Through bolts
2 Connecting rod	7 Cable rack	12 Brush boxes	17 Slip-ring
3 Steel washers	8 Gearbox	13 Armature	
4 Bronze bushes	9 Slip-ring contacts	14 Yoke	
5 Moulded gear	10 Terminal cover	15 Field magnets	

to park the windscreen wipers on the other side of the windscreen rotate the limit switch 180º clockwise. NOTE: The instructions in paragraphs 1 to 3 are for the DR3A type motor. On 12W and 14W type motors there is no provision for parking adjustment.

4. Should the windscreen wipers fail, or work very slowly, then check the current the motor is taking by connecting up a 1-20 volt voltmeter in the circuit and turning on the wiper switch. Consumption after a few seconds running should be as follows:-

a) 12W Motor; 11.5 volts. Or with an ammeter substituted for the voltmeter and the cable rack disconnected 1.4 amperes maximum.

b) DR3A Motor; 11.5 volts. Or with an ammeter substituted for the voltmeter and the cable rack disconnected 3.4 amperes maximum.

c) 14W Motor; 11.5 volts. Or with an ammeter substituted for the voltmeter and the cable rack disconnected 1.5 amperes maximum.

5. If no current is passing through check the wiring for breaks and loose connections.

6. If the wiper motor takes a very high current check the wiper blades for freedom of movement. If this is satisfactory check the gearbox cover and gear assembly for damage.

7. Check that excessive friction in the cable connecting tubes caused by too small a curvature is not the cause of the high current consumption.

8. If the motor takes a very low current ensure that the battery is fully charged. Check the brush gear after removing the commutator end bracket or cover and ensure that the brushes are bearing on the commutator. If not, check the brushes for freedom of movement and if necessary renew the tension spring.

9. Check the armature by substitution if this unit is suspected.

25. Windscreen Wiper Motor - Removal - 12W and 14W

1. The wiper motor will be found mounted on the left-hand wheel arch inside the boot. To gain access to the motor,

remove the fibreboard covering the wheel arch.

2. Disconnect the earth lead on the battery. Remove all electrical cables from their terminals on the motor.

3. Remove the 'U' clamp securing the motor to the body. Undo and remove the four screws retaining the gearbox cover and lift the cover away.

4. Lift the connecting rod from the gearbox and then disconnect the cable rack from the motor gearbox. The wiper motor can now be withdrawn.

26. Windscreen Wiper Motor - Removal - DR3A

1. The wiper motor is mounted on the left-hand wheel arch and access can be gained by removing the fibreboard wheel arch cover.

2. Disconnect the earth lead from the battery. Remove the three lucar connectors from their terminals on the motor.

3. Unscrew the retaining screws and remove the gearbox cover. Lift the connecting rod from the gearbox.

4. Disconnect the cable rack from the motor gearbox. The wiper motor can now be withdrawn.

27. Windscreen Wiper Motors - Replacement

1. Replacement is generally a reversal of the removal procedure. However, care should be taken to ensure that all earthing points are clean and that the cables are firmly held.

28. Windscreen Wiper Motor DR3A - Dismantling, Inspection and Reassembly

1. Mark the domed cover in relation to the flat gearbox lid, undo the four screws holding the gearbox lid in place and lift off the lid and domed cover.

2. Pull off the small circlip and remove the limit switch wiper (4). The connecting rod (5) and cable rack (12) can now be lifted off. Take particular note of the spacer (6) located between the final drive wheel (7) and the connect-

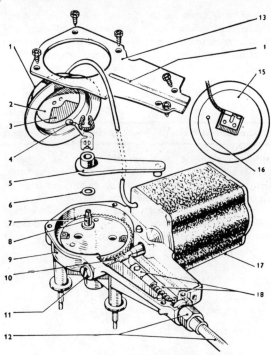

Fig. 9.12. EXPLODED VIEW OF THE DR3A WIPER MOTOR GEARBOX

1 Domed cover	11 Armature end-plate adjust-
2 Limit switch fixed contact	ing screw
3 Insulated sector	12 Protective tubing and securing
4 Limit switch moving	nut
contact	13 Gearbox cover
5 Connecting rod	14 Central groove
6 Pen-Steel washer	15 Plan view of domed cover
7 Final gear	16 Setting pip
8 Crank pin	17 Motor
9 Gearbox	18 Cross-head and guide
10 Worm gear	Channel

ing rod (5). All references are to Fig. 9.12.

3. Undo and remove the two through bolts from the commutator end cover. Pull off the end cover.

4. Lift out the brushgear retainer and then remove the brushgear. Clean the commutator and brush gear and if worn fit new brushes. The resistance between adjacent commutator segments should be .34 to .41 ohm.

5. Carefully examine the internal wiring for signs of chafing, breaks or charring which would lead to a short circuit. Insulate or replace any damaged wiring.

6. Measure the value of the field resistance which should be between 12.8 to 14 ohms. If a lower reading than this is obtained it is likely that there is a short circuit and a new field coil should be fitted.

7. Renew the gearbox gear teeth if they are damaged, chipped or worn.

8. Reassembly is a straightforward reversal of the dismantling sequence, but ensure the following items are lubricated:

a) Immerse the self aligning armature bearing in S.A.E. 20 engine oil for 24 hours before assembly.

b) Oil the armature bearings in S.A.E. 20 engine oil.

c) Soak the felt lubricator in the gearbox with S.A.E. 20 engine oil.

d) Grease generously the worm wheel bearings, cross head, guide channel, connecting rod, crankpin, worm, cable rack and wheelboxes and the final gear shaft.

29. Windscreen Wiper Motors - 12W and 14W - Dismantling and Reassembly

1. Unscrew and remove the four screws retaining the gearbox cover and remove the cover.

2. Remove the circlip and flat washer securing the connecting rod to the crankpin.

3. Remove the connecting rod noting the washer beneath it.

4. Remove the circlip and washer retaining the shaft and gear.

5. Clean any burrs from the gear shaft. Withdraw the gear. Note the washer fitted under it.

6. Mark the motor yoke and gearbox to ensure correct reassembly. Unscrew and remove the two fixing bolts. Remove the yoke and armature assembly. Take care to keep the yoke away from loose metallic pieces which will adhere to its poles.

7. Remove the brush gear and terminal and switch assembly which are interconnected by electrical cables, after removing the securing screws. Dismantling is now complete.

8. Reassembly is a reversal of the dismantling procedure.

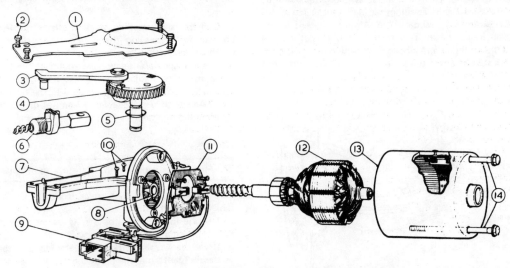

Fig. 9.13. EXPLODED VIEW OF THE 14 W WIPER MOTOR AND GEARBOX

1 Gearbox cover	5 Dished washer	9 Limit switch assembly	13 Yoke assembly
2 Gearbox cover screw	6 Cable rack and crosshead	10 Switch fixing screws	14 Yoke fixing bolts
3 Connecting rod	7 Gearbox	11 Brushgear	
4 Shaft and gear	8 Self-aligning bearing	12 Armature	

However, if either the brush gear or switch assembly requires replacing, unsolder the motor supply leaks at the brush boxes.

9. If a new switch is to be fitted to a single speed motor remove the third wire at the switch terminal. High melting point solder should be used to reconnect the leads to the brush boxes. Ensure that the leads are inside the recess in the switch unit moulding when refitting it to the gearbox.

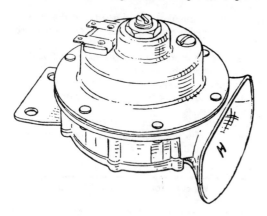

Fig. 9.14. The model 9H Lucas windtone horn.

30. Horns - Fault Tracing and Rectification

1. If a horn works badly or fails completely, first check the wiring leading to it for short circuits and loose connections. Also check that the horn is firmly secured and that there is nothing lying on the horn body.

2. The horn should never be dismantled but it is possible to adjust it. This adjustment is to compensate for wear of the moving parts only and will not affect the tone. To adjust the horn proceed as follows:-

a) Lucas 'windtone' horn, models 9H and 6H. At the rear of the horn is a small adjustment screw on the broad rim, nearly opposite the two terminals. Do not confuse this with the large screw in the centre.

b) Turn the adjustment screw anti-clockwise until the horn just fails to sound. Then turn the screw a quarter of a turn clockwise, which is the optimum setting.

c) Clearhooter horn, model F725. Almost adjacent to the two electrical terminals is a small screw. This should be rotated slowly in an anti-clockwise direction until the horn is restored to its correct volume of sound. NOTE: With both

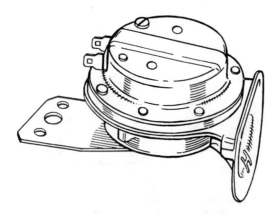

Fig. 9.15. The clear hooter model F725 horn.

types of horn if two are fitted then the horn which is not being adjusted should be disconnected while adjustment of the other takes place. The horns are located in a resonance box at the front of the car, together with the heater intake. To gain access to the interior of this box the louvred cover should be removed from beneath the front bumper after unscrewing its retaining screws.

31. Fuel Contents Gauge - Fault Tracing and Rectification

1. The fuel contents gauge can mis-read in four different ways. There can be no reading at all; there can be intermittent reading; the needle on the gauge can read too high or too low. The main components of the system comprise a fuel contents gauge, a tank sender unit, and a voltage stabiliser unit. Unfortunately, if any of these items become defective they cannot be repaired but must be exchanged for new units.

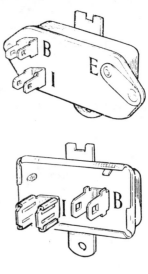

Fig. 9.16. Showing the two types of instrument voltage stabilizer in service.

2. If there is no reading at all check for loose electrical connections. Providing the wiring is in order check the components one at a time by substitution.

3. The voltage stabiliser will be found at the back of the speedometer case adjacent to the speedometer drive cable. The fuel tank sender unit is located in the top of the fuel tank. Access to the latter is by removal of the fibreboard covering the fuel tank.

32. Fuel Gauge Sender Unit - Removal and Replacement

1. Remove the fibreboard cover from the top of the fuel tank inside the boot.

2. Pull the lucar connector off its terminal on the sender unit and insulate it with tape.

3. Undo the screws which hold the sender unit to the tank.

4. Carefully lift the complete unit away making sure that the float lever is not bent or damaged in the process.

5. Replacement of the unit is a reversal of the above process. To ensure a fuel tight joint scrape both the tank and sender gauge mating flanges clean, and always use a new joint gasket, together with sealing compound.

33. Temperature Gauge - Fault Tracing and Rectification

1. If the temperature gauge fails to work or works incorrectly, it will be necessary to test for circuit continuity using an ohmmeter. Alternatively units can be tested by substitution.

2. The system comprises a temperature transmitter located in the thermostat housing, a voltage stabiliser and the temperature gauge itself.

3. None of these items can be repaired and if any are defective they must be exchanged for replacement units.

34. Headlamp Units - Removal, Replacement and Focusing - Two Headlamp System

Models with the two headlamp system are fitted with F700 Mk 10 headlamps of 7 inch diameter. The actual headlamps are of the sealed beam type and are therefore non-repairable and if defective must be replaced by a new unit.

1. Open the boot lid and remove the two screws securing each light unit bracket to the lip on the top of the front body panel.

2. Swing the lamp bracket on its hinge back into the luggage compartment. The lamp can now be pulled from its locating pin after freeing the spring clamp at the base of the lamp.

4. Withdraw the light unit after undoing the three screws securing the lamp rim. Detach the cable connector plug.

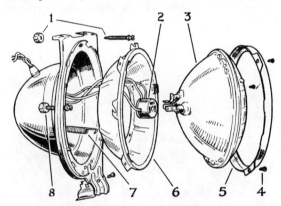

Fig. 9.17. EXPLODED VIEW OF THE F700 MK.10 HEADLAMP UNIT

1 Beam adjusting screw (Vertical)	5 Front rim
2 Cable connector plug	6 Seating rim
3 Sealed beam light unit	7 Tensioning spring
4 Rim retaining screw	8 Beam adjusting screw (Horizontal)

5. Replacement is a reversal of the removal procedure. When refitting is complete the lamp should be readjusted.

6. To adjust the lamps park the car 25 feet away from a suitable wall. It is important that the front of the car is parallel with the wall.

7. Mark the lines shown in Fig. 9.18. clearly in chalk on the wall. It is important that the lines should be as accurate as possible.

8. Switch the lamps on main beam, cover the one which is not being adjusted. Two screws are provided for lamp adjustment, one on the side of the lamp unit and the other on the top (see 1 and 8 in Fig.9.17). The too screw provides vertical adjustment while the other provides horizontal.

9. Proceed to adjust the lamp until the beams are as shown in Fig. 9.18. NOTE: It is important that the top of the concentrated area of light is just below the line 'B'. Repeat the process on the other lamp.

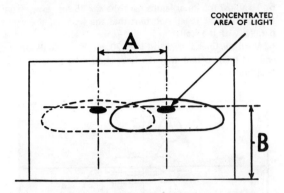

Fig. 9.18. Beam setting diagram for main beams of the two headlamp system.
'A' Distance between headlamp centres.
'B' Height of headlamp centres from the ground.

35. Headlamp Units - Removal, Replacement and Focusing - Four Headlamp System

Two pairs of headlamps of 5¾ inch diameter are used in this arrangement. The inner lamps provide main beam only at 50 watts each whilst the outer lamps provide both main beam at 37½ watts each and dipped beam at 50 watts each. Therefore, main beam from all lights totals 175 watts and dipped 100 watts. The inner and outer lamps are marked '1A' and '2A' respectively to help identification. The lamps are of the sealed beam type and are therefore non-repairable and must be replaced with new units when the need arises.

1. Unscrew and remove the screws retaining the headlamp bezel to the body. Remove the bezel.

2. Slacken the three screws securing the rim and light unit. Turn the rim in a clockwise direction until it comes free. Withdraw the rim at the same time holding the light unit on its location.

3. Remove the light unit and disconnect the cable adapter from the rear of the unit.

4. Replacement is a reversal of the removal sequence. If the adjustment screws have not been altered it should not be necessary to readjust the lamps.

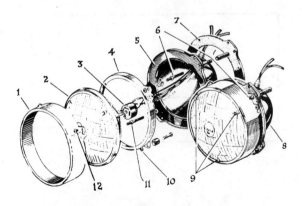

Fig. 9.19. EXPLODED VIEW OF THE F575 DUAL HEADLAMP UNITS

1 Front rim	7 Sealing gasket
2 Light unit (2A)	8 Lamp body
3 Cable adapter	9 Aiming pads
4 Seating rim	10 Retaining ring
5 Lamp body	11 Beam adjusting screw (Vertical)
6 Beam adjusting screw (Vertical)	12 Rim retaining screw

5. To adjust the inner lamps park the car 25 feet away from a suitable wall. It is important that the front of the car is parallel with the wall.

6. Mark the lines shown in Fig. 9.20. clearly in chalk on the wall. It is important that the lines should be as accurate as possible.

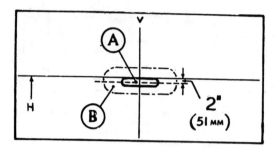

Fig. 9.20. Beam setting diagram - inner lamps. A. 'Hot spot'. B. High intensity zone H. Lamp centre-line (Horizontal). V. Lamp centre-line (Vertical)

7. Turn the light on main beam and mask the three lights which are not being adjusted. Adjust the lamp unit by means of the two adjusting screws, one at the top of the unit for vertical adjustment and another at the side for horizontal adjustment. When a light pattern as shown in Fig. 9.20. is achieved then adjustment is complete. Repeat this process on the other inner lamp.

8. To adjust the outer lamps, follow the instructions given in paragraphs 5 and 6.

9. Turn the lamps on to dipped beam and cover the three lamps which are not being adjusted. Alter the adjusting screws until the light pattern in Fig. 9.21. is achieved. Repeat this process on the other outer lamp. Adjustment is then complete.

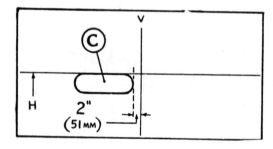

Fig. 9.21. Beam setting diagram - outer lamps (Left hand rule of the road). C. High intensity zone. H. Lamp centre-line (Horizontal). V. Lamp centre-line (Vertical).

10 For left-hand drive cars and right-hand drive cars used abroad, inner lamp adjustment is exactly the same. However, the outer lamps should be adjusted until the beams are as shown in Fig. 9.22. Adjustment procedure is exactly the same as described.

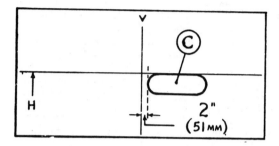

Fig. 9.22. Beam setting diagram - outer lamps (Right hand rule of the road)

36. Front, Side and Flasher Lamps - Bulbs - Removal and Replacement

1. Remove the two screws holding the lamp lens to the body. Remove the lens and gasket.

2. The defective bulb can now be removed by a single push and twist action.

3. Replacement is a reversal of the removal procedure. However, ensure the bulb is firmly located before replacing the lens.

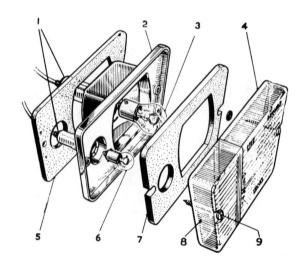

Fig. 9.23. EXPLODED VIEW OF THE L717 SIDE AND FLASHER LAMP UNIT - L.H.

1 Bulb holders
2 Diecast metal lamp body
3 Flasher bulb (single filament)
4 Flasher lens portion (amber)
5 Rubber mounting gasket
6 Side lamp bulb (single filament)
7 Rubber lens seal
8 Side lamp lens portion (clear)
9 Lens fixing screw

37. Stop/Tail and Rear Flasher Bulbs - Removal and Replacement

1. Unscrew and remove the two screws which retain the appropriate lens. Remove the lens.

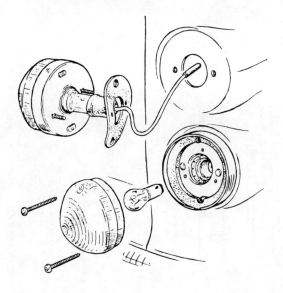

Fig. 9.24. Exploded view of the stop/tail and rear flasher lamps.

2. The bulb can be removed by a single push and twist action.

3. Replacement is a reversal of the removal procedure. However, check that the bulb is firmly located before replacing the lens.

38. Rear Number Plate Lamp Bulb - Removal and Replacement

1. Remove the two screws retaining the domed glass lens. Remove the lens.

2. The bulb can now be removed by a single push and twist action.

3. Replacement is a reversal of the removal procedure. However, ensure that the bulb is firmly located before replacing the lens.

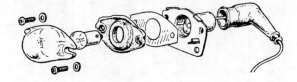

Fig. 9.25. Exploded view of the rear number plate lamp.

39. Panel and Warning Light Bulb - Removal and Replacement

1. Disconnect the earth lead from the battery.

2. The bulbs are accessible for renewal without removing the instrument panel. Tilt the bulbholder sideways and withdraw it from the rear of the instrument.

3. Remove the faulty bulb from the holder and fit the new bulb in its place.

4. Refit the bulb holder and reconnect the battery.

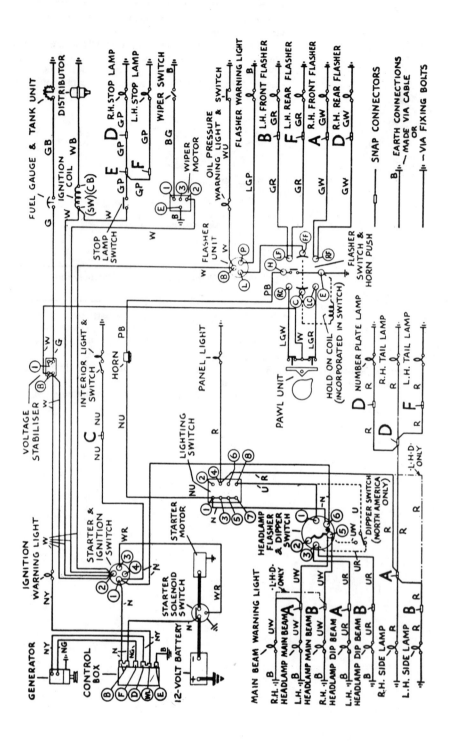

IMP Mk.I WIRING DIAGRAM

COLOUR CODE

R. red. W. white. Y. yellow. N. brown. G. green. U. blue. P. purple. B. black. L.G. light green.

SNAP CONNECTOR LOCATIONS

A—On right-hand front wing valance beneath glass-fibre moulding   C—Above parcel shelf on extreme right-hand side   E—In engine compartment, central above power unit

B—On left-hand front wing valance beneath glass-fibre moulding   D—In engine compartment at right-hand side   F—In engine compartment at left-hand side

NOTE: Combined binnacle-mounted headlamp flasher and dipper switch is replaced by a floor-mounted dipper switch for North America export. In this instance, the UW and UR cables from the headlamps which are normally connected to the headlamp flasher and dipping switch, are joined by in-line connectors and the N leads which connect at terminal six of this same switch, are deleted.

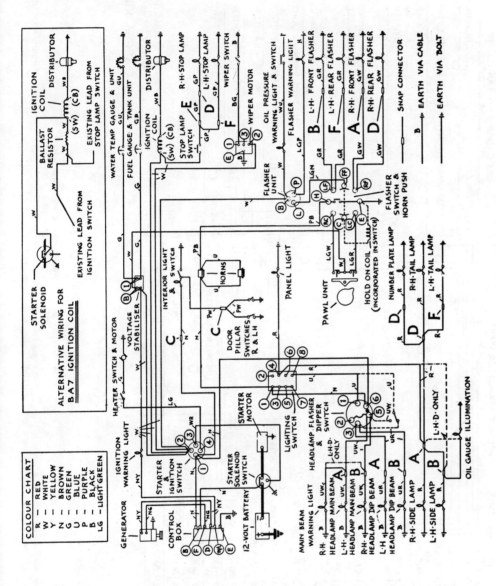

CHAMOIS Mk.I WIRING DIAGRAM
SNAP CONNECTOR LOCATIONS

A—On right-hand front wing valance beneath glass-fibre moulding   C—Above parcel shelf on extreme right-hand side   E—In engine compartment, central above power unit
B—On left-hand front wing valance beneath glass-fibre moulding   D—In engine compartment at right-hand side   F—In engine compartment at left-hand side

NOTE: Combined binnacle-mounted headlamp flasher and dipper switch is replaced by a floor-mounted dipper switch for North America export. In this instance, the UW and UR cables from the headlamps which
are normally connected to the headlamp flasher and dipping switch, are joined by in-line connectors and the N leads which connect at terminal six of this same switch, are deleted.

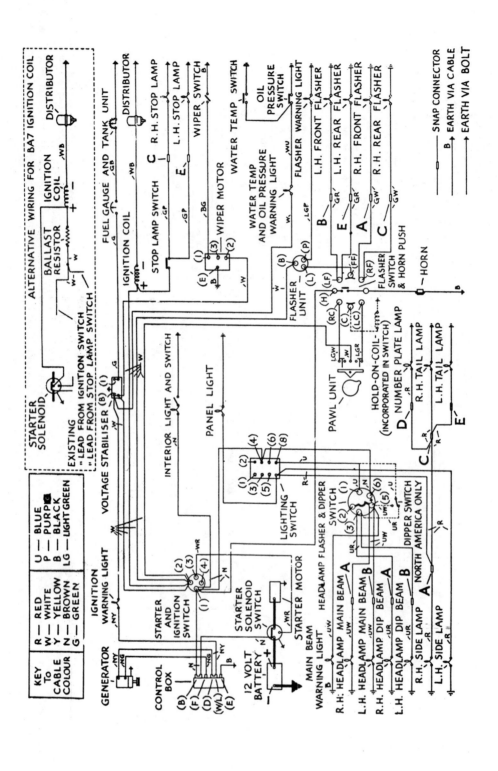

IMP DELUXE Mk. II. IMP BASIC Mk.II WIRING DIAGRAM
SNAP CONNECTOR LOCATIONS

A—On right-hand front wing valance beneath glass-fibre moulding
B—On left-hand front wing valance beneath glass-fibre moulding

C—In engine compartment at right-hand side
D—Central in engine compartment lid

E—In engine compartment at left-hand side

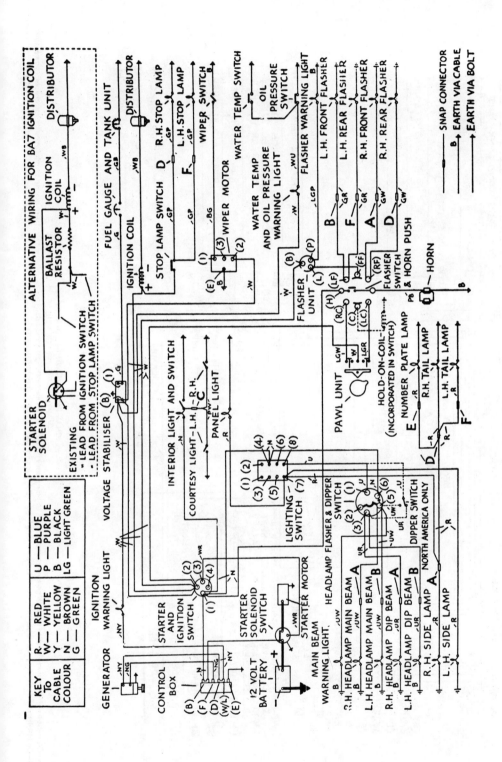

IMP SUPER Mk.II WIRING DIAGRAM
SNAP CONNECTOR LOCATIONS

A—On right-hand front wing valance beneath glass-fibre moulding
B—On left-hand front wing valance beneath glass-fibre moulding

C—Above parcel shelf on extreme right-hand side
D—In engine compartment at right-hand side

E—Central in engine compartment lid
F—In engine compartment at left-hand side

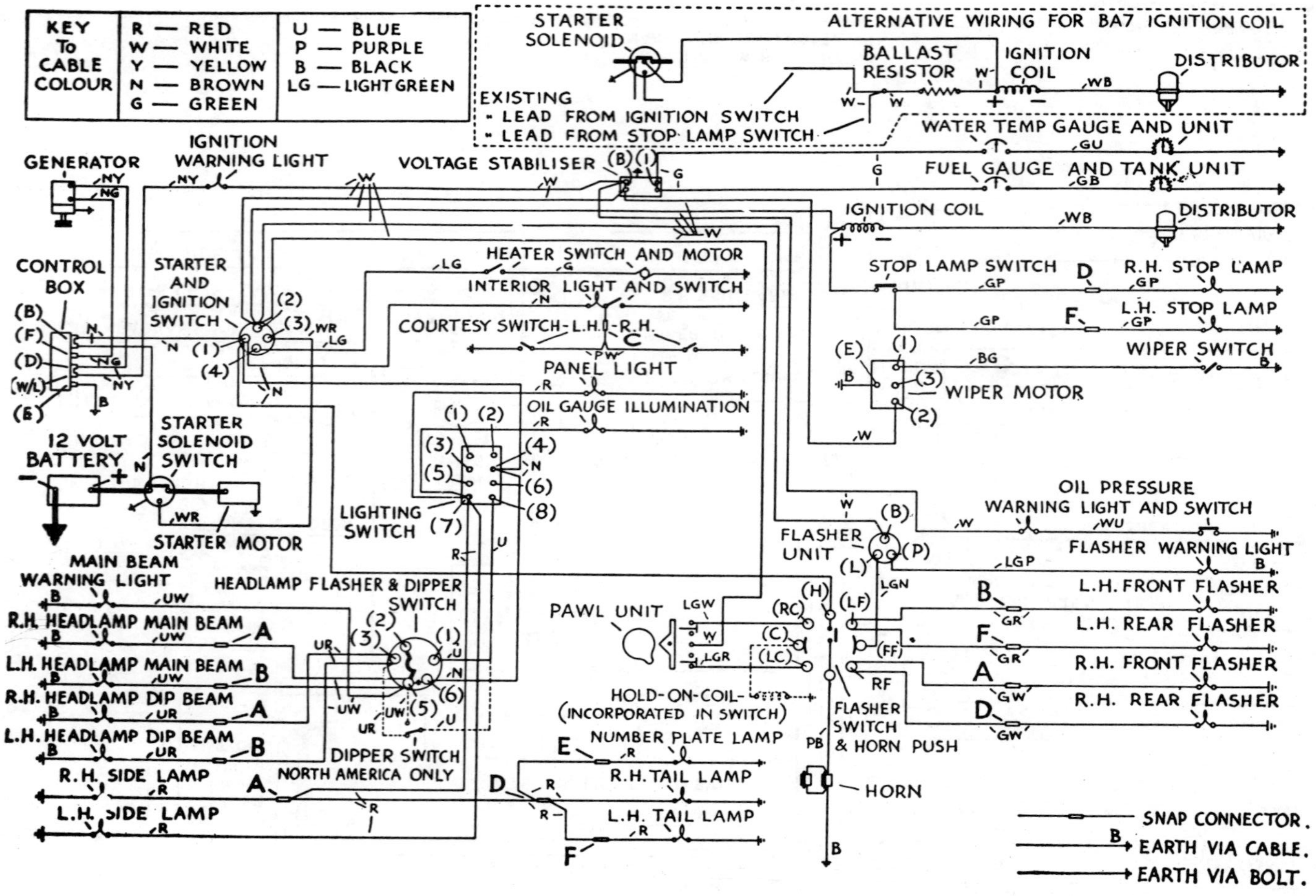

CHAMOIS Mk. II WIRING DIAGRAM
SNAP CONNECTOR LOCATIONS

KEY To CABLE COLOUR		
R — RED	U — BLUE	
W — WHITE	P — PURPLE	
Y — YELLOW	B — BLACK	
N — BROWN	LG — LIGHT GREEN	
G — GREEN		

ALTERNATIVE WIRING FOR BA7 IGNITION COIL

BALLAST RESISTOR
IGNITION COIL
DISTRIBUTOR

EXISTING
• LEAD FROM IGNITION SWITCH
• LEAD FROM STOP LAMP SWITCH

STARTER SOLENOID

WATER TEMP GAUGE AND UNIT
FUEL GAUGE AND TANK UNIT
IGNITION COIL
DISTRIBUTOR
STOP LAMP SWITCH
R.H. STOP LAMP
L.H. STOP LAMP
WIPER SWITCH
WIPER MOTOR

OIL PRESSURE WARNING LIGHT AND SWITCH
FLASHER WARNING LIGHT
L.H. FRONT FLASHER
L.H. REAR FLASHER
R.H. FRONT FLASHER
R.H. REAR FLASHER
FLASHER UNIT
FLASHER SWITCH & HORN PUSH
HORN
HOLD-ON-COIL (INCORPORATED IN SWITCH)
PAWL UNIT
NUMBER PLATE LAMP
R.H. TAIL LAMP
L.H. TAIL LAMP

IGNITION WARNING LIGHT
VOLTAGE STABILISER
HEATER SWITCH AND MOTOR
INTERIOR LIGHT AND SWITCH
COURTESY SWITCH—L.H. & R.H.
PANEL LIGHT
OIL GAUGE ILLUMINATION
LIGHTING SWITCH

HEADLAMP FLASHER & DIPPER SWITCH
DIPPER SWITCH
NORTH AMERICA ONLY

GENERATOR
CONTROL BOX
STARTER AND IGNITION SWITCH
STARTER SOLENOID SWITCH
STARTER MOTOR
12 VOLT BATTERY

MAIN BEAM WARNING LIGHT
R.H. HEADLAMP MAIN BEAM
L.H. HEADLAMP MAIN BEAM
R.H. HEADLAMP DIP BEAM
L.H. HEADLAMP DIP BEAM
R.H. SIDE LAMP
L.H. SIDE LAMP

— SNAP CONNECTOR.
— EARTH VIA CABLE.
— EARTH VIA BOLT.

A—On right-hand front wing valance beneath glass-fibre moulding
B—On left-hand front wing valance beneath glass-fibre moulding
C—Above parcel shelf on extreme right-hand side
D—In engine compartment at right-hand side
E—In engine compartment, central above power unit
F—In engine compartment at left-hand side

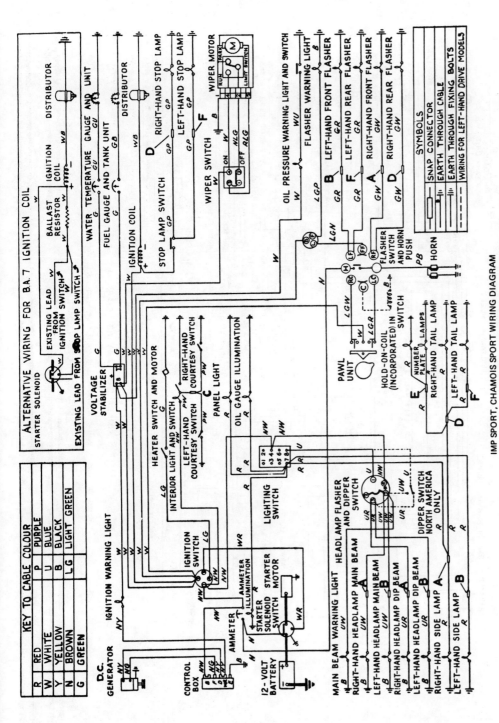

IMP SPORT, CHAMOIS SPORT WIRING DIAGRAM

COLOUR CODE

R. red. W. white. Y. yellow. N. brown. G. green. U. blue. P. purple. B. black. L.G. light green

SNAP CONNECTOR LOCATIONS

A—On right-hand front wing valance beneath glass-fibre moulding
B—On left-hand front wing valance beneath glass-fibre moulding

C—Above parcel shelf on extreme right-hand side
D—In engine compartment at right-hand side

E—In engine compartment, central above power unit
F—In engine compartment at left-hand side

NOTE: Combined headlamp flasher and dipper switch is replaced by a single dipper switch for North America export with cables UR and UW joined by an in-line connector. Connections to terminals 3 and 5 on the headlamp flash-and-dip switch are reversed for all left-hand-drive export except North America and Finland, and foot dip-lead 'N' from lighting switch terminal 4 to headlamp flash switch terminal 6 deleted.

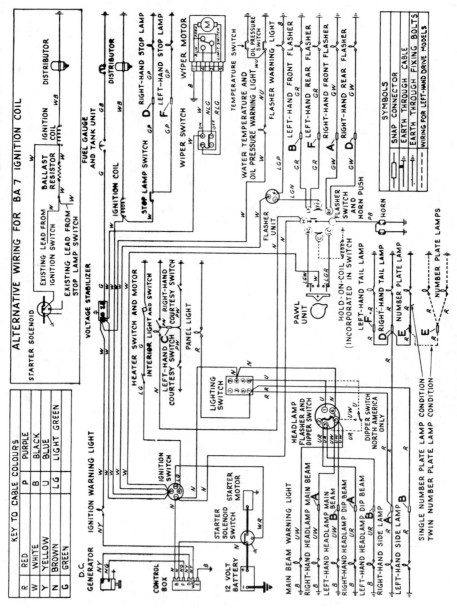

ALTERNATIVE WIRING FOR BA7 IGNITION COIL

IMP CALIFORNIAN WIRING DIAGRAM
COLOUR CODE
R. red. W. white. Y. yellow. N. brown. G. green. U. blue. P. purple. B. black. L.G. light green

SNAP CONNECTOR LOCATIONS

A—On right-hand front wing valance beneath glass-fibre moulding
B—On left-hand front wing valance beneath glass-fibre moulding

C—Above parcel shelf on extreme right-hand side
D—In engine compartment at right-hand side

D—In engine compartment, central above power unit
F—In engine compartment at left-hand side

NOTE: Combined headlamp flasher and dipper switch is replaced by a single dipper switch for North America export with cables UR and UW joined by an in-line connector. Connections to terminals 3 and 5 on the **headlamp flash-and-dip switch** are reversed for all left-hand-drive export except North America and Finland, and foot dip-lead 'N' from lighting switch terminal 4 to headlamp flash switch terminal 6 deleted.

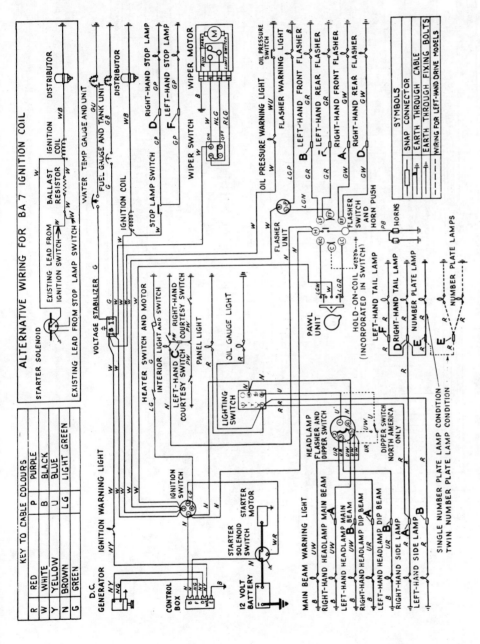

CHAMOIS COUPE WIRING DIAGRAM

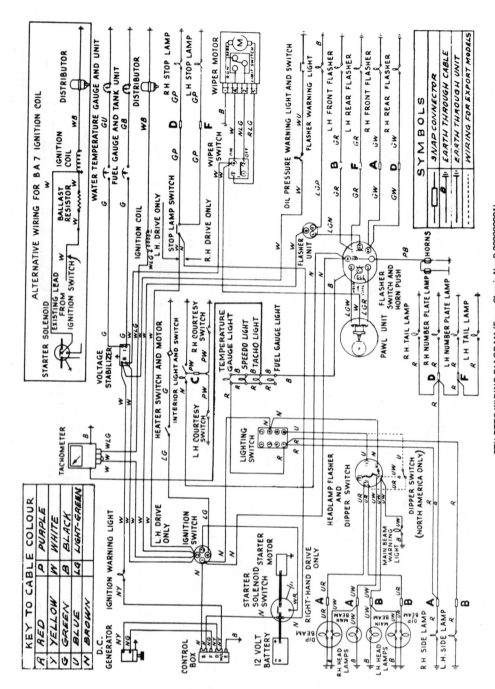

STILETTO WIRING DIAGRAM (From Chassis No. B.3020000001)
SNAP CONNECTOR LOCATIONS

A—On right-hand front wing valance beneath glass-fibre moulding
B—On left-hand front wing valance beneath glass-fibre moulding
C—Behind fascia at extreme right-hand side

D—In engine compartment at right-hand side
E—In engine compartment at left-hand side

F—In luggage compartment at front near blower
G—At door pillar switch

NOTE: Cables 'UR' and 'UW' to terminals 3 and 5 respectively on headlamp flash-and-dip switch
are reverse connected for left-hand-drive cars.

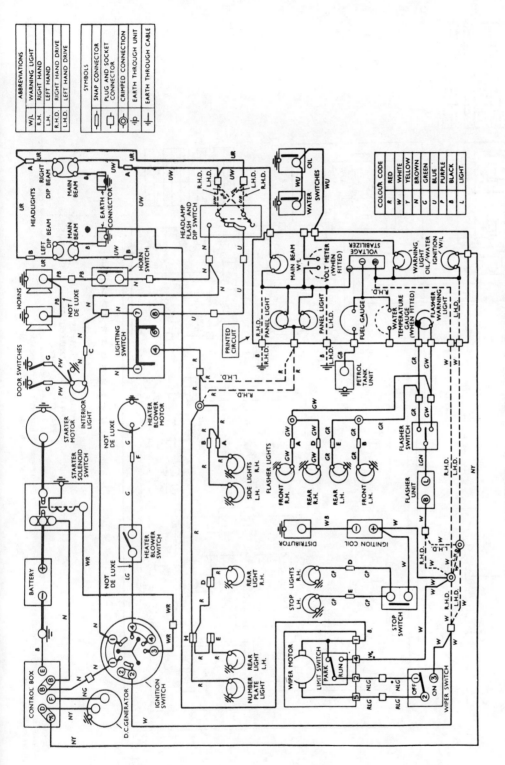

IMP DELUXE, IMP SUPER AND IMP CALIFORNIAN

(From chassis no. B.413000001 (Deluxe), 443000001 (Super), B.402000001 (Californian))

SNAP CONNECTOR LOCATIONS

A—On right-hand front wing valance beneath glass-fibre moulding

B—On left-hand front wing valance beneath glass-fibre moulding

C—Behind fascia at extreme right-hand side

D—In engine compartment at right-hand side

E—In engine compartment at left-hand side

F—In luggage compartment at front near blower

G—At door pillar switch

H—In engine compartment at right-hand side near hinge

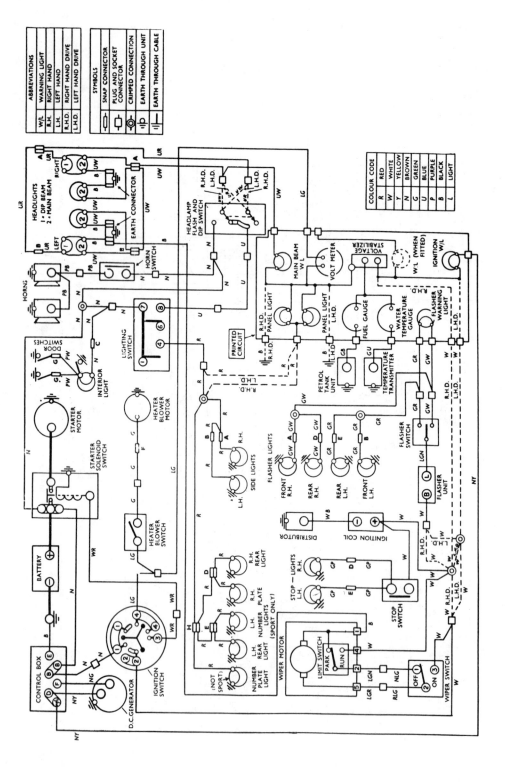

CHAMOIS SALOON, CHAMOIS COUPE, CHAMOIS SPORT WIRING DIAGRAM
(From chassis no. B.733000001 (Saloon) B.722000001 (Coupe), B.793000001 (Sport))

SNAP CONNECTOR LOCATIONS

A—On right-hand front wing valance beneath glass-fibre moulding
B—On left-hand front wing valance beneath glass-fibre moulding
C—Behind fascia at extreme right-hand side

D—In engine compartment at right-hand side
E—In engine compartment at left-hand side
F—In luggage compartment at front near blower

G—At door pillar switch
H—In engine compartment at right-hand side near hinge

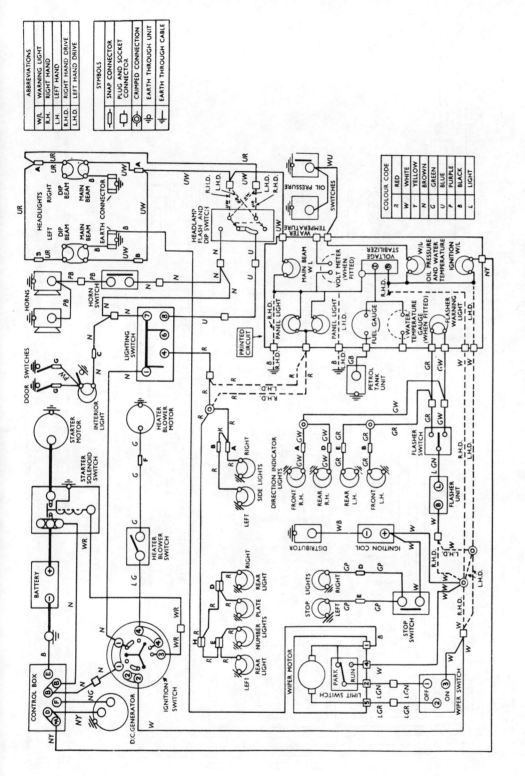

IMP SPORT WIRING DIAGRAM (From Chassis No. B.493000001)

SNAP CONNECTOR LOCATIONS

A—On right-hand front wing valance beneath glass-fibre moulding
B—On left-hand front wing valance beneath glass-fibre moulding
C—Behind fascia at extreme right-hand side

D—In engine compartment at right-hand side
E—In engine compartment at left-hand side
F—In luggage compartment at front near blower

G—At door pillar switch
H—In engine compartment at right-hand side near hinge

ABBREVIATIONS	
W/L	WARNING LIGHT
R.H.	RIGHT HAND
L.H.	LEFT HAND
R.H.D.	RIGHT HAND DRIVE
L.H.D.	LEFT HAND DRIVE

SYMBOLS	
	SNAP CONNECTOR
	PLUG AND SOCKET CONNECTOR
	CRIMPED CONNECTION
	EARTH THROUGH UNIT
	EARTH THROUGH CABLE

COLOUR CODE	
R	RED
W	WHITE
Y	YELLOW
N	BROWN
G	GREEN
U	BLUE
P	PURPLE
B	BLACK
L	LIGHT

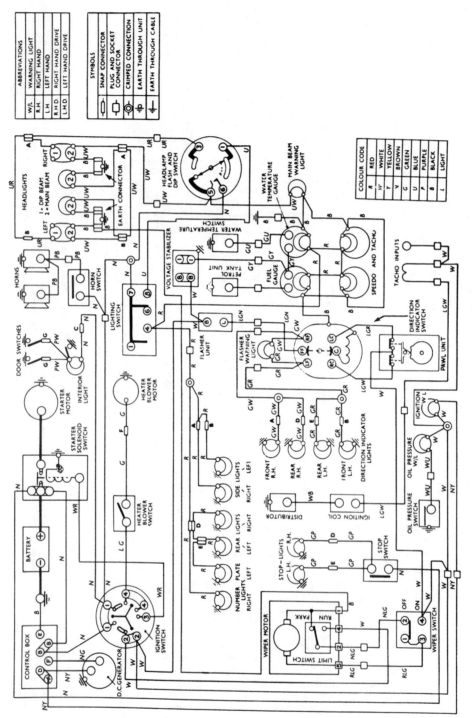

STILLETTO WIRING DIAGRAM (up to Chassis No. B.3020000001)

COLOUR CODE

R. red. W. white. Y. yellow. N. brown.. G. green. U. blue. P. purple. B. black. L.G. light green

A—On right-hand front wing valance beneath glass-fibre moulding
B—On left-hand front wing valance beneath glass-fibre moulding

C—Above parcel shelf on extreme right-hand side
D—In engine compartment at right-hand side

SNAP CONNECTOR LOCATIONS

E—In engine compartment, central above power unit
F—In engine compartment at left-hand side

NOTE: Combined headlamp flasher and dipper switch is replaced by a single dipper switch for North America export with cables UR and UW joined by an in-line connector. Connections to terminals 3 and 5 on the headlamp flash-and-dip switch are reversed for all left-hand-drive export except North America and Finland, and foot dip-lead 'N' from lighting switch terminal 4 to headlamp flash switch terminal 6 deleted

Cause	Trouble	Remedy
SYMPTOM: STARTER MOTOR FAILS TO TURN ENGINE		
No electricity at starter motor	Battery discharged	Charge battery.
	Battery defective internally	Fit new battery.
	Battery terminal leads loose or earth lead not securely attached to body	Check and tighten leads.
	Loose or broken connections in starter motor circuit	Check all connections and tighten any that are loose.
	Starter motor switch or solenoid faulty	Test and replace faulty components with new.
Electricity at starter motor: faulty motor	Starter motor pinion jammed in mesh with flywheel gear ring	Disengage pinion by turning squared end of armature shaft.
	Starter brushes badly worn, sticking, or brush wires loose	Examine brushes, replace as necessary, tighten down brush wires.
	Commutator dirty, worn, or burnt	Clean commutator, as recommended.
	Starter motor armature faulty	Overhaul starter motor, fit new armature.
	Field coils earthed	Overhaul starter motor.
SYMPTOM: STARTER MOTOR TURNS ENGINE VERY SLOWLY		
Electrical defects	Battery in discharged condition	Charge battery.
	Starter brushes badly worn, sticking, or brush wires loose	Examine brushes, replace as necessary, tighten down brush wires.
	Loose wires in starter motor circuit	Check wiring and tighten as necessary.
SYMPTOM: STARTER MOTOR OPERATES WITHOUT TURNING ENGINE		
Dirt or oil on drive gear	Starter motor pinion sticking on the screwed sleeve	Remove starter motor, clean starter motor drive.
Mechanical damage	Pinion or flywheel gear teeth broken or worn	Fit new gear ring to flywheel, and new pinion to starter motor drive.
SYMPTOM: STARTER MOTOR NOISY OR EXCESSIVELY ROUGH ENGAGEMENT		
Lack of attention or mechanical damage	Pinion or flywheel gear teeth broken or worn	Fit new gear teeth to flywheel, or new pinion to starter motor drive.
	Starter drive main spring broken	Dismantle and fit new main spring.
	Starter motor retaining bolts loose	Tighten starter motor securing bolts. Fit new spring washer if necessary.
SYMPTOM: BATTERY WILL NOT HOLD CHARGE FOR MORE THAN A FEW DAYS		
Wear or damage	Battery defective internally	Remove and fit new battery.
	Electrolyte level too low or electrolyte too weak due to leakage	Top up electrolyte level to just above plate.
	Plate separators no longer fully effective.	Remove and fit new battery.
	Battery plates severely sulphated	Remove and fit new battery.
Insufficient current flow to keep battery charged	Fan/dynamo belt slipping	Check belt for wear, replace if necessary, and tighten.
	Battery terminal connections loose or corroded	Check terminals for tightness, and remove all corrosion.
	Dynamo not charging properly	Remove and overhaul dynamo.
	Short circuit causing continual battery drain	Trace and rectify.
	Regulator unit not working correctly	Check setting, clean, and replace if defective.
SYMPTOM: IGNITION LIGHT FAILS TO GO OUT, BATTERY RUNS FLAT IN A FEW DAYS		
Dynamo not charging	Fan belt loose and slipping or broken	Check, replace, and tighten as necessary.
	Brushes worn, sticking, broken, or dirty	Examine, clean, or replace brushes as necessary.
	Brush springs weak or broken	Examine and test. Replace as necessary.
	Commutator dirty, greasy, worn, or burnt	Clean commutator as recommended.
	Armature badly worn or armature shaft bent	Fit new or reconditioned armature.
	Commutator bars shorting	Clean commutator as recommended.
	Dynamo bearings badly worn	Overhaul dynamo, fit new bearings.
	Dynamo field coils burnt, open, or shorted	Remove and fit rebuilt dynamo.

Cause	Trouble	Remedy
	Commutator worn	Turn down on lathe or renew.
	Pole pieces very loose	Strip and overhaul dynamo. Tighten pole pieces.
Regulator or cut-out fails to work correctly	Regulator incorrectly set	Adjust regulator correctly.
	Cut-out incorrectly set	Adjust cut-out correctly.
	Open circuit in wiring of cut-out and regulator unit	Remove, examine, and renew as necessary.

Failure of individual electrical equipment to function correctly is dealt with alphabetically, item by item, under the headings listed below:

FUEL GAUGE

Cause	Trouble	Remedy
Fuel gauge gives no reading	Fuel tank empty!	Refill fuel tank
	Electric cable between tank sender unit and gauge earthed or loose	Check cable for earthing and joints for tightness.
	Fuel gauge case not earthed	Ensure case is well earthed.
	Fuel gauge supply cable interrupted	Check and replace cable if necessary.
	Fuel gauge unit broken	Replace fuel gauge.
Fuel gauge registers full all the time	Electric cable between tank unit and gauge broken or disconnected	Check over cable and repair as necessary.

HORN

Cause	Trouble	Remedy
Horn operates all the time	Horn push either earthed or stuck down	Disconnect battery earth. Check and rectify source of trouble.
	Horn cable to horn pushed earthed	Disconnect battery earth. Check and rectify source of trouble.
Horn fails to operate	Cable or cable connection loose, broken or disconnected	Check all connections for tightness and cables for breaks.
	Horn has an internal fault	Remove and overhaul horn.
Horn emits intermittent or unsatisfactory noise	Cable connections loose	Check and tighten all connections.
	Horn incorrectly adjusted	Adjust horn until best note obtained.

LIGHTS

Cause	Trouble	Remedy
Lights do not come on	If engine not running, battery discharged.	Push-start car, charge battery.
	Light bulb filament burnt out or bulbs broken	Test bulbs in live bulb holders.
	Wire connections loose, disconnected or broken	Check all connections for tightness and wire cable for breaks.
	Light switch shorting or otherwise faulty	By-pass light switch to ascertain if fault is in switch and fit new switch as appropriate.
Lights come on but fade out	If engine not running battery discharged	Push-start car, and charge battery.
	Light bulb filament burnt out or bulbs broken	Test bulbs in live bulb holder.
	Wire connections loose, disconnected or broken	Check all connections for tightness and wire cable for breaks.
	Light switch shorting or otherwise faulty	By-pass light switch to ascertain if fault is in switch and fit new switch as appropriate.
Lights come on but fade out	If engine not running battery discharged	Push-start car, and charge battery.
Lights give very poor illumination	Lamp glasses dirty	Clean glasses.
	Reflector tarnished or dirty	Fit new reflectors.
	Lamps badly out of adjustment	Adjust lamps correctly.
	Incorrect bulb with too low wattage fitted	Remove bulb and replace with correct grade.
	Existing bulbs old and badly discoloured	Renew bulb units.
	Poor earth	Check earth terminals, clean and tighten as necessary.
Lights work erratically - flashing on and off, especially over bumps	Battery terminals or earth connection loose	Tighten battery terminals and earth connection.
	Lights not earthing properly	Examine and rectify.
	Contacts in light switch faulty	By-pass light switch to ascertain if fault

Cause	Trouble	Remedy
		is in switch and fit new switch as appropriate.

WIPERS

Cause	Trouble	Remedy
Wiper motor fails to work	Wire connections loose, disconnected, or broken	Check wiper wiring. Tighten loose connections.
	Brushes badly worn	Remove and fit new brushes.
	Armature worn or faulty	If electricity at wiper motor remove and overhaul and fit replacement armature.
	Field coils faulty	Purchase reconditioned wiper motor.
Wiper motor works very slowly and takes excessive current	Commutator dirty, greasy or burnt	Clean commutator thoroughly.
	Drive to wheelboxes too bent or un-lubricated	Examine drive and straighten out severe curvature. Lubricate.
	Wheelbox spindle binding or damaged	Remove, overhaul, or fit replacement.
	Armature bearings dry or unaligned	Replace with new bearings correctly aligned.
	Armature badly worn or faulty	Remove, overhaul, or fit replacement armature.
Wiper motor works slowly and takes excessive current	Brushes badly worn	Remove and fit new brushes.
	Commutator dirty, greasy, or burnt	Clean commutator thoroughly.
	Armature badly worn or faulty	Remove and overhaul armature or fit replacement.
Wiper motor works but wiper blades remain stationary	Driving cable rack disengaged or faulty	Examine and if faulty, replace.
	Wheelbox gear and spindle damaged or worn	Examine and if faulty, replace.
	Wiper motor gearbox parts badly worn	Overhaul or fit new gearbox.

Chapter 10/Suspension - Dampers - Steering

Contents

Specifications

Front Suspension

Type	Independant by coil springs and wishbones

Coil Spring Diameter:

Early saloons	3.123 in. (7.9 cm)
Later saloons and sport	3.123 in. (7.9 cm)

Coil Spring Static Laden Length (Off Car)

Early saloons	7.56 in. (19.2 cm)
Later saloons and sport	7.84 in. (19.19 cm)

Coil Spring Static Laden Load (Off Car)

Early saloons	490 lbs. (222 Kg)
Later saloons and sport	490 lbs. (222 Kg)

Coil Spring Free Length:

Early saloons	10.07 in. (25.6 cm)
Later saloons and sport	10.35 in. (26.3 cm)

Camber Angle:

Original Suspension	$5\frac{1}{2}^{o}$ Positive $\pm$ $1\frac{1}{2}^{o}$
Low pivot suspension	$2\frac{1}{4}^{o}$ Positive $\pm$ $1\frac{1}{2}^{o}$

Caster Angle   ... ... 9° Positive $\pm$ 1°

Toe-in (at wheel rim)... ... ... $1/8 \pm 1/16$ in. (3 ± 1.5 mm) or $\frac{1}{2}^{o} \pm \frac{1}{4}^{o}$

Toe-out on turns (Ackerman) ... ...   Nil

Swivel pin inclination:

Original suspension	$5\frac{1}{2}^{o} \pm 1\frac{1}{2}^{o}$
Low pivot suspension	$8\frac{3}{4}^{o} \pm 1\frac{1}{2}^{o}$

Hub bearing end float   ... ...   .002/.004 in. (.05/.10 mm)

Dampers:

Make	Woodhead Munroe
Type	Telescopic, direct acting

Mountings ... ...   Rubber bushed

Rear Suspension:
Type   ... ...   Independant coil, trailing arms

Springs, Early Saloons:
Paint colour code	Black
Outer diameter	4.02 in. (10.2 cm)
Free length	9.14 in. (23.2 cm)
Laden length	7.10 in. (18 cm)
Laden load	940 lbs. (426 Kg)

Springs, Later saloons and sport:
Paint colour code	Grey or white
Outer diameter	4.02 in. (10.2 cm)
Free length...	9.30 in. (23.6 cm)
Laden length	7.35 in. (18.7 cm)
Laden load	940 lbs. (426 Kg)

Springs, Early sport slaoons:
Paint colour code	Orange
Outer diameter	4.02 in. (10.2 cm)
Free length	9.20 in. (23.4 cm)
Laden length	7.35 in. (18.7 cm)
Laden load	940 lbs. (426 Kg)

Springs, Saloons (Heavy Duty):
Paint colour code	Blue
Outer diameter	4.02 in. (10.2 cm)
Free length	9.45 in. (24 cm)
Laden length	7.60 in. (19.3 cm)
Laden load	940 lbs. (426 Kg)

Toe-in at wheel rim ... ... $3/16 \pm 1/16$ in. (4.8 ± 1.5 mm) or $\frac{3}{4}^{o} \pm \frac{1}{4}^{o}$

Camber Angle   ... ... $\frac{1}{2}^{o}$ Positive $\pm \frac{3}{4}^{o}$

Dampers:
Make	Woodhead Munroe
Type	Telescopic, direct acting
Mountings	Rubber bushed

Steering:
Make	Engineering products
Type	Rack and pinion
Total angular movement	70°
Turns lock-to-lock	$2^{5}/8$
Adjustment:	
Pinion endfloat...	Shims
Rack and pinion (backlash)	Screw and locknut

Wheels and Tyres:
Wheels, type	Pressed steel disc, four stud fixing
Size	12L x 4J or 4½ J
Tyres, type	Tubeless
Size:	
Saloon and coupe	5.50 x 12 (Optional 155 x 12)
Sport saloon	155 x 12

	Front	Rear & Spare
Pressures	15 lbs.in.^{2}(1.1 Kg.cm^{2})	30 lbs.in.^{2}(2.1 Kg.cm^{2})
Spare wheel, location	Front luggage compartment	

Lifting jack, type   ... ...   Scissor

Jacking locations:
Front	Central, below suspension front pivots
Rear	Pegs at either end of the rear crossmember

NOTE: The tyre pressures quoted are for Dunlop C.41 or Goodyear G.8 tyres as fitted by Chrysler.
If tyres other than the above are fitted they should be inflated to the pressures recommended by their manufacturers.

Torque Wrench Settings:

King pin carrier to wishbone:		
Horizontal	74 lb.ft (10.2 Kg.m)	
Vertical	48 lb.ft (6.6 Kg.m)	
Wishbone pivot bolts	25 lb.ft (3.4 Kg.m)	
Suspension support bracket:		
Front	27 lb.ft (3.7 Kg.m)	
Rear	27 lb.ft (3.7 Kg.m)	
Road wheel nut	48 lb.ft (6.6 Kg.m)	
Shock absorber to suspension	43 lb.ft (5.9 Kg.m)	
Suspension member to body	20 lb.ft (2.7 Kg.m)	
King pin retainer nut...	6 lb.ft (.8 Kg.m)	
Front hub adjusting nut	6 lb.ft (.8 Kg.m)	
Front hub locknut	13 lb.ft (1.7 Kg.m)	
Crossmember to body	27 lb.ft (3.7 Kg.m)	
Engine mounting to crossmember	27 lb.ft (3.7 Kg.m)	
Damper to body	14 lb.ft (1.9 Kg.m)	
Damper to suspension	25 lb.ft (3.4 Kg.m)	
Suspension pivot bolts	43 lb.ft (5.9 Kg.m)	
Steering unit retaining 'U' bolts	14 lb.ft (1.9 Kg.m)	
Steering unit to track rod	37 lb.ft (5.1 Kg.m)	
Track rod ball joint	20 lb.ft (2.7 Kg.m)	
Steering arm to stub axle:		
3/8 in. U.N.F.	33 lb.ft (4.5 Kg.m)	
7/16 in. U.N.F.	47 lb.ft (6.5 Kg.m)	
Inner column pinch bolt:		
¼ in. U.N.F. (Head not marked)	8 lb.ft (1.1 Kg.m)	
¼ in. U.N.F. (Head marked with 'V')	10 lb.ft (1.4 Kg.m)	
5/16 in. U.N.F. (Through bolt)	13 lb.ft (1.7 Kg.m)	
Tie-rod to steering arm	15 lb.ft (2.1 Kg.m)	
Steering wheel to column	24 lb.ft (3.3 Kg.m)	
Road wheel nuts	47 lb.ft (6.5 Kg.m)	

1. General Description

The suspension is independent on each of the four wheels. The front suspension is of the 'swing axle' type by means of a large single wishbone to each stub axle with a coil spring mounted vertically at the outer end. The inner ends of each of the two wishbones are adjacent to each other along the centre line of the car and swivel in metalastic bushed brackets which are bolted to the underframe.

Each stub axle is held to its wishbone by a vertical swivel pin sometimes called a kingpin.

Suspension damping is provided by telescopic dampers contained in the centre of the coil springs.

Rear suspension is provided by semi-wishbone type trailing arms and coil springs. The trailing arms are supported by four pivot brackets mounted on a subframe bolted to the rear floorpan. Each of the bracket ends of the trailing arms pivots on a pressed in bush. Damping is provided by telescopic type dampers. Camber, caster and steering axis inclination angles are set during manufacture, therefore, adjustment is not necessary and is not provided for. Wheel alignment can be adjusted by altering the length of the right hand track rod.

The steering gear is of the rack and pinion type, the actual rack and pinion assembly being mounted on the rear support bracket of the front suspension.

2. Routine Maintenance

1. Very little maintenance is required as there are no greasing points in either the suspension or steering systems.
2. Every 5,000 miles check the tightness of the rack and pinion unit mounting bolts. The correct torque is given at the end of the specifications.

3. Also check the rack and pinion unit for signs of leakage. If leakage is present details for renewal of the convolute and conical rubber covers and oil replenishment are given in Sections 19 and 20.
4. The outer column fixing bolts and inner column to pinion pinch bolt should also be checked for tightness. If loose they should be tightened to the specified torque.
5. Check front and rear suspension pivot bolts and mounting to floor bolts for tightness; again, if loose tighten to the specified torque.
6. Every 30,000 miles visually inspect all the rubber bushes incorporated in the front and rear suspension for damage or deterioration. Details of bush renewal are given in Section 10.
7. Clean and repack the front hub bearings with the specified grease as described in Section 5.

3. Inspecting the Suspension, Steering and Dampers for Wear

1. To check for wear in the outer ball joints of the tie-rods place the car over a pit, or lie on the ground looking at the ball joints, and get a friend to rock the steering wheel from side to side. Wear is present if there is play in the joints.
2. To check for wear in the kingpins and wheel bearings jack up the front of the car until the wheels are clear of the ground. Hold each wheel in turn, at the top and bottom and try to rock it. If the wheel rocks continue the movement at the same time inspecting the suspension to determine where play exists.
3. If the movement occurs between the wheel and the brake backplate then providing the wheel is on tightly the hub bearings will require replacement. However, if the play is further in (i.e. behind the backplate) then it is likely that the kingpin is worn; if the movement is excessive then the kingpin should be renewed. NOTE: There should be a small

amount of play in the wheel assembly, approximately 1/32 inch at both the top and bottom of the wheel.

4. How well the dampers function can be checked by bouncing the car at each corner. After each bounce the car should return to its normal ride position within 1½ up-and-down movements. If the car continues to move up-and-down in decreasing amounts it means that the dampers are worn and must be replaced.

5. Excessive play in the steering gear will lead to wheel wobble, and can be confirmed by checking if there is any lost movement between the end of the steering column and the rack. Rack and pinion steering is normally very accurate and lost motion in the steering gear indicates a considerable mileage or lack of lubrication.

6. If backlash develops it is quite possible to take up the wear which will have occured between the teeth on the rack and the pinion by adjusting the pinion damper.

7. The outer ball joints at either end of the tie-rods are the most likely components in the suspension to wear first.

8. At the rear end, bangs, clonks and squeaks can arise from a variety of sources and to determine the exact point of trouble is not difficult as long as a methodical and thorough check is made.

9. Start by checking the trailing arm pivot bushes for play. If excessive movement is present the bushes should be replaced. The damper bushes may also have worn and should be checked by heavy bouncing.

10 Rear wheel bearings can be checked for wear by jacking up the rear of the car and grasping the top and bottom of each of the rear wheels in turn. Try rocking the wheels; if any lateral movement is apparent then in all probability the rear hub bearings are in need of renewal.

4. Front Hubs - Removal, Replacement and Adjustment

1. To remove a front hub first check the rear wheels and jack up the front of the car until the wheel to be worked on is clear of the ground. NOTE: Before jacking the car slacken the wheel retaining nuts.

2. Remove the roadwheel. Withdraw the brake drum after unscrewing the single retaining screw.

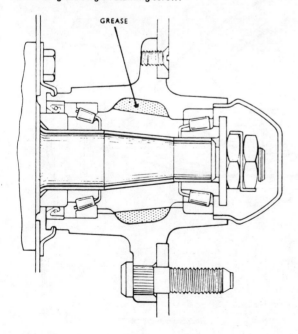

Fig. 10.1. Sectioned view of the front hub showing the correct level of grease.

3. Using a screwdriver as a lever, prise off the hub dust cap. NOTE: If the nearside hub is being removed, withdraw the speedometer cam, which will be seen protruding from the stub axle, after removing the hub dust cap.

4. Knock back the tabs of the tab washer and using a suitable spanner undo and remove the locknut from the end of the stub axle, followed by the tab washer, adjusting nut and 'D' shaped washer.

5. Grasp the hub firmly in both hands and pull it off the stub axle together with its bearings. NOTE: If the inner hub bearing is left on the stub axle it can be withdrawn using a suitable puller, or it may be possible to lever it off with a pair of screwdrivers. Great care should be taken to ensure that the backplate is not distorted if it is used as a fulcrum for the levers.

6. Replacement is a straightforward reversal of the removal procedure. However note the following points:-

a) The hub endfloat should be correctly adjusted before refitting the tab washer and locknuts.
b) Remember to refit the speedometer cam if the nearside hub was removed.
c) The hub dust cap should be empty of all grease on refitment.

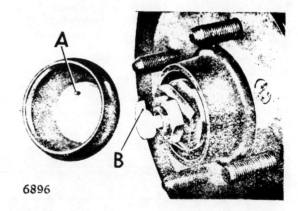

6896

Fig. 10.2. View of the front hub showing speedometer drive. A. Peg in hub dust cap. B. Speedometer cam.

7. To adjust the hub endfloat (with the wheel and brake-drum in position) pin the wheel and simultaneously tighten the hub adjusting nut to the setting given in the Specifications. Next slacken off the adjusting nut two flats. Refit the tab washer and locknut.

5. Front Hubs - Dismantling and Reassembly

1. Remove the hubs as described in the previous section.
2. Prise the oil seal at the rear of the hub out with a suitable lever. Withdraw the inner race from the inner and outer bearings on a finger.
3. The bearing outer races can be tapped out of the hub by using a narrow drift. Insert the drift through the opposite end of the hub from that of the bearing; hold the drift in contact with the rear face of the race to be removed. Then gently tap the race out of the hub.
4. All parts of the hub should be thoroughly washed in paraffin.
5. The bearings should be checked for excessive looseness in their cages and the bearing races checked for grooves or

scoring. If any part is in doubtful condition it should be re-placed. NOTE: The hub grease seal should be replaced regardless of its apparent condition.

6. Reassembly commences by packing the hubs with Castrol LM grease to the level shown in Fig. 10.1.

6. The outer bearing races can be refitted to the hub in the following manner:-

Place the race squarely on the outside of its bore. Place a block of wood over the race. Tap the block of wood with a hammer until the outside of the race is flush with the end of the hub.

7. Continue to drift the race into the hub utilising the same drift as was used to remove it. When the race contacts the internal shoulder of the hub the race is in its correct position.

8. The remaining reassembly is a simple reversal of the removal procedure. Once reassembly is complete the hub can be refitted to the stub axle as described in the previous section.

6. Front Suspension Assembly - Removal and Replacement

1. Check the rear wheels, loosen the front wheel nuts and jack up the front of the car. Support the car on sturdy supports which should bear on the outside of the floor ribs 2 to 3 ft. behind each wheel arch. Remove the jack.

2. Remove the two roadwheels. Remove the flexible pipes between the body and brake backplates on each side of the car as described in Chapter 8/8.

3. Mark the end of the inner steering column and the splined pinion of the steering unit at the point where they are joined. This will facilitate correct reassembly. Remove the pinch bolt from the clamp and separate the column from the steering unit by lifting the steering wheel about two inches.

4. Detach the speedometer cable from the rear of the near-side stub axle by removing the single screw holding the forked cable retaining plate.

5. Using suitable stands and a plank of wood passed transversely under the two wishbones, support the weight of the suspension assembly.

6. Unscrew and remove from the centre of the car just behind the front valence the four bolts and washers which hold the support bracket for the front half of the two wishbones to the underside of the car. This is done from beneath the car.

7. Inside the car, roll back the carpet from the front bulk-head. Unscrew and withdraw the four bolts and washers holding the rear edge of the wishbones rear support bracket to the floorpan. From beneath the car unscrew and remove the remaining four bracket retaining bolts on the front edge of the rear bracket. The entire weight of the suspension assembly will now be supported on the transverse plank.

8. Detach the lower ends of the dampers from the top faces of the wishbones by removing the bolt which passes through the lower eye of each damper, after undoing its retaining nut and washer.

9. It should now be possible for two strong men to take the weight of the suspension assembly, push away the support-ing blocks and carefully lower the unit, at the same time easing the speedometer cable through the left hand side of the rear member. This done the unit can be withdrawn from beneath the car.

10 Replacement is generally a reversal of the removal procedure. Note the following points:-

a) When the suspension assembly is in position beneath the car the forward edge of the rear wishbone support bracket should be attached to the car first. THIS IS ESSENTIAL. This is then followed by the rear edge of the rear support bracket and finally the front wishbone support bracket.

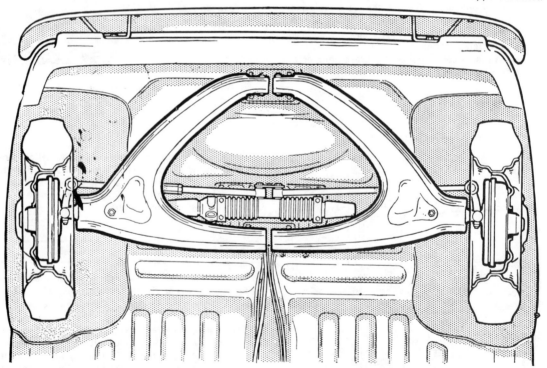

Fig. 10.3. View of the front suspension and steering mechanism from beneath the car.

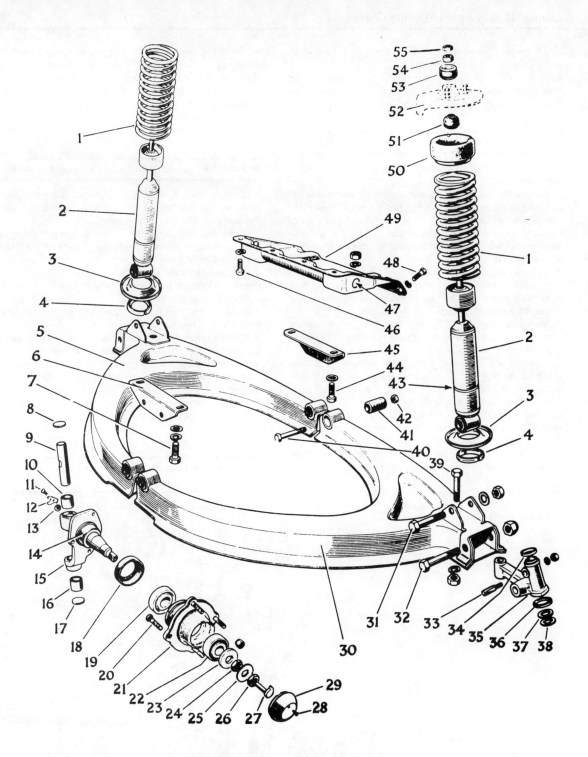

Fig. 10.4. EXPLODED VIEW OF THE FRONT SUSPENSION

1 Front Spring
2 Shock absorber
3 Lower spring seat
4 Split collets
5 Right hand wishbone
6 Rear section of front bracket
7 Front bracket bolt
8 Upper welch washer
9 King pin
10 P.T.F.E. bush bearing
11 Speedometer cable retaining screw
12 Speedometer cable retaining fork
13 Rubber washer

14 Pressed-on distance piece
15 Stub axle
16 P.T.F.E. bush bearing
17 Lower welch washer
18 Grease seal
19 Inner roller bearing
20 Wheel stud
21 Hub shell
22 Outer roller bearing
23 'D' washer
24 Adjusting nut
25 Tabwasher
26 Locknut
27 Speedometer cam
28 Speedometer driving peg
29 Hub dust cap

30 Left hand wishbone
31 Shock absorber bolt
32 Stub axle carrier bolt
33 Cotter pin
34 Small sealing ring
35 Stub axle carrier
36 Large sealing ring
37 P.T.F.E. washer
38 Bearing washer
39 Stub axle carrier bolt
40 Wishbone pivot bolt
41 Wishbone pivot bush
42 Special locking nut
43 Split collet locating groove
44 Front section bracket bolt

45 Front section of rear bracket
46 Rear bracket bolt
47 Speedometer cable aperture
48 Rear bracket bolt (inside car)
49 Rear bracket
50 Upper spring seat
51 Shock absorber bush and cup washer
52 Shock absorber upper bracket
53 Shock absorber bush and cup washers
54 Shock absorber nut
55 Shock absorber lock nut

b) Ensure that the rubber washer on the end of the speedometer outer casing is not omitted.

c) The nuts and bolts securing the wishbone support brackets and the lower ends of the dampers should NOT be finally tightened until the car is back on the ground.

7. Front Suspension Assembly - Dismantling and Reassembly

1. Remove the front suspension assembly as described in the previous section.

2. Detach the track rods from the steering arm ball joints by unscrewing each ball joint nut until it is flush with the top of the threaded ball pin. Give the nut and pin a sharp tap with a hammer. This should free the track rod. Finish unscrewing the nut from the pin and lift the track rod off the ball joint pin.

3. The steering rack unit can be removed from the wishbone rear support bracket by unscrewing and removing four nuts and washers and the two reinforcing plates and bridge pieces from the rack retaining 'U' bolts.

4. Withdraw the two 'U' bolts from the support bracket, after collecting the other two bridge pieces from beneath the rack unit.

5. Unscrew and remove the two nuts, bolts and washers, retaining the hub and kingpin assembly to the end of each wishbone. Drift the assembly out of the end of each wishbone with a suitable brass drift.

6. Unscrew and remove the four through bolts, nuts and washers, retaining the two wishbones to the front and rear support brackets. Dismantling is now complete.

7. Reassembly is a reversal of the dismantling procedure. However, the following points should be noted:-

a) The rear wishbone support bracket must be refitted so that the weld-nuts and also the heads of the wishbone pivot bolts face towards the rear of the car.

b) The four 'Nyloc' nuts from the wishbone pivot bolts should be renewed. NOTE: These nuts should NOT be fully tightened until the car is back on the ground.

c) The hub and kingpin assemblies must be refitted to the wishbones so that steering arms point forwards.

d) The 'U' bolts retaining the rack unit are left slack until the steering column has been secured to the splined shaft.

8. Front Springs and Dampers - Removal and Replacement

1. Slacken the wheel nuts and place a jack beneath the wishbone on the side of the car from which the spring/damper assembly is to be removed.

2. Raise the jack until the wheel is clear of the ground. Place a sturdy support beneath the outside of the floor rib 2 to 3 feet behind the wheel arch.

3. Remove the road wheel. NOTE: The jack must be left raised and in position beneath the wishbone.

4. Detach the damper from its top support bracket by unscrewing and removing a locknut, a second nut, rubber bush and two cup washers.

5. Gently lower the jack until the spring is no longer in a compressed condition. Unscrew and remove the nut, bolt and washer securing the damper to its lower mounting. Withdraw the spring/damper assembly from the car.

6. Replacement is a reversal of the removal procedure. NOTE: The nut and bolt retaining the damper to its bottom mounting should not be fully tightened until the car is back on the ground.

9. Kingpins and Bushes - Removal, Inspection and Replacement

Bracketed letters refer to Fig. 10.4.

1. Slacken the wheelnuts and place a jack beneath the

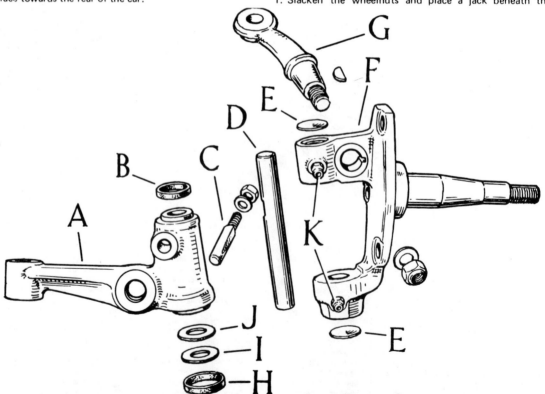

Fig. 10.5. EXPLODED VIEW OF THE KING PIN & STUB AXLE

A King pin carrier
B Small sealing ring
C Cotter Pin
D King pin
E Welch washer
F Stub axle
G Steering arm & locating key
H Large sealing ring
I Bearing Washer
J P.T.F.E. Washer
K Lubrications

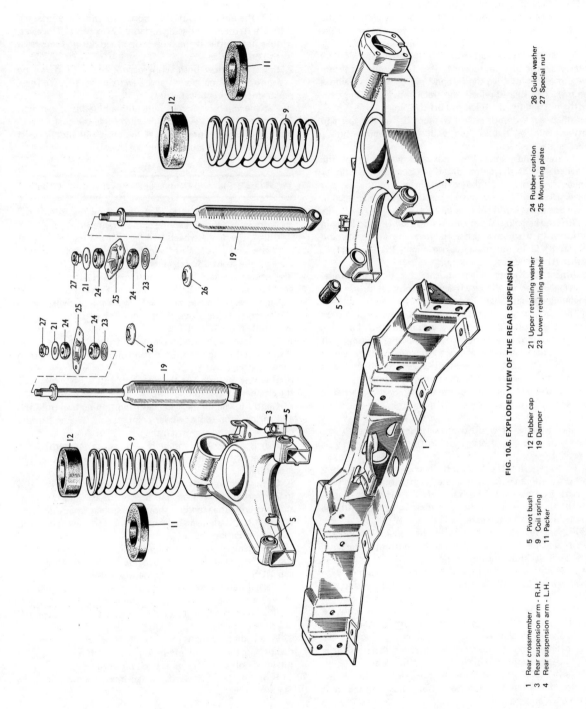

FIG. 10.6. EXPLODED VIEW OF THE REAR SUSPENSION

1	Rear crossmember	5	Pivot bush	12	Rubber cap	21	Upper retaining washer	24	Rubber cushion	26	Guide washer
3	Rear suspension arm - R.H.	9	Coil spring	19	Damper	23	Lower retaining washer	25	Mounting plate	27	Special nut
4	Rear suspension arm - L.H.	11	Packer				

wishbone on the side of the car from which the kingpin is to be removed. Raise the jack, remove the roadwheel and fit a stand for safety reasons.

2. Unscrew the single retaining screw and remove the brake drum. Withdraw the hub as described in Section 4.

3. Unscrew and remove the three nuts, bolts and washers holding the brake backplate to the stub axle. Withdraw the backplate and suspend it on a piece of wire nearby. Take care not to strain the flexible brake hose.

4. Detach the track rod from the steering arm (G) by unscrewing the ball pin nut until it is flush with the top of the threaded pin. Give the nut and pin a sharp tap with a hammer. This should release the track rod. Finish unscrewing the nut and lift the track rod off the pin.

5. Collapse the domed welch washers (E) at the top and bottom ends of the kingpin with light hammer blows. Remove the washers.

6. Unscrew and remove the nut and washer from the threaded end of the cotter pin (C). Using an old bolt or similar as a drift, drift the cotter pin out of the kingpin carrier (A). NOTE: If the cotter pin threads are damaged in the process the pin must be renewed.

7. Drift the kingpin (D) out of the stub axle (F) and kingpin carrier with a suitable drift. Remove the stub axle and collect the large and small sealing rings (H & B), P.T.F.E. washer (I) and bearing washer (J).

8. Inspect the kingpin and bushes for excessive wear, grooving or bad scratching. If any of these are present the kingpin and bushes should be renewed.

9. The kingpin bushes can be removed by clamping each bush carrier of the stub axle in a vice in turn, and drifting the bushes out of their bores with a small chisel or similar. It does not matter if the bushes are damaged, as they will be renewed. NOTE: If grease nipples (K) are fitted they should be removed before attempting to remove the bushes.

10 Refit the new bushes by clamping each bearing carrier in the vice in turn. Place the bearing squarely on top of its bore.

11 Place a block of wood over the bearing and gently tap the block with a hammer, thus drifting the bush into its bore.

12 To countersink the bush into its correct position use a soft drift with an external diameter slightly smaller than the internal diameter of the bush bore. NOTE: If grease nipples are fitted ensure that the holes in the bushes align with the nipple holes in the stub axle.

13 Fit the smaller sealing ring to the top of the kingpin carrier and the large sealing ring to the bottom. A smear of grease will facilitate this operation.

14 Liberally smear the kingpin, bushes and washers with Shell Spirax E.P. oil. Position the kingpin carrier and stub axle together.

15 Place the washers in their correct positions as shown in Fig. 10.4. NOTE: The P.T.F.E. washer must be fitted darker face downwards above the bearing washer.

16 Drift the kingpin into position, ensuring that the cotter pin flat aligns with the hole in the kingpin carrier.

17 Refit the cotter pin from the rear, drive it home and tighten the nut and washer. Paint both ends with shellac to form a water tight seal.

18 Place the new welch washers in position and secure by tapping their domed centres, taking care not to collapse the washers. Further retention can be gained by staking the stub axle flange above the washers in four positions. Paint around the periphery of the washers to obtain a water tight joint.

19 The remainder of the replacement is a reversal of the removal procedure. NOTE: When replacement is completed visit your Chrysler dealer to have the steering alignment checked.

10. 'Metalastic' Bushes - Removal and Replacement

The procedure for the removal and replacement of metalastic bushes is the same no matter from where they come on the car.

1. Drift the old bush out of its bore. This may be extremely difficult if the bush has distorted or broken up. However, it does not matter if the bush is damaged during removal as it is to be renewed.

2. Smear the new bush with soap or brake fluid (on no account use oil or grease) and also its bore. This will ease replacement a great deal.

3. Tap the new bush into its bore with a hide faced hammer. Of if possible use a vice as a press to force the bush into its bore. The latter is preferable as the bush will slide into its bore more easily if movement is continuous.

11. Rear Springs and Dampers - Removal and Replacement

1. Loosen the wheel nuts of the wheel on the side of the car from which the coil spring is to be removed.

2. Check the front wheels and jack up the rear of the car until the wheel is clear of the ground. Place sturdy supports beneath the rear body crossmember.

3. Remove the jack and re-position it beneath the trailing arm just behind the brake backplate. Raise the jack until it just contacts the trailing arm. Remove the roadwheel.

4. Disconnect the drive shaft from the rotoflex coupling as described in Chapter 7/2.

5. Disconnect the handbrake cable from the brake backplate by removing the split pin and clevis pin retaining it to the actuating arm.

6. Unscrew and remove the nut, bolt and washer retaining the damper to the trailing arm.

7. Gently lower the jack beneath the trailing arm until the coil spring is no longer under compression. The coil spring can now be withdrawn from the car.

8. If it is wished to completely remove the damper this can be achieved by removing the bolts retaining it to its top mounting.

9. Some cars were fitted with longer springs. NOTE: If a longer spring is fitted on one side of the car and the outer side has only the standard short spring then a packing piece will be fitted between the short spring and the trailing arm to equalise car height.

10 Replacement commences by fitting the rubber cap to the top of the coil spring. Although the spring is reversable the cap MUST always be fitted to the top of the spring.

11 Place the spring in its correct position. Raise the jack and at the same time ensure that the spring is correctly seated in its housing top and bottom. Check that the rubber cap has not been disturbed.

12 When the spring is sufficiently compressed refit the damper to its bottom mounting. Do not fully tighten the retaining bolt until the car is back on the ground.

14 From this point onwards, replacement is a reversal of the removal procedure.

12. Rear Suspension Assembly - Removal and Replacement

1. The following description covers the removal of a rear suspension assembly from either side of the car. Remove the coil spring as described in the previous section.

2. Remove the handbrake cable guide brackets from the trailing arms by undoing the two bolts or drilling out the hollow rivets and cutting the track weld.

3. Disconnect the flexible hose between the brake backplate

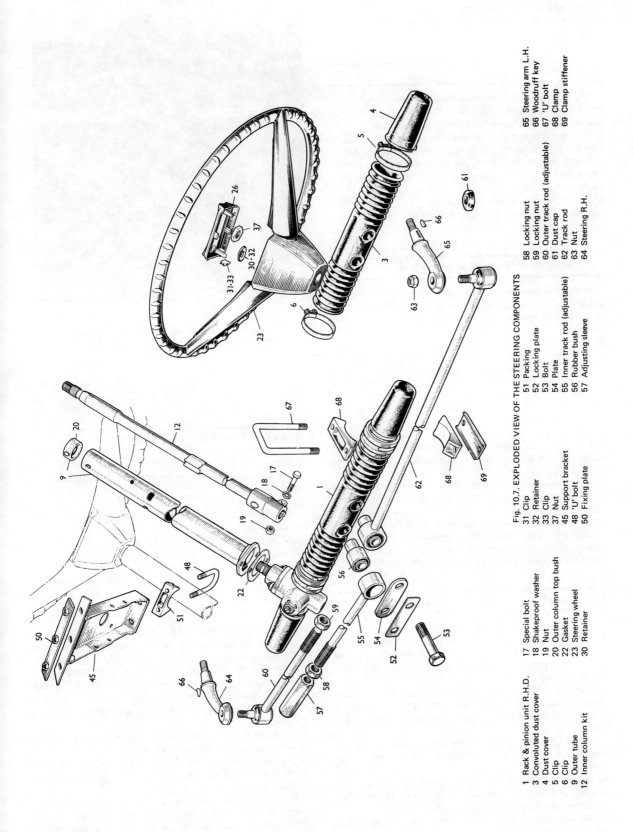

Fig. 10.7. EXPLODED VIEW OF THE STEERING COMPONENTS

1	Rack & pinion unit R.H.D.	17	Special bolt	31	Clip	51	Packing	58	Locking nut	65	Steering arm L.H.
3	Convoluted dust cover	18	Shakeproof washer	32	Retainer	52	Locking plate	59	Locking nut	66	Woodruff key
4	Dust cover	19	Nut	33	Clip	53	Bolt	60	Outer track rod (adjustable)	67	'U' bolt
5	Clip	20	Outer column top bush	37	Nut	54	Plate	61	Dust cap	68	Clamp
6	Clip	22	Gasket	45	Support bracket	55	Inner track rod (adjustable)	62	Track rod	69	Clamp stiffener
9	Outer tube	23	Steering wheel	48	'U' bolt	56	Rubber bush	63	Nut		
12	Inner column kit	30	Retainer	50	Fixing plate	57	Adjusting sleeve	64	Steering R.H.		

and body as described in Chapter 8/9.

4. Support the trailing arm. Remove the two nuts, bolts and washers holding the arm to its pivot brackets. The trailing arm can now be lifted away from the car.

5. Replacement is a straightforward reversal of the removal procedure.

13. Front Wheel - Alignment

1. The front wheels are correctly aligned when they turn in at the front 1/8 inch ± 1/16 inch. Adjustment is effected by altering the length of the RIGHT HAND track rod.

2. This is a job that your local Chrysler agent must do, as accurate alignment requires the use of expensive base bar or optical alignment equipment. On no account try to do this job yourself, using planks of wood or other make shift implements.

3. If the wheels are not in alignment, tyre wear will be excessive and uneven, and the steering will be heavy and unresponsive.

14. Steering Wheel - Removal and Replacement

1. Prise the centre motif from the steering wheel. Remove and retain the two spring clips from the motif. Note that on some cars they are positioned in holes in the steering wheel hub.

2. Unscrew and remove the nut from the inner column. Mark the steering wheel and centre column to facilitate correct positioning of the wheel on replacement.

3. Pull the steering wheel off the inner column. If the wheel appears to be stuck do not use hammer blows to assist its removal as the inner column pinch bolt and steering unit pinion are easily damaged.

4. Replacement is a reversal of the removal procedure. NOTE: If it is wished to alter the position of the steering wheel relevant to the inner column, each spline represents 10°.

5. If fitting a new steering wheel, position the front wheels so that they are in the straight ahead position and parallel with the rear wheels.

6. Offer up the steering wheel so that its two yokes are parallel with the instrument binnocle. To engage it on the nearest spline turn the wheel slightly in an anti-clockwise direction (clockwise on left-hand drive cars).

15. Steering Column - Removal and Replacement

All bracketed letters refer to Fig.10.8.

1. Detach the pawl unit (A) from the steering column by removing the two retaining screws and washers and also the single clip. Remove the steering wheel as described in the previous section.

2. Remove the two nuts and washers securing the outer column bracket (C) to the floor and unscrew and remove the 'U' bolt (B) and bridge piece securing the column to the fascia.

3. Beneath the car mark the inner column and steering unit pinion to facilitate correct replacement. Slacken the clamp bolt.

4. From inside the car withdraw the inner and outer steering column together. If they are not removed together the indicator cancelling system may be affected.

5. Replacement is a reversal of the removal procedure. However, note the following:-

a) The inner and outer column must be refitted together, otherwise cancelling of the direction indicators may be im-

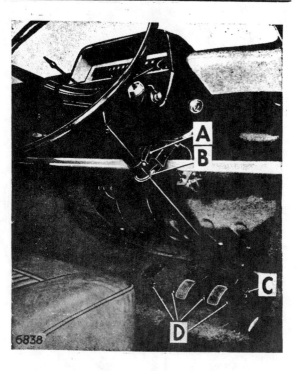

Fig. 10.8. View of steering column from car interior. A. Pawl unit. B. 'U' bolt. C. Outer column flange. D. Rear support bracket bolts.

paired.

b) See Section 16.

16. Inner Column/Pinion Unit Clamp - Modifications

Three different types of assembly have been used to secure the inner column to the pinion unit. These are as follows:-

a) A ¼ inch U.N.F. pinch bolt and washer having an unmarked head.

b) A ¼ inch U.N.F. pinch bolt and washer with a 'V' marked on its head. This bolt permitted a greater tightening torque to be used.

c) A 5/16 inch U.N.F. through bolt, washer and 'Wedglok' nut. This permitted an even greater tightening torque to be used.

The shanks of these bolts locate in a groove formed in the splines of the steering unit pinion. On some steering units this groove is not concentric. Therefore, any resulting misalignment of the spring driver clip or bush and the outer column aperature must be rectified before the direction indicator pawl is refitted. To ensure the correct inner column and steering unit pinion alignment proceed as follows:-

1. Examine the splines of the steering unit pinion and also the inner column for damage or corrosion.

2. Apply a liberal coating of Shell Retinax 'A' grease to both sets of splines. This will protect the splines from corrosion.

3. Lower the inner and outer steering columns into position simultaneously. The outer column to the floor and the inner onto the steering unit pinion. The inner column may need slight rotation to align the pinch bolt hole to the groove in the steering unit pinion when the groove in the pinion is not concentric. To facilitate assembly the top of the pinion is chamfered immediately above the groove. Fit

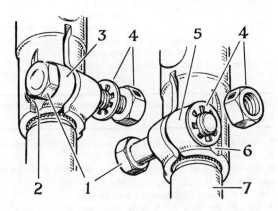

Fig. 10.9. SHOWING THE ATTACHMENT OF THE INNER COLUMN TO THE STEERING UNIT PINION

1 Through bolt
2 Shoulder to lock bolt head
3 Thinner lug
4 Washer and 'Wedgelok' nut
5 Thicker lug
6 Spot face for nut
7 Steering unit pinion

the pinch bolt assembly to the inner column as follows:-

a) Type A and B. The pinch bolt and washer is fed through one lug of the inner column, so that it picks up the thread in the opposite lug.

b) Type C. The through bolt is fed through the inner lug of the inner column until the bolt head becomes captive. A NEW 'Wedglok' nut and washer must then be fitted. Tightening torques are given in the specifications.

17. Rack and Pinion Steering Unit - Removal and Replacement

1. Check the rear wheels and jack the front of the car off the ground.
2. Remove the steering column as described in Section 15.
3. Detach the track rods from the steering arms by unscrewing the ball pin nuts until they are flush with the tops of the threaded pins. Give the nuts and pins a sharp tap. This should free the track rods. Finish undoing the nuts and lift the track rods off the steering arms.
4. Unscrew and remove the four nuts and washers, two reinforcement plates and lower bridge pieces from the steering unit retaining 'U' bolts. Lower the steering unit and collect the upper bridge pieces.
5. Manoeuvre the steering unit complete with the two track rods from beneath the car through the wishbones.
6. To replace the unit start by holding the steering unit in position beneath the car. Refit the curved bridge pieces. These are fitted above and below the steering unit accommodating its cylindrical shape.
7. Offer up the unit to the 'U' bolts. The four threaded shanks should locate in the grooves of the steering unit.
8. Refit the reinforcement plates, raised edges first. Fit the four 'U' bolt nuts and do them up finger tight.
9. Refit the inner and outer steering columns to the car and at the same time clamp the inner column to the steering unit pinion (see Section 16).
10 From this point replacement is a reversal of the removal procedure. However, the points listed below should be noted.

a) Check the convolute and conical covers for leakage, wear or perishing. If any of these faults are present the covers should be renewed.

b) When the pawl unit is refitted to the steering column, ensure that the cable is uppermost and the pawl (protruding through its fitting face) is situated centrally in the most vertical aperature of the outer steering column.

c) Visit your local Chrysler dealer to have the steering alignment checked.

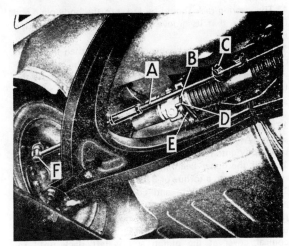

Fig. 10.10. Underneath view of the right hand side of the steering layout.

A Adjustable track rod
B 'U' bolt
C Track rod bolt
D Lower bridge piece
E Reinforcing Plate
F Ball joint

18. Rack and Pinion Steering Unit - Dismantling, Reassembly and Adjustment

1. Detach the two track rods from the steering unit. This is accomplished by releasing the lock plate, withdrawing two bolts and the strut plate and prising the extended bushes of the track rods from the convolute cover.
2. Release the four metal clips retaining the convolute and conical covers. Remove the two conical covers, and slide the convolute cover off the opposite end of the steering unit to the pinion.
3. Unscrew and remove the damper screw and locknut and on some steering units a sealing ring. Prise out the closure cap from the opposite side of the body.
4. Unscrew and remove the two bolts and washers or on some models the two nuts and washers which retain the upper bearing assembly in place. Remove the upper bearing together with the shim pack and paper joints from the pinion.
5. Withdraw the pinion and thrust washer from the body by applying pressure to the steering rack against the damper spring.
6. With pressure still applied to the rack, move the rack into the body until the end of it is clear of the damper pad. Remove the damper pad, washer and damper spring through the closure cap aperature.
7. Withdraw the steering rack from the pinion end of the body. In this way the rack teeth will not score the bush in the opposite end of the body. Dismantling is now complete.
8. Reassembly is generally a reversal of the removal procedure but note the following paragraphs.
9. Before reassembly commences give all components a liberal coating of Shell Spirax 80 E.P. oil.
10 The paper joints used in the original shim pack must be discarded and replaced with metal shims.
11 Before the shim pack is fitted each shim MUST be smeared

with jointing compound and also the rim of the closure cap.

12 Fit the thrust washer (flat face downwards) pinion and upper bearings into the empty body without the shim pack. The oil film is broken and the pinion seated by gently tapping the splined end with a mallet. Measure the gap between the upper bearing flange and the body. Select a shim pack .001 in. to .004 in. (.02 to .10 m.) thicker than the measured gap with a preference for the lower limit. Remove the upper bearing pinion and thrust washer from the body.

13 The steering rack should be fed into the body plain end first. Ensure that its groove aligns with the damper spring tapping.

14 The damper spring washer and pad are then fitted and compressed. This enables the steering rack to be moved outwards from the pinion end when its groove will house the tongue of the damper pad.

15 Place the thrust washer (flat face downwards) on its seat and insert the pinion.

16 Apply pressure to the steering rack against the damper spring. As the pinion goes home the thrust washer will move fully onto its seat.

17 Refit the upper bearing and shim pack and tighten the retaining nuts to a torque of 3 lbs.ft. (42 Kg.Cm.).

18 When the convolute and conical covers are refitted, ensure that the boltheads of the retaining clips are in a position that will be vertically downwards when the steering unit is refitted to the car. NOTE: The clip securing the conical cover at the pinion end is left slack until reassembly is complete. This will enable the unit to be filled with oil.

19 Refit the damper screw, seal, washer and locknut. Set the damper endfloat by traversing the rack until it is in its tightest spot.

20 Tighten the damper screw until it contacts the washer, then slacken off the damper screw and locknut half a flat to obtain .003 in. (.08 mm) damper pad endfloat.

21 Hold the damper screw still whilst tightening the locknut to a torque of 3.5 lbs.ft. The closure cap is then pressed in, recessed side first, until it becomes flush with the body.

22 Ensure that the starting torque required to rotate the pinion to the full lock position does not exceed 14 lbs.in. (15 Kg.Cm.).

23 Refit the track rods to the steering unit noting that the adjustable track rod is fitted on the right.

24 Set both track rods so that they run parallel with the centre line of the steering unit and tighten the track rod retaining bolts to the specified torque.

25 Fill the unit with oil as described in Section 20.

19. Convolute and Conical Covers - Removal and Replacement

1. Remove the steering unit complete with track rods from the car as described in Section 17.

2. Slacken the two metal clips securing the conical covers to each end of the steering unit. Have a receptacle ready to catch the oil and withdraw the two covers.

3. Detach the two track rods from the steering unit by releasing the lock plate, withdrawing the two bolts, strut plate and prising the extended metal bushes of the track rods from the convolute cover.

4. Slacken the two clips retaining the cover and slide the convolute cover off the steering unit at the opposite end to the pinion.

5. Replacement is a reversal of the removal procedure. Leave the conical cover at the pinion end slack until the unit has been filled with oil (see Section 20).

20. Steering Unit - Oil Replenishment

1. Remove the steering unit from the car as described in Section 17.

2. Inspect the conical and convolute covers for any signs of oil leakage. Any faults should be rectified before re-filling the unit with oil.

3. Slacken the retaining clip and remove the conical cover from the pinion end of the steering unit.

4. Drain off the old oil into a suitable receptacle.

5. Hold the steering unit vertical, pinion end upwards. Refill the unit with ½ pint (.3 litre) of Shell Spirax 80 E.P. oil.

6. Refit the conical cover and tighten the retaining clip firmly. Oil replenishment is now complete.

Cause	Trouble	Remedy
SYMPTOM: STEERING WANDERS - IMPRECISE		
Lack of maintenance and general wear	Tyre pressures incorrect	Check pressures.
	Worn ball joints or suspension bushes	Renew.
	Wheel alignment incorrect	Check.
	Different types of tyres fitted	Arrange tyres as recommended.
	Bent tie rods	Renew.
	Bent knuckle or steering arm	Renew.
	Worn steering gear	Overhaul or renew.
	Worn steering shaft coupling	Renew.
	Front brakes binding	Check and adjust as necessary.
SYMPTOM: STIFF AND HEAVY STEERING		
Lack of maintenance and general wear	Tyre pressures low	Check pressures.
	Steering ball joints worn or seized	Renew.
	Steering geometry incorrect	Check on wheel alignment gauge.
	Steering gear stiff due to leakage of oil from rack housing from broken rubber end boots	Renew oil as recommended and check for wear. Replace rubber covers if necessary.
	King pins insufficiently lubricated	Grease as necessary.
	Incorrect tyres fitted to front wheels	Fit correct tyres.
SYMPTOM: VIBRATION AND WHEEL WOBBLE		
Lack of maintenance and general wear	Worn suspension bushes	Check and renew.
	Worn steering ball joints	Check and renew.
	Maladjusted or worn out front wheel bearings	Adjust or renew.
	Steering gear badly worn	Renew.
	Broken front spring	Renew.
	Wheel nuts loose	Tighten.
SYMPTOM: CORNERING VERY POOR. CAR CONTINUES TO BOUNCE FOR A LONG TIME AFTER HITTING A BUMP		
General wear	Spring very weak	Replace weak spring with ı new unit.
	Worn dampers	Replace worn units with new ones.

Chapter 11/Bodywork and Underframe

Contents

1. General Description

The combined body and underframe is of steel welded construction. This makes a very strong and torsionally rigid shell.

Two doors are fitted with hinges at the front. On some models forward hinging quarter lights are fitted to the doors and are held shut by catches. The windows in the doors wind down completely. A hinged window is fitted at the rear to allow access to the rear luggage compartment.

2. Maintenance - Body and Subframes

1. The condition of your car's bodywork is of considerable importance as it is on this that the second hand value of the car will mainly depend. It is much more difficult to repair neglected bodywork than to renew mechanical assemblies. The hidden portions of the body, such as the wheel arches and the underframe and the engine compartment are equally important, though obviously not requiring such frequent attention as the immediately visible paintwork.

2. Once a year or every 12,000 miles, it is a sound scheme to visit your local main agent and have the underside of the body steam cleaned. This will take about 1½ hours and cost about £4. All traces of dirt and oil will be removed and the underside can then be inspected carefully for rust, damaged hydraulic pipes, frayed electrical wiring and similar maladies. The car should be greased on completion of this job.

3. At the same time the engine compartment should be in the same manner. If steam cleaning facilities are not available then brush 'Gunk' or a similar cleanser over the whole engine and engine compartment with a stiff paint brush, working it well in where there is an accumulation of oil and dirt. Do not paint the ignition system and protect it with oily rags when the Gunk is washed off. As the Gunk is washed away it will take with it all traces of oil and dirt, leaving the engine looking clean and bright.

4. The wheel arches should be given particular attention as undersealing can easily come away here and stones and dirt thrown up from the road wheels can soon cause the paint to chip and flake, and so allow rust to set in. If rust is found, clean down the bare metal with wet and dry paper, paint on an anti-corrosive coating such as Kurust, or if preferred, red lead, and renew the paintwork and undercoating.

5. The bodywork should be washed once a week or when dirty. Thoroughly wet the car to soften the dirt and then wash the car down with a soft sponge and plenty of clean water. If the surplus dirt is not washed off very gently, in time it will wear the paint down as surely as wet and dry paper. It is best to use a hose if this is available. Give the car a final wash-down and then dry with a soft chamois leather to prevent the formation of spots.

6. Spots of tar and grease thrown up from the road can be removed with a rag dampened with petrol.

7. Once every six months, or every three months if wished, give the bodywork and chromium trim a thoroughly good wax polish. If a chromium cleaner is used to remove rust on any of the car's plated parts remember that the cleaner also removes part of the chromium so use sparingly.

3. Maintenance - Upholstery and Carpets

1. Remove the carpets or mats and thoroughly vacuum

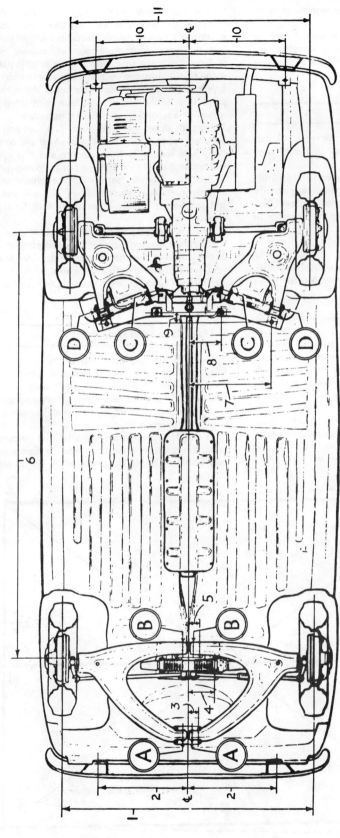

Ȼ of pivot above ground — Ⓐ 9.90 in. Ⓑ 9.90 in. Ⓒ 10.18 in. Ⓓ 10.37 in.
(4 up - static laden condition) (25.1 c.m.) (25.1 c.m.) (25.8 c.m.) (26.3 c.m.)

1 — 49.1 in. (124.6 c.m.)   2 — 17.63 in. (44.8 c.m.)   3 — 2.25 in. (5.7 c.m.)
4 — 5.34 in. (13.6 c.m.)   5 — 2.25 in. (5.7 c.m.)   6 — 82.0 in. (208.3 c.m.)
7 — 16.15 in. (41.0 c.m.)   8 — 6.5 in. (16.5 c.m.)   9 — 1.97 in. (5.0 c.m.)
10 — 19.0 in. (48.26 c.m.)   11 — 47.9 in. (121.6 c.m.)

Fig. 11.1. DIAGRAM OF PRINCIPAL UNDERFRAME DIMENSIONS

clean the interior of the car every three months or more frequently if necessary.

2. Beat out the carpets and vacuum clean them if they are very dirty. If the upholstery is soiled apply an upholstery cleaner with a damp sponge and wipe off with a clean dry cloth.

4. Minor Body Repairs

1. At some time during your ownership of your car it is likely that it will be bumped or scraped in a mild way, causing some slight damage to the body.

2. Major damage must be repaired by your local Hillman agent, but there is no reason why you cannot successfully beat out, repair and respray minor damage yourself. The essential items which the owner should gather together to ensure a really professional job are:-

a) A filler such as Holts 'Cataloy'.

b) Paint whose colour matches exactly that of the bodywork, either in a can for application by a spray gun, or in an aerosol can.

c) Fine cutting paste.

d) Medium and fine grade wet and dry paper.

3. Never use a metal hammer to knock out small dents as the blows tend to scratch and distort the metal. Knock out the dent with a mallet or rawhide hammer and press on the underside of the dented surface a metal dolly or smooth wooden block roughly contoured to the normal shape of the damaged area.

4. After the worst of the damaged area has been knocked-out, rub down the dent and surrounding area with medium wet and dry paper and thoroughly clean away all traces of dirt.

5. The plastic filler comprises a paste and a hardener which must be thoroughly mixed together. Mix only a small portion at a time as the paste sets hard within five to fifteen minutes depending on the amount of hardener used.

6. Smooth on the filler with a knife or stiff plastic to the shape of the damaged portion and allow to thoroughly dry; a process which takes about six hours. After the filler has dried it is likely that it will have contracted slightly so spread on a second layer of filler if necessary.

7. Smooth down the filler with fine wet and dry paper wrapped round a suitable block of wood and continue until the whole area is perfectly smooth and it is impossible to feel where the filler joins the rest of the paintwork.

8. Spary on from an aerosol can, or with a spray gun, an anti-rust undercoat, smooth down with wet and dry paper, and then spray on two coats of the final finishing using a circular motion.

9. When thoroughly dry polish the whole area with a fine cutting paste to smooth the resprayed area into the remainder of the wing and to remove the small particles of spray paint which will have settled round the area.

10 This will leave the wing looking perfect with not a trace of the previous unsightly dent.

5. Major Chassis and Body Repairs

1. Major chassis and body repair work cannot be successfully undertaken by the average owner. Work of this nature should be entrusted to a competent body repair specialist who should have the necessary jigs, welding and hydraulic straightening equipment as well as skilled panel beaters to ensure a proper job is done.

2. If the damage is severe it is vital that on completion of repair the chassis is in correct alignment. Less severe damage may also have twisted or distorted the chassis although this

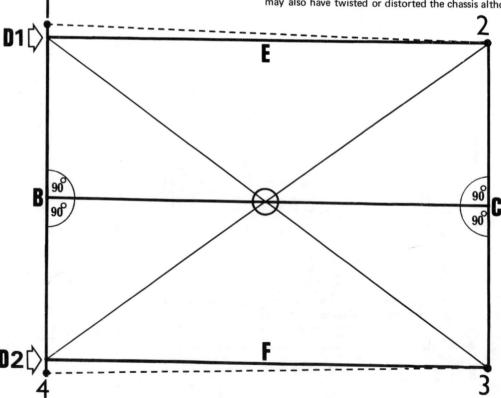

Fig. 11.2. BODY ALIGNMENT TEST, DIMENSIONS AND ANGLES

may not be visible immediately. It is therefore always best on completion of repair to check for twist and squareness to ensure that all is correct.

3. From beneath the car check all the body and underframe dimensions shown in Fig. 11.1. Measurements taken should be identical on both sides of the car and if they are not it will become fairly evident that the body and subframe are out of true.

4. A further check for squareness can be made by placing the car on level ground which is hard and smooth. Hang a plumb weight from the centre of each hub cap in turn. Mark the point where the plumb weight contacts the ground with a chalked dot. Move the car away so that the four dots are on open ground.

5. Join the four dots thus making a shape which is almost rectangular. Find and mark the lines '1' and '4' also '2' and '3'. (All references are for Fig. 11.2.) Join these two centres with a chalk line.

6. Find the measurement between 'C' and '2' and also 'C' and '3'. Mark these measurements in the corresponding positions on the line '1' to '4'. The two new points resulting are 'D1' and 'D2'.

7. Mark a new line between 'D' and '2' also 'D' and '3'. Letter these lines 'E' and 'F' respectively. The resulting shape will be rectangular. Erase the lines '1' to '2' and '4' to '3' to avoid confusion.

8. Join the points 'D1' and '3' also 'D2' and '2' diagonally. The bisecting point of these diagonals should occur exactly on the centre line between points 'B' and 'C'. Also check that the angles shown in Fig. 11.2 are in fact 90°. If the two points do not correspond or the angles are not 90° it is a sure indication that the body/subframe is out of true. If this is the case it should be rectified immediately.

6. Maintenance - Hinges and Locks

Once every six months or 5,000 miles the door, rear window, bonnet and boot hinges should be oiled with a few drops of engine oil from an oil can. The door striker plates can be given a thin smear of grease to reduce wear and ensure free movement.

7. Door Trim Panels, Handles and Map Pocket - Removal and Replacement

1. Unscrew and remove the self tapping screws holding the map pocket to the doors. Remove the pocket.

2. Press the handle escutcheon inwards. This will reveal a pin retaining the handle to its square shaft. Push the pin out with a thin screwdriver or similar; the handle, escutcheon and spring can now be removed. This procedure is for both window winder and door handles.

3. Remove the screws from around the periphery of the door trim panel. Withdraw the panel.

Replacement is a reversal of the removal removal sequence.

8. Door Locks - Removal and Replacement

1. Remove the door trim panel as described in Section 7.

2. Unscrew and remove the four screws holding the door lock in position (three on later models) from the rear edge of the door (see Fig. 11.3.).

3. Remove the remote door handle mechanism by removing its securing screws and washers. If a remote control guide is fitted this can be removed by levering out of the door panel.

4. Withdraw the whole lock assembly including the remote

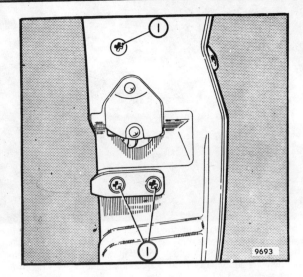

Fig. 11.3. Showing door lock attachment - later models.

control through the aperture in the inner door panel.

5. Replacement is a straightforward reversal of the removal sequence

9. Striker Plate - Removal, Replacement and Adjustment

1. If it is wished to renew a worn striker plate mark its position on the door pillar so a new plate can be fitted in the same position.

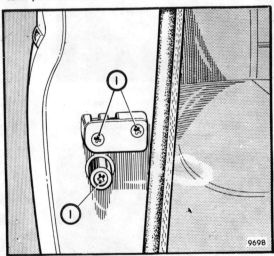

Fig. 11.4. Showing door lock striker unit - later models.

2. To remove the plate simply undo the three Phillips screws which hold the plate in position. Replacement is equally straightforward.

3. To adjust the striker plate first slacken the three screws and remove the striker plate slightly. Retighten the screws and close the door, noting the position of the door. Repeat this process until the door is 'flush' with the adjacent rear body panel. The crease in the door panel should be level with the crease in the rear body panel as well.

4. Check that the door closes easily without lifting or dropping and that on the road it does not rattle. NOTE: Although the appearance of earlier and later door strikers differs the removal, replacement and adjusting procedures are identical.

This sequence of photographs deals with the repair of the dent and paintwork damage shown in this photo. The procedure will be similar for the repair of a hole. It should be noted that the procedures given here are simplified — more explicit instructions will be found in the text

In the case of a dent the first job — after removing surrounding trim — is to hammer out the dent where access is possible. This will minimise filling. Here, the large dent having been hammered out, the damaged area is being made slightly concave

Now all paint must be removed from the damaged area, by rubbing with coarse abrasive paper. Alternatively, a wire brush or abrasive pad can be used in a power drill. Where the repair area meets good paintwork, the edge of the paintwork should be 'feathered', using a finer grade of abrasive paper

In the case of a hole caused by rusting, all damaged sheet-metal should be cut away before proceeding to this stage. Here, the damaged area is being treated with rust remover and inhibitor before being filled

Mix the body filler according to its manufacturer's instructions. In the case of corrosion damage, it will be necessary to block off any large holes before filling — this can be done with aluminium or plastic mesh, or aluminium tape. Make sure the area is absolutely clean before ...

... applying the filler. Filler should be applied with a flexible applicator, as shown, for best results; the wooden spatula being used for confined areas. Apply thin layers of filler at 20-minute intervals, until the surface of the filler is slightly proud of the surrounding bodywork

Initial shaping can be done with a Surform plane or Dreadnought file. Then, using progressively finer grades of wet-and-dry paper, wrapped around a sanding block, and copious amounts of clean water, rub down the filler until really smooth and flat. Again, feather the edges of adjoining paintwork

The whole repair area can now be sprayed or brush-painted with primer. If spraying, ensure adjoining areas are protected from over-spray. Note that at least one inch of the surrounding sound paintwork should be coated with primer. Primer has a 'thick' consistency, so will find small imperfections

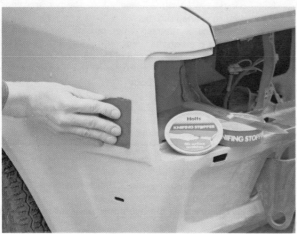

Again, using plenty of water, rub down the primer with a fine grade wet-and-dry paper (400 grade is probably best) until it is really smooth and well blended into the surrounding paintwork. Any remaining imperfections can now be filled by carefully applied knifing stopper paste

When the stopper has hardened, rub down the repair area again before applying the final coat of primer. Before rubbing down this last coat of primer, ensure the repair area is blemish-free — use more stopper if necessary. To ensure that the surface of the primer is really smooth use some finishing compound

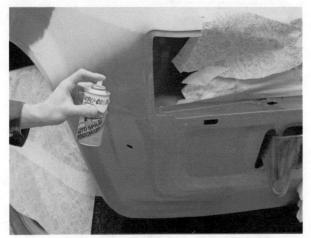

The top coat can now be applied. When working out of doors, pick a dry, warm and wind-free day. Ensure surrounding areas are protected from over-spray. Agitate the aerosol thoroughly, then spray the centre of the repair area, working outwards with a circular motion. Apply the paint as several thin coats

After a period of about two weeks, which the paint needs to harden fully, the surface of the repaired area can be 'cut' with a mild cutting compound prior to wax polishing. When carrying out bodywork repairs, remember that the quality of the finished job is proportional to the time and effort expended

10. Door Rattles - Tracing and Rectification

1. The commonest cause of door rattle is a misaligned, loose or worn striker plate nut other causes may be:-

a) Loose door handles, window winder handles or door hinges.
b) Loose, worn or misaligned door lock components.
c) Loose or worn remote control mechanism.
d) Loose trim panels or map pockets.

2. It is quite possible for door rattles to be the result of a combination of the above faults, so a careful examination must be made to determine the causes of the fault.
3. If the nose of the striker plate is worn and as a result the door rattles, renew and then adjust the plate as described in Section 9.
4. Should the inner door handle rattle this is easily cured by fitting a rubber washer between the escutcheon and the handle.
5. If the nose of the door lock wedge is badly worn and the door rattles as a result, then fit a new lock as described in Section 8.
6. Should the hinges be badly worn, then they must be replaced.

11. Windscreen Glass - Removal and Replacement

1. If you are unfortunate enough to have a windscreen shatter, fitting a replacement windscreen is one of the few jobs which the average owner is advised to leave to a professional mechanic. The owner who wishes to do the job himself will need the help of a friend.
2. Take off the windscreen wiper arms and blades, disconnect the earthed battery lead and remove the interior light and mirror.

3. Remove the bright metal windscreen surround trims. The ends of the trims will be exposed by sliding to one side the escutcheon in the centre of the surround top and bottom. The mouldings and escutcheons should then be carefully eased out of the rubber channel.
3. Work all round and under the outside edge of the windscreen sealing rubber with a screwdriver to break the Seelastik seal between the rubber and the windscreen frame flange.
4. Spread a blanket over the bonnet and with a friend steadying the glass from the outside sit in the passenger's seat and press out the glass and rubber surround with one foot. Place rag between your foot and the glass. The glass is started most easily at one of the corners.
5. Clean off all the old Seelastik from the windscreen flange with petrol.
6. The windscreen is replaced after having smeared Seelastik sealing compound on the outside edge of the glass where it is covered by the rubber surround.
7. With the rubber surround and finisher fitted to the windscreen so that the joint is at the bottom insert 16 ft. of cord all round the channel in the rubber which will sit over the windscreen aperture flange. Allow the two free ends of the cord to overlap slightly.
8. Fit the windscreen from outside the car and with an assistant pressing the rubber surround hard against the body flange, slowly pull one end of the cord out moving round the windscreen so drawing the lip of the rubber over the windscreen flange on the body.

12. Imp Mk. I Instrument Binnacle, Instruments and Switches - Removal and Replacement

To remove an instrument it will first be necessary to remove the binnacle.

1. Before removing the binnacle disconnect the battery earth cable.
2. Then remove the two upper bolts securing the binnacle

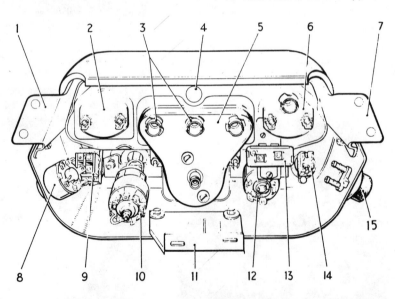

Fig. 11.5. REAR VIEW OF THE INSTRUMENT BINNACLE - EARLY IMP & CHAMOIS
(on some cars the lighting and wiper switch positions are vice versa)

1 Mounting bracket	6 Water temperature gauge (when fitted)	10 Direction indicator-horn switch	13 Voltage stabilizer
2 Fuel gauge	7 Mounting bracket	11 Lower mounting bracket	14 Windscreen wiper switch
3 Warning light locations	8 Ignition switch	12 Headlamp flash-and-dip switch	15 Windscreen washer pump
4 Panel light location	9 Lighting switch		
5 Speedometer case			

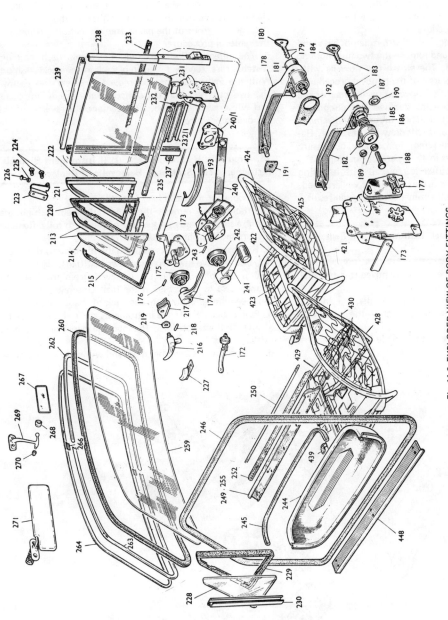

Fig. 11.6. EXPLODED VIEW OF BODY FITTINGS

172	Check link	186	Spring
173	Door lock & remote control	187	Spring clip
174	Inside handle	188	Contactor screw
175	Handle escutcheon	189	Lock nut
176	Cross pin	190	Brass washer
177	Door striker	191	Seating washer
178	OUtside door handle	192	Seating washer
179	Lock cylinder	193	Door pull
180	Key	213	Inner frame & glass
181	Push button	214	Glass
182	Outside door handle	215	Inner frame glazing rubber
183	Lock cylinder	216	Locking handle R.H.
184	Key	217	Bracket
185	Push button	218	Grooved pin

219	Wave washer	232/1	Channel & cam plate
220	Weatherstrip R.H.	233	Channel & cam plate
221	Outer frame R.H.	235	Inner waist seal
222	Centre chanel	237	Glass run channel R.H.
223	Top pivot R.H.		front
224	Screw	238	Glass run channel R.H.
225	Spacer		rear
226	Pivot pin	239	Glass run channel-top
227	Catch striker R.H.	240	Window regulator R.H.
228	Fixed light glass	240/1	Support bracket
229	Weatherstrip R.H.	241	Regulator handle
230	Centre channel R.H.	242	Handle escutcheon
231	Glass	243	Cross pin
232	Glazing rubber & cam plate	244	Door pocket

245	Door pocket finisher	268	Clamping nut
246	Door seal	269	Stem unit
249	Waist finisher L.H.	270	Buffer sun visor
250	Waist finisher moulding	421	Seat frame R.H.
252	Wood capping L.H.	422	Long cushion strap
255	Waist finisher L.H.	423	Short strap
259	Zone-toughened glass (R.H.)	424	Long squab strap
260	Weatherstrip	425	Short strap
262	Moulding R.H.	428	Seat frame
263	Moulding L.H.	429	Spring cushion case
264	Moulding	430	Spring case
265	Moulding	439	Seat adjustment cover
266	Clip		
267	Mirror		

to the fascia rail.

3. Unscrew and remove the two screws with nuts which hold the lower side of the binnacle to the steering column bracket. The binnacle can then be withdrawn sufficiently to allow access to the cables at the rear.

4. Unscrew the drive cable from the rear of the speedometer. Remove the panel warning lights, after disconnecting the instrument and switch cables.

5. Pull off the screenwasher pipes and then withdraw the binnacle from the fascia. Refitment of the binnacle is a reversal of the removal procedure.

6. To remove the direction indicator/headlamp flash and dip switches first unscrew and remove the two nuts holding either switch to the panel. The switch can now be withdrawn. Replacement is a reversal of the removal procedure.

7. The voltage stabiliser unit is located on the rear of the speedometer case. To remove the stabiliser first disconnect the cables leading to the unit. Then unscrew and remove the single retaining screw and withdraw the stabiliser. Replacement is a reversal of the removal procedure, but ensure that the cables are replaced in their correct positions. It is also essential that the stabiliser is replaced with its fixing lug in an upright position and that the lug is well earthed. If this is not done incorrect instrument readings will result.

13. Stiletto Instrument Panel, Instruments and Switches - Removal and Replacement

1. Before the instrument panel can be removed it is essential to disconnect the battery earth cable.

2. Lower the steering column slightly at the top end by removing the 'U' bolt and clamp which holds the column to the bulkhead bracket.

3. Disconnect the drive cable and trip cable from the rear of the speedometer.

4. Unscrew and remove the five screws holding the instrument panel to the fascia. Pull the panel away from the fascia enough to allow the cables to be pulled off the instruments, switches and panel lights. Withdraw the panel from the car. Refitting is a reversal of the removal procedure but check with the wiring diagram to ensure that all cables are reconnected to their correct positions.

5. To remove an instrument (with the instrument panel removed) unscrew the finger nuts retaining the 'U' shaped slamp and remove the clamp. Withdraw the instrument through the front of the panel. Replacement is a reversal of the removal procedure.

6. The direction indicator and headlamp flash and dip switches are renewed and replaced in identical fashion. With the instrument panel removed, unscrew and remove the two nuts securing the switch to the rear of the panel and withdraw the switch. Replacement is a reversal of the removal procedure.

14. Imp Mk. II, Chamois Mk. 1, II Instrument Binnacle, Instruments and Switches - Removal and Replacement

1. Disconnect the earth lead from the battery.

2. Unscrew and remove the wing nuts from behind the fascia, also the screws on the face of the crash rolls. Remove the left and right-hand fascia crash rolls.

3. Remove the four bolts securing the binnacle to the fascia rail, also the two lower fixing screws (if fitted).

4. Pull the binnacle far enough away from the fascia to allow access to the cables at the rear. Unscrew and remove the speedometer cable from the back of the speedometer.

5. Pull the cables off the instruments and switches, making a note of their positions. Remove the panel and warning lights.

6. Pull off the screenwasher pipes and withdraw the binnacle

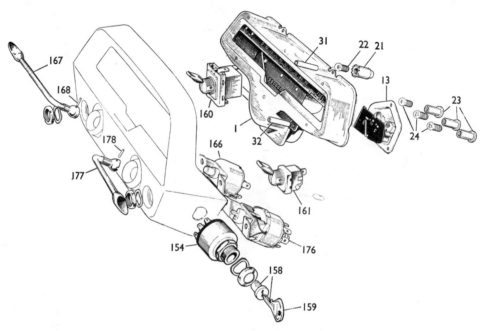

Fig. 11.7. EXPLODED VIEW OF THE EARLY IMP AND CHAMOIS INSTRUMENT BINNACLE

1 Speedometer assembly	24 Bulb 12v. 2.2 watt	160 Lighting switch	176 Direction indicator and
13 Petrol gauge	31/32 Spacer tube	161 Windscreen wiper switch	horn switch R.H.D.
21 Bulb holder	154 Ignition and starter switch	166 Dip & flasher switch R.H.D.	177 Knob and lever
22 Bulb 12v. 2.2 watt	158 Lock barrel	167 Knob and lever	178 'Roll' pin
23 Warning light bulb holders	159 Key	168 'Roll' pin	

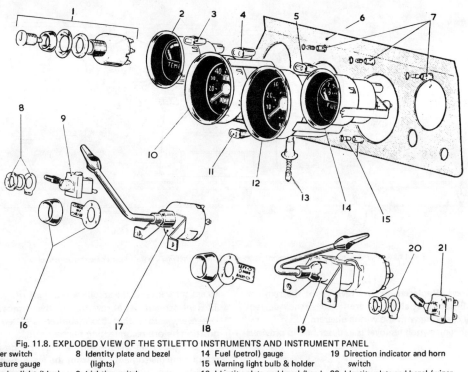

Fig. 11.8. EXPLODED VIEW OF THE STILETTO INSTRUMENTS AND INSTRUMENT PANEL

1 Ignition/Starter switch
2 Water temperature gauge
3 Headlamp warning light (blue)
4 Oil warning light (amber)
5 Flasher warning light (green)
6 Instrument panel
7 Warning light bulb and holder

8 Identity plate and bezel (lights)
9 Lighting switch
10 Speedometer
11 Ignition warning light (red)
12 Tachometer (rev counter)
13 Speedometer trip control

14 Fuel (petrol) gauge
15 Warning light bulb & holder
16 Identity plate and bezel (headlamp flash-and-dip switch)
17 Headlamp flash-and-dip switch
18 Identity plate & bezel (direction indicator & horn switch)

19 Direction indicator and horn switch
20 Identity plate and bezel (wiper switch)
21 Windscreen wiper switch

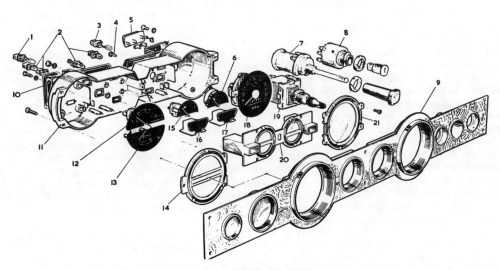

Fig. 11.9. EXPLODED VIEW OF THE NEW INSTRUMENT PANEL ARRANGEMENT - LATER IMP AND CHAMOIS MODELS EXCEPT STILETTO

1 Panel illumination
2 Warning lights
3 Panel illumination
4 Plastic stud
5 Voltage stabilizer
6 Oil pressure gauge

7 Windscreen wiper-washer switch
8 Ignition starter switch
9 Instrument panel
10 Printed circuit
11 Instrument case

12 Fuel (petrol) gauge
13 Water temperature gauge
14 Outer lens (fuel and temperature gauges)
15 Voltmeter
16 Warning light lens (red)

17 Warning light lens (amber)
18 Speedometer
19 Lighting switch
20 Centre lens and mask assembly
21 Outer lens (speedometer)

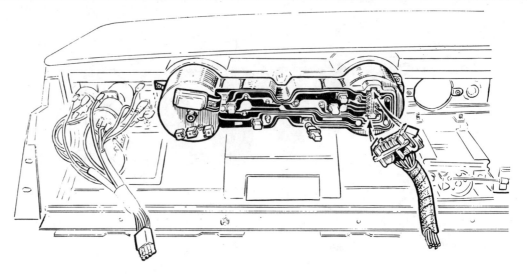

Fig. 11.10. Rear view of the new instrument panel arrangement, showing the instrument case and printed circuit.

from the fascia. Replacement is a reversal of the removal procedure. Ensure that all cables are fitted in their correct locations by checking with the wiring diagram.

7. Instrument and switch removal is as described in previous sections.

15. Imp and Chamois Models (Except Stiletto) New Instrument Panel, Instruments and Switches - Removal and Replacement

1. Disconnect the battery earth cable.

2. Remove the trim cappings from both ends of the panel, or from one end if only one is fitted.

3. Unscrew and remove the six screws retaining the panel to the fascia. Remove the cable harness plugs from behind the panel. Note the plug which supplies the instruments is located immediately behind the fuel gauge. It can be removed by depressing its upper and lower claws which engage in slots in the instrument case. The other plug which supplies the controls and switches is of the twopiece interconnecting type which can be pulled apart by hand.

4. Pull off the pipes at the rear of the windscreen washer pump. Unscrew and remove the pipe from the rear of the oil pressure gauge (if fitted).

5. Unscrew and remove the cable from the rear of the speedometer. Disconnect the cables from any other accessories which may be fitted, cigar lighter, clock, etc.

6. Withdraw the panel from the fascia. Replacement is a reversal of the removal procedure. Care should be taken to ensure that the instrument panel retaining screws are not overtightened. Note that the supply plug to the instruments fits one way only into the instrument case.

7. Printed circuit removal (with instrument panel removed). Place the instrument panel on a bench with the printed circuit upwards. Remove the panel and warning lights and voltage stabiliser.

8. Remove the two white plastic studs securing the printed circuit.

9. Undo the three screws securing the recessed voltage stabiliser terminals to the instrument case.

10 Withdraw the printed circuit by lifting it from the instrument case. Replacement is a reversal of the removal procedure.

11 To remove the voltage stabiliser first disconnect the battery earth cable. Pull the stabiliser from the rear of the instrument case. A wedge shaped piece of wood can be used

to assist removal if the stabiliser is a tight fit.

12 Replacement is a reversal of the removal sequence. However, ensure that the stabiliser is fitted squarely in position before reconnecting the battery.

13 To remove an instrument it will first be necessary to remove the instrument case from the instrument panel.

14 With the instrument panel removed from the car unscrew and remove the five screws securing the instrument case to the panel. Withdraw the case complete with instruments.

15 Remove the outer lens from the instrument which is to be removed.

16 If it is a centre instrument it will be necessary to withdraw the sliding warning light lens before proceeding further.

17 If the voltmeter is being removed undo the two circular shouldered nuts from the rear of the case and withdraw the instrument. The same procedure is used when removing the speedometer as that for the voltmeter. However, it will be necessary to remove the voltage stabiliser as described previously to allow access to one of the screws. The oil pressure gauge is removed by unscrewing and removing the two screws from its bore flange. These screws are accessible from inside the case. Withdraw the instrument.

18 Replacement of all instruments is a reversal of the removal procedure. Care should be taken not to overtighten the instrument retaining screws. Insulate any printed circuit contacts not in use with insulating tape.

16. Window Regulator Mechanism - Removal and Replacement

1. If the window glass is very difficult to wind up and down try oiling the joints in the mechanism before removing the mechanism.

2. If the mechanism is badly worn it will have to be replaced. To remove it from the car first remove the interior handles and trim as described in Section 7.

3. Temporarily replace the window winding handle and lower the window to its approximate half way position. Support it in this position with a block of wood. Remove the handle.

4. Unscrew and remove the three screws (1) surrounding the window winder shaft; these retain the regulator mechanism.

5. Slide the operating arm from its location in the bottom channel (complete). Withdraw the regulator from the door.

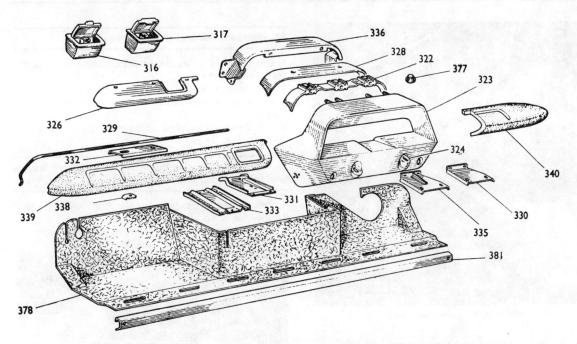

Fig. 11.11. EXPLODED VIEW OF THE IMP AND CHAMOIS Mk. I FASCIA FITTINGS

316 Ash tray	324 Binnacle bezel	331 Fascia support bracket	338 Fixing plate
317 Ash tray	326 Panel filler R.H.D.	332 Stay	339 Centre crash roll
322 Rear extension	328 Back cover	333 Stay	377 Fixing bush
323 Instrument binnacle and bezel	329 Fascia finisher	335 Binnacle support stay	378 Parcel tray
	330 Binnacle support stay	336 Binnacle rear cover	381 Parcel tray rail

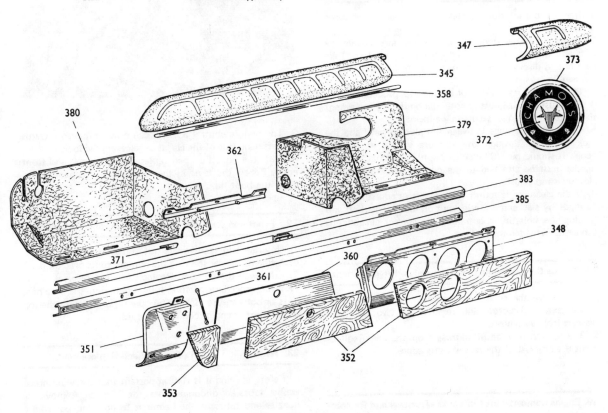

Fig. 11.12. EXPLODED VIEW OF THE CHAMOIS AND SPORT FASCIA FITTINGS

345 Crash roll	352 Wood capping	361 Check strap	373 Bezel plaque
347 Crash roll	353 Wood capping	362 Closing strip	380 Parcel tray
348 Fascia centre panel	358 Fascia moulding	371 Lock striker	383 Parcel tray rail
351 Fascia end panel	360 Glove box lid	372 Clock aperture plaque	385 Parcel tray rail

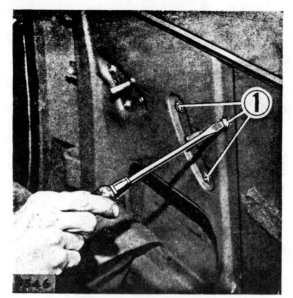

Fig. 11.13. Window regulator removal

Replacement is a reversal of the removal procedure.

17. External Door Handles - Removal, Replacement and Push Button Adjustment

1. Remove the interior handles and trim pad as described in Section 7.
2. From inside the door casing unscrew and remove the nuts and washers which retain the handle to the door. Take care not to displace the door handle seating pads. Remove the handle.
3. Replacement is a reversal of the removal procedure.
4. To adjust the pushbutton note that on the reverse side of the button is a plunger secured by a locknut.
5. Check the clearance between the plunger head and the lock contactor through the aperture in the inner door panel. It should be 1/32 inch (.79 mm). Note that the door handle must be attached to the door when checking this clearance and adjusting.
6. If the clearance is found to be incorrect adjustment can be made by slackening the locknut on the plunger bolt and turning the bolt in or out until the correct clearance is achieved. Retighten the locknut.

18. Engine Compartment Lid - Removal and Replacement

1. To remove the engine compartment lid open it to its fullest extent. Unscrew and remove the two nuts and washers from each hinge.
2. The lid can now be lifted away from the car. Replacement is a reversal of the removal procedure.

19. Engine Compartment Lid Locks - Removal and Replacement

1. Unscrew and remove the locknut and nut from the reverse end of the handle. (On some models only one nut is fitted.)
2. Unscrew and remove the two screws and lockwashers retaining the lock to the lid. Withdraw the lock.
3. Replacement is a reversal of the removal procedure.

20. Boot Lid - Removal and Replacement

1. Open the lid to its fullest extent and hold it in this position with a sling.
2. Remove the two nuts and washers from the reverse side of the hinges on each side of the lid. Lift the lid away from the car.
3. Replacement is a reversal of the removal procedure.

21. Method of Opening the Boot Lid when Lock Release Mechanism has Failed

1. Remove the screws securing the front grille in place. Remove the grille.
2. From inside the aperture behind the grille push the large grommet (1) out of its location.

21.2

3. The remote control arm (2) can now be moved towards the left hand side of the car, thus releasing the lock.
4. With the boot lid open replace the grommet and front grille. Repair the fault in the lock release mechanism and close the boot lid.

22. Front and Rear Bumpers - Removal and Replacement

1. Unscrew and remove the nut and washer (or bolt) on each side of the car securing the bumper to its bracket.
2. Lift away the bumper. Replacement is a reversal of the removal procedure. Before fully tightening the retaining nuts or bolts ensure that the bumper is parallel with the top of the boot or engine compartment lid.

23. Heater Mk. I and II - Removal and Replacement

Before starting it is very important that the windscreen washer tubes are disconnected at the 'T' piece. Remove the nozzles and tubes. If the heater is being removed from a Chamois it is necessary to remove the instrument panel on which the heater control is mounted, together with the ashtray and oil pressure gauge as described in Section 14.
1. Disconnect the earth lead from the battery. Remove the luggage compartment bulkhead trim and open the bleed valve (if fitted).
2. Drain the cooling system as described in Chapter 2.
3. Disconnect the upper hose and remove the bleed valve.

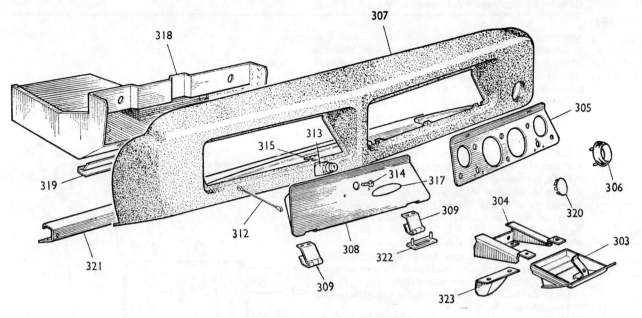

Fig. 11.14. EXPLODED VIEW OF THE CALIFORNIAN, STILETTO
AND COUPE FASCIA FITTINGS

303	Ash tray	308	Glove box lid	315	Lock striker	321	Parcel tray rail

303 Ash tray	308 Glove box lid	315 Lock striker	321 Parcel tray rail
304 Support bracket	309 Hinge	317 Finger pull	322 Mounting plate
305 Instrument panel	312 Check strap	318 Glove box tray	323 Quadrant panel
306 Bezel	313 Push button lock	319 Bracket	
307 Crash roll	314 Key	320 Blanking plug	

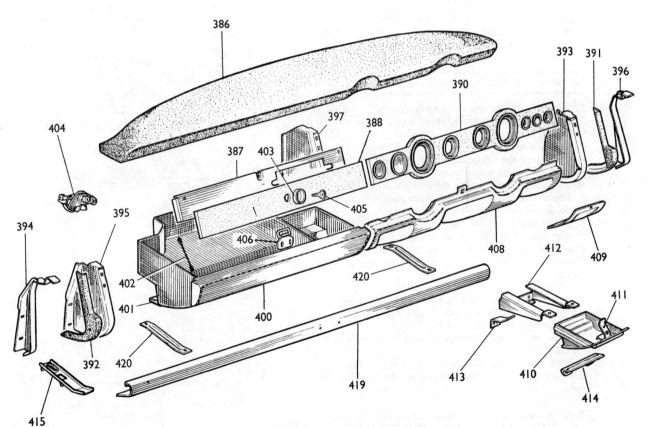

Fig. 11.15. EXPLODED VIEW OF THE LATER IMP, CHAMOIS,
SUPER SALOON AND SPORT FASCIA FITTINGS

386 Crash roll	394 Fascia end finisher	403 Escutcheon	411 Ash tray stubber
387 Support panel	395 End panel	404 Lock assembly	412 Support bracket
388 Finisher	396 Fascia end finisher	405 Key	413 Support bracket
390 Instrument panel	397 Fascia centre panel	406 Catch	414 Control quadrant
391 End capping	400 Glove box assembly	408 Lower fascia panel	415 Bonnet control bracket
392 End capping	401 Hinge	409 Mounting panel	419 Parcel rail
393 End panel	402 Check strap	410 Ash tray	420 Rail reinforcement

Also disconnect the lower hose.

4. Release the control cable from the water valve. Undo the water valve union nut and remove the two crosshead screws. Remove the water valve assembly.

5. Loosen the hexagon nut on the stud which holds the polythene air inlet pipe (if fitted) to the bulkhead.

6. Remove the auxiliary instrument panel (if fitted). Disconnect the blower switch (if fitted).

7. Remove the parcel shelf.

8. Loosen the two screws which retain the polythene air inlet pipe (if fitted) to the bulkhead. Do not entirely remove the pipe, but secure it loosely in place.

9. Some models are fitted with a continuous air hose between the air box (or blower if fitted) and the air inlet of the heater. Withdraw this hose from the heater by compressing it.

10 Remove the heater control unit (Imp models only).

11 Screw off the control lever knob. Remove the control from its mounting bracket, after unscrewing the two retaining screws. Withdraw the control and cable.

12 Undo the six screws and remove the mounting bracket and escutcheon.

13 Unscrew and remove the three screws which hold the demister manifold to the fascia stiffener panel. To accomplish this it will be necessary to remove the crash roll (if fitted) and instrument panel as described in previous sections.

14 Remove the three screws securing the heater to the bulkhead. Withdraw the heater unit by easing the left-hand side down first, keeping it away from the air inlet pipe.

15 Replacement is a reversal of the removal procedure. Note that the air inlet pipe is entered into the heater as it is replaced, the flange being finally tightened when the heater is in position. Refill the cooling system and bleed as necessary. The bleeding procedure is described in Chapter 2. Reconnect the windscreen washer apparatus

---

24. Heater 1969 Models - Removal and Replacement

1. Disconnect the battery at the earth terminal.

2. Remove the centre and left-hand luggage compartment trims.

3. Drain the cooling system as described in Chapter 2.

4. Disconnect the upper hose and then the water valve elbow hose at the heater pipe. Remove the water valve securing screws and withdraw the water valve and hose.

5. Remove the instrument panel as described in Section 15. Undo and remove the steering column 'U' bolt.

6. If it is found that the luggage compartment lid interior remote control retains the parcel shelf or cubby box, it should be released and the slotted retainer removed.

7. Remove the fascia panel and crash roll complete as follows:-

a) Remove the two screws at each end of the crash roll, also the three underneath and the one which retains each support stay at the bulkhead end.

b) Withdraw the indicator harness and plug over the fascia rail.

c) Withdraw the control cable into the car. The fascia assembly can now be withdrawn to the passenger side of the car.

8. Disconnect the windscreen washer tubes from their 'T' piece and release the 'T' piece from the heater casing.

9. Unscrew and remove the two screws securing the demister manifold. Remove the three screws retaining the heater assembly. Withdraw the heater unit from the car.

10 Replacement is a reversal of the removal procedure. Care should be taken when re-routing the indicator harness and

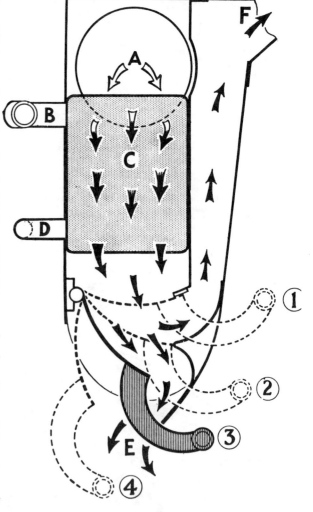

Fig. 11.16. SCHEMATIC SECTION OF THE HEATER AIR DISTRIBUTION CONTROL

A   Air inlet
B   Water inlet pipe
C   Heater element
D   Water outlet pipe
E   Air to car
F   Air to screen
1   Heater control position (uppermost) - Off
2   Heater control position - Air to screen
3   Heater control position - Air to screen and car
4   Heater control position - Air to car

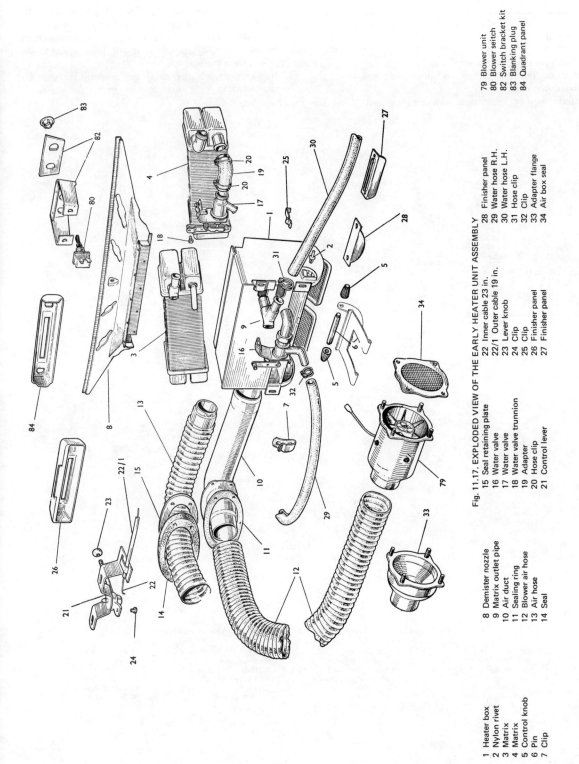

Fig. 11.17. EXPLODED VIEW OF THE EARLY HEATER UNIT ASSEMBLY

1 Heater box	8 Demister nozzle	22 Inner cable 23 in.	28 Finisher panel
2 Nylon rivet	9 Matrix outlet pipe	22/1 Outer cable 19 in.	29 Water hose R.H.
3 Matrix	10 Air duct	23 Lever knob	30 Water hose L.H.
4 Matrix	11 Sealing ring	24 Clip	31 Hose clip
5 Control knob	12 Blower air hose	25 Clip	32 Clip
6 Pin	13 Air hose	26 Finisher panel	33 Adapter flange
7 Clip	14 Seal	27 Finisher panel	34 Air box seal
	15 Seal retaining plate		79 Blower unit
	16 Water valve		80 Blower seitch
	17 Water valve		82 Switch bracket kit
	18 Water valve trunnion		83 Blanking plug
	19 Adapter		84 Quadrant panel
	20 Hose clip		
	21 Control lever		

plug over the fascia rail. Also ensure that the windscreen washer tubes are not trapped and that the 'T' piece is vertical. Refill the cooling system and bleed as described in Chapter 2.

25. Heater Blower Motor (If Fitted) - Removal and Replacement

1. Disconnect the battery earth cable.
2. Remove the spare wheel and disconnect the air hose at the blower end.
3. Undo the two retaining screws and remove the louvred

grille beneath the front humper.
4. From inside the chamber which will now be exposed, unscrew and remove the four nuts and washers retaining the blower and intake gauze. Withdraw the blower complete with gauze.
5. Disconnect the blower electrical cable from its switch inside the car. Release the cable from its retaining clips in the luggage compartment and draw the cable through the bulkhead into the luggage compartment. Remove the blower and cable from the car.
6. Replacement is a reversal of the removal procedure but before refitting the gauze ensure that it is clean and unblocked.

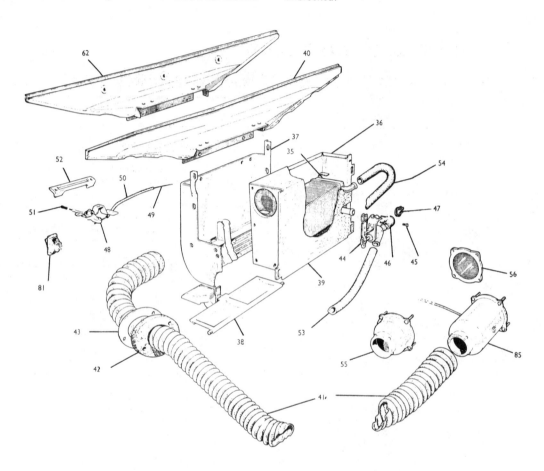

Fig. 11.18. EXPLODED VIEW OF THE HEATER UNIT ASSEMBLY - 1969 ONWARDS

35 Matrix	42 Seal retainer	48 Lever and quadrant	54 Water hose L.H.
36 Matrix case	43 Seal retaining plate	49 Inner cable 23 in.	55 Adapter flange
37 Distributor box	44 Water valve	50 Outer cable 19 in.	56 Air box seal
38 Flap and control	45 Water valve trunnion	51 Lever knob	62 Demister nozzle
39 Fibre back panel	46 Adapter	52 Heat control indicator	81 Blower switch
40 Demister nozzle	47 Hose clip	53 Water hose R.H.	85 Blower unit
41 Air hose			

Chapter 12 Supplement
and Revision for later Cars, Husky and Van models

Contents

1 Introduction

The purpose of this Supplement to the Owner's Workshop Manual is to bring the information up-to-date with current manufacturing specifications, to fill a few gaps in information found in the first editions and lastly to include certain details applicable to the Husky and Van models.

The author would like to thank Mr. A.J. Purchase of Martock, Somerset for assistance with the compilation of the Transmission Unit Section.

2 Routine maintenance

In addition to the tasks listed on pages 6, 7 and 8 of the manual, the following should be added, where applicable.

5000 miles
At intervals of 5000 miles (8000 km) or six months, whichever occurs first:
1 Apply a grease gun charged with Castrol LM Grease to the nipples of the steering swivel pins and the driveshaft outer (Hardy Spicer) couplings. Three or four strokes of the grease gun is normally sufficient until grease is just seen to exude from the joints.

10000 miles
Every 10000 miles (or every year if 10000 miles (16000 km) are not exceeded)
1 Where a brake servo is fitted, renew the filter element.
2 Examine the seatbelts and their attachment points for deterioration.

40000 miles
Every 40000 miles
1 Where a Girling Mk IIB brake servo is fitted it should be renewed.

Fig. 12.1. Hillman Imp De - Luxe Saloon, 1974 model

3   General Data

Cooling system
Thermostat starts to open ...   .   85 to 89°C (185 to 192°F)
Radiator pressure cap setting   ...   . 7 lb/in^2 (0.5 kg/cm^2)

Fuel system and carburation
Solex carburettors - jet differences for altitudes above 400 ft (1200 m)

	Mk I (H.C.)	Mk I (L.C.)	Mk II (H.C. and L.C.)
Main jet	102	102	112.5
Air correction	165	190	220

For Mk I (H.C. and L.C.) with automatic choke, the choke cover should be turned 5 mm anticlockwise from the datum. For temperatures above 20°C accelerator pump rod SK. 3151 should be used.
For Mk II H.C. and L.C. the strangler (choke) spring should be in its weakest position.

Jet differences for Solex carburettors where a heavy duty or B— post intake air cleaner is fitted

	Up to 4000 ft (1200 m)	Above 4000 ft (1200 m)
Mk I (I.C.):		
Air correction	200	215
Econostat	45	45
Mk I (H.C.):		
Air correction	180	195
Econostat	45	45
Mk II (H.C. and L.C.) using Mk I carburettor adapter elbow:		
Main jet	105	105
Air correction	190	220
Econostat	Blank	Blank
Pilot	40	40
Mk II (H.C. and L.C.) using Mk II carburettor adapter elbow:		
Main jet	100 (102 may be required in cold climates)	100
Air correction	180	195 (220 above 7500 ft (2300 m))

Note: Ignition should be set to optimum according to local conditions and fuel grades.

Stromberg carburettors:
Metering needle for altitudes between 5000 and 10000 ft
(1500 to 3000 m)   ...   .   5U (B.17751 Z)
Metering needle for altitudes above 10000 ft (3000 m)   ...   5V (B.17752Z)

Solex carburettor details for 1973/74 models:
Type ...   .   B.30 P.I.H. - 5
Reference number   3652
Choke tube   ...   .   19 mm
Main jet 97.5
Air correction jet   160
Slow running jet   40
Air bleed jet   180
Econostat jet   120
Needle valve seat 1.6
Strangler control   ...   .   Manual

Ignition system
Ignition distributor type   ...   .   Lucas 45D4
Spark plug type ...   .   Champion RN9Y or AC

Rear hubs - Driveshafts - Universal joints
Torque wrench settings (all models):
Rear hub nuts   ...   .   175 lb ft (24.3 kg m)

Braking system
Master cylinder bore:
Van   ...   .   5/8 in. (15.875 mm)
Front wheel cylinder bore:
Husky   ...   .   0.7 in. (17.78 mm)
Van   ...   .   5/8 in. (15.875 mm)

Electrical system

Starter motor:	Lucas M35J
Number of brushes	4
Lock torque	7 lb ft (0.97 kg m) at 350 to 370 amps
Drive	Inertia, inboard type
Brush spring tension	28 oz (800 gm)
Alternator:	
Type	Lucas 10AC or 11AC (positive earth) or Lucas 16 AC or 16 ACR (negative earth)

Suspension - Dampers - Steering

Front suspension:	
Coil spring diameter, Husky	3.123 in (7.9 cm)
Coil spring static laden length, (off car) Husky	7.84 in (19.19 cm)
Coil spring static laden load, (off car) Husky	490 lb (222 kg)
Coil spring free-length, Husky	10.35 in (26.3 cm)
Coil spring diameter, Van	3.153 in (8.0 cm)
Coil spring static laden length, (off car) Van	8.35 in (21.21 cm)
Coil spring static laden load, (off car) Van	3.70 lb (168 kg)
Coil spring free-length, Van	9.94 in (25.24 cm)
Caster angle, Husky	9° positive ± 1°
Caster angle, Van	8° positive ± 1°

Rear suspension:		
Springs:		
Husky	As for heavy duty Saloon (see Chapter 10)	
Van:		
Paint colour code	Pink (early models), Yellow or brown (later models)	
Outer diameter	4.02 in (10.2 cm)	4.02 in (10.2 cm)
Free-length	9.40 in (23.8 cm)	9.90 in (25.1 cm)
Laden length	6.98 in (17.7 cm)	7.48 in (19 cm)
Laden load	1332 lb (604 kg)	1332 lb (604 kg)
Camber angle:		
Husky	½° positive ± ¾°	
Van	1 ¾° positive ± ¾°	

Wheels and tyres:	
Wheel size, Van	12H x 4J
Tyre size:	
Husky and late model Saloons	155 x 12 radial
Van	5.50 x 12 (cross ply), Dunlop Van G.72 or Goodyear 4/6 ply nylon
Tyre pressures (all models):	
Front	18 lb/in^2
Rear and spare *	30 lb/in^2

Rear tyre pressures should be increased by 15 lb/in^2 for Vans when fully laden and 6 lb/in^2 for Husky models when fully laden.

Torque wrench settings (all models:	
King pin carrier to wishbone:	
Horizontal	80 lb ft (11.1 kg m)
Vertical	54 lb ft (7.5 kg m)
Rear hub nut	175 lb ft (24.3 kg m)
Steering arm to stub axle (½ in. U.N.F.)	80 lb ft (11.1 kg m)
Rear suspension, crossmember to body	31 lb ft (4.3 kg m)

---

4 Engine

1 Engine - removal (Vans and Husky Models)

1 When it is required to remove an engine from a van, the following procedure is to be adopted since the transaxle must be removed also.

2 Initially raise the rear end of the vehicle by means of a trolley jack or similar device beneath the rear body crossmember. Now place axle stands or suitable blocks under the body sills just forward of the rear wheels.

3 Drain the cooling system (refer to Chapter 2, if necessary) and disconnect the battery leads.

4 Working from beneath the car, disconnect the gearshift coupling at the transaxle end. This is done by working through the hole in the chassis member then folding back the tab on the retaining bolt, unscrewing the nut from the bolt and withdrawing the latter.

5 Disconnect the earth strap at the forward end of the transaxle.

6 Remove the bolt from each mounting rubber under the transaxle.

7 Disconnect the Rotoflex couplings, by reference to Chapter 7, Section 2, if necessary.

8 Now remove the engine tray. This is secured by 3 drive screws at the front, 4 number 10 bolts at the sides and 2 drive screws at the rear.

9 Slacken the clip which secures the fan cowl rubber hose and roll the hose on to the radiator cowl.

10 Now, working from above the engine, disconnect the rear number plate lamp leads and remove the rear bumper.

11 Disconnect the starter motor leads, the engine coolant thermostatic switch leads, the coil leads and the generator leads.

12 Remove the lower fixing bolts from the rear crossmember.

13 Remove both water hoses from the front end of the cylinder head.

14 Remove the clutch slave cylinder and tie it up clear of the engine. Do not disturb the hydraulic connection.

15 Disconnect the hoses from the water pump.

16 Remove the dipstick and its rubber (not the dipstick tube) from the engine.

17 Take off the inlet pipe to the fuel pump.

18 Take off the choke and throttle cables at the carburettor.

19 Take off the engine oil filler hose from the filler neck at the body end.

20 Raise the rear of the vehicle, remove the stands or blocks from beneath the body sills, then lower to the floor.

21 Now place a suitable trolley beneath the engine to permit its withdrawal after the rear crossmember has been removed. Note - an alternative method is to lower the vehicle carefully (paragraph 20) so that the engine sump just rests on suitable wooden or concrete blocks, then very carefully push the vehicle away after the rear crossmember has been removed.

22 Remove the single nut securing the rear engine mounting bolt then the remaining crossmember securing bolts. Take off the rear crossmember.

23 Remove the engine/transaxle from the vehicle and at the first opportunity tie the two differential shaft flanges together, over or under the transaxle, to prevent them inadvertently falling out and causing damage to the splines. As soon as the assembly is clear of the car and on a suitable workbench these shafts can be pulled out for convenience and placed on one side for safety.

24 Refitting is the reverse of removal but reference should be made to the appropriate Sections of Chapter 7 and Chapter 2, when refitting the Rotoflex couplings and refilling the cooling system. If the engine has been dismantled the sump should be filled with the appropriate amount and grade of engine oil.

2 Oil Pump Driven and Driving Gears - Renewal

1 Oil pump driven and driving gears may only be renewed as a pair. If one gear requires renewal, even if the other is apparently satisfactory, they must both be renewed.

2 When fitting a new oil pump it will be necessary to either renew both gears or remove the existing driven gear from the old pump. Whichever you do, you will have to drill the pump driveshaft and fit the driven gear.

3 If the fixing pin holes of a new driven gear do not line up with the fixing pin holes on an existing pump, the pump must be renewed.

4 When fitting new gears, remove any burrs with a fine oilstone before assembly.

5 Remove the pump end cover and support the end of the shaft to prevent the inner rotor/shaft pin from shearing.

6 Now press the gear on to the spindle until it is 3/32 in. (2.5 mm) from the pump body as gauged using a twist drill shank of the correct size (see Fig. 12.2).

7 Drill through the shaft (and through the remaining side of a new gear) in two places using a 1/8 in. drill and fit a new fixing pin in each hole. The ends of the pins should be rivetted over afterwards.

8 Before fitting the end cover liberally coat the working parts of the pump with engine oil.

---

5 Fuel System and Carburation

---

1 Dry element type air cleaner - intake tube position

1 Later model air cleaners have a body fixing bracket with two holes to enable the intake tube to be positioned towards the exhaust manifold in cases of carburettor icing. The earlier type fixing bracket can be replaced by the later version (Part number 7100305), if necessary.

2 Air cleaner - large dry element type

1 Cars supplied for certain territories have a large dry element air cleaner. In some cases the inlet is connected to a hose that passes inside the body to an air intake grille in the right-hand door post.

2 To remove the element, unscrew the long wing headed through-bolt from below the unit and lift off the top cover. Note that joint rings are fitted both above and below the element.

3 Cleaning is carried out as for the standard type of dry element air cleaner.

4 It is important to maintain a leak-free joint at the air intake tube. If necessary, the joint should be wrapped round with adhesive tape to achieve this condition.

3 Pneumatically Operated Throttle Control - Description

1 Early model Imps were equipped with a pneumatically

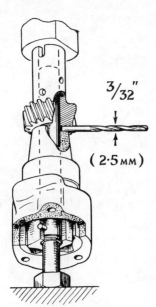

Fig. 12.2 Positioning the oil pump driven gear

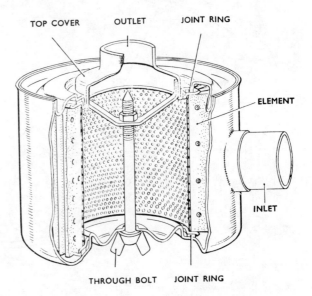

Fig. 12.3 Large dry element type air cleaner

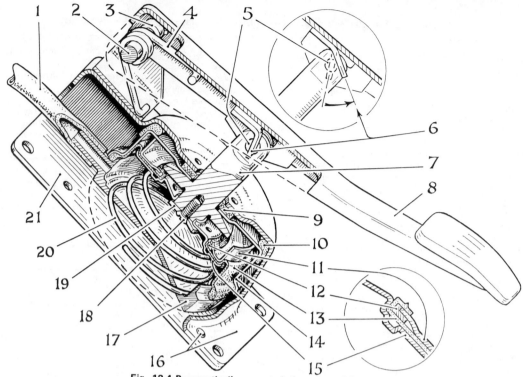

Fig. 12.4 Pneumatically operated throttle pedal unit

1   Plastic air pipe
2   Pedal pivot pin (long)
3   Pedal bush (two)
4   Pedal return spring
5   Pivot pin (short)
6   Short pin retaining tag

7   Piston
8   Accelerator pedal
9   Dust seal
10 Rubber clamping ring
     (or circular spring ring)
11 Metal clip

12 Nylon locating ring
13 Rubber diaphragm
14 Cylinder
15 Spring retainer
16 Rivet and cover pressing

17 End cap
18 Countersink screw or circlip
19 Washer or circlip
20 Diaphragm return spring
21 Base plate

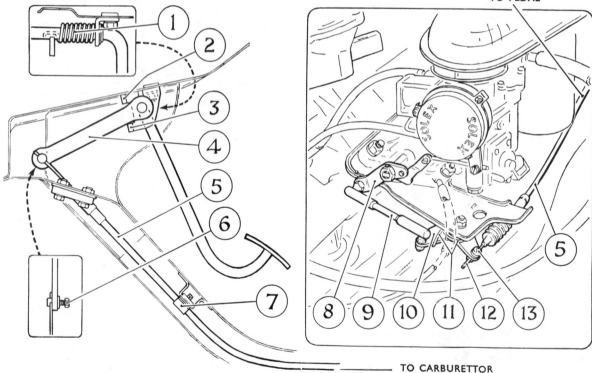

Fig. 12.5 The cable operated throttle linkage

1   Torsion spring
2   Upper limit of lever travel
3   Lower limit of lever travel
4   Lever
5   Outer cable

6   Cable securing screw
7   Cable fixing clip
8   Throttle operating lever
9   Connecting rod

10 Cranked lever
11 Torsion spring
12 Inner cable
13 Cable securing screw

operated throttle control system. This comprised a pedal unit which was in effect a piston and diaphragm mounted below the throttle pedal. This was linked via a tube to another smaller piston mounted on a bracket at the carburettor.

2 Although operating on a very much lower pressure, the operation can be compared with the hydraulic brake circuit except that the pressure medium is air. When the throttle pedal is depressed, pressure beneath the diaphragm is passed to the piston on the carburettor via the interconnecting tube. This in turn will open the throttle by an amount dependant upon the amount by which the pedal is depressed. When the pedal is released the throttle will close under spring action.

4 Pneumatically Operated Throttle Control - Removal and Replacement

1 To remove the throttle unit, take off the securing clip and the air pipe then remove the carburettor, as described in Chapter 3, Section 13.

2 Disconnect the ball joint on the carburettor operating link and remove the throttle unit.

3 Replacement is simply a reversal of the removal procedure but ensure that no oil or grease is allowed to enter the unit. **Note:** do not attempt to dismantle the unit. If it is faulty it must be renewed complete.

4 The pedal unit can be removed by taking out the two bolts and two crosshead screws securing it to the floor, then pulling off the interconnecting pipe.

5 Replacement is simply a reversal of the removal procedure but as with the throttle unit it cannot be dismantled for repair, and oil or grease must not be allowed to enter it.

5 Cable Operated Throttle Control - Description

1 Later model Imps have a conventional cable operated throttle. A heavy torsion spring on the pedal pivot shaft is used to return the pedal and cable to the normal position after being depressed, with a small additional spring on the carburettor linkage.

6 Cable Operated Throttle Control - Cable renewal

1 The inner throttle cable can be renewed as a separate item by disconnecting it at the carburettor and pedal operating lever then drawing out the existing cable. However, it is recommended that the outer cable is also renewed with the inner one since the lubricating film on the inner walls of the outer cable wears after a high mileage has been completed, thus resulting in a 'sticky' throttle action.

2 To remove the complete cable, detach both ends as detailed in paragraph 1, then raise the car to provide access to the outer cable run beneath.

3 Release the cable fixing clips along the run of the outer cable, then withdraw it from the front abutment plate and the hole where it passes into the engine compartment.

4 Refitting is the reverse of the removal procedure.

6 Ignition system

1 Lucas 45D4 distributor - description and application

1 This distributor was introduced in 1973 to replace the earlier 25D4 type. It provides better sealing against the entry of dampness and dust, gives less contact breaker noise and is not fitted with a vernier adjuster. It is slightly smaller than its predecessor.

2 Lucas 45D4 distributor - maintenance and adjustment

1 Every 5000 miles (8000 km) release the two spring clips which retain the distributor cap. Remove the cap and pull off the rotor arm. Apply two or three drops of engine oil to the felt pad which is located in the recess on top of the cam.

2 Remove the moving contact breaker arm by lifting the spring out of the white nylon insulator and the contact point from its

Fig. 12.6 The Lucas 45D4 distributor

Fig. 12.7 The Lucas 45D4 distributor with the cap removed

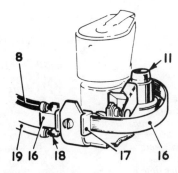
Fig. 12.8 Details of LT terminal on type 45D4 distributors

8 LT lead
11 Pivot post
16 Moving contact spring arm

17 Insulator
18 LT connecting plate
19 Capacitor lead

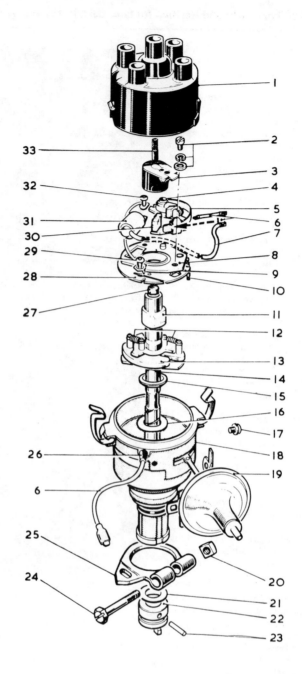

Fig. 12.9 Exploded view of Lucas type 45D4 distributor

1 Cap
2 Contact securing screw
3 Rotor
4 Pivot post
5 Movable contact arm
6 LT lead and terminal plate
7 Condenser (capacitor) lead
8 Movable baseplate
9 Fixed baseplate
10 Baseplate locating prongs
11 Cam

12 Centrifugal advance springs
13 Centrifugal advance mechanism
14 Shaft
15 Nylon washer
16 Steel washer
17 Vacuum capsule or blanking plate screws
18 Body
19 Vacuum capsule
20 Pinch bolt nut
21 Thrust washer
22 Driving dog

23 Pin
24 Pinch bolt
25 Clamp plate
26 Insulating sleeve
27 Felt lubricating pad
28 Baseplate expanding section
29 Wedge screw
30 Cam lubricating wick
31 Capacitor (condenser)
32 Retaining screw
33 Carbon brush

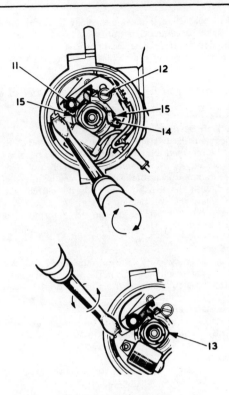

Fig. 12.10 Contact breaker gap adjustment (Lucas type 45D4 distributor)

11 Pivot
12 Fixed contact locking screw
13 Cam
14 Felt lubricating wick
15 Lubrication holes

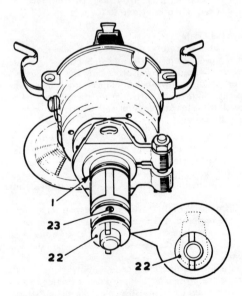

Fig. 12.11 Location of driving dog relative to rotor arm (Lucas type 45D4 distributors)

1 'O' ring seal
22 Driving dog
23 Pin

hollow pivot. Apply a thin smear of high melting point grease to the outer surface of the hollow pivot.

3 Apply a similar smear of high melting point grease to the distributor cam surface.

4 Apply one drop of oil through the centre plate holes.

5 Prise the contact points apart and check their faces for pitting. Minor 'pips' and 'craters' may be removed by dressing them carefully on an oilstone but the contacts must be renewed if badly pitted or burnt. When dressing the contact points it is important that the faces are kept flat and square or slightly domed to minimise wear and pitting after replacement.

6 To remove the contacts, push the LT and condenser lead connecting plate from the looped end of the movable contact spring arm.

7 Unscrew and remove the locking screw and washers which secure the fixed contact breaker arm and lift the complete contact set from the distributor baseplate.

8 Separate the two contact points by pulling the movable arm from the hollow pivot.

9 Refitting the points is a reversal of the removal procedure but do not tighten the fixed contact screw fully at this stage.

10 Rotate the crankshaft until the heel of the moving contact breaker arm is on top of one of the peaks of the cam. Now, using a screwdriver in the adjustment slots, move the contacts until a gap of 0.015 in. (0.38 mm) exists between the contact faces as determined with a feeler gauge. With the contacts set in this position, tighten the fixed contact securing screw and recheck the gap.

11 Check the ignition timing, as described in the following sub-Section.

3 Ignition Timing where a Lucas 45D4 distributor is fitted

1 Ignition timing where a 45D4 distributor is fitted, is identical to the procedure given in Chapter 4, Section 10, except that any reference to the vernier adjustment should be ignored. Where any alteration to the timing is deemed necessary the whole of the distributor body must be moved after slackening the clamp bolts.

4 Lucas 45D4 distributor - removal and refitting
Refer to Chapter 4, Section 6.

5 Lucas 45D4 Distributor - Dismantling and Reassembly

1 Remove the distributor cap, rotor arm and lubrication pad (from the top of the cam spindle).

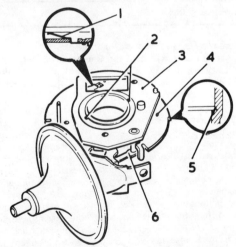

Fig. 12.12 Details of movable and fixed baseplate (Lucas type 45D4 distributors)

1 Bearing spring
2 Lubrication holes
3 Movable plate
4 Fixed plate
5 Locating groove in distributor body
6 Vacuum unit connecting link

2   Remove the vacuum unit securing screws, noting the two baseplate prongs which locate beneath one screw.

3   Push back the LT lead and rubber sleeve into the centre of the distributor.

4   Remove the baseplate wedge screw and then use a small screwdriver to prise the expanded segment of the fixed baseplate inwards so that the complete baseplate/contact breaker assembly can be lifted from the distributor body.

5   Carefully drive out the pin which secures the drive dog, then pull off the dog and thrust washer.

6   The shaft, complete with centrifugal advance mechanism can now be withdrawn through the distributor body. Retain the O-ring if undamaged.

7   If there is undue wear of the centrifugal advance mechanism it should be renewed as a complete shaft/advance mechanism assembly. Any servicing should be limited to renewal of the springs if they have stretched or broken.

8   Check the shaft for side-movement in the bearings. If evident, then the complete distributor should be renewed on an exchange basis.

9   Reassembly is a reversal of the removal procedure but the following points should be observed. Smear all friction surfaces of internal components with a molybdenum based general purpose grease before assembly. Insert the baseplate assembly into its approximate position in the distributor body so that the two prongs are located either side of the hole through which the vacuum unit securing screw passes. Connect and screw the vacuum unit into position and then snap the baseplate into the body ensuring that it is pressed down against the ledge inside the body so that the chamfered edges will engage the undercut in the body side. If there is any tendency for the baseplate to be a loose fit in the body, the former item must be renewed. Fit and tighten the securing screw.

10 Fit the thrust washer (raised side of pips towards the dog) and the drive dog, noting particularly the alignment of the large and small segments in relation to the electrode of the rotor arm.

11 Fit the dog retaining pin and stake the holes at each end. If a new shaft is being used, it will have been supplied undrilled and should now be drilled with a 3/16 in. (4.76 mm) drill. Use the dog as a guide to position the hole and press down on the cam end of the shaft whilst drilling to compress the dog and washers against the shank. Where a new thrust washer is being used, assemble the drive dog, washer and pin, and then tap the end face of the dog to slightly compress and flatten the 'pips' on the thrust washer to obtain the correct endfloat of 0.010 to 0.020 in. (0.254 to 0.508 mm).

7   Transmission Unit

1   Transaxle Repairs - Cautionary Note

1   It must be understood that the transaxle is a complex piece of machinery which requires a great deal of special tooling and 'know-how' to be accurately assembled in the event of major repairs being necessary.

2   With reference to Chapter 6, Sections 4, 6 and 15, the procedure given is satisfactory provided that no new parts are required for the hypoid assembly and its bearings, or the output (pinion) shaft, the components directly assembled on to the shaft and the shaft bearings. If these items are in need of repair you should contact your Chrysler dealer or one of the engineering companies specializing in transaxle repairs who will have the necessary equipment to do the job.

3   When a transaxle is removed from a vehicle you should tie the two differential shaft flanges together, over or under the transaxle, to prevent them inadvertently falling out and causing damage to the splines. (This does not apply if it is already known that the differential shafts are of the early type where a circlip is used at the inner ends to retain them). At the earliest opportunity after removing the transaxle, when it is on a suitable workbench, pull out the shafts (where this is possible) and place them on one side for safety.

4   At first sight it may seem that renewal of the pinion tail bearing and subsequent re-shimming is a straightforward operation. You are strongly advised not to attempt this job since the shimming and bearing preload are related to the tolerances of the gears and synchro units on the shaft.

2   Items which can be renewed without special equipment

a)   Input Shaft Bearings

The needle roller bearing at the clutch shaft end of the input shaft can be removed after the clutch shaft has been taken out (Chapter 6, Section 4, paragraphs 1 to 16) provided that a suitable extractor is available. The inner race on the shaft **must** be refitted with the two holes towards the clutch end of the shaft. To renew the ball bearing at the reverse gear end of the shaft, the gearbox must be dismantled; refer to Chapter 6, Section 9.

b)   Input Shaft

This can be renewed by following the procedure of Chapter 6, Section 4, paragraphs 1 to 17, but it is recommended that the bearings (see previous paragraph) are renewed at the same time.

c)   Reverse pinion and gear

These items can be renewed by following the procedure given in Chapter 6, Section 4, paragraphs 1 to 10.

d)   Selector Shafts

These items can be renewed by following the procedure given in Chapter 6, Section 4, paragraphs 1 to 25.

e)   Baulk Rings (and Synchro Parts)

When the components on the output (pinion) shaft have been removed (see Chapter 6, Section 4) it is quite in order to renew the baulk rings without renewing the synchro units. On any transaxle which has been in service for more than 30000 miles (48000 km) this is advisable anyway. **Note:** It is not normally possible to renew a synchro sleeve since it is purchased as a set with the hub, springs, etc. However, if parts can be obtained and are known to be serviceable, they may be fitted provided that the original synchro hub is refitted to the shaft.

f)   Differential Gears

Differential gears can be renewed after the hypoid assembly has been removed. Refer to Chapter 6, Section 4, paragraphs 1 to 14 for the hypoid removal procedure and to the following Section for the differential gears removal procedure. **Note:** It is not impossible (but rather difficult) for the differential gears to be removed with the differential still fitted, also refer to the following sub-Section.

3   Differential Gears - Removal and Replacement

Note: If it is wished to attempt to remove the differential gears from the transaxle after it has been removed from the car, refer to paragraph 6 onwards in this sub-Section.

1   Remove the hypoid assembly as described in Chapter 6, paragraph 15.

2   If the differential shafts have circlips at their inner ends these must first be removed. Withdraw the shafts just far enough to clear the differential gears. (The aim is to disturb things as little as possible to preclude damage to the oil seals and the necessity for re-shimming).

3   With an assistant supporting the assembly, drive out the pin which retains the cross pin, then push out the latter followed by the gears. In certain cases thrust washers are fitted between the gears and hypoid casing whilst on others the gears run against a machined face in the casing. Thrust washers can be used with either type of casing on reassembly.

4   Inspect all the parts for wear and damage, renewing as necessary. If any parts are to be renewed they should be of the latest type available and fitted as a complete kit.

5   Reassembly is the reverse of the removal procedure but

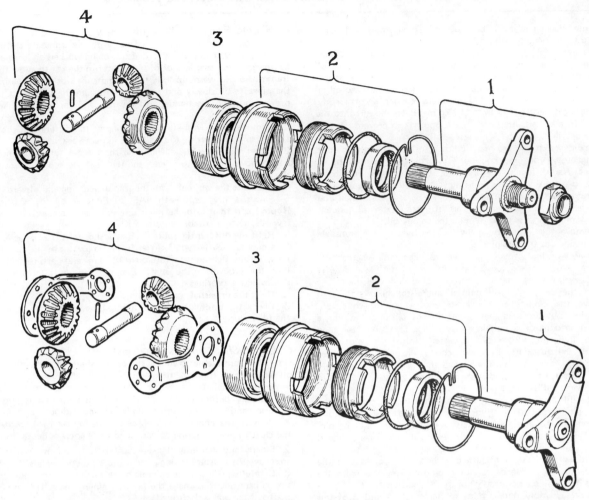

Fig. 12.13 Alternative later types of differential flange assemblies

1 Flange assembly (spider)
2 Screwed sleeve assembly
3 Bearing
4 Differential gears and cross pin assembly

In the upper illustration which was the first type not to be fitted with a circlip at the inner end, the nut is a redundant feature although fitted.

Fig. 12.14 Extracting the input shaft needle roller bearing after removing the clutch shaft

Fig. 12.15 The inspection cover, circlip and O-ring in the transaxle casing

absolute cleanliness must be observed at all times and parts should be lubricated with SAE 80 EP gear oil (eg; Castrol Hypoy Light) immediately prior to assembly. It is essential that a new locking pin is used to retain the cross pin. On the earlier types of differential shafts there is no need to replace the circlips at the inner ends provided that should the nut have been removed at the drive flange (spider) end, a new item is fitted and correctly torque tightened to 130 lb ft (18 kg m). Peen the nut into the groove in the shaft afterwards but support it to prevent damage to the bearings.

6 Provided that you are prepared to resort to a certain amount of ingenuity you may consider it worthwhile to attempt to remove the differential gears once the transaxle has been removed from the car, by referring to the following paragraphs.

7 Drain the transaxle oil. If the engine is still connected you will need to be extremely careful during the subsequent manhandling and also need to drain the engine oil.

8 Remove the inspection cover on the base of the transaxle after taking out the retaining circlip.

9 Now, working through the aperture, check the whereabouts of the cross pin and locking pin in the hypoid assembly. If necessary it may be rotated by turning the differential shaft.

10 On the early type differential shafts the next step is to remove the circlips at the inner ends. They are not very accessible but provided that pieces do not fall into the unit, a certain amount of brute force may be used. If you have long nosed circlip pliers, so much the better. With this type of shaft, due to the possibility of slight scoring when the circlips are removed, it is recommended that they are not completely removed since they may damage the oil seals, but withdrawn to just clear the differential gears.

11 The difficult part now, is to remove the locking pin from the cross pin. Provided that you can make up a suitable tool, cranked at the end to fit against the end of the locking pin, leverage can be carefully applied through the aperture provided that care is taken not to damage the O-ring or sealing face.

12 With the locking pin pushed clear of the cross pin, the differential gears can be carefully removed (together with the shims if fitted - see paragraph 3 of this Section).

13 For reassembly details refer to paragraph 4 and 5 of this Section, then finally refit the inspection cover and its circlip. Smear a little SAE 80 EP gear oil on the sealing surface of the cover to prevent damage to the O-ring. **Note:** Up to chassis numbers B41/100373 (De-luxe) and B42/1000100 (Basic) fit circlip number 7104213. After these chassis numbers fit circlip 7104200.

4 Hypoid Flange Oil Seals - Renewal

1 This operation can be carried out with the transaxle still in the car provided that the side which is being worked on is raised to prevent excessive loss of oil. Initially run the car to allow the transmission to warm up fully then commence work by releasing the pressure by **slowly** and **carefully** removing the filler plug, to prevent burning the hands with the hot oil. Replace the filler plug hand-tight.

2 Remove the driveshaft and coupling at the differential shaft flange (spider) referring to Chapter 7, as necessary.

3 Either withdraw the differential shaft (later types) or undo and remove the nut to release the flange (early types). Discard the nut.

4 Prise out the oil seal from the transaxle casing and discard it.

5 Smear a new seal with SAE 80 EP gear oil (eg; Castrol Hypoy) and fit it into the inner screwed sleeve in the casing, lip inwards, using a suitable tubular drift.

6 Refit the differential shaft (later types) or refit the flange and fit a new nut (early types). After fitting a new nut of the correct type, torque tighten it to 130 lb ft (18 kg m) and peen the collar into the groove in the shaft. Support the shaft to prevent damaging the bearings.

7 Refit the driveshaft and coupling.

8 Check the transaxle oil level, top-up if necessary then replace the filler plug.

5 Clutch Shaft Oil Seal - Renewal

Note: It is preferable to renew the clutch shaft oil seal with the oil at normal running temperature if at all possible. It is recommended that the car is taken on a 'warming-up' run immediately before commencing if only the oil seal requires attention and no other dismantling is to be carried out.

1 Remove the engine and transaxle from the car then remove the clutch release bearing as described in Chapter 5, Section 11.

2 Slowly and carefully slacken the filler plug on the transaxle to relieve the pressure taking care not to burn your hands.

3 Carefully prise out the existing oil seal from the shaft housing taking care not to damage the housing sealing faces. It does not matter if the seal is destroyed.

4 Smear a little SAE 80 EP gear oil on the new seal and fit it carefully (lip inwards), taking care not to damage it on the clutch shaft splines. Press it home using a suitable tubular drift.

5 Replacement is now a reversal of the removal procedure.

6 Check the transaxle oil level, top-up if necessary then replace the filler plug.

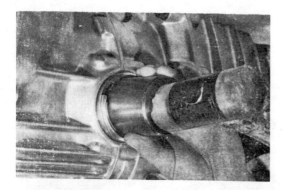

Fig. 12.16A Fitting an hypoid flange oil seal

Fig. 12.16B Fitting a clutch shaft oil seal

6 Fault diagnosis

Note: It is sometimes difficult to decide whether it is worthwhile removing and dismantling the transaxle for a fault which may be nothing more than a minor irritant. Transaxles which howl, or where the synchromesh can be 'beaten' by a quick gear change, may continue to perform for a long time in this state. A worn unit usually needs a complete rebuild to eliminate noise because the various gears, if re-aligned on new bearings, will continue to howl when different wearing surfaces are presented to each other.

The decision to overhaul, therefore, must be considered with regard to time and money available, relative to the degree of malfunction that the driver has to suffer.

Symptom	Reason/s	Remedy
'Notchy' gearchange	Detent tube incorrectly assembled or loose	Check that the detent tube in the rear cover protrudes approximately 0.015 in (0.38 mm) into the counterbore.
	Gearchange control shaft flexible coupling loose or damaged	Check tightness and condition.
	Cross pin in gear lever ball off-centre	Check cross pin and re-position if necessary.
'Sticky' moving across gate	Interlock plate too thick	Check interlock plate thickness for a maximum thickness of 0.2495 in (6.33 mm) and renew if necessary.
	End cover boss too shallow	Renew end cover.
	O-ring groove in main selector shaft too shallow	Remove O-ring and check. If now satisfactory, change the selector shaft.
	Bent selector shaft	Renew selector shaft.
Heavy pressure needed to engage first gear when moving, but satisfactory when stationary	Worn or damaged baulk rings	With the baulk ring pressed on to the gear cone there should be at least 0.025 in (0.63 mm) gap between the baulk ring and the face of the gear. Renew the baulk ring if this gap is too small. Also carefully remove the peak of the cone by stoning.
Difficulty in engaging first/second gears, but easier if the lever is held away from the reverse stop	Fault in interlock plate, reverse plunger or main selector	Renew parts as necessary.
'Notchy' movement across gate	Relationship between milled slots and selector shaft/fork is incorrect	Renew the shaft and fork assembly.
Reverse latch too hard or reverse plunger sticks in	Burrs or wear on plunger and bore in casing	Remove burrs and replace parts as necessary.
	Interlock plate too thin	Exchange interlock plate with one at least 0.001 in (0.025 mm) thicker.
	Wear or damage in associated selector fork, synchro hub, gear, bush, Woodruff key (third/fourth gear), pinion shaft (third/fourth gear)	Examine and renew parts as necessary.
	Worn/damaged detent mechanism in end cover	Examine and renew parts as necessary.
No drive in any gear (muff coupling on clutch shaft adrift or broken)	Muff coupling moved due to circlip not seating in groove	First ensure that the needle bearing is fully home in the housing, then replace the circlip. Note: provided that the reverse gear end of the input shaft can be **very** solidly supported, it is permissible to lightly tap the needle bearing inner sleeve.
	Insufficient radial movement of the clutch shaft	Screw clutch shaft fully home then slacken back at least one spline. When fully assembled there must be at least 0.1 in (2.7 mm) up and down movement.
No drive in third and fourth gears	Third and fourth gears rotating on shafts	Examine and renew shaft and gears as necessary.
Excessive travel across gate	Faulty or loose gearchange control shaft flexible coupling	Check condition and tightness of pinch bolt.
Difficult selection (all gears)	Gearchange tube bearing dry	Lubricate bearing with Castrol LM Grease.
	Selector shaft binding in casing bore	Clean rust from shaft surface.

	Misalignment of rear cover	Bore out the stud holes to 23/64 in (9.1 mm) to permit better alignment.
	Faulty synchro dogs or hubs	Examine and renew parts as necessary.
	Incorrectly assembled detent tube	Rectify as necessary.
Difficulty in selecting first gear	Dog teeth burred on first gear	Renew first gear. Also carefully remove the peak of the cone by stoning.
All gears unobtainable	Bent selector, seized bushes, selector fork insecure on shaft, detent ball jammed or detent tube moved	Examine and renew parts as necessary.
Rattling under light load	Muff coupling rattle	See earlier Symptom - No drive in any gear (muff coupling on clutch shaft adrift or broken).
Excessive noise in reverse gear	Worn teeth on reverse gears	Examine and renew as necessary.
Whine when idling but stops when clutch is depressed	Worn ball race on input shaft	Renew bearing.

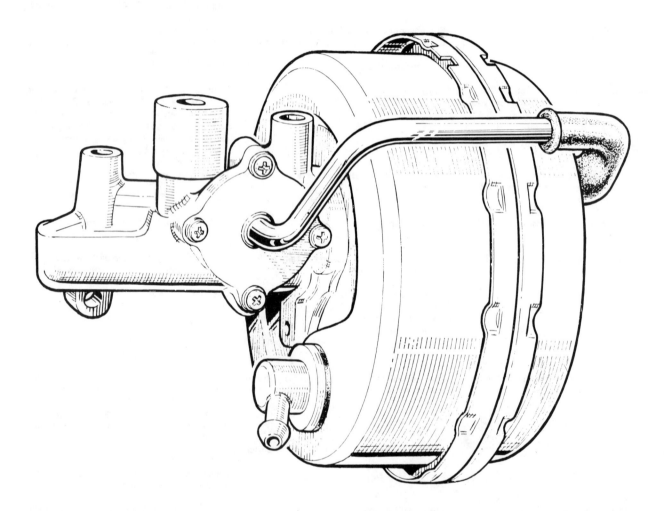

Fig. 12.17 The Girling Mk II B Servo unit

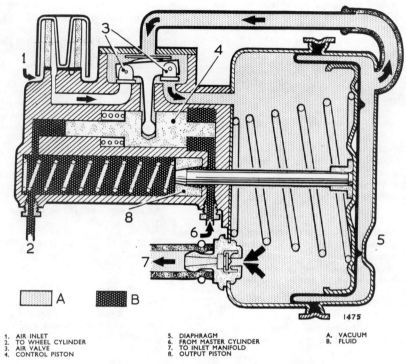

1. AIR INLET
2. TO WHEEL CYLINDER
3. AIR VALVE
4. CONTROL PISTON

5. DIAPHRAGM
6. FROM MASTER CYLINDER
7. TO INLET MANIFOLD
8. OUTPUT PISTON

A. VACUUM
B. FLUID

Fig. 12.18 Schematic diagram in 'at - rest' position

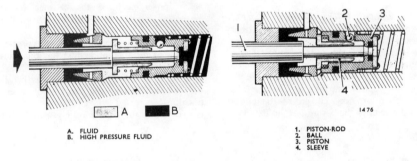

A. FLUID
B. HIGH PRESSURE FLUID

1. PISTON-ROD
2. BALL
3. PISTON
4. SLEEVE

Fig. 12.19 The operation of the output piston

8 Braking System

1 Girling Mk IIB Servo Unit - Description

1 A modified vacuum servo is fitted on later models of the Sport Saloon. A rolling diaphragm replaces the original vacuum piston and, unlike its predecessor which could be dismantled by unscrewing the bolts around the end cover, it is a sealed unit. The unit should be renewed at intervals of 40000 miles (64000 km).

2 In Fig. 12.18 the unit is shown 'at rest' with no pressure in the hydraulic system. The valve is open to the inlet manifold and there is no differential pressure across the diaphragm. When pedal pressure is applied, the hydraulic pressure is exerted throughout the whole system and equally on both ends of the composite valve control piston. Since one end of the piston is larger than the other a greater thrust is exerted on the large end and the piston moves to the left; the T-shaped lever therefore opens the valve to the atmosphere. The air which is admitted to the right-hand end of the vacuum cylinder moves the diaphragm

to the left and the piston rod moves te output piston down the bore. During operation the output piston remains in contact with the piston rod. The piston sleeve remains stationary during the initial movement and thus permits the ball to drop and seal off the fluid port in the piston (see Fig. 12.19). With further movement the piston applies pressure on the fluid proceeding to the wheel cylinders and to the small end of the valve control piston. The output piston continues to move until the thrust on the small end of the plunger due to the higher pressure of the fluid, overcomes the thrust of the fluid pressure on the large end. Thus the valve control piston is moved back, closing off the air valve. Both valves are now closed and the brakes are therefore held on. If the brake pedal is now released the control piston moves to the right as the pressure is reduced at the large end. The valve rocker opens the vacuum valve and air is sucked out of the cylinder causing the diaphragm and piston to return; the pressure to the wheel cylinders is now relieved. The ball is now lifted by the piston sleeve and permits unrestricted movement of the fluid between the supply tank and the wheel cylinders.

If the pressure on the foot pedal is increased there is additional assistance from the diaphragm until the limit of the available vacuum is reached. Conversely, with a reduction of pedal pressure there will be a reduction in the pressure at the wheel cylinders until a state of balance of the control piston is reached. Due to the difference in area between the two opposed ends of the control piston there will be a proportionate difference in assistance provided by the unit.

2 Mk IIB Vacuum Servo air filter - removal and replacment

1 The procedure for this is similar to that given for the earlier type of servo in Chapter 8, Section 19.

3 Mk IIB Vacuum Servo non-return valve - removal and replacement

1 Lever out the non-return valve by carefully using a broad, thin bladed screwdriver, taking care that the grommet does not fall into the vacuum cylinder.
2 Fit a new grommet to the rear shell, smear the ribs of the new non-return valve with the grease provided and press the item fully home.

4 Mk IIB Vacuum Servo - removal and replacement

1 Remove the vacuum hose connection.
2 Unscrew the hydraulic connections. Mop up any spillage of fluid before it has a chance to damage any paintwork.
3 Unscrew the four bolts and remove the servo complete with its fixing bracket.
4 The bracket can be removed from the servo by taking out the three screws.
5 Refitting is a reverse of the removal procedure, following which it will be necessary to bleed the braking system of air as described in Chapter 8, Section 5.

9 Electrical System

1 Regulator adjustment where a C40-L dynamo is fitted

1 Where a C40-L dynamo is fitted, as indicated by a current value of 25 amperes marked with yellow crayon on the regulator cover, revised figures are now given for the dynamo check. **Note:** A current value of 22 amperes is marked with yellow crayon on the regulator cover where a C40-1 dynamo is fitted.
2 Refer to Section 19, paragraph 7 onwards in Chapter 9. A C40-L dynamo should be able to provide a current of 25 amps at 4500 rpm irrespective of the state of the battery, as indicated by

an ammeter reading of 24 to 26 amps when the voltage regulator contacts are shorted out with a bulldog clip, the Lucar connectors are removed from the 'B' terminals and an ammeter capable of reading up to 40 amps is connected between the two cables and one of the 'B' terminals. Regulator adjustment is otherwise the same as for the C40-1 dynamo.

2 Lucas M35J Starter Motor - General Description

The starter motor is a four brush, four pole, series wound machine and is of the non-ventilated, windowless yoke type.

The face type commutator is a moulded assembly mounted on one end of the armature. Brushes are axially mounted and are located in a plastic brush box rivetted to the commutator end bracket.

One end of the field winding is earthed to the yoke by a rivetted connection and the other end is connected to one pair of brushes. The other pair of brushes is connected to the insulated supply terminal which is mounted on the commutator end bracket.

An inboard inertia drive is fitted to one end of the armature shaft.

3 Lucas M35J Starter Motor - Removal and Replacement

Refer to Chapter 9, Section 13.

4 Lucas M35J Starter Motor - Dismantling and Reassembly

1 To gain access to the brushes and commutator for inspection, remove the two screws securing the commutator end bracket and pull it gently away from the yoke. Take the field winding brushes out of the brush box and completely remove the bracket.
2 Remove the armature thrust washer.
3 If no other dismantling is required, check that the brushes are free to move in the brush box, cleaning if necessary with a little petrol on a cloth. If the brushes are worn down to their minimum permissible length of 3/8 in. (9.5 mm) they must be renewed.
4 To renew the commutator end bracket brushes, note the position of the long and short flexible leads, then cut each lead at the terminal post.
5 File, or saw cut, a groove in the head of the terminal just deep enough to take the new flexible leads then solder them in position.
6 To renew the field winding brushes, again note the position

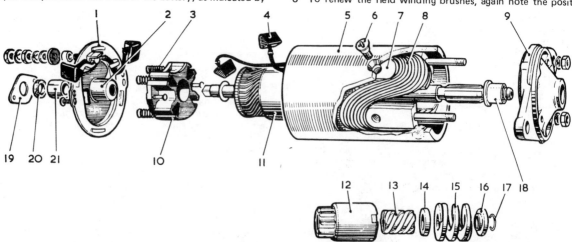

Fig. 12.20 The Lucas M35J Starter Motor

1 Commutator end bracket		
2 Bush housing	7 Pole shoe	12 Pinion and barrel	17 Jump ring
3 Brush springs	8 Field coils	13 Screwed sleeve	18 Bearing
4 Brushes	9 Drive end brackets	14 Buffer washer	19 Bush cover
5 Yoke	10 Brush box moulding	15 Main spring	20 Felt washer
6 Pole screw	11 Armature assembly	16 Cup spring	21 Bearing

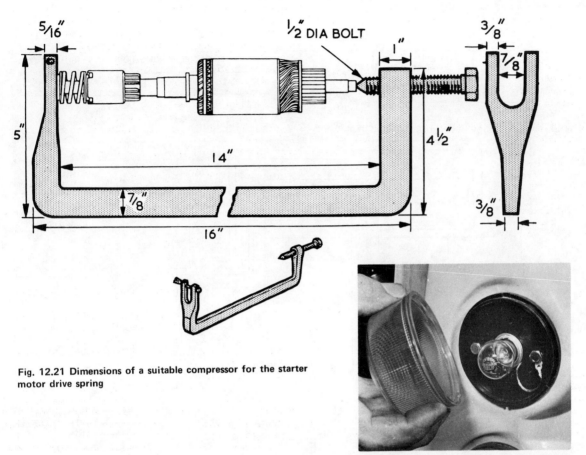

Fig. 12.21 Dimensions of a suitable compressor for the starter motor drive spring

Fig. 12.22 Removing a later type rear lamp lens

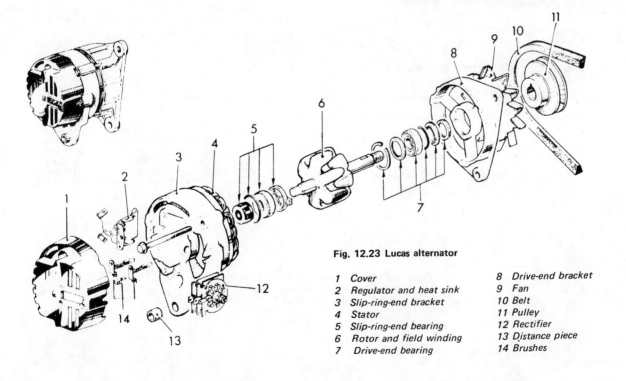

Fig. 12.23 Lucas alternator

1 Cover	8 Drive-end bracket
2 Regulator and heat sink	9 Fan
3 Slip-ring-end bracket	10 Belt
4 Stator	11 Pulley
5 Slip-ring-end bearing	12 Rectifier
6 Rotor and field winding	13 Distance piece
7 Drive-end bearing	14 Brushes

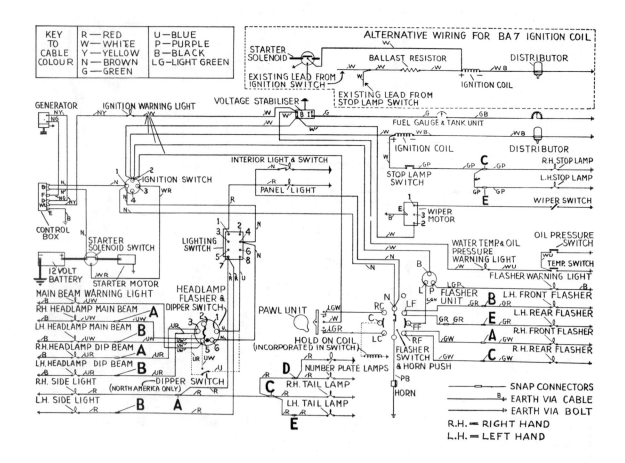

SNAP CONNECTOR LOCATIONS

A — On right-hand front wing valance beneath glass-fibre moulding.

B — On left-hand front wing valance beneath glass-fibre moulding.

C — In engine compartment at right-hand side.

D — Central behind rear bumper.

E — In engine compartment at left-hand side.

COMBINED HEADLAMP FLASHER AND DIPPER SWITCH IS REPLACED BY A SINGLE DIPPER SWITCH FOR NORTH AMERICA EXPORT WITH CABLES UR AND UW JOINED BY AN IN-LINE CONNECTOR. CONNECTIONS TO TERMINALS 3 AND 5 ON THE HEADLAMP FLASH-AND-DIP SWITCH ARE REVERSED FOR ALL LEFT-HAND-DRIVE EXPORT EXCEPT NORTH AMERICA AND FINLAND, AND FOOT DIP-LEAD "N" FROM LIGHTING SWITCH TERMINAL 4 TO HEADLAMP FLASH SWITCH TERMINAL 6 DELETED.

Fig. 12.24 Wiring diagram
Imp Van and Husky up to Chassis number
B 463000000 (Van) and B 482000000 (Huskey)

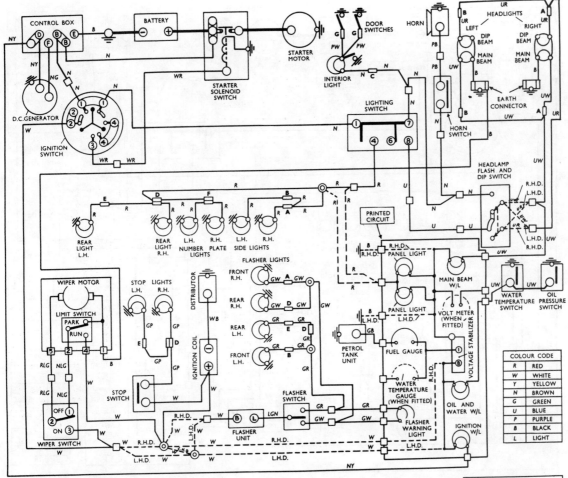

SNAP CONNECTOR LOCATIONS

A —On right-hand front wing valance beneath glass-fibre moulding.

B —On left-hand front wing valance beneath glass-fibre moulding.

C —Behind facia at extreme right-hand side.

D —In engine compartment at right-hand side.

E —In engine compartment at left-hand side.

F —Central behind rear bumper.

G —At door pillar switch.

COLOUR CODE	
R	RED
W	WHITE
Y	YELLOW
N	BROWN
G	GREEN
U	BLUE
P	PURPLE
B	BLACK
L	LIGHT

ABBREVIATIONS	
W/L	WARNING LIGHT
R.H.	RIGHT HAND
L.H.	LEFT HAND
R.H.D.	RIGHT HAND DRIVE
L.H.D.	LEFT HAND DRIVE

SYMBOLS	
	SNAP CONNECTOR
	PLUG AND SOCKET CONNECTOR
	CRIMPED CONNECTION
	EARTH THROUGH UNIT
	EARTH THROUGH CABLE

Fig. 12.25 Wiring diagram
Imp Van and Husky from Chassis number
B 463000001 (Van) and B 4820000001 (Husky)

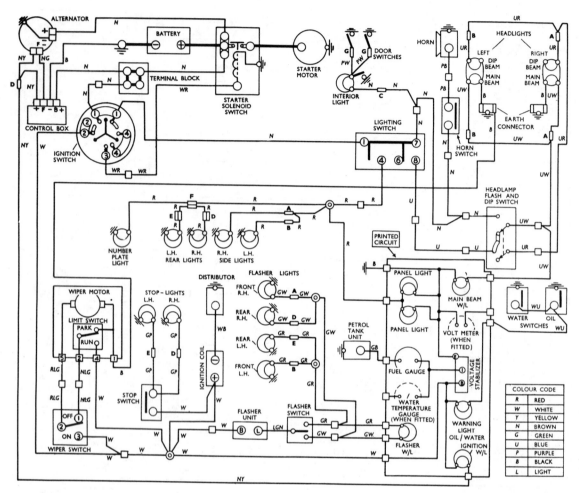

SNAP CONNECTOR LOCATIONS

A —On right-hand front wing valance beneath glass-fibre moulding
B —On left-hand front wing valance beneath glass-fibre moulding.
C —Behind facia at extreme right-hand side.
D —In engine compartment at right-hand side.
E —In engine compartment at left-hand side.
F —In engine compartment at right-hand side near hinge.
G —At door pillar switch.

COLOUR CODE	
R	RED
W	WHITE
Y	YELLOW
N	BROWN
G	GREEN
U	BLUE
P	PURPLE
B	BLACK
L	LIGHT

ABBREVIATIONS	
W/L	WARNING LIGHT
R.H.	RIGHT HAND
L.H.	LEFT HAND
R.H.D.	RIGHT HAND DRIVE
L.H.D.	LEFT HAND DRIVE

SYMBOLS	
	SNAP CONNECTOR
	PLUG AND SOCKET CONNECTOR
	CRIMPED CONNECTION
	EARTH THROUGH UNIT
	EARTH THROUGH CABLE

Fig 12.26 Wiring diagram, Imp (Police specification)

of the long and short flexible leads, then cut each lead about ¼ in. (7 mm) from the field winding joint.

7 Solder the new leads to their respective ¼ in. (7 mm) ends, ensuring that the insulating sleeve provides adequate protection against short circuits when the motor is assembled. Also ensure that the yoke insulation is in place.

8 Brush springs can only be renewed with the brush box and end bracket assembly but after fitting new brushes check that a pressure of 28 oz (800 gm) is required to depress the brush into the box so that only 2/16 in. (1.5 mm) protrudes.

9 To remove the armature if it should be necessary, remove the bolts from the drive end bracket, noting their respective lengths. Now withdraw the armature complete with the drive assembly and end bracket.

10 Inspect the armature and field windings for obvious damage and deterioration. The armature commutator should be burnished to a dark chocolate colour and free from pitting and burning. A petrol moistened cloth may be used for cleaning. With regard to the field coils, examine for obvious signs of insulation breakdown (eg; charred insulation), in particular the insulating piece between the field winding brush joint and the yoke. If the condition of either the armature or field windings is unsatisfactory, you are advised to consult your Chrysler dealer or car electrical specialist for a proper check. Although it is permissible to skim the armature commutator to a minimum thickness of 0.080 in. (2.05 mm), provided that the insulation slots are not undercut, there is a likelihood that this will only be a temporary cure if it is in poor condition, since there is a possibility of a hidden fault. In general, the most satisfactory thing to do is to obtain a replacement starter motor on an exchange basis.

11 After any dismantling, reassembly is the reverse procedure.

5 Lucas M35J Starter Motor Bushes - Inspection, Removal and Replacement

Refer to Chapter 9, Section 16.

6 Lucas M35J Starter motor Drive Assembly - Inspection, Removal and Replacement

1 The pinion and barrel should rotate freely on the screwed sleeve without signs of excessive clearance. The pinion, barrel and sleeve are selectively assembled and must be renewed as a set in the event of wear or damage.

2 To dismantle the drive it is best to entrust the job to your Chrysler dealer or car electrical specialist, although if a suitable spring compressor is available (see Fig. 12.21) it is fairly straightforward. Compress the spring and cup to expose the jump ring, then prise out the latter. Reassembly is the reverse procedure to removal, but it is extremely important that the jump ring is properly seated in its groove.

7 Rear Lamp Lenses on Later Models - Removal and Replacement

1 On later models the rear lamp and rear flasher lamp lenses are a push fit on to the plastic baseplate. To remove the lens, gently squeeze the sides and pull.

2 When refitting, the lens can be pushed back on using the palm of the hand but take care to align the key on the rim of the lens with the slot in the baseplate.

8 Alternator

The latest series production cars and those built to police specifications use an alternator instead of the DC generator. This needs no cut-out. Its regulator is inbuilt. To protect the regulator and rectifier disconnect the alternator leads when using electric arc welding equipment on the car, or a mains battery charger.

Removal, and fan belt tensioning is the same as with a generator.

No lubrication is needed.

There is no commutator to clean: the brushes on the simple slip ring last longer, and should not need cleaning more than once every 50,000 miles.

---

10 Suspension - Dampers - Steering

---

1 Steering Column Bush - Removal and Replacement

1 Remove the steering column from the car, as described in Chapter 10, Section 15.

2 Lay the upper end of the outer steering column on a bench with one bush spigot uppermost, then use a blunt tool to press the spigot into and upwards, out of the column. Repeat for the other spigot.

3 Refitting is a reversal of the removal procedure, but note that with the early metal and rubber bush it is fitted with the metal insert end first and the end face then becomes flush with the end of the outer column. With the later bush it remains below the top of the outer column when fitted.

4 Lubricate the chamfer in the top face of the bush with petroleum jelly then reassemble the steering column.

2 Rack and Pinion Steering Unit fitted with Ball Bearing Pinion - Dismantling and Reassembly

1 Later model cars have a slightly modified steering rack where the pinion runs in two ball races and the damper mechanism is replaced by Belleville spring washers.

2 In general, the dismantling procedure is the same as for the earlier type described in Chapter 10, Section 18, with the pinion and upper ball bearing assembly being removed together. This bearing can be removed by simply inverting the housing.

Fig. 12.27 Steering column lock markings
O Ignition 'off', steering locked when key is withdrawn
I Ignition 'off', auxiliaries 'on'
II Ignition and accessories 'on'
III Ignition/start

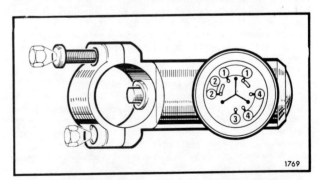

Fig. 12.28 Rear view of ignition switch and steering lock

Terminal	Colour Code	Connected to
1	Brown	Control box B
2	White	Ignition Coil
3	White/Red	Starter solenoid
4	Light green	Blower motor

3   To remove the pinion bottom ball bearing assembly, carefully heat the body around the bearing. Turn the body over, tap the pinion end on a wooden block and the bearing will come out.

4   When reassembling, if either of the studs in the body have been removed, they should be torque tightened to 3.5 lb ft (50 kg cm).

5   To ensure that the pinion bearings have the correct preload, press the pinion and top ball race assembly into the empty body followed by the original shim pack and cover plate but **without** a paper joint and breaking the oil film by gently tapping its splined end with a mallet. Now measure the gap between the cover plate and body, and calculate the thickness of shim pack required to produce a preload of zero to 0.002 in (0.000 to 0.050 mm), including the thickness of one paper joint. Remove the cover plate, shim pack and top ball race assembly from the body.

6   Feed the rack into the body, plain end first, ensuring that the groove aligns with the damper screw tapping and until the end just clears the damper pad housing.

7   Fit the pressure plate and two Belleville washers (raised centre edges together) inside the damper pad with a smear of general purpose grease to hold them in position.

8   Coat the paper joint with a non-setting gasket sealant such as Golden Hermitite, fit it beneath the end cover and secure with two nuts tightened to a torque of 3.5 lb ft (50 kg cm).

9   Coat the edge of the closure cap with the gasket sealant then press it in too, with the recessed side first until it becomes flush with the body.

10 The remainder of the reassembly procedure is now to be carried out in accordance with the requirements of paragraphs 18, 22, 23, 24 and 25 of Section 18, in Chapter 10.

3 Steering Column Lock (including Steering Column Assembly) - Removal and Replacement

Note: It is not recommended that the steering column lock is removed unless the column has been removed from the car.

1   Disconnect the earth lead from the battery.

2   Pull back the gaiter which protects the switch to the rear of the lock.

3   Withdraw the switch and support it in the most convenient way for the duration of the operation.

4   Remove the screws and clamp which secure the two halves of the cowl to the steering column.

5   Withdraw the flasher unit from its retaining spring clip and support it in the most convenient way for the duration of the operation.

6   Disconnect the harness plug for the headlamp/horn/indicator control.

7   Now take off the nut and bolt which secure the inner column to the pinion shaft.

8   Remove the setscrews and bracket used to secure the outer column to the dash and toe-board.

9   Remove the inner and outer column complete with the steering wheel and place it on a suitable bench.

10 Now centre punch the ends of the shear head screws and drill a ¼ in. (6.5 mm) hole in each bolt head to a depth of 1/8 in. (3.2 mm).

11 The clamp can now be released from the lock unit and the bolt shanks removed using mole grips or pliers.

12 When reassembling the lock initially loosely assemble the parts to the column using the correct type of shear-head screws obtained from a Chrysler dealer. When the parts are correctly aligned, pinch the shear-head screws up lightly, so as not to shear the head, then fit the key and check the lock for correct action.

13 When the locking and unlocking action is satisfactory, tighten the screws to shear the heads.

14 Reassembly of the column to the car is now a reversal of the removal procedure. The direction of fitting the inner column clamp is shown in Fig. 10.9 in Chapter 10, but when fitting always use a new washer and 'Aero-tight' nut. Before finally tightening the inner column clamp, fit the outer column securing bolts and clamp loosely.

15 Finally replace the switches and check the operation of all the associated equipment.

11 Bodywork and Underframe

1 Glovebox Lid Lock - Dismantling and Reassembly

1   Initially remove the lock by unscrewing the large nut on the inside of the lid then, once the lock body is free, unscrewing the bezel ring. The lock assembly can then be withdrawn.

2   Take out the two screws in the lock body and withdraw the bolt, bridge piece, spring and bellcrank lever.

3   When reassembling, locate the loop of the spring and the leg of the bellcrank lever in the slot in the bolt.

4   Next fit the bridge piece (which must be pushed downwards and retained against the spring so that the bolt can be fitted over it.)

5   Now fit the outer cover with its two screws.

6   Before refitting the lock to the glovebox lid, check for correct locking and unlocking.

2 Seatbelts - General Note

1   The latest production series Imps have 'one-handed' seatbelts of the lap/diagonal type. Earlier cars which were fitted with Chrysler or Rootes belts were of the lap/diagonal type with either a magnetic buckle or latch-type buckle. All the afore-mentioned types have two floor mounting points and one side panel mounting point. Early cars, which were not fitted with seatbelts as standard equipment, may have one of several types including a two point, floor fixing, lap/diagonal type where one of the diagonal straps passes through a clip at the top of the front seatback.

2   If stowage hooks are provided they should always be used to prevent damage to the belts whilst they are not in use.

3   In the event of an accident where a seatbelt has been subjected to extreme strain, it should be renewed.

4   For cleaning the seatbelt webbing, all that is requires is soap and warm water. Excess water should be wiped off and the belts then allowed to air-dry. Detergents and cleaning fluids can cause irreparable damage to the belt material and should never be used.

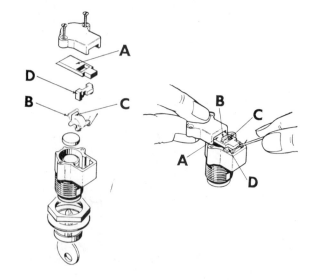

Fig. 12.29 Glovebox lid lock

A Bolt   C Bell crank lever
B Spring   D Bridge piece

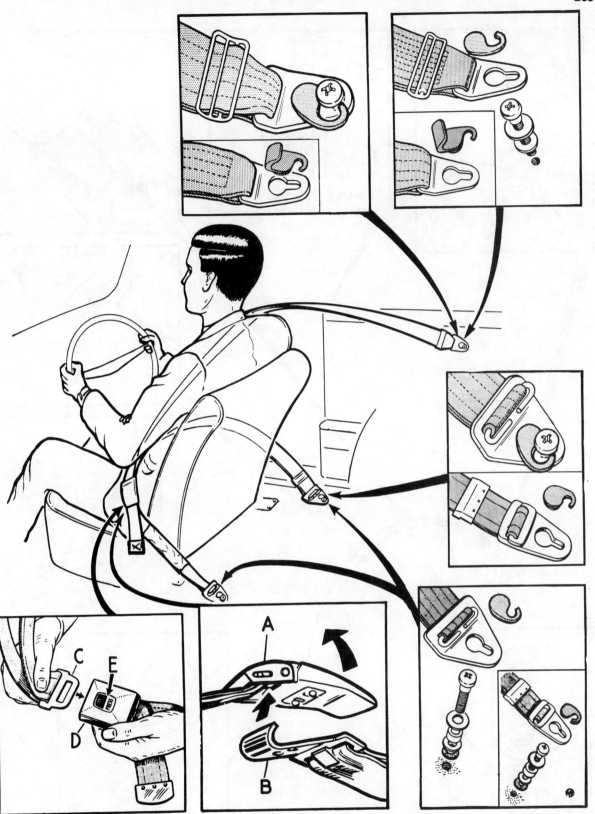

Fig. 12.30 Magnetic Buckle and Latch type Buckle safety belts

A Buckle   C Connector   E Release plate
B Connector   D Buckle

210

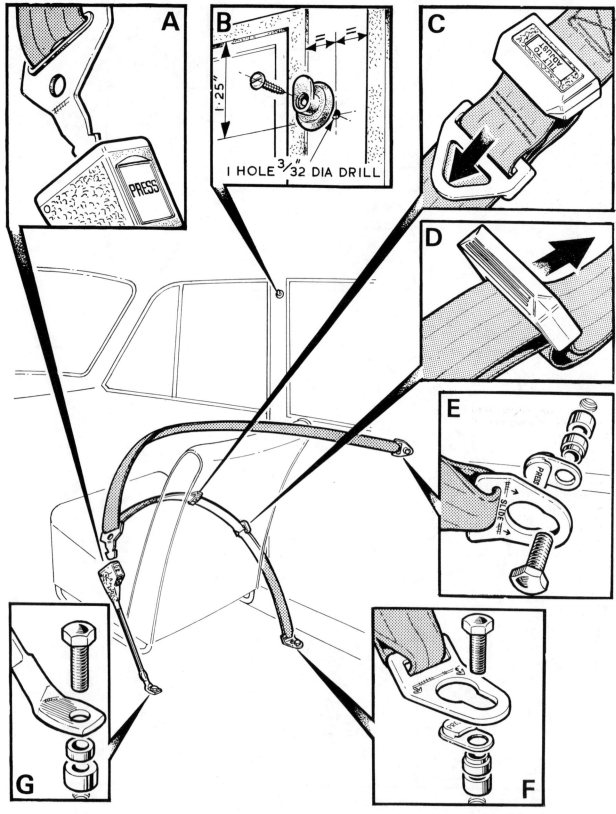

Fig. 12.31 'One - handed' seat belts
A Locking assembly
B Dimension for fitting door pillar stowage clip
C,D Belt adjusters
E,F,G Attachment points

Index

Printed by
Haynes Publishing Group
Sparkford Yeovil Somerset
England